The Impeachment of Chief Justice David Brock

The Impeachment of Chief Justice David Brock

Judicial Independence and Civic Populism

John Cerullo and David C. Steelman

LEXINGTON BOOKS
Lanham • Boulder • New York • London

Published by Lexington Books
An imprint of The Rowman & Littlefield Publishing Group, Inc.
4501 Forbes Boulevard, Suite 200, Lanham, Maryland 20706
www.rowman.com

Unit A, Whitacre Mews, 26-34 Stannary Street, London SE11 4AB

British Library Cataloguing in Publication Information Available

Library of Congress Cataloging-in-Publication Data

Names: Cerullo, John J., 1949- author. | Steelman, David C., author.
Title: The impeachment of Chief Justice David Brock : judicial independence and civic populism / John Cerullo and David C. Steelman.
Description: Lanham : Lexington Books, 2017. | Includes bibliographical references and index.
Identifiers: LCCN 2017042136 (print) | LCCN 2017040266 (ebook) | ISBN 9781498565905 (Electronic) | ISBN 9781498565899 (cloth : alk. paper)
Subjects: LCSH: Brock, David A.—Impeachment. | Trials (Impeachment)—New Hampshire. | Judges—New Hampshire—Discipline. | Justice, Administration of—New Hampshire.
Classification: LCC KFN1725.5.I4 (print) | LCC KFN1725.5.I4 C47 2017 (ebook) | DDC 347.742/014—dc23
LC record available at https://lccn.loc.gov/2017042136

∞™ The paper used in this publication meets the minimum requirements of American National Standard for Information Sciences—Permanence of Paper for Printed Library Materials, ANSI/NISO Z39.48-1992.

Printed in the United States of America

Contents

List of Tables

Preface

The optimal locus of judicial institutions and the proper boundaries of judicial action have been contested throughout American history and remain so today. Not surprisingly, the bulk of scholarly work (not to be confused with political polemic) on the subject has addressed the U.S. Constitution and the federal courts. State-level inquiries have been plentiful enough, but mainly focused on state-specific circumstances. In the last couple of decades, however, a provocative sub-genre of legal history has emerged through the work of scholars such as Jed Shugerman, John Dinan, Paul Carrington, and others.[1] Practitioners essentially bridge the gap between federal and state perspectives by highlighting the relevance of state-level actions to developments at a national level, as well as the impact of national trends in particular states. With this study, we hope to contribute to that literature.

That ambition, it must be acknowledged, is not a particularly humble one. The question of judicial power, after all, is one of the central concerns of representative democracy itself. No permanent, formulaic resolution may be possible or even desirable, precisely because the role of the judiciary implicates two equally compelling democratic values, in ongoing tension with one another. Put broadly and bluntly, they are, on the one hand, the sovereignty of the people; and, on the other, "rule of law not men." To a degree, that tension is built into the foundational American commitment to separate and compartmentalized governmental powers, each checking the other. In classic Madisonian thought, consolidated power is by definition unaccountable power; and over the course of American history, a fully independent judiciary came to be deemed an essential part of the arrangements minimizing that possibility. But how is that judiciary itself to be held accountable? What exactly is it to be independent of? "Politics?" Or the will of the people? And what exactly is the difference?

Is popular sovereignty to be exercised directly and constantly? Or is it to be filtered and mediated? Are all governing institutions to be immediately responsive to prevailing public sentiment? Or does that stricture apply to the elected branches alone, with judicial agencies deliberately exempted? Those sorts of issues have long been salient in New Hampshire. From the beginning, this has been a state committed to maximizing the powers of ordinary citizens and deeply mistrustful of the role of purported experts, including those called to the administration of justice. Indeed, the authors of this study hope that its title will suggest the sheer force of populism as counterbalance to judicial independence in New Hampshire.

Any usage of the term 'populism' will and should raise questions. One of the most loosely defined terms in political analysis, it has been associated with the political left and right; applied to groups ranging from the *Narodniks* of nineteenth-century Russia to the adherents of President Donald Trump today; applauded as the fulfillment of democracy's promise and deplored as mechanism of authoritarianism.[2] Yet, somehow, it remains indispensable as a descriptor. "There can be no doubt about the importance of populism," wrote two influential analysts in 1969. "But no one is quite clear just what it is."[3]

Crystal clarity may not be in the offing, but scholars can claim at least some general sense of what populism is, thanks in part to scholars such as English political theorist Margaret Canovan.[4] Canovan confirms certain common, core aspects of populist movements: an appeal to "ordinary" people; hostility to both "the established structure of power" and "the dominant ideas and values of the society," each of which those ordinary people have determined to be threatening.[5] Populists, then, can be expected to pursue both an expressly political and a wider sociocultural program. But those programs' precise nature is a function of the "elites" they oppose, hence their ideological heterogeneity. If those elites are seen as, for instance, cosmopolitan and liberal, populists' posture will likely be militantly parochial and traditionalistic.

But Canovan provides more than a rough taxonomy. Drawing on political philosopher Michael Oakeshott, she argues that what might be called the populist temperament, whatever form it happens to publicly manifest in any particular time and place, is an integral a part of democratic life precisely because its primeval antagonists, complacent officialdom, and entrenched privilege are similarly inherent to democratic practice. Populism, Canovan proposes, thus occupies the space between what she calls the "redemptive" promise of democracy (visible affirmation of the worth of the masses) and its "pragmatic," mundane, and bureaucratized operations (the maintenance of order, traditional rights, and extant institutions), waiting to be triggered by some event or development. In this book, we have tried to explain how that dynamic has operated in New Hampshire.

But the most crucial part of that story, to us, is what all this has meant for the rule of law here. For as Canovan reminds us, the rule of law is crucial to defenders of those pragmatic functions of government in general.[6] Given populists' standard impatience with "legalistic restrictions" on the realization of the people's will, it is hardly surprising that they would so often target standing legal institutions and the credentialed (i.e., "elite") personnel staffing them. There is now a substantial literature on the subject of "legal" and "constitutional" populism as well, reflecting a variety of political perspectives.[7] This literature encompasses state-level studies, and that is probably the body of work into which our own most comfortably fits.[8]

But we have selected the term "civic populism" rather than "legal populism" or "constitutional populism" for a reason. With it, we are describing a populist stance toward all organs of government and all aspects of civic culture, not just judicial institutions and legal culture.[9] By "civic populists," we simply mean those New Hampshire citizens whose commitment to direct citizen engagement in the act of governance is the prime directive. They would certainly disclaim any hostility to the rule of law. But they might well acknowledge some toward lawyers and judges, and deny that law degrees and bar membership automatically confer a superior understanding of justice. They have certainly opposed the professionalization of government on all levels, in all branches. We understand that our term "civic populism" connotes the mistrust of elites and enthusiasm for citizen empowerment generally associated with populism. But we mean to denote a broad, multilevel political orientation, perhaps even a general social stance—and then to interpret its consequences for the principle of judicial independence, as they have played out in the State of New Hampshire.

We hope we have done this adequately. If so, we believe the implications of our study will be clear.

NOTES

1. See, for example, Jed Shugerman, *The People's Court: Judicial Independence in America* (Cambridge, MA: Harvard U. Press, 2012); John Dinan, *Keeping the People's Liberties: Legislators, Citizens, and Judges as Guardians of Rights* (Lawrence, KS: University Press of Kansas, 1998); and Paul Carrington, "Judicial Independence and Democratic Accountability in Highest State Courts," *Law & Contemp. Probs.* 61, no. 3 (1998): 79–126. The entirety of the latter publication was devoted to the subject, and contains a number of valuable considerations of it.

2. On the *Narodniki* and populist agitation against tsarism in imperial Russia, see Richard Wortman, *The Crisis of Russian Populism* (Cambridge: Cambridge University Press, 2008). American analysts of populism include historian Michael Kazin, whose *The Populist Persuasion: An American History* (New York: Basic

Books, 1995) addresses in detail the disassociation of movements and leaders fitting the rough designation "populist" from the political left to the political right.

3. Ghita Ionescu and Ernest Gellner, eds., *Populism: Its Meaning and National Characteristics* (London: Weidenfield and Nicholson, 1969), 9.

4. Margaret Canovan, *Populism* (New York: Harcourt Brace Jovanovich, 1981).

5. Canovan, "Trust the People! Populism and the Two Faces of Democracy," *Political Studies*, 47, no. 1 (1999): 2, 3.

6. Ibid., 8.

7. See, most recently, Charles Geyh, *Courting Peril: The Political Transformation of the American Judiciary* (New York: Oxford U. Press, 2016). In the 1990s, the Critical Legal Studies (CLS) movement inspired much of this literature, both in defense of CLS principles—for example, Mark Tushnet, *Taking the Constitution Away from the Courts* (Princeton, NJ: Princeton University Press, 1999)—and in opposition to them—for example, John Batt, "Special Essay: American Legal Populism: A Jurisprudential and Historical Narrative, Including Reflections on Critical Legal Studies," *N. Ky. L. Rev.* 22, no. 3 (1995): 651–752. See, also, the literature on "popular constitutionalism" and "constitutional democracy"—for example, Larry Kramer, *The People Themselves: Popular Constitutionalism and Judicial Review* (New York: Oxford University Press, 2004); John Finn, *Peopling the Constitution* (Lawrence, KS: University Press of Kansas, 2014); and Elizabeth Beaumont, *The Civic Constitution: Civic Visions and Struggles in the Path Toward Constitutional Democracy* (New York: Oxford University Press, 2014).

8. The key work here is G. Alan Tarr, *Without Fear or Favor: Judicial Independence and Judicial Accountability in the States* (Stanford, CA: Stanford University Press, 2012). See also, Douglas Reed, "Popular Constitutionalism: Toward a Theory of State Constitutional Meanings," *Rutgers L. J.* 30 (1999): 871–932.

9. The idea has been explored in detail by political scientist Harry Boyte. See, for example, *Civic Agency and the Cult of the Expert* (Dayton, OH: Kettering Foundation, 2009); *Everyday Politics: Reconnecting Citizens and Public Life* (Philadelphia: University of Pennsylvania Press, 2004); and "Civic Populism," *Perspectives on Politics* 1, no. 4 (2003): 737–42.

Acknowledgments

A work like this cannot be accomplished without the assistance of a great many people. We gratefully acknowledge the contributions of the following—and sincerely hope this list does not omit more than the limitations of human memory and awareness necessitate.

Karen Wadsworth, former administrative assistant at the New Hampshire General Court, directed us to essential archival materials in the initial stages of our research. Michael York, New Hampshire State Librarian, and the entire staff of the state library in Concord, went to extraordinary lengths to facilitate access to materials housed there. Former Rep. Peter Bergin, Judge Robert Rowe, and Charles Putnam, Esq., now clinical professor of Justice Studies at the University of New Hampshire (UNH), were all kind enough to discuss their personal recollections of the impeachment process, discussions that produced insights we could have achieved no other way.

We especially appreciate the contributions of the friends and colleagues who read all or portions of our manuscript and provided extremely valuable suggestions and support. These include, in alphabetical order: Alex Aikman, Esq., court management consultant and former Western Regional Vice President of the National Center for State Courts (NCSC); Todd DeMitchell, John and Irene Peters Professor of Education and Professor of Justice Studies at UNH; Victor E. ("Gene") Flango, retired Executive Director for Program Resource Development at NCSC; Peter Haebler, former Dean of Academic Affairs, UNH-Manchester; Jack Resch, Professor Emeritus (History), UNH-Manchester; Susan Siggelakis, Associate Professor of Political Science, UNH; Dick Van Duizend, Esq., former Deputy Director of the State Justice Institute and retired Principal Court Management Consultant at NCSC; and Catharine Wells, Professor of Law and Law School Fund Research Scholar at Boston College Law School. Each of these individuals offered detailed, highly perceptive commentary on our manuscript, and each improved it. We are deeply grateful to all of them for their critical advice.

We acknowledge in a special way the contribution of Robert F. Williams, Distinguished Professor of Law at Rutgers-Camden Law School and Director of the Center for State Constitutional Studies at Rutgers. Bob was among the first to see a completed draft of our manuscript. By inviting us to submit an article based on a portion of it for an upcoming issue of *Rutgers Law Review* on state constitutional law, he has both encouraged us and helped us to sharpen our thinking. We much appreciate being referred to him by Prof. Charles ("Buzzy") Baron, retired Professor of Law at Boston College Law School.

John Phillip Reid, Russell D. Niles Professor of Law Emeritus at the New York University School of Law, gave our final manuscript a close and critical reading, and we are both enormously grateful for the quality of his effort and the many copy-edit improvements that he suggested. We also wish to thank Blair Gerold, Editor-in-Chief, and Michael Stoolman, Managing Editor, and their colleagues at the 2017 Rutgers University Law Review, for identifying errors in some factual details in an article derived from our work on this book, leading us to make corresponding fact corrections here.

Finally, we would like to reserve our most heartfelt statement of gratitude for our wives, Shawn and Ginny. Their patience with and support for what must have sometimes seemed our interminable labors have been more important than either of them will probably ever know.

John Cerullo and David C. Steelman
September 27, 2017

Introduction

The impeachment of a judge, at either the state or federal level, is a rare event. Even more rare is the impeachment of a chief justice. (See Appendix A.) Yet on July 12, 2000, New Hampshire's House of Representatives voted by an overwhelming, bipartisan majority of 253–95 to impeach not just a judge, but the very highest judge on the state bench. The object of their wrath was no less a personage than chief justice of the New Hampshire Supreme Court, David A. Brock.

THE CRISIS OF 2000: "PROFESSIONALIZED" JUDICIARY VERSUS "POPULIST" LEGISLATURE

On April 13, the state's House of Representatives had charged the House Judiciary Committee (HJC) to investigate Brock and other justices. House members, like the rest of the state, had been shocked by a report issued on March 31 by the state's attorney general, Philip McLaughlin—itself catalyzed by prior revelations from the clerk of the New Hampshire Supreme Court, the Judicial Conduct Committee, and justices themselves.[1] The McLaughlin Report, as it came to be called, had concentrated on apparent attempts by a particular Justice, Stephen Thayer, to influence cases in which he himself was personally involved, and a possibly criminal willingness to accommodate him by Chief Justice Brock and others.[2] But it had also gone beyond these particular actions to suggest that current but unspecified practices of the court at large merited scrutiny.

The House's charge to HJC had been to inquire more deeply into points raised by the McLaughlin Report and, for good measure, to pursue "any information arising out of the judiciary committee's [own] investigation."[3]

That is, HJC was empowered to follow as far as it chose whatever leads it considered potentially important. Employing its subpoena powers quite liberally for the better part of four months, committee members had followed a great many leads indeed. A majority of them members decided that all of them led directly to David Brock.

On April 9, HJC concluded its labors by drafting a recommendation that the House adopt three articles of impeachment against the chief justice. The charges encompassed improper contacts Brock was accused of having had with a Superior Court judge thirteen years earlier, regarding the disposition of a case involving a state senator (Article 1); *ex parte* communications Brock was accused of having had with recused justices regarding one of their number's divorce proceedings, most egregiously with the divorcing Justice himself (Article 2); and claims that Brock had lied in his testimony to the HJC during its investigation of these matters (Article 3).[4] So agitated were House representatives when they received the HJC's recommendations that they had added another charge: that the recusal policy over which Brock had presided enabled recused or disqualified justices to unduly influence cases where potential conflicts of interest were manifest and acknowledged (Article 4).[5]

It was a remarkable moment. Prior to it, only one state judge had ever been impeached in New Hampshire: Woodbury Langdon, in 1790.[6] Langdon, however, had resigned before his constitutionally mandated trial in the state Senate could begin, leaving Brock the only New Hampshire judge to have ever experienced that ordeal.[7] In fact, David Brock is the only chief justice of a state supreme court to have actually undergone an impeachment trial in more than 70 years.[8]

Like other state-level impeachments, this one was driven by state-specific concerns, concerns which by 2000 had generated widespread mistrust of New Hampshire's Supreme Court in general and its chief justice in particular. Among some legislators, that mistrust was metastasizing into rage. The most immediate and inflamed issue was certainly a recent set of Court decisions overturning New Hampshire's traditional method of financing its public schools almost entirely through local property taxes. The initial case was brought in 1993 by the Claremont school district and four others, all comparatively poor. The plaintiffs (a student and a property taxpayer from each school district) argued that the New Hampshire constitution established a state duty to provide an adequate education to all its citizens, which the state had illicitly shunted off to local taxing districts. By those plaintiffs' reckoning, property valuations and tax rates varied so wildly across the state that reliance on local property taxes to finance public schools overtly violated the state's constitutional stricture that all public levies be "reasonable and proportionate." In practical terms, property-poor school districts were unable to adequately fund their schools even while imposing higher tax rates than did property-rich districts. That is: taxpayers in poorer districts were forced to pay more for less.

Chief Justice Brock himself authored the crucial decisions on those claims, known as *Claremont I* and *Claremont II*. In *Claremont I* (1993), Brock and his entire Court concluded that New Hampshire's constitution did, in fact, confer the right to an adequate public education on all citizens of the state; and that the responsibility to provide that education did rest with the state, which could not simply hand it over to districts of widely varying financial means.[9] The court left to the elected branches of state government the task of meeting that responsibility, including the designation of "reasonable and proportionate" statewide revenues to underwrite whatever educational standards were eventually deemed adequate. But therein lay the rub. The tradition of local control and local funding of public schools was a very strong one in New Hampshire, as was (and is) the state's aversion to broad-based, statewide taxes. Elected officials determined to maintain those traditions were about to collide with a supreme court equally determined to defend a newly recognized constitutional right.

In *Claremont II* (1997), the court found by a 4–1 vote that the state's initial effort at compliance with its prior ruling, which conceded a larger state role in the provision of public education while avoiding state-level financing of it, simply did not pass constitutional muster.[10] *Claremont II* may actually have been even more controversial a decision than *Claremont I*, since it directly challenged legislators' historically grounded expectations of an entirely free hand in the formation of social policy. With *Claremont II*, the court essentially announced that state legislators would not only have to undertake a duty they had not previously recognized, but would have to do so within parameters set not by local voters but by the New Hampshire Supreme Court. This, to New Hampshire legislators, was an entirely new world. Few welcomed it.

Between *Claremont II* and Brock's impeachment in 2000, his Court would issue a set of decisions (*Claremont III* through *Claremont VI*) and advisory opinions rebuffing other schemes the elected branches put forward, as well as initiatives aimed at vitiating or mitigating the effects of earlier *Claremont* holdings. With each new ruling, legislative frustration and rancor deepened. To its opponents, the court was systematically violating the separation of powers by meddling in policy questions (public finances, educational standards) that were clearly entrusted to the peoples' representatives. But none of the efforts to undo its *Claremont* holdings ever deterred the court, which refused to waver from its initial commitments. Indeed, the consistency of its rulings on school funding arguably justifies the local practice of lumping the entire corpus of litigation together, conveniently if imprecisely, under the all-purpose term "*Claremont.*" By 2000, mere mention of that word was enough to raise tempers in New Hampshire. In much of the state, it still is.

The depth of this rancor is remarkable. New Hampshire, after all, was hardly the only state to face litigation on education funding at the time. By 1998, in fact, over thirty had coped with similar rulings, usually complying with judicial findings akin to those of David Brock's Supreme Court.[11] But the special intensity of the conflict in New Hampshire drew national attention. The Granite State, reported the *New York Times*, "seems to stand out as more defiant and more intent on defending its local tradition than any other state."[12] The Washington *Post* echoed that view, noting that "no state has the unique ingredients that make the court's rulings so volatile as New Hampshire," since "The decision threatens profound changes in a state where individualism and local autonomy are core values and low state taxes are the hallmark of its conservative approach to state government."[13]

With the *Claremont* controversy in mind, a number of analysts have seen the impeachment of David Brock as simply an attempt to wreak political vengeance on a judge whose real offense was overturning long-standing fiscal arrangements, and greatly discomfiting politicians left with the task of finding new ones.[14] Certainly, a legislative-judicial imbroglio as bitter and extended as *Claremont* could hardly fail to loom large in the minds of the legislators who would bring Brock to task, and deliberate his fate. Indeed, its significance is perhaps best indicated by the very strenuousness of the efforts that fair-minded critics had to make to exclude it from their consideration of his case.[15]

Yet there were deeper reasons for the impeachment, with roots that trace back roughly to the years between 1966 and 1978. In 1966, New Hampshire became the last state in the country to grant constitutional status to its judiciary, thereby putting the state's supreme and superior courts beyond the reach of legislative power to abolish and create judicial bodies for the very first time. That change was mandated by voters, who approved the constitutional amendment required for it. In 1978, they approved another constitutional amendment making the chief justice of that reconfigured supreme court the administrative head of the entire state judiciary, greatly diminishing the legislature's role in shaping or even monitoring the daily dispensation of justice in New Hampshire. Much happened between and shortly after those remarkable developments to persuade some legislators that these alterations in the status of the judicial branch had been ill-advised, even dangerous. In fact, the evidence suggests that the impeachment charges were brought against Brock for actions which critics felt confirmed their suspicion that the judiciary under his leadership could not be trusted to exercise its newly granted institutional independence in a manner that would serve the best interests of New Hampshire citizens.

That is: the importance of the *Claremont* controversy in catalyzing overt hostility to David Brock is undeniable, but his impeachment cannot be waved away as nothing more than retribution for controversial court decisions. The *Claremont* litigation forms a vital part of the story we tell here. But it is not its entirety. Indeed, that broader, deeper story is precisely what makes the impeachment of Chief Justice David Brock a matter of much more than local significance. For the story is really one of crucial shifts in state government—shifts that were occurring not only in New Hampshire but across the nation.

One of them was the movement toward judicial "modernization" that had begun around the middle of the twentieth century. The movement's proponents aimed to enhance the efficiency (and minimize the corruptibility or "politicization") of state courts by, for example, securing administrative and fiscal consolidation under fully constitutionalized high courts; detaching courts from counties, municipalities, and other local governance units; and the like. Significantly, they also aimed for the sort of institutional autonomy vis-à-vis the elected branches of government that the federal judiciary had long modeled. In 1966 and 1978, New Hampshire's citizens approved constitutional amendments that enabled their judiciary's leaders to align their courts with that movement. By the end of the century, judicial modernization had dramatically remolded New Hampshire's judiciary.

But those citizens were less willing to approve changes allowing the elected branches to align *their* institutions with similar movements that were being embraced for legislatures and executives in other states. As in the judicial branch, proponents of elected-branch modernization aimed to essentially professionalize those bodies. Favored measures included longer terms of office for governors and expanded gubernatorial veto powers; reducing the size of lower houses; increasing legislators' salaries and staff support; and authorizing longer legislative sessions. In New Hampshire, however, that movement was resisted by opinion leaders and voters mindful of the state's civic traditions of proudly *non*-professional citizen-legislators and direct, active citizen engagement in town and local politics as means of maintaining popular control over the cost and power of government.

In short, our story is about a tectonic clash between a modernizing judiciary and a defiantly traditional legislature and executive—in effect, a conflict between "professionalizers" in the former branch and "populists" in the latter two. The depth and dimensions of the conflict are indicated by the nature of the critique elaborated by those who organized and directed the Brock impeachment, a critique that both preceded and exceeded anything in either the McLaughlin Report or the HJC's bill of impeachment.

Their broad claim was that under Brock's leadership the supreme court had grossly exceeded the powers constitutionally ascribed to it, all in the name of a misbegotten notion of judicial independence. In the floor debate that preceded the House's vote approving articles of impeachment against Brock, Rep. Paul Mirski, one of Brock's most determined antagonists, insisted that the framers of the state constitution had actually "hated the idea of an institutional judiciary," and deliberately accompanied constitutional provisions affirming judges' independence with others that "left the judiciary and all its aspects up to this House and the Senate behind us." Mirski closed by flatly declaring that "There is no such thing as an institutional separate co-equal branch of government called the judiciary in New Hampshire."[16] Rep. Henry Mock, then chair of HJC, argued that the court's dereliction "began 40 or 50 years ago under the disguise of judicial independence. ... Slowly the court has become so independent that it has gotten itself in trouble." *Claremont*, by such legislators' reckoning, was simply the most egregious transgression of a supreme court run amok—a Court, and indeed a judiciary, whose internal ethical chaos should surprise no one aware of its infuriating disregard for the state constitution, civic culture, and all conventional boundaries of judicial action. Thanks to the McLaughlin Report, the rot had finally come to light in clear and indictable form.

Ironically, it may have been unfortunate for Brock that New Hampshire's judges are comparatively well-insulated from quotidian political pressures: the state is one of only three (along with Massachusetts and Rhode Island) where judges' tenure in office was subject to neither the direct judgment of the electorate nor formal and periodic review by either elected branch of government.[17] What this meant in practice was that critics of Brock and his Court had no means of acting on their views short of forcibly removing the offending judge from office, by either impeachment or legislative address (whereby officials can be ousted for causes apart from those that would trigger an impeachment, should a legislative committee approve and secure the agreement of the executive to that action).

The impeachment of David Brock was, then, an explosion of rocket-fire illuminating a larger battlefield, where contending forces struggled to determine what judicial modernization was to actually mean for state-level democracy in New Hampshire. It is that battle, we submit, that merits attention by historians both within and beyond New Hampshire, and indeed by anyone interested in the dynamics of American state government.

Yet there are additional questions here, which we find worthy of the most careful consideration. They lie beyond the impeachment's historical context or institutional determinants, and involve its actual merits. These are essentially normative, even philosophical questions. But they are hardly less significant for that.

The first is simply: was the impeachment of David Brock an appropriate, responsible legislative action—the best available response by legislators to disturbing information that had recently come to light? Brock, after all, would be acquitted in open trial by the New Hampshire Senate (although later admonished by the state's Judicial Conduct Committee). Was the House of Representatives' action invalidated by that outcome? Or was it, rather, the Senate that erred, averting its eyes from what the House in general and the HJC in particular had dutifully, and unflinchingly, recognized? Secondly: did the impeachment contribute positively to a reordering of legislative-judicial relations in New Hampshire? Was it in some sense cathartic? Did it help bring inter-branch tensions more or less to an end? Or did it, rather, intensify those tensions? Did the conclusion of the event represent merely the end of one phase of an endless dispute, and the inception of another?

We are asking, in short, whether the impeachment of New Hampshire's Chief Justice represented, overall, a proper and productive use of the impeachment power. It would be irresponsible to avoid this question. But it would be equally irresponsible to address it until the full story has been told.

It is a story should be prefaced with a brief consideration of impeachment itself: its purpose, its history, its implications.

IMPEACHMENT IN THEORY AND PRACTICE

It is a truism that impeachment is an extreme measure, to be used only when exceptionally dangerous or difficult circumstances have arisen for which no alternative measures avail. Yet it is also a vital feature of stable constitutional rule, clearly established on both the federal and state levels. Impeachment is, in fact, among the most paradoxical provisions of constitutional law, simultaneously reassuring and unsettling. It is a vital safeguard of rule of law that, when actually undertaken, is nearly always held to mark a crisis *in.* the rule of law. That is because impeachment challenges one of the most important ideals in American political thought and practice.

The ideal holds that "law" and "politics" are distinct realms of civic life—each assigned its own domain, which must be carefully defended against encroachments by the other. It was perhaps promoted most effectively by Harvard Law School's Christopher Langdell, whose entire "case method" of legal instruction, still practiced today, was based on it.[18] By this vision, the realm of law, both theorized and applied, lies on one side of a rather bright line. What we should see there is the protection of stipulated, fundamental rights and civic principles, a task that must be entrusted to a separate and independent judicial branch of government lest those rights and principles be compromised by political expediency. On the other side of that line is the political universe. Here, we are to determine our social and economic policies, which we understand to be mutable, properly shaped by clashes and compromises among contending interests, and negotiated by legislators kept closely accountable to the will of their constituents.[19] The notion of a clear and sustainable split between legal and political realms of action has, of course, been disputed by theoreticians from Oliver Wendell Holmes through the "legal realists" of the 1920s to the Critical Legal Studies (CLS) school of the 1970s. The ideal survives nonetheless, and with reason. We recognize that the line separating the legal and political worlds can, and sometimes must, be crossed. But we respect and normally maintain the distinction because we fear, quite rationally, the consequences of casual admixture of those categories. The politicization of law can be a form of corruption. The judicialization of politics threatens a kind of tyranny.

Yet in providing for impeachment, the framers of both state and federal constitutions created an act that is simultaneously juridical *and* political, and challenged future generations to maintain the proper balance between them in specific cases.[20]

An impeachment is a formalized proceeding by which an elected or appointed public official is held to account for alleged abuse of power or violations of his or her duties to the public. At the inception of the American republic, Alexander Hamilton acknowledged that such offenses "may with peculiar propriety be denominated POLITICAL, as they relate chiefly to injuries done immediately to the society itself."[21] From the beginning that categorization raised the question of whether those "political" offenses could or should be confined to acts formally designated indictable by criminal or civil codes. Those arguing for a more expansive view note that delimiting impeachable offenses to criminal acts would allow gross incompetence, dereliction of duty, even chronic alcoholism or other personal behaviors clearly deleterious to the public interest to escape censure.[22] The debate goes on, but the modern historical record seems to favor the broader view, at least on the federal level.[23]

As such, impeachment is perhaps the ultimate expression of popular sovereignty in a democratic order. It serves notice to all and sundry that it is the citizenry that rules—not just at election time, but always; and that no public official, ever, can assume immunity from public scrutiny. The action is entrusted to elected legislators for the simple reason that they and they alone are the citizenry's designated spokesmen. [24] In this instance, ordinary judges and juries will not do. No conventional judge or court is similarly attuned to the people's voices (on the contrary, conventional judges and courts are, in general, deliberately insulated from them); and lay jurors, for their part, are charged to exercise their own best judgment of the case before them, not channel the general public's broadest concerns. That defense of the public interest, as defined by citizens themselves and communicated to the officials they have chosen to represent them, is perhaps the very essence of "politics" in any democratic order. Indeed, an impeachment trial is not an *impeachment* trial if all political considerations, understood in that sense, are left at the courtroom door.

Yet for all that, an impeachment trial remains a *trial*. It is an official act of reckoning with alleged wrongdoing, and constitutions calling for it, including New Hampshire's, clearly require a particular set of legislators to reconstitute themselves as a *court*, albeit an unconventional one. That command carries an undeniable resonance. Court trials are not political referenda, or policy judgments. They are intended to yield justice, not secure partisan victory. Courts generally assess individual, not institutional or categorical, behaviors. They render their decisions on the basis of public and contestable evidence, after trials conducted in adversarial mode, with procedures carefully designed to protect the rights of all involved. Nothing less would be expected of the court that conducts an impeachment.

This taken together is what makes an impeachment trial *sui generis*. It is unlike other trials in that it departs quite deliberately from the ideal of a fully de-politicized justice that prevails in other adjudicative settings. But it is not a purely political act, or beyond the reach of due-process legalisms, either. Its outcome should be a distinct brand of justice, one incorporating broad and basic political considerations. Yet it must be justice nonetheless, politicized in proper form and measure only: a kind of "people's justice," perhaps, but justice all the same. If effective steps are taken to see that it isn't simply a venting of popular resentments, fears, and immediate partisan agendas, it might be "people's justice" at its best. But that is hardly assured. Indeed, legal scholar Richard Neumann, Jr., has argued that, in modern times, the quality of justice yielded by impeachments, at least on the federal level, has not often attained that high-minded, nonpartisan quality.[25]

The practice traces back to fourteenth-century England, when it was used by Parliament to remove officials allegedly engaged in criminal acts under cover of governmental functions. There was, from the beginning, an adherence to legal forms: the House of Commons assumed the equivalent of a grand-jury function, deciding whether grounds for impeachment existed; the House of Lords served as the trial court, with due observance of normal common-law procedures. But the act of impeachment, for all its legal trappings, was usually a rather overtly political act, generally aiming to augment the power of Parliament over agents of the crown. That political cast was even more evident in colonial America—especially during the pre-revolutionary era, where the impeachment proceedings regularly undertaken by colonial assemblies against royal officers were effective means of mobilizing anti-royalist sentiment (albeit less effective in actually compelling action by the king).

But when the time came for Americans to write constitutions of their own, framers of both federal and state versions were prepared to reconsider the political dimension of impeachment. Granted, it was essential to find some means of acting outside normal electoral or appointive processes to remove an official whose corruption, irresponsibility, or disloyalty presented a serious and imminent threat to the common good. It was equally clear that, in the republican order the Americans aimed to construct, only the people's elected representatives could decide just when that extraordinary action was warranted. But steps must also be taken to address "the greatest danger:" impeachment actions undertaken not as high-minded defense of an imperiled citizenry but in the spirit of "factionalism," for tactical partisan gain.[26]

The framers of the federal constitution, in particular, were determined that impeachment not be allowed to serve as politics by other means. The delicate balance among branches of government they aimed to establish would be undone if legislators were constitutionally licensed to unseat executive and judicial officers at will. Restraints, it was recognized, must be imposed, lest stable republican government prove the pipe dream its critics alleged.

One of them was conferring the responsibility to actually conduct impeachment trials on the upper chamber of the legislature alone. The House of Representatives would be the body to bring impeachment charges; but only the Senate, carefully designed to be less roiled by partisan passions than the lower chamber, could be entrusted to actually try the case, and do justice to both complainants and defendants. When conducting those proceedings, senators "shall be on oath or affirmation," that is, expected to conduct themselves by the same standards of impartiality and probity that jurists were customarily held to.[27]

In addition, constitutional provisions set the bar for the impeachment of any federal official quite high: the requirement of a two-thirds vote in the Senate to impeach a president, for example; or the decision by delegates to the constitutional convention not to allow impeachment for "maladministration" or "malpractice," terms deemed too loose and too easily politicized.[28] In 1787, the framers vigorously debated whether to grant Congress the power to remove, by means of "bill of address" (i.e., a simple petition to the chief executive), any official whose actions had sufficiently displeased a majority of legislators, even if those actions did not rise to the level of the "high crimes and misdemeanors" that might trigger formal impeachment proceedings.[29] By bypassing formal trial in the Senate, of course, removal by address also minimized the possibility of a vigorous public defense by the accused. The idea was rejected.

The steps taken to protect federal officials from removal for partisan reasons, and thus to maintain the stability of the federal government, proved especially beneficial to federal judges, who have only rarely been the subject of impeachment proceedings.[30] But in fact, impeachments of state judges, too, have grown increasingly rare over the course of American history.[31] This might have surprised the framers of those state constitutions where the impeachment power was considerably more robust than anything the authors of the nation's charter were prepared to countenance. Indeed, it might even have surprised the framers of New Hampshire's constitution most of all.

NOTES

1. New Hampshire, Attorney General Philip McLaughlin, *Report of the Attorney General: in re: W. Stephen Thayer, III and related matters* (Concord, NH: Office of Attorney General, 2000, (hereinafter, McLaughlin Report).

2. Associated Press, "2 Justices Broke Law, New Hampshire Attorney General Says," *New York Times*, April 1, 2000, http://www.nytimes.com/2000/04/01/us/2-justices-broke-law-new-hampshire-attorney-general-says.html.

3. See Journal 13 (April 13, 2000), in New Hampshire General Court, *Journal of the House of Representatives* [hereinafter, N.H. H.R. Jour.] (Concord, NH: The House, 2000), 571–76.

4. Judiciary Report Pursuant to HR50, N.H. H.R. Jour. 20 (July 12, 2000), 982–91.

5. See HR51, Floor Amendment 4796h, N.H. H.R. Jour. 20 (July 12, 2000), 1036–43.

6. Langdon was a judge on the N.H. Superior Court, then the state's highest court. His critics alleged that he was pursuing commercial interests in the city of Portsmouth, where he lived, rather than holding court in outlying counties. They may have been influenced, as well, by his criticism of them for interfering in court proceedings, and failing to set judicial salaries at a level he considered fair. See John Phillip Reid, *Legislating the Courts: Judicial Dependence in Early National New Hampshire* (DeKalb, IL: Northern Illinois University Press, 2009), 35–39.

7. The case of Judge John Pickering might be noted here. In the 1790s, Pickering was Chief Justice of New Hampshire's Superior Court of Judicature, then its highest state tribunal. Critics complained that his behavior on the bench was erratic, but they lacked the political support to force him from office. See Reid, *Legislating Courts*, 55–58. In 1795, they instead convinced President Washington to appoint him to the U.S. District Court for New Hampshire—where he was indeed impeached, convicted, and removed in 1803–1804. Ibid., 90–109.

8. Before David Brock in 2000, the only state court chief justices in American history who had articles of impeachment filed against them were Edward Shippen (PA, 1803); John McClure (AR, 1871 and 1874); David Furches (NC, 1901); Frederick Branson (OK, 1927); and Charles Mason (OK, 1929). See Appendix A for more information.

9. See Claremont School District v. Governor, 138 N.H. 183, 635 A. 2d 1375 (1993) [*"Claremont I"*].

10. See Claremont School District v. Governor, 142 N.H. 462, 703 A. 2d 1353 (1997) [*"Claremont II"*]. *Claremont I* and *II* were the first and second of seven separate decisions on issues associated with this litigation.

11. Carey Goldberg, "In the Live-Free-or-Die State, An Unpalatable Tax Decision," *New York Times*, July 29, 1998, http://www.nytimes.com/1998/06/29/us/statehouse-journal-in-the-live-free-or-die-state-an-unpalatable-tax-decision.html.

12. Ibid.

13. Dan Balz, "School vs. Property Tax Dilemma Testing New Hampshire Communities," *Washington Post*, January 10, 1998, https://www.washingtonpost.com/archive/politics/1998/01/10/school-vs-property-tax-dilemma-testing-new-hampshire-communities/829fca84-e0bd-494e-812a-a4bc0e506a06/?utm_term=.018eb2b21e79.

14. Kermit Hall, for instance, in considering the Brock impeachment flatly concluded that "the real basis for the attack was his court's decision mandating increased school funding and then rejecting legislative proposals to do so" (Kermit Hall, "Judicial Independence and the Majoritarian Difficulty," in Kermit Hall and Kevin McGuire (eds.), *Institutions of American Democracy: The Judicial Branch* (New York: Oxford University Press, 2005), 72. See also Tarr, *Without Fear or Favor*, 94, 98.

15. State Sen. Mary Brown, one of only two Senators to find Brock guilty of all four articles of impeachment voted by the House of Representatives, would publish a very valuable overview of the affair a year after its conclusion (*The Impeachment Trial of the New Hampshire Supreme Court Chief Justice,* Pittsfield, NH: Lynxfield Publishing, 2001). In it, Brown openly wondered "Did the New Hampshire Legislature overreact, venting pent-up resentment about the Supreme Court's Claremont ruling?" (Ibid., 1). Acknowledging that "the ghost of the *Claremont Case*" was present throughout the impeachment," Brown recalled the efforts required to keep *Claremont* out of the deliberations. "But of course, we all knew this impeachment was not about *Claremont*," she explained. "It couldn't be. That would be wrong." (Ibid., 259).

16. N.H. H.R. Jour. 20, HR51 Debate (July 12, 2000), 998.

17. For current information on the selection and retention of appellate and trial judges in state courts, see Shauna Strickland, Richard Schauffler, Robert LaFountain, and Kathryn Holt, eds., *State Court Organization* [last uploaded June 30, 2017], National Center for State Courts, Tables 2.3 and 3.3, www.ncsc.org/sco, as accessed July 20, 2017.

18. Basically, Langdell's view was that legal analysis was a kind of quasi-science, requiring a rationalism untainted by political concerns and passions. See Paul Carrington, "Hail! Langdell!" *Law & Social Inquiry* 20, no. 3 (1995): 691–760.

19. Judith Shklar's *Legalism* (Cambridge, MA: Harvard University Press, 1964) provides an especially careful, perceptive, philosophical consideration of both the boundaries and the interface between "law" and "politics." Otto Kirschner's influential *Political Justice: The Use of Legal Procedure for Political Ends* (Princeton, NJ: Princeton University Press, 1961) offers a somewhat different perspective, and remains a valuable provocative work as well.

20. The classic treatments of the purpose and nature of impeachment are Alexander Hamilton, "Federalist #65," in Alexander Hamilton, James Madison, and John Jay, *The Federalist Papers* (New York: New American Library, 1961), 396–401; and Joseph Story, *Commentaries on the Constitution of the United States* (Boston: Billiard, Gray, 1833), Vol. II, Chapter IX, §§686–87.

21. Hamilton, "Federalist #65," 396.

22. In *Impeachment in America, 1635–1805* (New Haven, CT: Yale University Press, 1984), 101–102 and 118–19, Peter Hoffer and N.E.H. Hull argue persuasively

that the American colonies had long subscribed to that broader view of impeachable offenses. Raoul Berger had previously argued that delegates to the U.S. Constitutional Convention in 1787 meant to adopt English precedent, and to confine those offenses to overt crimes (*Impeachment: The Constitutional Problems*, Cambridge: Harvard University Press, 1973). But, as Richard Posner notes, that would have meant that the convention's delegates were emulating the power they had just rebelled against, and ignoring their own colonial and state traditions. It also would have rendered presidents, vice presidents, and federal judges all but invulnerable, since the constitution provided no means other than impeachment for removing those officials. See Posner, *An Affair of State: The Investigation, Impeachment, and Trial of President Clinton* (Cambridge: Harvard University Press, 1999), 98–99.

23. In the nineteenth century, both Supreme Court Justice Samuel Chase and President Andrew Johnson were impeached but won acquittal with defenses stressing the non-indictable character of their alleged offenses. In the twentieth century, however, both Judge Robert Archibald (1913) and Judge Halsted Ritter (1936) were convicted for non-indictable offenses. An historical summary of the practice is provided at U.S. Senate, "Impeachment," http://www.senate.gov/artandhistory/history/common/briefing/Senate_Impeachment_Role.htm#2.

24. An impeachment is "designed as a method of NATIONAL INQUEST into the conduct of public men," argued Hamilton, and for that reason must be entrusted to the peoples' elected representatives ("who can so properly be inquisitors for the nation as the representatives of the nation themselves?"). Hamilton, "Federalist #65," 397. Joseph Story concurred that this was one adjudicative function that could not be entrusted to conventional courts precisely because they lacked a direct popular mandate. He wrote, "It is, perhaps, one of the circumstances most important in the discharge of judicial duties, that they rarely carry with them any strong popular favor, or popular influence." Story, *Commentaries*, Vol. II, Ch. X, §759.

25. Neumann attributes a "dual personality" to the impeachments he has studied, proposing that the practice has served both the legitimate political purpose intended by the founders ("to oust in a nonpartisan or bipartisan manner a corrupt official who abuses power") and less high-minded, more baldly partisan ones ("to inflict, for partisan reasons, a political blow on an official whose conduct the impeaching Representatives simply dislike"). Notably, he finds that "Because the second purpose is much less acceptable, the impeaching Representatives attempt to disguise their purpose even when voting on strictly party lines." See Neumann's "The Revival of Impeachment as a Partisan Political Weapon," *Hastings Const. L. Q.* 34, no. 2 (2007): 161–62.

26. Hamilton, "Federalist #65," 396–97. Hamilton was acutely mindful that, to the degree that they indeed are political acts, impeachment actions "will seldom fail to agitate the passions of the whole community, and to divide it into parties more or less friendly or inimical to the accused … there will always be the greatest danger that the decision will be regulated more by the comparative strength of the parties than by the real demonstration of innocence or guilt." That was precisely why, in Hamilton's view, the best adjudicators of impeachment charges would be senators. "Where else than in the Senate," he asked, "could have been found a tribunal sufficiently dignified,

or sufficiently independent? What other body would be likely … to preserve, unawed and uninfluenced, the necessary impartiality between an INDIVIDUAL accused, and the REPRESENTATIVES OF THE PEOPLE, HIS ACCUSERS?" Ibid., 398.

27. In 1833, Joseph Story would laud this as "a provision which, as it appeals to the conscience and integrity of the members by the same sanctions which apply to judges and jurors, who sit in other trials, will commend itself to all persons, who deem the highest trusts, rights, and duties, worthy of the same protection and security, at least, as those of the humblest order." Story, *Commentaries*, Vol. II, Chapter X, §774.

28. Hoffer and Hull, *Impeachment in America,* 101. In recognition of the gravity of impeachment, virtually all states also require a two-thirds vote for conviction. See Council of State Governments, *The Book of the States, Volume 42* (Lexington, KY: the Council, 2010), Table 4.8.

29. For more on removal by address, see Charles Geyh, James Alfini, Steven Lubet, and Jeffrey Shaman, *Judicial Conduct and Ethics, 5th ed.* (Newark, NJ: Matthew Bender, 2013), §14.05.

30. See Warren Grimes, "Hundred-Ton Gun Control: Preserving Impeachment as the Exclusive Removal Mechanism for Federal Judges," *UCLA L. Rev.* 38, no. 5 (1991): 1209.

31. For details on the grounds for impeachment in each state, see Connecticut General Assembly, Office of Legal Research, "Constitutional and Statutory Impeachment Provisions in 50 States," OLR Research Report 2004-R-0146 (2004), https://www.cga.ct.gov/2004/rpt/2004-R-0146.htm.

Part I

LEGISLATIVE-JUDICIAL RELATIONS: THE HISTORICAL RUPTURE

Chapter 1

The Historical New Hampshire Civic Culture

In June 1778, in the midst of the revolutionary war, New Hampshire's voters established the very first constitutional convention in American history.[1] Its delegates hoped to replace the essentially ad hoc document assembled in 1776, upon the collapse of royal government, with something more considered and more permanent. But the task would prove vexing: the state's electorate would not actually approve a founding charter for themselves until 1784. The document they finally endorsed in that year, as well as the revised version they brought forth in 1792, reflected no great caution regarding deployment of the impeachment power. In New Hampshire, "maladministration" and "malpractice" *were* specifically included as grounds for impeachment.[2] In addition, delegates to the 1784 Constitutional Convention *did* grant legislators additional means of removing offending officials by establishing the "bill of address" that their counterparts in Philadelphia would eschew.[3]

The measures lowering the bar to impeachment in New Hampshire in 1784 were consistent with the general political philosophy that prevailed in several states at the time, a philosophy shaped by hard historical experience. It was not a philosophy that prioritized the protection of judges, or anyone else, from the judgment of the peoples' chosen representatives. The authors of New Hampshire's constitution, while formally committed to a separation of powers, were considerably less emphatic on that point than their counterparts in Massachusetts.[4] New Hampshire's framers, profoundly marked by the long struggle with royal governors and, especially, royal courts, were frankly committed to a strong legislative branch, and unafraid to expand its prerogatives vis-á-vis the others.[5] Not until 1792 was the legislative leviathan somewhat tamed by a range of constitutional revisions, which mainly elevated the power of the governor. Only then, for example, was the chief executive granted any veto authority whatsoever, or fully uncoupled from the legislature.[6]

LEGISLATIVE SUPREMACY AND "PEOPLE'S JUSTICE" IN NEW HAMPSHIRE

But the judicial branch was not similarly strengthened or distanced from legislative control in 1792.[7] In fact, it would remain for all intents and purposes mainly a creature of the legislature (the latter designated, as in Massachusetts, the state's "General Court") for well over a century. The main reason was that the constitution granted the legislature full power to establish courts and set their jurisdictions as it saw fit.[8] The constitution of 1784 did allow that judicial impartiality is an important consideration ("It is the right of every citizen to be tried by judges as impartial as the lot of humanity will admit").[9] To secure that impartiality, the constitution's framers were even prepared to grant that "judges of the supreme judicial court [then the state's highest court] should hold their offices so long as they behave well."[10] But ostensibly generous tenure was no guarantee of judicial autonomy. The authority to determine transgressive behavior, after all, was left to the legislature.

New Hampshire voters, for their part, showed scant interest in alternative arrangements when presented with them. In fact, they unambiguously rejected one particular reform intended to liberate courts from the control of legislative bodies, a reform that was quite popular elsewhere in the country. That was the popular election of judges. Historians continue to assess the motivations behind those measures. Some argue, from the direct manifestation of Jacksonian democracy that judicial elections appear to be, that they were actually born of a desire to fortify rather than diminish judicial power by granting judges the same popular mandates legislators enjoyed. The idea, at least as articulated in numerous states' constitutional debates, was endowing judges with the democratic legitimacy they needed to maintain constitutional constraints on legislators, many of whose actions had proven so short-sighted and self-interested in the economic panics of the 1830s.[11] By the outbreak of the Civil War, twenty-four of thirty-four states had established elected judiciaries.[12]

New Hampshire, however, was not one of them (joining Massachusetts and Rhode Island as the only states to reject the idea). Its voters effectively ended debate on the matter after the 1850 Constitutional Convention.[13] Delegates to that conclave endorsed no fewer than fifteen constitutional revisions providing for the popular election of various judges and court functionaries (high court judges, county judges, probate judges, registers of probate, police magistrates, and trial justices in towns), for terms of office ranging from two to six years. But when voters were called on to ratify the proposals in town meetings, all fifteen measures were easily defeated.[14] The question has not been seriously entertained in New Hampshire since then.

Indeed, New Hampshire's legislators were so confident of the rightness of legislative supremacy over the judiciary that in the state's early history they maintained the revolutionary tradition whereby the adjudication of particular cases was directly monitored, and often undone, by the people's assembly.[15] As in other states, New Hampshire litigants dissatisfied by the judgment of regular courts could and often did invoke the legislature's "redress of grievances" function, whereupon the people's assembly might set aside court decisions and order a new trial, or even announce a decision of its own.[16] The democratized or "common-sense" justice thus delivered may not have been as unashamedly political as the brand that had been meted out by the New Hampshire Committee of Public Safety during the revolution (the latter likened by one historian to the notorious peoples' tribunals of the French Revolution).[17] But in the view of another scholar, it was "not law," either. It was, rather, "unequal, crude, uncertain, and often unfair, for partisan and corrupt interests sometimes entered into judgment."[18]

Be that as it may, the state's court arrangements and legal practice simply reflected the general belief that law and justice issued more reliably from the common sense of the common man than from the circumlocutions of trained lawyers. It followed that the powers of those lawyers should be quite deliberately circumscribed as well. No one in early-republican New Hampshire (or, for that matter, in many other states at the time) thought it improper that probate and other local courts should be entrusted to laymen, and juries empowered to rule on points of law in addition to fact. It was thought right and proper that legal professionals, certainly including judges, be kept on a leash, in fact a rather short one. That was simply the operational concomitant of the philosophical commitment to legislative supremacy by which legislative-judicial relations in New Hampshire were shaped until well into the twentieth century.

Clearly, the state's founders felt little ardor for judicial independence in institutional terms, and positive revulsion toward judicial overreach. For roughly the first century and a half of the state's post-colonial history, most of its political class and citizenry gave little indication that they felt otherwise.

NEW HAMPSHIRE JUDICIARY UNDER LEGISLATIVE SUPREMACY

New Hampshire's judicial history, however, is not monochromatic. For there has always been another current in New Hampshire civic life—robust if not dominant, palpable within the judicial branch if not always welcomed outside it—that saw the principle of judicial subordination as something closer to heresy than holy writ.

That current has manifested itself in ongoing efforts to de-politicize or professionalize the administration of justice, a process that has required granting thicker insulation to judges against the wrath of legislators or even citizens. This has not been an easy argument to make in New Hampshire. Yet its proponents have had considerable success, especially in recent decades. In fact, much of New Hampshire's legal history has revolved around the question of how, and sometimes whether, those two notions of justice—"people's" versus "professionalized"—can coexist.

Even the early judicial history of the state witnessed vigorous efforts by reformers such as the remarkable Jeremiah Smith, a U.S. District Attorney and eventual Chief Justice of the N.H. Supreme Judicial Court, to expand the power of judges both within their own courtrooms (by, e.g., bringing juries more firmly under their control) and outside them (by, for example, establishing the precedential value of published judicial decisions, a deliberate move toward judge-made law). The intent was to render justice more uniform, more predictable, less arbitrary—in brief, to substitute the rule of law, administered by law-trained personnel, over the people's sometimes ad hoc notions of justice and equity.[19]

The episode that best illustrates some state judges' commitment to the notion that the people's will could be exercised only within parameters set by trained judges may have been the remarkable "Ten Pounds Act" cases of 1786–1787. In 1785, the legislature had passed a law empowering local justices of the peace to settle actions for debt or trespass under ten pounds, if title to land was not involved. Previously, any claim over two pounds required a jury trial. The change was intended to help the state's many debtors in the years following the revolutionary war by reducing the expense of defending themselves from creditors' claims: bench trials before a local justice were cheaper than jury trials conducted in distant courts, and court costs were assessed against the losers. But a series of appeals went to the Inferior Court of Common Pleas for Rockingham County, and judges there repeatedly declared the Ten Pound Act a violation of the state constitution's guarantee of a right to trial by jury in civil cases.[20] The judges' defiance of the legislature nearly got them impeached. But they held their ground, and in the end they had enough defenders in the legislature to not only survive but prevail. The law was rescinded.[21]

That victory, however, was neither easy nor easily forgotten. The Ten Pounds Act controversy "fueled a political and constitutional crisis of significant proportions" in New Hampshire.[22] It also helped fix in the public mind an association of judicial assertiveness with "elitism," that is, with opposition to popular rule, as constitutionally mandated, by the permanent and unqualified supremacy of the peoples' elected representatives. That, in fact, may help explain why an effort to secure full constitutional status for the state's highest court in 1791 failed. Legislators were every bit as committed to the proposition that the judiciary ought properly to be subordinate to their own will in 1791 as they had been in 1784, if not more so.[23]

Yet if New Hampshire judges could not achieve institutional independence in terms of constitutional status, they were hardly supine. A turning point of sorts was reached in 1818, when, in *Merrill v. Sherburne,* N.H.'s Superior Court of Judicature (then the state's highest court) went beyond the facts of that particular case to declare that the legislature's habit of granting new trials (somewhat disingenuously labeled "restoration to law") was "not within the legitimate exercise of legislative power."[24] The decision, written by Justice Levi Woodbury, represented the culmination of an extended period of resistance by New Hampshire courts to the state legislature's ongoing interventions in judicial affairs, with which some courts had simply refused to comply. What Woodbury did was elucidate a constitutional basis for that resistance. By his reckoning, the separation of powers proposed by the state's constitution was meaningless unless adjudicative responsibilities were assigned to courts alone. Woodbury then went somewhat further. By granting each branch of government the right and power to defend its realm from encroachments by the others, he argued, the constitution authorized the judiciary to declare this entire practice a form of legislative overreach.

Merrill v. Sherburne was not really New Hampshire's *Marbury v. Madison*, as is sometimes claimed. Woodbury's ruling was more defensive than offensive in nature, fending off legislative incursions into actions that properly belonged to trained judges and claiming just enough power vis-á-vis that legislature as was necessary to do so.[25] In fact, the case's historical significance may lie less in the (relatively modest) blow it struck for judicial independence than in its call for a more fully professionalized judiciary. Woodbury's ruling was, in essence, a plea for "decisional" independence: letting judges rule on each case without external influence from the elected branches of government.[26]

That agenda, neither more nor less, would motivate some of New Hampshire's most ambitious judges for the next century and a half. Indeed, the core historical struggle of the state judiciary until the mid-twentieth century would be for justice ascertained by legally trained personnel, following established legal procedures, in settings that had been sufficiently de-politicized so that legal reasoning and legal reasoning alone might carry the day. Real judicial independence (as modeled in, for example, the federal constitution) was simply not attainable, or probably even imaginable, until well into the twentieth century. Judicial professionalization, however, could be advanced by means short of that.

One of them was influence over the state bar—repository of professional standards and values to judges, incubator of legal elitism to New Hampshire's

Jacksonian democrats. In 1842, the latter sought to democratize the bar with legislation granting admission to any twenty-one-year-old man of good character. The superior court of judicature responded with a series of judgments securing to itself some concurrent powers in determining at least when members' claim to "good character" had lost credibility.[27]

The reforms of the celebrated Charles Doe, Chief Justice from 1876 to 1896, can be understood as attempts to take judicial professionalization a step (actually, a rather long stride) further. Doe focused on court procedures (pleadings, rules of evidence, the use of various writs) in both civil and criminal actions. He blithely cut away a number of the common-law procedural protocols that he felt rendered many civil actions, in particular, needlessly burdensome for litigants, and therefore all too likely to sacrifice justice to procedural form. At first glance, it would seem that Doe's actions effectively *un*did much of what prior professionalizers, including Jeremiah Smith, had already done. But his actions actually took the New Hampshire judiciary further down the trail those predecessors had blazed. For, anti-formalist as he was, Doe's judicial life was one broad rebuke of legal populism, and elevation of the role of the legal expert. His jurisprudence flowed logically from the sort of philosophically-informed (in this case, Lockean) interpretation of the state constitution that only a trained judge could or would internalize, and from his own deep conviction that the function of judges was the protection of substantive common-law rights rather than *pro forma* practices—whether legislators recognized that or not.[28] No specific statute authorized Doe to alter court procedures; in fact, critics lambasted him for terminating standing court practices without legislative warrant.[29] But it was his belief that justice emerged from courts alone, and that judges' role there is maintaining the rules that best secure it. Understood in those terms, his storied career is a kind of case study in the merits and/or perils of judicial professionalization.

All this could be (and probably had to be) accomplished without upsetting the state's long-standing tradition of legislative primacy; after all, separate powers had not, in New Hampshire, ever meant *equal* powers. Certainly, throughout the nineteenth century the state legislature showed little reluctance to exercise that mastery. Responding to shifts in political currents, the legislature abolished and remade entire courts no fewer than five times between 1813 and 1876.[30] In each of these "court clearings," sitting judges were dismissed and new ones appointed. In addition, while no judge was impeached, no fewer than sixty-four were removed by means of legislative address.[31]

As the nineteenth century neared its end, the two main themes around which the legislative-judicial dynamic operated in New Hampshire seemed fairly well set. Within the judicial branch, the impulse to professionalize continued apace. New Hampshire's bare handful of state courts and judges had once assumed fluid, overlapping functions (e.g., the resolution of both law and equity cases). Over time, and with legislative approval, more specialized duties were articulated. The number of judges and jurisdictions grew, and court protocols were specified and standardized. In sum, judicial institutions and the judiciary as a whole were more fully elaborated, refined, formalized—arguably, bureaucratized. Legislators, for their part, maintained their oversight, and guarded their supremacy. That is, they simply conducted business as usual, unburdened by fears of serious judicial constraints on their traditional fields of action or policy choices.

To be sure, judicial rebuffs did occasionally occur, sometimes in cases where constitutional limitations on the taxing power of the state, or provisions for the basic separation of powers, were at issue.[32] Those cases did multiply somewhat in the post–Civil War era,[33] as state government coped with the social and economic changes attendant on industrialization.[34] Yet the great majority of the decisions affirmed the constitutionality of statutes, and none of the cases finding statutes unconstitutional were as consequential as the *Merrill* decision. As Table 1.1 indicates, there were 74 reported New Hampshire cases with judicial decisions on challenges to the constitutionality of legislative action rendered in the entire nineteenth century, with only 16 holding legislation unconstitutional.[35]

ADVISORY OPINIONS

Still other decisions on the constitutionality of legislative or executive action have taken the comparatively benign form of advisory opinions, rendered at the request of the legislature or the executive and representing only the viewpoints of individual justices rather than the judgment of the high court as an institution. New Hampshire is one of only a handful states to adopt that practice, whereby overt and definitive rejections of duly enacted legislation were eschewed and conflicts among legislature, executive, and judiciary softened.[36]

Table 1.1 Percent of New Hampshire Cases with Legislation Found Unconstitutional, 1817–1900

Time Period	*Total Judicial Review Cases*	*Legislation Found Unconstitutional*	*Percent Found Unconstitutional (%)*
1817–1865	19	1	5.3
1866–1900	55	15	27.3
Nineteenth century Total	74	16	21.6

Source: case-by-case analysis (on file with the authors) of 74 reported New Hampshire judicial review cases, 1817–1900. For more information, see Appendix B.

New Hampshire's high court rendered its first advisory opinion in 1816. It was requested by the governor and executive council, asking about the constitutionality of legislation that would amend the charter of Dartmouth College. Acting in their individual capacity and not as a court to offer authoritative advice, the justices replied that the state constitution does not authorize a request for advice on a question involving vested private rights, which justices accurately anticipated might soon be litigated in the courts. The governor also asked about his power with the executive council to fill vacancies on the Dartmouth College Board of Trustees. The justices responded that the governor and council had no authority to fill vacancies occurring after the date of the Board's first scheduled meeting.[37]

After the justices responded to the request for an advisory opinion, the matter was indeed litigated, and the court held in 1817 that the legislation, which would result in Dartmouth being converted from a private to a public institution of higher education, was valid under the New Hampshire constitution. Yet that decision was subsequently reversed on separate grounds by the U.S. Supreme Court in 1819, which rendered a landmark decision invalidating the New Hampshire legislation as a retroactive impairment of private contract rights in violation of the contract clause of the U.S. constitution.[38]

Requests for advisory opinions in New Hampshire were infrequent before the Civil War but they increased during and after it, usually at the requested of the legislature. See Table 1.2.

As Table 1.2 shows, there were occasions when the justices declined to answer the questions posed, and others where the questions involved only the interpretation of a statute, with no constitutional question presented. In the requests that remained, the justices responded more often than not that the contemplated action would indeed be constitutional.

Table 1.2 New Hampshire Advisory Opinions, 1816–1900

Action Taken by Justices on Advisory Opinion Requests	*Cases Reported*	*Percent Of Opinions Requested (%)*
• Proposed action found constitutional	14	50.0
• Proposed action found only partially constitutional	0	0.0
• Proposed action found not constitutional	9	32.1
• Justices declined to render opinion	3	10.7
• Statutory interpretation only	2	7.1
Grand Total of Advisory Opinion Requests	28	99.9[a]

Source: case-by-case analysis (on file with the authors) of 28 reported New Hampshire advisory opinions, 1816–1900. For more information, see Appendix C.

[a] Cumulative total does not equal 100.0 percent because of rounding.

With so little judicial resistance in any form to actions of the elected branches of state government, it is hardly surprising that none of the court clearings of the nineteenth century represented legislative retaliation for an unfriendly appellate court decision or advisory opinion. Rather, those were functions of raw, partisan politics: judicial appointments were among the spoils of war seized by victorious parties and that, far more than judicial professionalization, was what threatened the stability of legislative-judicial relations in New Hampshire well into the twentieth century.[39]

NOTES

1. Massachusetts would have had the honor of being first, but the revolutionary-era Massachusetts legislature rejected requests by various towns to call a special convention to draft a state constitution, opting in 1777 to attempt the job itself. The constitution it produced would be rejected by Massachusetts voters in June 1778. In that same month and year, New Hampshire voters did elect a convention of delegates for the purpose of writing a constitution for their state (New Hampshire had adopted a provisional constitution in 1776, but it was understood as a temporary response to the disintegration of royal government). Massachusetts, however, did formally adopt its constitution prior to New Hampshire, whose voters would reject drafts offered in 1781 and 1782 before finally approving one in 1784. In fact, the Massachusetts version heavily influenced New Hampshire's. In particular, the latter chose to embrace their Massachusetts counterparts' notion that a constitution should foreground citizens' rights and derive the architecture of government from them—in marked contrast to the federal constitution, which reversed those priorities and incorporated a bill only after considerable debate. For a fine, concise summary of N.H.'s early constitutional history, see Susan Marshall, *The New Hampshire State Constitution* (New York: Oxford University Press, 2011), 3–38.

2. New Hampshire's constitution treats the impeachment power in Part 2, Articles 17, 38, and 39. Those provisions designate the lower house of the legislature as the "grand inquest of the state"; require that "all impeachments made by them, shall be heard and tried in the senate"; describe the investigatory and decisional powers of the Senate, on the one hand, and the procedural rights of defendants in impeachments hearings, on the other; and distinguish impeachment from normal civil or criminal actions by limiting the effect of a conviction to removal from office (Part 2, Articles 17, 38, 39). See Marshall, *State Constitution,* 149–51, 168–69.

3. Part 2, Article 73 originally read, "The governor [changed from 'the president' in 1792] with consent of the [executive] council may remove any commissioned officer for reasonable cause upon the address of both houses of the legislature, provided nevertheless that the cause for removal shall be stated fully and substantially in the address and shall not be a cause which is a sufficient ground for impeachment." In fact, no fewer than sixty-five judicial officers (including prosecutors as well as judges) would be removed from office in New Hampshire by that method prior to 1966. Ibid, 199.

4. Article XXX of the Massachusetts constitution ("Separation of Legislative, Executive and Judicial Departments") reads "In the government of this commonwealth, the legislative department shall never exercise the executive and judicial powers; or either of them: the executive shall never exercise the legislative and judicial powers, or either of them: the judicial shall never exercise the legislative and executive powers or either of them, to the end it may be a government of laws and not of men." Article 37 of New Hampshire's constitution offers decidedly less assertive, vaguer language: "In the government of this state, the three essential powers thereof, to wit, the legislative, executive, and judicial, ought to be kept as separate from, and independent of, each other, as the nature of a free government will admit, or as is consistent with that chain of connection that binds the whole fabric of the constitution in one indissoluble bond of unity and amity." As 23 of the 37 articles in the Bill of Rights that constitute Part 1 of New Hampshire's constitution are copied almost word for word from Massachusetts' 1780 constitution, this contrast is especially notable. See Richard McNamara, "The Separation of Powers Principle and the Role of the Courts in New Hampshire," *N.H. Bar J.* 42, no. 2 (2001): 66, 69.

5. N.H. Const. Pt. 1, Art. 37. Susan Marshall acknowledges that, despite Part 1 Article 37's stipulation regarding separate and independent powers, "the executive and judicial branches were weak and subservient to the legislature." Marshall, *State Constitution*, 19.

6. Even today, New Hampshire's Governor shares appointive and other executive powers with an elected Executive Council, and legislative duties with the third largest legislative body in the English-speaking world, behind only the British Parliament and U.S. Congress.

7. This, despite the efforts of reformers such as future governor and U.S. Sen. William Plumer. Plumer's proposals to strengthen the judiciary, including granting it sole power to grant new trials, were in fact included in the draft constitution prepared in 1791, but rejected by voters in that year. See Timothy Lawrie, "Interpretation and Authority: Separation of Powers and the Judiciary's Battle for Independence in New Hampshire, 1786–1818," *Am. J. Legal Hist.* 39, no. 3 (1995): 310, 319–20.

8. Part 2, Article 4 of the N.H. constitution reads "The General Court shall forever have full power and authority to erect and constitute judicatories and courts of record, or other courts, to be beholden, in the name of the state, for the hearing, trying, and determining all manner of crimes, offenses, pleas, processes, plaints, actions, causes, matters and things whatsoever arising or happening within the state, or between or concerning persons inhabiting or residing, or brought, within the same, whether the same be criminal or civil, or whether the crimes be capital, or not capital, and whether the said pleas be real, personal, or mixed, and for the awarding and issuing execution thereon." The only court mentioned in the constitution was the already-extant Superior Court of Judicature, but was not established by the constitution nor exempted from the provisions of Part 2, Article 4. It had been established by the monarchy in 1692, and was retained with minor changes when the revolution broke out.

9. N.H. Const. Pt. 1, Art. 35 (Marshall, *State Constitution*, 110). It is worth noting that New Hampshire's constitution speaks of "impartial" judges, but not the "free, impartial, and independent" judges described in the Massachusetts Constitution.

10. Ibid. The only explicit constitutional qualification of tenure so long as good behavior is not breached is found in Part 2, Article 78, adopted in 1792. It stipulates a mandatory retirement at age 70 for judges of any court, and sheriffs of any county.

11. This interpretation was first proposed by Kermit Hall, who saw legal professionals as the main promoters of judicial elections. See Hall, "The Judiciary on Trial: State Constitutional Reform and the Rise of an Elected Judiciary, 1846–1860," *Historian 45,* no. 3 (1983): 337–54. It was reiterated the following decade by Caleb Nelson, who shared Hall's view of such elections' purpose but saw them as a popular, rather than lawyer-driven, reform. See Nelson, "A Re-Evaluation of Scholarly Explanations for the Rise of the Elective Judiciary in Antebellum America," *Am. J. Legal Hist.* 37, no. 2 (1993): 190–224. The general thesis that such elections were intended to advance, rather than constrict, judicial authority has been re-asserted more recently by Jed Shugerman, in "Economic Crisis and the Rise of Judicial Elections and Judicial Review," *Harv. L. Rev.* 123, no. 5 (2010): 1061–1150, and again in *The People's Court: Judicial Independence in America.*

12. Tarr, *Without Fear or Favor.* See also, Robert Tobin, *Creating the Judicial Branch: The Unfinished Reform* (Williamsburg, VA: National Center for State Courts, 1999), 27–32.

13. Larry Berkson, Rachel Caulfield and Malia Reddick, "Judicial Selection in the United States: A Special Report," American Judicature Society (2010), 1. Available at http://www.judicialselection.us/uploads/documents/Berkson1196091951709.pfd.

14. Rejection of those measures may have reflected voters' general suspicion that the 1851 Constitutional Convention had been too radical overall, rather than a more focused opposition to judicial elections themselves. Susan Marshall has noted that the *New Hampshire Patriot and State Gazette* openly recanted its initial support for the convention, arguing that if the sum total of its work would be a "new Constitution" which left "scarcely a feature of the old one" recognizable. Marshall, *State Constitution*, 24.

15. In the pre-revolutionary period, New Hampshire's and other colonies' legislatures had strenuously resisted royal grants of chancery powers to governors and their councils. Equity, argued colonists, should be determined by peoples' assemblies, which claimed the same powers Parliament enjoyed *vis-á-vis* English courts, or even expanded ones. See Mary Clark, *Parliamentary Privilege in the American Colonies* (New Haven: Yale University Press, 1943).

16. John Phillip Reid, *Legislating the Courts.* See also Reid's *Controlling the Law: Legal Politics in Early National New Hampshire* (DeKalb, IL: Northern Illinois University Press, 2004), and *Legitimating the Law: The Struggle for Judicial Competency in Early National New Hampshire* (DeKalb, IL: Northern Illinois University Press, 2012). Taken together, the three works constitute the most thorough and penetrating investigation of the judiciary in New Hampshire during the early-republican period, and especially of the state's legislative-judicial relations in that era.

17. Richard Upton, *Separation of Powers in New Hampshire*, unpublished thesis, Harvard Law School, cited by Richard McNamara, "Separation of Powers," at 68.

18. John Phillip Reid, "From Common Sense to Common Law to Charles Doe: The Evolution of Pleading in New Hampshire," *N.H. Bar J.* 1, no. 2 (1959): 27–44, cited by Richard McNamara, "Separation of Powers," 71.

19. Reid's trilogy (*Controlling the Law*, *Legislating the Courts*, and *Legitimating the Law*) explores the process, including resistance to it, in great depth. Reid notes that, while the early legal history of other states has not been studied as extensively as has New Hampshire's and Massachusetts's, available evidence suggests that most of them probably mirrored New Hampshire's preference for "common sense jurisprudence" over judge-made or professionalized law.

20. The Rockingham County bar maintained a reputation for excellence well into the nineteenth century. See John Phillip Reid, "The Arena of Giants: Rockingham County, Hew Hampshire," *ABAJ* 46, no. 2 (1960): 163–66, 214–16.

21. The full record of New Hampshire's "Ten Pound Act" cases was unearthed by Richard Lambert in the course of researching his 1985 Master's thesis at the University of New Hampshire. Lambert published an excerpt from his thesis as "The 'Ten Pound Act' Cases and the Origins of Judicial Review in New Hampshire," *N.H. Bar J.* 43, no. 1 (2002): 37–54. In "Ten Pound Acts: An Introduction to Original Research on the Origins of Judicial Review," *N.H. Bar J.* 43, no. 1 (2002): 34, Eugene Van Loan described the cases as "the earliest and the most important precedent for the doctrine of judicial review," as articulated in 1803 by Chief Justice John Marshall in *Marbury v. Madison* in 1803. For more on the Ten Pound Act cases, see Scott Gerber, *A Distinct Judicial Power: The Origins of an Independent Judiciary 1606–1787* (New York: Oxford University Press, 2011), 116–22; William Treanor, "Judicial Review Before Marbury," *Stanford L. Rev.* 58, no. 2 (2005): 455–562; and Lawrie, "Interpretation and Authority."

22. Lambert, "'Ten Pound Act' Cases," 47.

23. Constitutional amendment resolutions to exempt the state's highest court from the legislative power to create and abolish courts were considered again in the constitutional conventions of 1889 and 1902, but they were rejected each time. See Constance Rinden and Janet Lyman, *New Hampshire Constitutional Amendment Proposals, Third Edition* (Concord, N.H.: State Law Library, 1984), 32 and 34. When New Hampshire amended its constitution in 1966 to grant constitutional status to the Supreme and Superior Courts, it was the last state in the country to do so. See Table 2.2.

24. Merrill v. Sherburne, 1 N.H. 199 (1818). For an excellent discussion of the case, see Lawrie, "Interpretation and Authority."

25. Most modern historians agree that the powers of judicial review claimed by Woodbury were far more modest than what is claimed for modern constitutional courts. John Phillip Reid sees the case as marking the passing of full legislative supremacy, but cautions that "judiciary supremacy lay more than a half century in the future" (Reid, *Legitimating the Law,* 202). Timothy Lawrie interprets the authority Woodbury asserted as "less 'supreme' than balanced between extremes," claiming independence for the judicial branch but not denying concurrent powers of constitutional interpretation still claimed by the legislature. Lawrie, "Interpretation and Authority," 330–31. Richard Hesse, however, suggests that a rather firmer power of judicial review had been established by Dartmouth College v. Woodward, 1 N.H. 111 (1817), rev'd on other grounds, 17 U.S. (4 Wheat.) 518 (1819), a year before the decision in *Merrill*. In that case, the Court found unconstitutional a legislative act reconstituting Dartmouth College. Hesse argues that, although its finding was reversed by the U.S. Supreme Court in 1819, the Court had confirmed its role as guardian

of New Hampshire's constitutional values, a claim that would never be seriously challenged. Hesse, "The Legislature, the Court, and the Constitution," *N.H. Bar J.* 41, no. 1 (2000): 38–45.

26. On the distinction between "decisional and "institutional" judicial independence, see William Batchelder, "The Independence of the Judiciary in New Hampshire Revisited," *N.H. Bar J. 39,* no. 2 (1998): 62–71.

27. Richard McNamara, "The Separation of Powers Principle and the Role of the Courts in New Hampshire," *N.H. Bar J.* 42, no. 2 (2001): 66, 73.

28. John Phillip Reid, *Chief Justice: The Judicial World of Charles Doe* (Cambridge: Harvard University Press, 1967). Reid sees Lockean principles as the basis of Doe's thinking. To Doe, the N.H. constitution represented Locke's version of the "social contract." Its whole raison d'etre was preserving the broadest manifold of personal rights and liberties consistent with social order, which meant that its mandate to courts was the realization of that goal in individual cases. It should be noted that Doe carried out many of his varied reforms of legal practice not only without benefit of legislation but, often enough, without benefit of legal precedent either. See also Reid, "Doe of New Hampshire: Reflections on a Nineteenth Century Judge," *Harv. L. Rev.* 63, no. 3 (1950): 513–22.

29. McNamara, "Separation of Powers," 75.

30. Marshall, *State Constitution*, 198.

31. Robert Dishman, *A New Constitution for New Hampshire?* (Durham, N.H.: University of New Hampshire, 1956), 68. See also Richard Upton, "The Independence of the Judiciary in New Hampshire," *N.H. Bar J.* 39, no. 2 (1998): 56–61.

32. On the taxing power of the state, for example, the Court held in State v. U.S. & Canada Express Co., 60 N.H. 219 (1880), that a statute providing for taxation and licensing of commercial transport companies was unconstitutional because it imposed taxation in a manner that was not proportional and reasonable; and in Curry v. Spencer, 61 N.H. 624 (1882), the Court found that a law on taxation of legacies and successions was similarly unconstitutional because it imposed taxes that were not proportional and reasonable. On separation of powers, the Court wrote in Concord Railway v. Greeley, 17 N.H. 47 (1845), that the interpretation of the Bill of Rights is a matter for judicial decision. The opinion of the legislature is not final, they continued, but depends on whether the act of that body is in conflict with the constitution. And in Deming v. Foster, 42 N.H. 165, 178–179 (1860), the Court allowed that court rules would be subordinate to an act of the legislature within its constitutional powers, but that the courts have inherent authority to make rules of practice and to regulate their proceedings "as justice may require."

33. From 1818 (the year that official reports of New Hampshire decisions were first published) through the end of the Civil War, the high court rendered only 19 decisions on the constitutionality of legislation, or an average of one every two or three years. After the Civil War, the incidence of constitutional decisions per year quadrupled (a total of about 55 from 1866 through 1900). See Appendix B.

34. See, for example, Charter of Manchester, 47 N.H. 277 (1867) (statute on voting in new urban municipality found constitutional); Amoskeag Mfg. v. Head, 56 N.H. 386 (1876) (statute on textile mill found constitutional); State v. Campbell, 64 N.H. 402, 13 Atl. 585 (1887) (statute on regulation of milk sold commercially found

constitutional); State v. Hayes, 61 N.H. 264 (1884) (statute on minority rights in corporations found unconstitutional); Durkee v. Moses, 67 N.H. 115 (1891) (statute regulating liquor commerce found to impose impermissible constraint on interstate commerce); and Boston & Maine Railroad v. Concord, 69 N.H. 91, 44 Atl. 808 (1896) (one of several decisions holding legislation promoting railroads to be constitutional).

35. For examples of the comparatively mundane nature of some decisions, see East Kingston v. Towle, 48 N.H. 57 (1868) (statute on town recovery of costs in dog bite cases found unconstitutional); and Bliss's Petition, 63 N.H. 135 (1884) (statute denying peddlers' licenses to non-residents found a violation of federal constitution).

36. See Mel Topf, *A Doubtful and Perilous Experiment: Advisory Opinions, State Constitutions, and Judicial Supremacy* (New York: Oxford University Press, 2011), 8–17. Influenced by the English experience, Massachusetts was the first state in 1780 to authorize advisory opinions by constitution, perhaps as a way to address some of the problems of plural office-holding. The Massachusetts example was followed by New Hampshire in 1784. In the nineteenth century, Maine, Rhode Island, Missouri, Florida, Colorado, and South Carolina would follow; in the twentieth century, only Michigan would provide for advisory opinions by constitutional provision. There were also twelve additional states that considered or used advisory opinions without a constitutional mandate. By the end of the nineteenth century, however, there was a tendency in those states "to put a stop to the giving of extra-judicial advice where it is not required by the constitution" (Albert Ellingwood, *Departmental Cooperation in State Government* [New York: Macmillan, 1918], 30–55). Today, there are eleven states in which advisory opinions are authorized by constitution, statute, or custom (Ibid., 64–78). Retaining their nineteenth-century constitutional provisions for advisory opinions are Florida (1868), Colorado (1886), and South Dakota (1889). In 1875, Missouri repealed its 1852 constitutional authorization of advisory opinions. Only two states, Delaware (1852) and Alabama (1922), provide for them by statute. Finally, North Carolina has allowed advisory opinions since the mid-nineteenth century with neither a constitutional nor a statutory provision. See Topf, *Doubtful Experiment,* 17–27.

37. See Opinion of the Justices (1816), 62 N.H. 704 (published 1883).

38. Dartmouth College v. Woodward, 1 N.H. 111 (1817), *rev'd on other grounds,* 17 U.S. (4 Wheat.) 518 (1819). On the Contract Clause, see U.S. Const. art. I, §10, cl. 1.

39. At different times in the nineteenth century, the highest court of New Hampshire was called the "Superior Court of Judicature" (1776–1813, 1816–1855, and 1874–1876), the "Supreme Judicial Court" (1813–1816 and 1855–1874), and finally the "Supreme Court" (1876–present). Charles Douglas and Jay Surdukowski, "The New Hampshire Supreme Court: A History of Change," *N.H. Bar J.* 51, no. 2 (2010): 10, 13. Nineteenth-century General Court reconstruction of the judiciary under Part II, Article 4, of the New Hampshire Constitution was always a consequence of partisan political disputes, with judicial appointments as part of the "spoils of victory" for the party gaining the upper hand. For the national context for the first reconstruction in 1813, see McNamara, "Separation of Powers Principle," 66, and Upton, "Independence of Judiciary," 56–57. For a late nineteenth-century perspective, see Charles Corning, "The Highest Courts of Law in New Hampshire—Colonial, Provincial, and State," in Horace Fuller, *Green Bag* 2 (1890), 469–89.

Chapter 2

Twentieth-Century Reforms

Reconfiguring Only the Judiciary

It is not surprising that, as the Republican and Democratic parties took their modern forms and competed for power, each would find tempting opportunities for the advancement of partisan agendas in judicial institutions—as repositories of patronage positions, arenas for political retribution, and more. But yielding to those temptations meant chronically unsettling a judiciary that was striving mightily to establish its own institutional identity and role within the state's system of governance, and thus to change an identity and role that had thus far proven quite acceptable to legislators *qua* legislators.

A turning point of sorts was reached after the 1902 Constitutional Convention, one of seventeen in the state's history. The state's courts had been reorganized yet again in 1901, this time by establishing the New Hampshire Supreme Court as the state's highest appellate court and its Superior Court as its general trial court (previously, the Supreme Judicial Court held both trial and law terms, which had raised objections within the Bar). At the 1902 convention, constitutional amendments were proposed to render that arrangement permanent and to limit removal of judges by legislative address to cases of "physical or mental disability."[1] But neither amendment secured the approval of voters. At that point, leaders of the two major parties decided that, after the tumults of the nineteenth century, the stabilization of the judiciary was really in each party's interests. Since that end could not be reached by constitutional amendment, an informal understanding would have to do.

The result was a kind of "gentlemen's agreement" regarding the composition of at least the state's supreme and superior courts. Each bench was to contain representatives of both parties, with the party in power retaining only a bare overall majority.[2] It worked. From 1901 through 1966, there were no more court clearings, and nearly no removals by address.[3] To be sure, those powers remained in legislators' hands, to be wielded if and when the informal

Table 2.1 New Hampshire Judicial Review Outcomes, 1901–1966

Time Period	Total Judicial Review Cases	Legislation Found Unconstitutional	Percent Found Unconstitutional (%)
1817–1900	74	16	21.6
1901–1966	108	17	15.7

Source: case-by-case analysis (on file with the authors) of 182 reported New Hampshire judicial review cases for 1817–1900 and 1901–1966. For further information, see Appendix B.

political understanding that had precluded them went the way of most informal political understandings. But the first half of the twentieth century would remain a period of notable calm in legislative-judicial relations, reflected in a further decline in the already low rate of judicial decisions overturning the constitutionality of legislative enactments. See Table 2.1.

This decline was rather remarkable, as constitutional challenges were even more numerous than in the nineteenth century. The reason was the quickening pace of social and economic change: lawmakers contemplating the state's role in New Hampshire's modern, industrializing economy often sought new revenues to provide for new services—always a difficult undertaking under the state's constitutionally limited taxing power.[4]

Not surprisingly, the social and economic changes also caused a dramatic increase in the number of advisory opinions requested from the justices of the supreme court. In the first two-thirds of the twentieth century, from 1901 until the supreme court was written into the constitution in 1966, the justices rendered 143 advisory opinions, or an average of about 2.2 per year, or almost seven times as many per year as in the nineteenth century.

In 1901–1966, Table 2.2 shows that the justices occasionally declined to respond, and sometimes no constitutional question was posed. When the justices did respond on a constitutional question, they answered more often than not (as they had in the nineteenth century) that the proposed legislative or executive action would be fully or largely constitutional.

Table 2.2 New Hampshire Advisory Opinions, 1901–1966

Action Taken by Justices on Advisory Opinion Requests	Cases	Percent Of Opinions Requested (%)
• Proposed action found constitutional	75	52.4
• Proposed action found only partially constitutional	6	4.2
• Proposed action found not constitutional	45	31.5
• Justices declined to render opinion	11	7.7
• Statutory interpretation only	6	4.2
Grand Total of Advisory Opinion Requests	143	100.0

Source: case-by-case analysis (on file with authors) of 143 reported New Hampshire advisory opinions, 1901–1966. For more information, see Appendix C.

Perhaps as a reflection of the "gentlemen's agreement" between political parties on the composition of the high court, even litigated cases on appeal showed a substantial consensus among legislators and justices about the constitutional parameters for legislation.[5] Oddly, just as political accord seemed to finally stabilize the state judiciary, the seeds of the reform movement that was eventually to remove it from the control of politicians entirely were being sown.

JUDICIAL INDEPENDENCE AT AN INSTITUTIONAL LEVEL

The sower was Roscoe Pound, Dean of Harvard Law School and the father of court reform in America. In 1906, Pound addressed the subject of popular discontent with courts in an important speech before the American Bar Association, noting a "widespread feeling that the courts are inefficient."[6] The most direct causes of dissatisfaction, he said, traced to archaic judicial organization and procedure, resulting in "uncertainty, delay, and expense" which "have created a deep-seated desire to keep out of court, right or wrong." Pound was a leading force behind the creation of the American Judicature Society, the country's first court reform organization, in 1913.[7] It focused on judicial selection and tenure; promoted the creation of judicial councils as planning and policy bodies for court systems; and, perhaps most significantly, encouraged courts to more broadly exercise their own rulemaking powers to foster greater coherence in court operations and procedures.[8]

Pound himself was clearly associated with the Progressive movement in the early twentieth century. His rightward turn during the New Deal era is often described as an inconsistency motivated by personal issues, but it may have simply reflected a tension regarding legal reform inherent to Progressivism itself. To the degree that state-level judicial power was associated with sociopolitical conservatism (e.g., by overturning legislation establishing minimum wages, or employer liability), movement adherents aimed to check it by expanding citizens' input into judicial action (e.g., popular recall of decisions and judges, or supermajority requirements for the exercise of judicial review). Yet at the same time, Progressives fought to de-politicize courts and emancipate judges from partisan political influence by, for instance, attempting to replace partisan with non-partisan judicial elections, or with early versions of a non-political, merit-based process for selecting judges.[9]

As the twentieth century neared its midpoint, that selection process would yield significant successes in a number of states, thanks in part to the organization Pound had created. In fact, state-level actions had coalesced into a national current for the transfer of administrative and financial control over trial courts from the county and municipal governments which had generally held those powers to judicial officers, usually representing high courts. The idea was to fully extricate local courts from local politics, and place their management in the hands of individuals who fully understood the requirements of a genuinely professionalized judiciary. Then and only then, reformers argued, could state courts achieve anything like the independence modeled by the federal bench, or dispense a brand of justice resembling that of federal courts.[10]

Arthur Vanderbilt of New Jersey was perhaps the single most influential and best-known representative of the movement, after Pound himself. When he became President of the American Bar Association in 1938, Vanderbilt created a special section on judicial administration, calling for national standards.[11] Appointed chief justice of the (newly constitutionalized) New Jersey Supreme Court in 1948, he was able to implement many of the ideas he had been promoting, including the establishment of a special administrative office authorized by the chief justice to carry out administrative policies established at that high-court level.[12] A few years later, Vanderbilt helped found the Institute of Judicial Administration at New York University School of Law to further promote judicial reform nationwide.[13] Beyond consolidating probate, specialized, and local trial courts under a single, state-level supervisory authority within the judiciary's own ranks (i.e., creating "unified" court systems), reformers associated with the Institute aimed to replace localized funding sources with a single, state-level one. They further aimed to upgrade the training and quality of entire state judiciaries, both bench and bar, through the creation or strengthening of educational and disciplinary committees directed by trained judges, not laymen.

This was a movement with deep appeal among certain elements of New Hampshire's judiciary, given the long-standing efforts of some jurists to fully professionalize the administration of law and dispensation of justice. But transplanting the national reform agenda to New Hampshire would mean departing from the traditional notion that the judicial branch should enjoy only a partial and qualified independence: independence in its adjudicative functions ("decisional" independence), yes, but not the sort of administrative and fiscal independence ("institutional" independence) that might loosen the supervisory powers of the people's elected representatives. Even the consolidation of New Hampshire's rather complex set of municipal courts and specialized jurisdictions into a comprehensive body of district courts, first recommended by legislative committee in 1956, would not secure legislative consent until 1963. A fully unified and self-administering court system would require even more strenuous efforts.

In recognition of their own vulnerability before the countervailing tradition of legislative supremacy, and their awareness that such success as they had enjoyed to date could easily be undone in the future, reformers turned their

Table 2.3 Elapsed Time in Years from Date of Statehood to Date Highest Court Was Vested with Constitutional Status

Description	*States (Years Before or After Statehood Date)*
Constitutional status *before* statehood date	VT (-14), NC (-13), MD (-12), DE (-11), GA (-11), NY (-11), PA (-11), MA (-7), IA (-2), KS (-2), MI (-2), OR (-2), MO (-1), NM (-1)
Constitutional status *on* statehood date	AL, AK, AZ, AR, CA, CO, HI, ID, IN, KY, LA, ME, MN, MS, MT, NE, NV, ND, OH, OK, SD, TX, UT, WA, WV, WI, WY
Constitutional status *after* statehood date	CT (30), TN (39), VA (42), RI (53), NJ (57), SC (80), NH (178)

Source: Historical records for statehood date and date of the earliest grant of constitutional status for highest court in each state.

attention to the state constitution itself.[14] They would be remarkably successful in their efforts to amend it. In fact, at the 1964 Constitutional Convention, proponents of judicial reform were able to secure the delegates' endorsement of genuinely momentous changes.

One aimed to permanently end the status of at least the state's highest court as a body whose very existence depended on legislative forbearance. Most state constitutions, ratified at or even before admission to statehood, had included a grant of constitutional status to one or more courts, usually the highest. New Hampshire was one of only five whose original constitutions had not formally established a judicial power fully independent of the legislative branch by the mid-nineteenth century or shortly afterward.[15] See Table 2.3.

In fact, New Hampshire remained the last holdout well past the mid-twentieth century. Reformers aimed to change that now. At the 1964 Constitutional Convention, they proposed that Part 2, Article 72 of the constitution be amended to include a new provision, Article 72(a), stipulating that "The judicial power of the state shall be vested in the supreme court, a trial court of general jurisdiction known as the superior court, and such lower courts as the legislature may establish under Article 4th of Part 2." In addition, reformers proposed that the language of Part 2, Article 73, which described the terms of judicial tenure (including its termination by bill of address), be changed. New language would stipulate that "the cause for removal shall be stated fully and substantially in the address and shall not be a cause which is a sufficient ground for impeachment, and provided further that no officer shall be so removed unless he shall have had an opportunity to be heard in his defense by a joint committee of both houses."[16]

The voters who confirmed those changes by referendum in 1966 gave New Hampshire the first constitutional courts in its history, and the first due-process protections its judges had ever had against removal by politically motivated bills of address. They had rendered the New Hampshire judiciary more independent than it had ever been. But that was just the beginning.

Reformers claimed another significant victory in 1968, when a supreme court ruling established a unified bar under its own supervision, despite the failure of legislation that had proposed to do exactly that in 1961.[17] One of that measure's purposes was to gradually close out the era of non-lawyer judges, who still sat on a number of municipal courts; hence, its stipulation that judges of the new district courts should be "qualified persons who are also members of the bar of New Hampshire" (while grandfathering the local civic leaders currently serving on local benches).[18] The reform was indeed a benchmark in New Hampshire's judicial history: the first time that a major jurisdictional reorganization had occurred here without the forced removal of sitting judges.[19]

The route to full court unification had to be statutory, but by this time judicial reformers had the wind at their backs, with support from executive and legislative department leaders. In June 1968, Gov. John W. King (who would later serve as Chief Justice of New Hampshire's Supreme Court) appointed a commission to study the New Hampshire court system and to recommend ways to improve performance, with particular attention to jury trials in superior court.[20] In 1971, the state legislature decided to "improve the administration of justice and the efficient operation of all the courts" by finally authorizing the fully unified court system that reformers had long sought. To render that victory permanent, those reformers turned their eyes once again to the state constitution. In March 1973, Gov. Meldrim Thompson appointed another commission on court system improvement, which studied court congestion, district courts, domestic relations, judicial selection and review, prosecution, and sentencing procedures.[21] Just months after the recommendations of that commission were submitted in a final report, the next constitutional convention began, and reformers would emerge from the 1974 conclave with yet another victory. This one, however, was perhaps somewhat Pyrrhic.

Arthur Vanderbilt had believed strongly that fully insulating the judicial branch from political interference required consolidating the administration of the unified court systems he aimed to fashion in the hands of judicial personnel and there alone.[22] In perhaps his most controversial decision, *Winberry v. Salisbury,* he had ruled that the New Jersey Supreme Court's rulemaking authority, while constitutionally "subject to law," was not subject to *statutory* law.[23] That view was shared by Maurice Geiger, a North Conway lawyer who worked with courts and criminal justice officials in New Hampshire and other New England states as an adjudication specialist for the Law Enforcement Assistance Administration ("LEAA") of the U.S. Justice Department.[24] As a Carroll County delegate to the 1974 Constitutional Convention, Geiger introduced a resolution relating to the exercise of administrative powers over the judicial branch of government, "Providing that the chief justice shall be the administrative head of the courts, and he shall assign judges to temporary duty in the superior courts and other courts of the state, and he shall appoint an administrative assistant to serve at his will and pleasure."[25]

Geiger's resolution was referred to the convention committee on the judicial department, chaired by Attorney Arthur Nighswander.[26] When Nighswander presented the results of the committee's deliberations on Geiger's resolution on June 28, 1974, he reported that the majority of the committee considered the resolution as proposed to be more specific than necessary, so that they had eliminated the last two sentences as proposed. In place of Geiger's proposal, they offered an amended version of the resolution.

> The chief justice of the supreme court shall be the administrative head of all the courts. He shall, with the concurrence of a majority of the supreme court justices, make rules governing the administration of all courts in the state and the practice and procedure to be followed in all such courts. The rules so promulgated shall have the force and effect of law.[27]

The amended version of the resolution also included the recommended wording of the ballot question to be considered by voters in the next general election if the convention delegates approved the resolution.

> Are you in favor of amending the constitution to provide that the chief justice of the supreme court shall be the administrative head of state courts, and that he may, with the concurrence of a majority of the supreme court justices, make rules governing procedure in the courts?[28]

This amended version of the resolution would be inserted as Article 73-a in Part II of New Hampshire's constitution. In the discussion of the resolution that followed, Delegate Martin Gross[29] had the following exchange with Nighswander about the effect that the adoption of the resolution might have on the powers of the state legislature in terms of court procedure.

> Del. Gross: The last sentence of the proposed amendment reads: 'The rules so promulgated shall have the force and effect of law.' Could you tell us what effect that sentence would have on the Legislature's ability to provide by statute for court procedures in the future?
>
> Del. Nighswander: It is my understanding that the courts now have rule-making power. The rules which they make for the orderly procedure within the courts are within the jurisdiction of the judiciary. All this does is to unify the place where the rules are promulgated; that is, in the Supreme Court. At the present time, for example, the Superior Court makes rules for themselves and then they

submit them to the Supreme Court for approval. But I don't think it changes the general principle that the rules of court, as far as procedure is concerned, have the effect of law.

Del. Gross: Is my understanding correct that this amendment, if adopted, would not deprive the Legislature of its right that it presently has, to regulate court procedure by statute?

Del. Nighswander: I would think any power that they now have, they would still have.[30]

Voters approved the amendment in 1978, conferring on the chief justice specifically and the court in general a high level of administrative authority over the entire judicial branch.

Article 73-a also established the supreme court as the face of the entire judicial branch of state government, in ways it had never been—and that change would come with costs. Misgivings regarding the judiciary in general would now focus on the high court specifically; and, reciprocally, misgivings about the court would feed disquiet regarding the entire judiciary. Over time, some legislators and citizens uncomfortable with what indeed was, in New Hampshire, an unfamiliar level of judicial assertiveness would come to focus on the amended Article 73-a, in particular, as the real source of all ills. Their claim would be that 73-a was illegitimately interpreted as the court's (i.e., the courts') mode of escape from all forms of legislative oversight and, indeed, public accountability—this in a state where the principle of separate powers had never been interpreted to deny all forms of overlapping or shared powers.[31]

For decades, in fact, critics have pointed to the fact that the voters' guide distributed prior to the 1978 referendum lacked the crucial final sentence of the proposed amendment, "The rules so promulgated shall have the force and effect of law." Their claim has been that the absence of that sentence from the voters' guide invalidated the entire referendum, that is, that Article 73-a was an act of shameless political chicanery.[32] As late as 1998, the process by which Articles 72-a and 73-a had been added to New Hampshire's constitution were still undergoing scrutiny by legislative committee.

That committee would hear these long-standing suspicions of deceit rebutted by no less a figure than chief justice David Brock.[33]

LEGISLATIVE AND EXECUTIVE BRANCHES: THE TRIUMPH OF TRADITIONAL CIVIC CULTURE

The approval of the ballot question for Article 73-a by New Hampshire voters was the logical culmination of the administrative reorganization that had begun over a decade earlier. In effect, what had happened was nothing less than the eclipse of a local civic norm by representatives of a national reform movement, that is, the "nationalization" of an aspect of New Hampshire's civic culture—a civic culture that had always been proudly, even defiantly distinctive.

At the same time, movements were underway to institute analogous changes to the status of the legislative and executive branches as well. But here, New Hampshire voters expressed a substantially different will. Overall, they would choose to keep the elected branches *more* closely attuned to the *vox populi*—even while granting the unelected branch a wider degree of autonomy.

One matter addressed was the nature of legislative representation, a question raised by the U.S. Supreme Court in its landmark *Baker v. Cross* ruling of 1962. In that case, the Supreme Court rejected the proposition that legislative redistricting is non-justiciable and created what has been called a "judicially-imposed 'reapportionment revolution'" by mandating "one person/one vote."[34] New Hampshire responded commensurately. At the Fifteenth New Hampshire Constitutional Convention of 1964, Resolutions 4, 29, and 2, all dealing with the apportioning of representatives, were agreed on by delegates and then approved by voters on November 3, 1964.[35] In 1965, both houses of the legislature enacted legislation in keeping with those constitutional amendments, replacing community representation in the House and representation by tax district (i.e., by income) in the Senate with straightforward representation by population in both.[36]

In addition to reapportionment, citizens also voted in 1964 to allow a change in how the state constitution might be revised or amended. In 1960, after the admission of Alaska and Hawaii to statehood, New Hampshire stood apart from every other state in that its state constitution could be amended by no means other than by the action of citizens themselves, as delegates to a constitutional convention.[37] In every other state, the constitution could also be amended by legislative vote and (except for Delaware) by submission of proposed amendment as a ballot question for approval by the voters.[38] In New Hampshire, after the 1964 Constitutional Convention, voters approved a ballot question amending the state constitution to authorize the legislature (by concurrent resolution of both houses) to periodically submit the prospect of a full constitutional convention to voter approval. Theoretically, this might have led to more conventions, thus expanding legislators' own opportunities to generate constitutional alterations.[39]

In practice, however, that has not happened. The state electorate has authorized no constitutional conventions since 1984, and proposals for constitutional amendment proposals have been considered as they were in the past: as individual ballot questions offered to voters only by concurrent resolution of both legislative chambers. Regarding how their constitution is to be altered, New Hampshire's voters have evidently decided to keep control in their own hands rather than devolving more of it on their legislators.[40]

Furthermore, they have consistently rejected a series of calls for dramatic renovations of both the legislative and executive branches—proposals advancing not a further democratization of the elected bodies but rather the sort of professionalization and modernization the judiciary was undergoing. Such proposals had multiplied since the end of the World War II.[41] In 1963, the state legislature finally responded by creating a committee to study the entirety of the state constitution.[42] That committee's recommendations, in fact, initiated the process whereby Articles 72-a and 73-a would eventually be adopted to protect the supreme and superior Courts from "political reorganization by the legislative and executive branches."[43] It was similarly willing to reconsider the role of the legislative and judicial branches. But the electorate that endorsed those recommendations regarding the state's judiciary would prove considerably less inclined to tamper with the modus operandi of their elected branches.

Regarding the executive, modernizers hoped "to increase governmental accountability and efficiency by giving the governor authority that matches his [or her] responsibility."[44] This would mean diluting or eliminating constitutional constraints on gubernatorial powers, constraints reflecting revolutionary-era framers' recollections of the arbitrary powers wielded by royal colonial governors.[45] In New Hampshire, Part 2, Article 41 of the constitution, as most recently amended in 1792, provided simply that "There shall be a supreme executive magistrate, who shall be styled the Governor of the State of New Hampshire." The 1963 constitutional-study committee recommended replacing the governor's two-year term with a four-year term, expanding his control over executive agencies' budgets, and granting him a line-item veto powers over the state budget.[46] Delegates to the 1964 constitutional convention ratified the general thrust of the committee's thinking on gubernatorial power, offering voters a ballot question whereby the language of Article 41 would be amended to fortify the governor's overall executive authority.[47]

But particular enhancements of gubernatorial power recommended by the study committee were rejected then and have been consistently rejected ever since, in apparent reflection of a civic culture determined to limit the power of government to intervene in the lives of its citizens.[48]

The governor of New Hampshire, the only state official chosen by statewide election, selects his or her own attorney general, unlike most other states.[49] That, however, is one of the very few ways in which New Hampshire's governor is empowered beyond national norms. Although there is no limit on how often its governor may be reelected, New Hampshire is now one of only two states, with Vermont, that retain a two-year term of office for its chief executive.[50] Extending the term of office for the governor from two years to four years was rejected seven times by delegates to constitutional conventions since 1956; twice (1971 and 1980) by voters on ballot questions submitted by the legislature; and eight times (most recently in 2009) by legislators themselves.[51] In New Hampshire, governors share the power of appointment and removal of executive-branch officials with an elected executive council, essentially an extension of the legislature. In fact, the only other state with that arrangement is Massachusetts, where the Council has much less involvement in important gubernatorial decisions, including fiscal matters.[52] A proposal to eliminate the executive council and create the position of lieutenant governor had been offered New Hampshire voters by delegates to the 1850 Constitutional Convention and rejected. Similar amendment proposals were considered but rejected by constitutional convention delegates eighteen times between 1879 and 1984, and ten times by state legislators since 1971 (most recently in 1999).[53]

The line-item veto recommended by the 1963 constitutional-study committee has also been rejected. The governor of every state has general veto power, and the governor of New Hampshire has had that power since 1792.[54] Yet New Hampshire is now one of only six states where he or she does not also have power to veto specific items without having to exercise a general veto.[55] Constitutional amendments have often been considered, but consistently rejected—four times (1912, 1918, 1930, and 1970) on ballot questions not approved by voters, nine times by constitutional convention delegates, and fifteen times by legislators.[56]

Regarding the legislative branch of state government, where, as one scholar has observed, reform efforts since the World War II have also been "characterized by incipient professionalization," New Hampshire voters have been similarly recalcitrant.[57] Here too, the specific recommendations of the 1963 constitutional-study committee simply did not gain traction within the electorate.

It recommended (1) an increase in the size of the Senate to 36 members and a reduction in the size of the House of Representatives to 300 members: (2) an increase in the salaries of legislators from the amount set in 1889 at $200 to $1,000, with mileage paid at the same rate as other state employees; and (3) more flexible taxing authority, giving the legislature "the same power to enact different classes and types of taxes which most other legislatures have."[58] These recommendations were echoed and extended by the Citizens Conference on State Legislatures, formed in 1965 to promote improved performance by state legislatures. In 1969, that organization's members began a study of all state legislatures resulting in recommendations for each state published in 1971.[59] New Hampshire's legislature was ranked 39th of 50 states in the study. Of 32 recommendations in the report for institutional improvement, the top three were: (1) reduce the size of the House; (2) increase legislative salaries; and (3) remove constitutional restrictions on length of sessions.[60] Those three recommendations for New Hampshire represent three aspects of what legislative reformers have called for in terms of improved "state legislative professionalism," referring to "the enhancement of the capacity of the legislature to perform its role in the policymaking process with an expertise, seriousness, and effort comparable to that of other actors in that process."[61]

But New Hampshire's voters would decide, repeatedly, that they simply did not want more professionalized legislators. To encourage citizen engagement in government and assure that New Hampshire's legislators remain close to their constituents, the state has more legislators in its House of Representatives than any other state. In 1877, citizens approved a constitutional amendment to base representation in the House on population, and the total number of representatives authorized for the House has been changed 27 times within constitutional parameters since 1900.[62] In 1942 voters approved an amendment to set the size of the House at 375–400 representatives,[63] but constitutional amendments to reduce its size have consistently been rejected a total of eight times by voters on ballot questions, thirty-five other times by constitutional convention delegates, and eleven times by legislators.[64]

Although the lower legislative chamber in New Hampshire is larger than that in any other state, its upper chambers is smaller than average. With the exception of Nebraska's unicameral legislature, the average upper chamber has 39.5 members, ranging from 20 (Alaska) to 67 (Minnesota).[65] Since the size of the New Hampshire Senate was set at 24 in 1877, voters have rejected constitutional convention proposals to increase its size even further on three occasions (1912, 1964, and 1974); twenty resolutions to increase senate size have not been adopted in constitutional convention sessions; and legislators have rejected eleven such proposals.[66]

As a way to attract talented people to state legislatures and reduce membership turnover, reformers have advocated that legislative pay be increased. In 1910, when New York state legislators (at $1,500 per year) were paid more than their counterparts in any other state, the legislators of New Hampshire were the lowest paid (at $100 per year). In 2003, when California had the highest-paid legislators (at $99,000 per year), New Hampshire legislators were still paid only $100 per year.[67] The pay level for legislators was set by voters at $100 per year in 1889, on recommendation of a constitutional convention after the scandalous 1887 legislative session.[68] Since then, New Hampshire voters have rejected proposals to improve legislative compensation four times on ballot questions, 35 times on constitutional convention resolutions, and 36 times on legislative bills proposing constitutional amendments.[69]

They have been no less hostile to recommendations that the state constitution be amended to provide for unlimited annual sessions in place of 90 legislative days per biennium.[70] Until 1877, New Hampshire legislators met each year. After the 1876 Constitutional Convention, voters approved a ballot question the following year to provide for biennial sessions for the legislature. In 1966, voters narrowly approved a ballot question proposed on concurrent resolution by the legislature to change legislative sessions back to annual meetings; but the vote was challenged, and the supreme court upheld a claim that the question submitted to the voters incorrectly stated the effect of the proposed amendment.[71] On recount, the proposed amendment fell just short of the two-thirds majority of voters required for approval. The matter has been put before the voters three times since, and failed each time by a small margin.[72]

Overall, the voters of New Hampshire have expressed their preferences with regard to the legislative branch quite unambiguously. As the authors of a recent comparison of state legislatures wrote,

> The New Hampshire General Court is considered one of the least professional legislatures in the country, with its low salary and limited staffing. … New Hampshire's legislators must be considered perhaps the closest thing to pure citizen legislators that can be found in the United States. … Citizens and legislators alike view their 'citizen's legislature' with pride. The legislative website encourages constituents to contact their legislators at home, listing their home numbers on the web page.[73]

The intensity of citizens' commitment to a legislature fully under their own control and substantially precluded from many of the initiatives that more modernized legislatures elsewhere might undertake is reflected in the debate on "unfunded mandates" in New Hampshire. They demonstrated a profound aversion to them in 1984, after delegates to the Constitutional Convention endorsed a constitutional amendment requiring full funding by the state, not localities, for any "new, expanded or modified" state programs requiring local expenditures.[74] That proposal, approved by 70 percent of the electorate, has been described as "the most sweeping constitutional prohibition against unfunded state mandates that exists anywhere in the United States."[75] Added as Part I, Article 28-a of the New Hampshire Constitution, it has been applied in litigation over municipal employees' workers compensation, solid waste disposal, and funding mechanisms for special education.[76]

The adoption of Part I, Article 28-a would prove consequential in additional ways. It did not relate specifically to matters of education funding, but it would help limit the range of acceptable options available to the legislature and the governor for the implementation of New Hampshire Supreme Court decisions in the *Claremont* education funding litigation beginning in 1993. As such, it constituted an important part of the landscape that both the court and the legislature would have to navigate in those years.

That landscape would witness a number of skirmishes prior to the major battle of 2000.

NOTES

1. Upton, "Independence of Judiciary," 59.

2. Upton cites William Sawyer, a former chief justice of the superior court, as his own source on this point. See also McNamara, "Separation of Powers," 71, 77.

3. Judge David Chase of the Seabrook Municipal Court was an exception. Upton, "Independence of Judiciary," 60.

4. Mel Topf has offered the following observation: "Different advisory opinion states may focus on different subjects. In New Hampshire, for example, taxes were for a while addressed incessantly in advisory opinions. Between 1913 and 1959, of ninety advisory opinions rendered, thirty-three covered taxes of all kinds, with at least one each on property, cigarettes, gasoline, income, inheritance, sales, airplane fuel, franchise, stock in trade, and dividend and interest." Topf, *Doubtful Experiment,* xi.

5. In 108 judicial review decisions between 1901 and 1966, there were only 17 in which the justices found legislation unconstitutional.

6. Roscoe Pound, "The Causes of Popular Dissatisfaction with the Administration of Justice," *Ann. Rep. ABA* 29 (1906): 395.

7. See David Steelman, John Goerdt, and James McMillan, *Caseflow Management: The Heart of Court Management in the New Millennium* (Williamsburg, VA: National Center for State Courts, 2004), xi–xiii.

8. See Robert Tobin, *An Overview of Court Administration in the United States* (Williamsburg, Va.: National Center for State Courts, 1997), 15–16.

9. Melvin Urofsky, "State Courts and Protective Legislation During the Progressive Era: A Reevaluation," *J. Am. History* 72, no. 1 (1985): 63–91; John Dinan, "Forward: Court-Constraining Amendments and the State Constitutional Tradition," *Rutgers L. J.* 38 (2006): 983. See, in particular, the discussion in Shugerman, *People's Courts,* 159–176. It is important to note that Progressives would be considerably less successful in their efforts to constrain judicial power through recalls and the like than they were in countering political influences on judicial institutions.

10. See Tobin, *Judicial Branch,* for a thorough treatment of the movement to reform state judiciaries. See also, Larry Berkson, Steven Hays, and Susan Carbon, eds., *Managing the State Courts: Text and Readings* (St. Paul, MN: West Publishing, 1977); and Tarr, *Without Fear or Favor.*

11. Under Vanderbilt's leadership, the National Conference of Judicial Councils compiled data for ten years on procedural practices in state courts, in order to measure each state's practices against the minimum standards prescribed by the ABA in such areas as the selection, conduct, and tenure of judges; the management of court

business; court rulemaking powers; juries; evidence; appellate practice; trial practice; and local courts of limited jurisdiction. See Arthur Vanderbilt, ed., *Minimum Standards of Judicial Administration* (New York: NYU Press, 1949).

12. Edward McConnell was thus appointed the first state court administrator in America, in 1948.

13. See Vanderbilt, *The Doctrine of the Separation of Powers and Its Present-Day Significance* (Lincoln, NE: University of Nebraska Press, 1953); *The Challenge of Law Reform* (Princeton, NJ: Princeton University Press, 1955); and *Judges and Jurors: Their Functions, Qualifications, and Selection* (Boston: Boston University Press, 1956). See also G. Alan Tarr, "Arthur T. Vanderbilt (1888–1957)," in *Great American Judges: An Encyclopedia*, ed. John Viles (Santa Barbara, CA: ABC-CLIO, 2003), Vol. 2, 775–82.

14. Both Chapter VI ("The Judiciary") of Dishman, *New Constitution,* and Upton's 1959 article, "Independence of Judiciary," were calls for a more clearly independent judiciary in New Hampshire. Both stressed the need for constitutional amendments granting constitutional status to the Supreme and Superior Courts.

15. As Table 2.2 shows, the others were New Jersey, South Carolina, Tennessee, and Virginia. Three of those adopted new constitutions between 1818 and 1844 that did give explicit constitutional status to the judiciary. In South Carolina, this came just after the end of the Civil War.

16. *[Journal of the] Convention to Revise the Constitution, May 1964* (Concord, N.H.: Evans Printing 1964), 185–87.

17. The court ruled that the legislature had earlier granted it authority to supervise the practice of law, including disciplinary power over those it admitted to the bar. In a 1986 ruling, however, it would also acknowledge that the legislature did hold concurrent statutory powers to control some aspects of the practice of law manifest in, for example, consumer-protection laws that might be applied to lawyers. McNamara, "Separation of Powers," 80.

18. The full transition would not be completed for another decade or so, and district courts were locally funded until the 1980s. Until that time, district-court judges were likely to be local notables well known to the citizens of a city or town.

19. Batchelder, "Independence Revisited," 63–64.

20. See "Report of Governor's Commission on Court System Improvement," *N.H. Bar J.* 11, no. 4 (1969): 217–61.

21. See "Report of Governor's Commission on Court System Improvement," *N.H. Bar J.* 16, no. 1 (1974): 1–125.

22. In the 1940s, researchers from the National Conference of Judicial Councils documented the procedural practices of state courts, for comparison to minimal standards the ABA had adopted under Vanderbilt's leadership. In the area of rulemaking, the ABA recommended "That practice and procedure in the courts should be regulated by rules of court; and that to this end the court should be given full rulemaking power." Researchers reported that N.H. was one of eleven states where courts' rulemaking powers were unsatisfactory, in that "procedure is probably regulated to a greater extent by statute than by court rule." See Vanderbilt, *Minimum Standards,* 90, 140–41.

23. Benjamin Kaplan and Warren Greene provided a thoughtful critique of that decision in "The Legislature's Relation to Judicial Rule-Making: An Appraisal of *Winberry v. Salisbury,*" *Harv. L. Rev.* 65, no. 2 (1951): 234–52. Alan Tarr notes that the Committee on the Judiciary at the convention that rewrote New Jersey's constitution had expressly indicated that it considered "subject to law" to mean subject to legislation. In his generally admiring retrospective of Vanderbilt, he acknowledges that "although Vanderbilt's position may have secured the independence of the judiciary and promoted better administration of the courts, it more closely resembled a usurpation than a faithful interpretation of the constitution." Tarr, "Arthur T. Vanderbilt."

24. Geiger had moved to North Conway in 1972 and become a member of the New Hampshire Bar in 1974. During the 1970s, he worked with Ernest Friesen, Dean of California Western University Law School, studying courts throughout the nation. See Beverly Rorick, "Maurice Geiger Dedicates Life to Judicial Reform," *N.H. Bar News,* May 7, 2004. Friesen had been the first dean of the National Judicial College, director of the Administrative Office of the United States Courts, and founder of the Institute for Court Management. Geiger became a protégé of Friesen's after Friesen was Assistant Deputy Attorney General in the U.S. Justice Department in 1965–1968.

25. Resolution No. 141, sponsored by Geiger. See *Journal of the Convention to Revise the Constitution, May 1974* (Concord, N.H.: Evans Printing, 1974), 41–42.

26. Nighswander was one of the state's most prominent attorneys. Three years before the 1974 convention, he had appeared on behalf of plaintiffs before the Supreme Court in Laconia Board of Education v City of Laconia, 111 N.H. 389, 285 A.2d 793 (1971). The principal issue in this case was whether the school board could legitimately compel city officials to provide funding for services and programs the school board considered essential for an adequate educational system. On behalf of twenty-eight school districts, Nighswander subsequently led a team of lawyers in the *Jesseman* case (N.H. Superior Court, Merrimack County, Docket No. 82-E-038, 1982), challenging the constitutionality of the state's reliance on property taxes to finance education. The state's adoption of a new funding approach (the "Augenblick" formula) led Nighswander and his team to file a "voluntary nonsuit." See J.R. Sirkin, "New Hampshire Districts Drop Finance Lawsuit," *Education Week* 5, no. 2 (1985): 9.But the state never fully funded the program, sparking yet another round of litigation that led to the *Claremont* decisions. When *Claremont I* was argued before the Supreme Court in 1993, Nighswander, then eighty-five, was seated among the supporters of the plaintiff school districts. See Charles DeGrandpre, "Lex Loci: A Survey of New Hampshire Supreme Court Decisions," *N.H. Bar J.* 35 no.1 (1994): 69. See also, Michael Kitch, "Legal Lion Arthur Nighswander Dies at 100," *N.H. Bar News,* January 16, 2009, https://www.nhbar.org/publications/display-news-issue.asp?id=4906.

27. *Constitutional Convention, 1974*, 261.

28. Ibid.

29. Attorney Martin Gross was a three-time mayor of Concord who died in 2016. See Obituary, "Martin L. Gross (1938–2016)," *Concord Monitor* (January 31, 2016). A prominent Democrat and legal counselor to two N.H. governors, he was later a

delegate to the 1984 Constitutional Convention, co-sponsoring a resolution that would make court rulemaking under Article 73-a subject to legislative override.

30. *Constitutional Convention, 1974,* 261–62.

31. In 1978, the supreme court itself stated "It is well established in our opinions that the three co-ordinate branches of government cannot be completely separate, and in the nature of things there must be some overlapping of power. . . . There exists what has been described as a 'region of authority, alternative and concurrent, the boundaries of which are fixed by no final rule.'" McNamara, "Separation of Powers," 77.

32. See, for instance, Richard Lessner, "Bait and Switch—Judicial Magic: Now You See It, Now You Don't," *Manchester Union Leader,* August 7, 1998, C1, and Bernadette Connolly, "The Judges' Trump Card," *Manchester Union Leader,* January 9, 2001, A8.

33. In 1998, Chief Justice Brock appeared before a legislative committee studying the procedures for the adoption of Articles 72-a and 73-a. In opposition to any suggestion of "chicanery," he observed that the delegates at the 1964 and 1974 conventions voted on both the specific language of the proposed constitutional changes and the specific language of the "plain English" ballot questions to be presented to the voters. "Although in some instances the ballot question may include the actual language of the proposed constitutional change," he said, "in many instances it does not." He continued, "If you review the journal of the 1964 and 1974 conventions you will find numerous instances in which the language of the ballot question differs from the constitutional language." Brock, "Remarks on August 11, 1998, to a legislative committee regarding the adoption of Part 2, Articles 72-a and 73-a of the N.H. Constitution," http://mainstream.net/nhpolitics/brock.html.In 2001, then-superior court justice Robert Lynn, later an Associate Justice of the Supreme Court, dismissed the notion that the omission of the sentence from the voters' guide of Article 73-a's final sentence fatally tainted the referendum approving it. Lynn noted, as had Chief Justice Brock in 1998, that the sentence *was* included in the amendment recommended by the convention's delegates to voters in 1974. He further noted that the sentence did not change the legal status of court rules anyway, since they had been endowed with the force of law for some time (courts could have hardly functioned, Lynn noted, if their rules were understood as merely advisory). But Lynn was nonetheless highly critical of later applications of the amendment, suggesting that "judicial supremacy over procedural law is fundamentally inconsistent with the separation of powers doctrine." He noted that the record of the 1974 Constitutional Convention would support a perception that delegates thought they were granting the judiciary powers concurrent with those the legislature had long enjoyed, and not exclusive administrative powers. Lynn, "Judicial Rule-Making and the Separation of Powers in New Hampshire: The Need for Constitutional Reform," *N.H. Bar J.* 42, no. 1 (2001): 44–69.

34. See Leroy Hardy, Alan Heslop, and Stuart Anderson, *Reapportionment Politics: The History of Redistricting in the 50 States* (Beverly Hills, CA, and London: Sage, 1981), 17.

35. See Rinden and Lyman, *Constitutional Amendment Proposals,* 59.

36. Janelle Hobbs and Blake Isaacson, "New Hampshire," in Hardy, *Reapportionment Politics,* 212.

37. In *The American State Constitutional Tradition* (Lawrence, KS: University Press of Kansas, 2006), John Dinan argues that the relative ease of altering most state constitutions, compared to that for the federal government, reflects a stronger democratic ethos at work in state-level constitutionalism.

38. On the history of state constitutional amendments, see John Jameson, *The Constitutional Convention: Its History, Powers, and Modes of Proceeding* (New York: Scribner, 1867), 486n. 1–4; Charles Bradley, *The Methods of Changing the Constitutions of the States, Especially That of Rhode Island* (Boston: Alfred Mudge & Son, 1885), 78–82; Walter Dodd, *The Revision and Amendment of State Constitutions* (Baltimore, MD: Johns Hopkins Press, 1910), 118; and Thomas White, "Amendment and Revision of State Constitutions," *U. Pa. L. Rev.* 100, no. 8 (1952): 1132–52. Eighteen states also allow constitutional amendment by voter initiative and referendum (see Ballotpedia, "Amending State Constitutions," https://ballotpedia.org/Amending_state_constitutions), but that option has never been submitted to N.H. voters as a ballot question. Resolutions for it have been rejected six times in constitutional conventions from 1889 through 1974 and at least twice by the General Court (in 1979 and 1981). See Rinden and Lyman, *Constitutional Amendment Proposals*, 17.

39. See N.H., *Manual for the General Court* (Concord, NH: Secretary of State, 1965), 701.

40. See Ballotpedia, "List of New Hampshire ballot measures," https://ballotpedia.org/wiki/index.php?title=List_of_New_Hampshire_ballot_measures&oldid=5330344.

41. See, for example, Ann Bowman and Richard Kearney, *The Resurgence of the States* (Englewood Cliffs, NJ: Prentice-Hall, 1986); and Jon Teaford, *The Rise of the States: Evolution of American State Government* (Baltimore, MD: Johns Hopkins Press, 2002).

42. N.H. Laws 1963, Ch. 186. See N.H. H.R. Jour. (1963), 1436.

43. See N.H. Commission to Study the State Constitution, *Report to the Fifteenth Constitutional Convention* (Concord, NH: Evans Printing, 1964). The report is summarized in Joseph Millimet, Richard Upton, and Stanley Brown, "A Modern Constitution for New Hampshire," *N.H. Bar. J.* 6, no. 3 (1964): 208–11.

44. Larry Sabato, *Goodbye to Good-time Charlie: The American Governorship Transformed, Second Edition* (Washington, DC: CQ Press, 1983), 57, 62.

45. Bowman and Kearney, *Resurges of the States*, 52.

46. Millimet, "Modern Constitution for New Hampshire."

47. Resolution 58 read "Are you favor of amending the Constitution to clarify and reinforce the executive powers of the governor by providing that he shall be vested with the executive power, shall be responsible for faithful execution of the laws and may by appropriate legal action enforce constitutional and legislative mandates within the executive branch?" See Rinden and Lyman, *Constitutional Amendment Proposals*, 61. Seventy percent of N.H. voters would approve that language and Article 41 would be formally amended in 1966. Law professor Lawrence Friedman confirms that "the people intended the 1966 amendment to vest in the governor strengthened executive power and responsibility, to be exercised within the dictates of the constitution and the lawful enactments of the legislative branch." Friedman, *The New Hampshire State Constitution* (New York: Oxford University Press, 2015), 154.

48. See Margaret Ferguson (ed.), *The Executive Branch of State Government: People, Process, and Politics* (Santa Barbara, CA: ABC-CLIO, 2006), 332.

49. That appointment is, like all other gubernatorial appointments, subject to the approval of the executive council. Regarding other states, Ferguson notes: "The vast majority of the attorneys general in the states (forty-three) are popularly elected in partisan elections. In all of these cases, the regular term of office is four years." Ferguson, *Executive Branch*, 177. In New Hampshire, there have been twenty-one times since 1971 when constitutional convention delegates (twice in 1984) or legislators (19 constitutional amendment bills) have considered proposals to change the selection and tenure of the attorney general, and none of them ever became a ballot question for voters to consider. See Rinden and Lyman, *Constitutional Amendment Proposals.*

50. New Hampshire is one of only three states, with New Jersey and Tennessee, whose only statewide elected official is the governor. Governors in every other state have a four-year term of office. See Robert Maddex, *State Constitutions of the United States, 2d. ed.* (Washington, DC: CQ Press, 2006), xxvi–xxx.

51. See Rinden and Lyman, *Constitutional Amendment Proposals*; N.H., *General Court Manual* (1985), 443–45; *N.H. Journal of Constitutional Convention of 1984* (1984); and N.H. H.R. Jour. (1983, 1985, 1986, and 1987).

52. See Ferguson, *Executive Branch*, 303–04 and 333–34, for a comparison of the executive councils of Massachusetts and New Hampshire.

53. See sources in note 51.

54. See N.H. Const. Pt. 2, Art. 44.

55. The other states whose governors lack item-veto authority are Indiana, Nevada, North Carolina, Rhode Island, and Vermont. See Maddex, *State Constitutions*, xxvi–xxx.

56. See sources in note 51.

57. Teaford, *Rise of the States,* 167. Peverill Squire has written extensively about measures of state legislative professionalization. See Squire, *The Evolution of American Legislatures: Colonies, Territories, and States, 1619–2009* (Ann Arbor, MI: University of Michigan Press, 2012). See also, Squire and Keith Hamm, *101 Chambers: Congress, State Legislatures, and the Future of Legislative Studies* (Columbus, OH: The Ohio State University Press, 2005).

58. Millimet, "Modern Constitution for New Hampshire."

59. The Conference operated from the premise that each citizen should expect his or legislature to be functional, accountable, informed, independent, and representative. To this end, those conducting the 50-state study looked at performance in nine basic fields: (1) staffing; (2) compensation; (3) time; (4) committee structure; (5) facilities; (6) leadership; (7) rules and procedures; (8) size; and (9) ethics. Citizens Conference on State Legislatures, *The Sometimes Governments: A Critical Study of the 50 American State Legislatures* (Kansas City, MO: The Conference, third printing, 1973), 40–42.

60. Ibid, 256–260.

61. Christopher Mooney, "Measuring U.S. State Legislative Professionalism: An Evaluation of Five Indices," *State & Local Govt. Rev.* 26, no. 2 (1994), 70–71.

62. Squire, *The Evolution of American Legislatures,* 266.

63. Rinden and Lyman, *N.H. Constitutional Amendment Proposals*, 15.

64. See sources in note 51.

65. See Maddex, *State Constitutions*, xxvii-xxxi.

66. These totals do not include twelve proposals that would combine a reduction in the number of representatives and an increase in the number of senators in the same constitutional convention resolution or legislative CACR bill. Nor do they include nine failed proposals for a unicameral legislature (four convention resolutions and five legislative CACR bills. See sources in note 51.

67. See Squire and Hamm, *101 Chambers,* 70–75.

68. As Leon Anderson wrote,

> Activities of the railroad lobbyists prolonged the session into a record 158 days, from June 1 through November 5. Each legislator collected an all-time record of $474 in wages. They then paid themselves $3 per day, including Sundays, although they actually worked only three or four days weekly. This was so shocking that eighteen months later the voters permanently pegged the legislative pay at $200 [per biennium], by a constitutional amendment, which has remained in effect to this day.

Anderson, *To This Day: The 300 Years of the New Hampshire Legislature* (Canaan, N.H.: Phoenix Publishing, 1981), 170.

69. See sources in note 51.

70. Citizens Conference, *Sometimes Governments*, 256–57.

71. Gerber v. King, 107 N.H. 495, 225 A.2d 620 (1967).

72. Rinden and Lyman, *Constitutional Amendment Proposals*, 14–15.

73. Thomas Little and David Ogle, *The Legislative Branch of State Government: People, Process, and Politics* (Santa Barbara, CA: ABC-CLIO, 2006), page 347.

74. See Marshall, *State Constitution*, 36.

75. John Andrews writes:

> Without painting delegates with too broad a brush, the motivations behind support for an amendment banning mandates were as varied as the ideologies of the delegates supporting passage of the amendment: conservatives wanted state government off the back of local government; liberals saw it as a way to force the State to be responsible for raising the money required to pay for programs it mandated, leading, perhaps, to tax reform; and local officials were just sick and tired of taking the heat for raising local property taxes to pay for programs and responsibilities foisted upon them by "the State," both legislatures and agencies.

Andrews, "So It's A Mandate! Whattya Goin' to Do About It?" *N.H. Hampshire Town & City,* November/December 2005, https://www.nhmunicipal.org/TownAndCity/Article8. The word "mandate" can be defined in general as a demand for action by "subordinate" governments, arising from a statute, constitutional provision, court decision, or administrative regulation that is enforceable by potential civil or criminal sanctions. See Advisory Commission on Intergovernmental Relations, *Mandates: Cases in State-Local Relations* (Washington, DC: The Commission, 1990), 2.

76. See Andrews, "So It's a Mandate!" See also, Marshall, *State Constitution*, 102–03.

Chapter 3

Interbranch Relations at Century's End

As a result of voter decisions to alter their judiciary while retaining their legislature and executive in traditional form, all three branches would enter a new era, to which past history could provide only the most uncertain guidance.

Certainly, judicial-legislative relations grew more sensitive as the 1980s progressed, in part because of a significant change in the funding of state courts. In 1983, after careful preparatory steps, New Hampshire did what most states that had opted for court unification had done, and moved to state-level funding for its newly consolidated judiciary.[1] Under the old system, the myriad municipal and probate courts of the state had been mainly supported by the various towns, cities, and counties that had housed them.[2] Now, legislators in a famously frugal state were expected to allot moneys to a body that was suddenly far less answerable to them than it had ever been—a body, in fact, that now seemed resistant to the kind of legislative direction willingly accepted by most of the other agencies that clamored for scarce public funds.

But if legislators found themselves in unfamiliar territory with the new funding arrangements, so did the courts—both the supreme court and the lower courts now more directly tied to it. The transition meant the judiciary would now have to rely for financial support not on local officials versed in the operations of local courts and personally familiar with local judges, but rather on state legislators who might lack any such direct experience and contacts, or indeed any particular sympathy with the judicial branch of government.[3] There was every reason to expect difficult negotiations ahead. Worse yet, the "gentlemen's agreement" that had protected the court from political attack since the beginning of the century had run its course by the 1970s.

CONFLUENCE OF 1966–1978 CONSTITUTIONAL REFORMS AND THE "RIGHTS REVOLUTION"

A different pattern of outcomes when the Supreme Court was asked to review the constitutionality of legislative actions may help explain that agreement's demise. The percentage of cases in which legislation was found unconstitutional between 1967 and 2000 was dramatically higher than it had been before the 1966 grant of constitutional recognition to the supreme court. This may not have been solely a result, however, of the courts having achieved institutional judicial independence as a result of the 1966 constitutional amendment. It was also a consequence of a different mix of cases before the supreme Court on appeal, particularly because of the "rights revolution" occasioned by the application of federal due process and equal protection provisions to the states.

The term "rights revolution" effectively denotes what was happening: a judicial turn toward a stronger, often counter-majoritarian defense of constitutional rights (and, arguably, identification of previously unrecognized ones).[4] It was a movement arguably catalyzed by the civil rights movement of the 1950s and 1960s, when activists turned to the judicial branch of government for relief from conditions that elected officials were unable or unwilling to address.

Table 3.1 compares the outcomes of such judicial review in the first two-thirds of the twentieth century (2001–1966), before the 1966 constitutional amendment, with those in the last third of the century (1967–2000), immediately after the constitutional amendment.

As one can see from Table 3.1, "rights revolution" issues dominated New Hampshire judicial review in 1967–2000. The most frequently raised constitutional question involved claims that the equal protection and due process provisions of the New Hampshire Constitution had been violated. In fact, nearly 80 percent of all judicial review cases (55 of 69) during that period involved state or federal issues of equal protection, due process, access to justice, or ex post facto laws. By contrast, the top three constitutional issues in 1901–1966 were presented much less often. The most frequently raised issue in 1901–1966 were relatively less important—the exercise of the state's police power fell to seventh place in the rankings; valid exercise of legislative power, from second to fifth; and valid delegation of legislative power from third to twenty-third.

Perhaps because of such changes as those evoked by the "rights revolution," the frequency of advisory opinion requests from the justices of the supreme court by the elected branches was much higher than during the nineteenth century and in the first two-thirds of the twentieth century. The justices issued 171 advisory opinions between 1816 and 1966, or an average

Table 3.1 New Hampshire Judicial Review Case Mix and Outcomes, 1901–2000

	1967–2000					*1901–1966*				
Constitutional Issue	*Rank 1967–2000*	*Cases*[a]	*Case Percent of Total (%)*[a]	*Unconstitutional Cases*	*Percent Unconstitutional (%)*	*Rank 1901–1966*	*Cases*[a]	*Case Percent of Total (%)*[a]	*Unconstitutional Cases*	*Percent Unconstitutional (%)*
NH Equal Protection	1	15	21.7	8	53.3	6	6	5.6	1	16.7
NH Due Process	2	12	17.4	5	41.7	5	8	7.4	1	12.5
NH Separation of Powers	3	9	13.0	4	44.4	4	10	9.3	2	20.0
US 14th Am Equal Protection	4	8	11.6	4	50.0	10	3	2.8	0	0.0
NH Exercise of Leg. Power	5	7	10.1	5	71.4	2	18	16.7	3	16.7
NH Access to Justice	6	6	8.7	4	0.0	28t	0	0.0	0	0.0
NH Police Power	7	4	5.8	0	0.0	1	29	26.9	3	10.3
US 14th Am DP-EP	8	4	5.8%	*0*	0.0	28t	*0*	0.0	0	0.0
NH Ex Post Facto Laws	9	3	4.3	0	0.0	28t	0	0.0	0	0.0
NH Reciprocity-Tax Share	10	3	4.3	2	66.7	18t	1	0.9	0	0.0
US 14th Am Due Process	11	3	4.3	1	33.3	11	3	2.8	0	0.0
US Ex Post Facto Laws	12	3	4.3	0	0.0	28t	0	0.0	0	0.0

(*Continued*)

Table 3.1 (*Continued*)

Constitutional Issue	*1967–2000*					*1901–1966*				
	Rank 1967–2000	*Cases*[a]	*Case Percent of Total (%)*[a]	*Unconstitutional Cases*	*Percent Unconstitutional (%)*	*Rank 1901–1966*	*Cases*[a]	*Case Percent of Total (%)*[a]	*Unconstitutional Cases*	*Percent Unconstitutional (%)*
NH Retrospective Laws	13	2	2.9	1	50.0	7	6	5.6	0	0.0
NH Eminent Domain	14	2	2.9	1	50.0	12	3	2.8	0	0.0
NH Unfunded Mandates	15	2	2.9	1	0.0	28t	0	0.0	0	0.0
US Interstate Commerce	16	2	2.9	2	100.0	8	6	5.6	3	50.0
Other Constitutional Issues [b]	17t	6	8.7	3	50.0	N/A	10	9.3	0	0.0
NH Delegation of Leg. Power	23t	0	0.0	0	0.0	3	15	13.9	2	13.3
Not Raised in 1967–2000 [c]	23t	0	0.0	0	0.0	N/A	16	2.8	3	18.8
Total Cases	N/A	69	100.0	31	44.9	N/A	108	100.0	17	15.7

Source: case-by-case analysis (on file with the authors) of 177 reported New Hampshire judicial review cases for 1901–1966 and 1967–2000. For further information, see Appendix B.

[a] In many cases, more than one constitutional issue was presented. Consequently, the cumulative total of cases with specific constitutional issues exceeds the actual number of judicial review cases.

[b] Each of the following state constitutional grounds was raised in just one case in 1967–2000: contract rights (2 cases in 1901-1966); right to jury trial (4 cases); excess punishment (3); education adequacy (0); and judicial disqualification (0). Under the federal constitution, the issue of cruel and unusual punishment was raised once in 1967–2000 and once in 1910–1966.

[c] The following state constitutional issues were raised in 1901–1966 judicial review cases, but they were not raised in any cases in 1967–2000: natural rights (3 cases in 1901–1966); free speech (3 cases); voting rights (2); religious freedom (1); the framework of state government (1); protection of competition (1); state legislative compensation (1); and powers of the governor (1). Under the federal constitution, the following issues were raised earlier in the twentieth century but not in 1967–2000: voting rights (1 case in 1901–1966); involuntary servitude (1 case); and free speech (1).

Table 3.2 New Hampshire Advisory Opinions, 1967–2000

Action Taken by Justices on Advisory Opinion Requests	*Cases Reported*	*Percent of Opinions Requested (%)*
• Proposed action found constitutional	62	43.7
• Proposed action found only partially constitutional	13	9.2
• Proposed action found not constitutional	50	35.2
• Justices declined to render opinion	11	7.7
• Statutory interpretation only	6	4.2
Grand Total of Advisory Opinion Requests	142	100.0

Source: case-by-case analysis (on file with authors) of 142 reported New Hampshire advisory opinions, 1967–2000. For more information, see Appendix C.

of just over one each year in the first 150 years. During the last third of the twentieth century, however, there were requests for 142 advisory opinions, or an average of more than four per year. See Table 3.2.

Table 3.2 indicates that the advisory opinions rendered by the justices in 1967–2000 were not as radical a departure from the pre-1966 era as their decisions were in cases involving judicial review of the constitutionality of legislative actions. Yet the advisory opinions did show a notable reduction in the number of cases in which the justices found proposed legislative or executive action to meet constitutional requirements. In the 151 years from 1816 through 1966, they opined that at least half of all proposed legislative or executive actions in question would be constitutional. In 1967–2000, however, they concluded that slightly more proposed actions would be at least partially unconstitutional than constitutional.

ADMINISTRATIVE CONFLICTS AND THE BACKDROP TO *CLAREMONT*

Navigating the *terra incognita* that both the legislature and the judiciary had entered would thus pose particular challenges to each. Could the legislature adapt to the loss of its traditional supremacy over the judicial branch, a supremacy that states throughout the nation seemed prepared, reluctantly or not, to yield? Could the judiciary use its new status to defend or even elevate the quality of justice it rendered without provoking counterreactions? In a sense, each branch had to contend with the weight of its own traditions, its own history; and each had to decide how much of that history it could and should retain in the present. The answers could only emerge in responses to particular circumstances.[5]

That is why a series of decisions the court rendered on administrative questions took on a significance they might not have been accorded in earlier times. They were highly fraught now, because they tested the real locus of the judiciary's new powers vis-á-vis the legislature, and seemed to suggest how far the court might go in expanding them. Would a court that was operationally liberated from legislative control seek to expand its jurisdictional and decisional powers, as well? Would the imperatives of professionalization require it to?

The first of these decisions, *In Re Mussman* had been rendered in 1972, but left a legacy that would trouble proponents of legislative supremacy long afterward.[6] The adjudicated question was whether the court itself had the power to investigate and, if necessary, discipline a district court judge, short of actual removal from office. But the broader issue was really whether the legislature (through the powers of impeachment and address) and the executive (through the power of address) would monopolize supervisory power over judicial personnel; or whether, alternatively, the judicial branch itself might be granted some means of policing its own ranks. While explicitly reaffirming that the power to actually remove a judicial officer belonged to the elected branches alone, the court cited a venerable New Hampshire statute confirming that "The supreme court shall have general superintendence of all courts of inferior jurisdiction to prevent and correct errors and abuses, including the authority to approve rules of court and prescribe and administer canons of ethics with respect to such courts." It also cited more recent findings in Michigan, Iowa, Oregon, and other states, and recent legal scholarship on the subject.[7]

The court took unto itself substantially more of the disciplinary function once held exclusively by legislators and the governor in 1977, when it created the state's first judicial conduct committee (JCC). Historically, the only means of dealing with misconduct by judges in most states had been impeachment, address, recall, or defeat in retention or competition elections. Those were blunt instruments, however, and not always optimal measures for dealing with misbehavior that didn't rise to the level of overt corruption or criminality.[8] To address that shortcoming, proposals had been advanced in the 1940s and 1950s to incorporate permanent disciplinary commissions into state judiciaries, and in 1960 California voters had amended their constitution to adopt one. The New Hampshire Supreme Court was among the first to adopt a code of conduct based on the ABA's Model Code of 1972, and its eleven-member JCC was created to enforce it.[9] The JCC in its original form was essentially an agency of the court, which appointed nine of its members and wrote the rules (Supreme Court Rules 38, 39, 40) by which the committee functioned.[10] No one yet knew how controversial that body would prove to be. What state legislators did perceive, however, was that the court's administrative domain was expanding, and arguably at their expense.

An opportunity to probe its limits emerged in *State v. LaFrance*, which tested whether the court's power to set rules for proceedings in courtrooms was independent of statutory oversight.[11] The 1983 case (the same year that state-level court funding took effect, oddly) concerned the attempt by a judge of the Belknap County Superior Court to enforce a policy preventing police officers from wearing their firearms on the stand, or even in court. The legislature had challenged that policy by passing a statute[12] that explicitly stipulated that law officers would be permitted to wear firearms in any courtroom in the state, "notwithstanding any other rule, regulation, or order to the contrary." On June 15, the Laconia Police Chief Bruce Cheney, citing the statute, refused to enter the courtroom when told to leave aside his weapon. Without his testimony, charges against defendant Timothy Clifton had to be dropped. Conversely, on July 12, defendant Arnold LaFrance claimed that his right to a fair trial would be violated if officers were permitted to testify against him while wearing guns.

It was not surprising that the constitutionality of the statute would be questioned. What evidently did surprise the legislation's supporters were the fourteen past presidents of the New Hampshire Bar Association who joined in the filing of an *amicus* brief.[13] If that suggestion of a legal community closing ranks in defense of court prerogatives was provocative, the supreme court's ruling on November 23, 1983, was no less so. It held that the separation of powers principle in general, and the established power to punish for contempt specifically, granted courts control over security measures within their own confines.[14] The decision is credited with helping build support for another constitutional convention the following year and, especially, with shaping some of the resolutions brought forth there: proposals for constitutional provisions on the election for judges, the dissolution of the unified bar, and others similarly aimed at what traditionalists saw as a judiciary spinning out of control.[15]

Although none of those resolutions would be adopted, one in particular was seen by its supporters as "sending the message" that judicial leaders must not ignore the need for suitable legislative involvement in the court rulemaking process. Resolution 100, "providing that supreme court rules are effective only when not inconsistent with statute," was offered by Delegate George Gordon of Merrimack County and seventeen cosponsors.[16] On June 20, 1984, Delegate Charles Bass, chair of the Committee on Judicial Power, presented the majority report recommending the adoption of Resolution No. 100, as amended with the support of a majority committee vote of 16-2. As amended, the resolution would require a two-thirds vote by each chamber of the legislature to override court rules adopted by the supreme court.[17]

Delegate Samuel Conti argued that the resolution should be rejected.[18] As one of the two dissenters from the committee majority, delegate Conti opened the floor debate on Resolution 100, arguing that it arose only in reaction against the New Hampshire Supreme Court's 1983 holding in *State v LaFrance*. In the absence of any evidence that the judiciary had generally abused its rulemaking power under Article 73-a, he claimed that the only purpose of Resolution 100 was to punish the courts for the "guns in court" decision. Rising in opposition to Conti was delegate Martin Gross, who argued that the resolution was not about the *LaFrance* decision, but instead about a critically important constitutional issue:[19] "The issue is whether authority of court procedures is to be allowed to slip into the exclusive control of the courts themselves," said Gross, "or whether we will continue to allow the legislature to step in to reform procedures when necessary." In a remark that may in retrospect be seen as prophetic, Gross went on to claim that there would be political consequences if the courts ignored Resolution 100.

> What we're saying here, is Resolution 100 is designed to preserve the legislature's authority to regulate and reform court procedures. There was a remark made during the hearings before the committee, that If the people approve Resolution 100 and the court won't take the message from it, then it would simply be because the court chooses not to take that message, that's what I'm trying to say to you. It was suggested before committee that the court won't take the message. That this resolution wouldn't do what it was intended to do. I guess I'd like to say again, that if the court chooses not to take the message, it will simply be because the court chooses not to take the message, and not because this resolution doesn't do the job. If that point ever comes, the Supreme Court of New Hampshire fails to take the message from a constitutional amendment, then there are other constitutional procedures available to send the message again. The court will simply have to bear the political cost.[20]

On a roll call vote, Conti's recommendation that Resolution 100 be rejected received support from only 41 percent of the voting delegates and was defeated.[21]

The committee majority then debated amending the resolution, a debate that came down to whether legislative override of Supreme Court rules should require a two-thirds majority or only a simple majority of the legislators. Speaking against the former idea, delegate Germain Bourdon of Nashua argued that it was "too stringent," and that it would "gut the intent" of the resolution as initially offered, which was

> to allow for representatives of the people, the general court and the senate, to say what is in their best interest, and not the courts. It was once devised that [of] the three branches of our government, the court system was the weakest, [and] unfortunately, through case law, become the strongest. What Resolution

> 100 would do, and what the amendment would not do, is put the power back where it belongs, where the people of this state, through their representative form of government, through their legislators and their senators, to allow them to express that which they want as a court rule.[22]

When there was a roll call vote on the amendment offered by the committee, it was supported by only 27 percent of the delegates voting and was overwhelming rejected.[23] A two-thirds legislative majority would be required to override the Supreme Court, if Resolution 100 were to become part of the state constitution.

Delegates then voted by roll call on whether to endorse it. Despite receiving the support of almost 60 percent of the voting delegates, the resolution failed to gain the necessary two-thirds majority required for its adoption.[24] Yet even though Resolution 100 had not been adopted in the constitutional convention, its proponents had indeed sounded a "warning alarm." Was it loud enough to be heard by judicial leaders?

It was sounded again in January 1995 (two years after the supreme court issued its first *Claremont* ruling), when a proposed constitutional amendment was filed in the House of Representatives by Reps. Roland Hemon and Normand Bergeron, both Democrats, with Republican Rep. Philip Cobbin as a third cosponsor.[25] This bill called for the repeal of three provisions of the N.H. constitution: Part 2, Articles 41 (expanded power for governor), 72-a (constitutional status for courts), and 73-a (administrative power of chief justice), thereby returning the constitution to its pre-1966 status in those areas. At a committee hearing on the bill, testimony by those supporting it included some reservations about the need to repeal Article 41. Supporters of the bill had no such reservations about Articles 72-a and 73-a, however, asserting that judges had exempted themselves from the law, that they "ignore our rights," that "the courts are destroying this country," that New Hampshire citizens have been "victims of judicial arrogance," and that the judiciary "has usurped the power of the Legislature."[26]

The committee struggled with the bill, voting only 9-7 in favor of it after the public hearing. It was re-referred for subcommittee work through 1995, and it was re-referred again in January 1996 for interim study. It was not until October 1996 that the committee concluded its work, deciding by a vote of 16-1 that it was "not recommended for future legislation."[27] But this was yet another warning signal, raising the question of whether it would be heeded by the judiciary.

Over time, the supreme court would confirm the principle of judicial administrative autonomy by, for example, invalidating, again on separation of powers grounds, a statute that transferred responsibility for security for district courts from the judicial branch to county sheriffs.[28] Critics charged that the separation of powers should not be evoked to justify judicial assumption of responsibilities which the executive or legislative branch was far better equipped to handle (and, indeed, usually had). For its part, the court did not consider itself more sensitive to the perils of executive and legislative incursion into its domain than it previously had been—simply more able and willing to ward them off. If the constitutional amendments of 1966 and 1978 had promised a more fully autonomous court in principle, decisions like these suggested what that would mean in practice. But disputes over who controlled courtroom security and ordinary procedures were mere skirmishes compared to the dispute that loomed over who controlled rules of evidence.

This time, it would be the champions of legislative prerogatives who could claim affiliation with a development on the national stage. In 1994, Congress was considering amending certain federal rules of evidence (Fed. R. Evid. 413, 414, and 415) so that evidence of prior sexual offenses of a defendant accused of sexual assault or child molestation would be admissible in a current trial "on any matter to which it is relevant."[29] The proposal broke with common law tradition, whereby the overall character of a defendant and/or evidence suggesting a propensity to crime is carefully excluded from consideration in court.[30] It was deemed necessary nonetheless, in part because of the difficulty securing testimony from victims who, aware of the defendant's history, feared retaliation. Congress's usual practice had been to request commentary by the U.S. Supreme Court and the Federal Judicial Conference before promulgating changes in federal rules of evidence. This time, however, it did so only after changing Rules 413, 414, and 415. Both advisory bodies recommended that Congress reconsider and retract. But it did not—which might help explain why 36 states have declined to incorporate the federal change into state law, despite a historic inclination of state judiciaries to follow the federal lead on overall changes in evidentiary norms (if not so frequently on particulars). See Appendix E.

In 1996, the New Hampshire Supreme Court was asked for an advisory opinion on a proposal inspired by the federal change. Supporters noted that legislative involvement in evidentiary questions was well within the state's traditions, and that judges would retain discretion to rule out evidence if its prejudicial threat seemed to outweigh its probative value.[31] But the "rebuttable presumption of admissibility" for such evidence stipulated in the New Hampshire proposal arguably went further than the federal change, in the near-automatic grounds for appealing such decisions that language seemed to provide.

More significantly, opponents of the measure submitted a constitutional problem with it. In 1985, the Supreme Court had formally adopted rules of evidence that made evidence of other crimes inadmissible to prove a criminal defendant's propensity to commit the present offense.[32] The proposed change would seem to invalidate that by legislative action—an incursion into the judiciary's newly constitutionalized rulemaking authority, claimed opponents, and hence a violation of the separation of powers.[33] The constitutional provision invoked, of course, was Article 73-a.

The court's *PSAE* (*Prior Sexual Assault Evidence*) opinion would be issued in 1997, the year of its second and far more controversial *Claremont* decision. If the latter, with its profound implications for the state budget, agitated a larger body of legislators, the former might have been even more disturbing to those troubled by what seemed the general trajectory of legislative-judicial relations.

The court found that the proposed bill did indeed violate the separation of powers of Part I, Article 37, of the New Hampshire Constitution.[34] Justices drew a distinction between "substantive" laws ("which have for their purpose to determine the rights and duties of the individual and to regulate his conduct and relation with the government and other individuals"), which were unquestionably the domain of the legislature; and "procedural" ones ("which have for their purpose … to prescribe machinery and methods to be employed in enforcing these positive provisions"), which the court claimed for itself alone.[35] The distinction itself may well have been, and may well remain, constitutionally and philosophically defensible, or even conventional (although perhaps murkier in practical application).[36] What troubled critics, however, was that the determination of what actually constituted a "procedural" matter in the first instance would now have to be assigned fully and exclusively to the court. The future role of the legislature on questions once understood to lie fully or at least partially within its bailiwick seemed much less clear.[37] In the context of the times, what mistrustful legislators saw in the *PSAE* opinion was a significant aggrandizement of the court's jurisdictional and decisional authority, under cover of procedural (i.e., administrative) independence.

NOTES

1. Jeffrey Leidinger, "The Move Toward State Financing: A New Hampshire Approach," *Just. Sys. J.* 7, no. 1 (1982): 103–23. New Hampshire was the last state in the nation to have a state court administrator. Chief Justice Frank Kenison had appointed James Gainey to be his administrative assistant in about 1978, but it was not until 1980 that Mr. Leidinger was appointed to be New Hampshire's first official full-time director of administrative services for the courts. Leidinger had previously worked for the Crime Commission, the state agency responsible for receiving grant funds from the Law Enforcement Assistance Administration, whose New England representative had been Maurice Geiger—the Carroll County delegate to the 1974 Constitutional Convention who sponsored the resolution that as amended became Article 73-a in Part II of the state constitution. Both Gainey and Leidinger came to the

court system after working for the National Center for State Courts, a non-profit organization created in 1971 to assist state and local courts in the improvement of judicial administration, and whose president at the time was Edward McConnell, who earlier had been America's very first state court administrator. For more information on the history of state court administrators, see David Steelman and Anne Skove, "Creation of State Court Administrative Offices and Selection of State Court Administrators: Technical Assistance Report" (Denver, CO: National Center for State Courts, 2007). Regarding the effects of the transition to state funding of a unified court system, see Robert Tobin, "Managing the Shift to State Court Financing," *Just. Sys. J.* 7, no. 1 (1982): 70–102.

2. John Vernhoff, *New Hampshire State Court Organization Profile* (Williamsburg, VA: National Center for State Courts, 1978).

3. See John Hudzik, *The Effects of State Financing: Summary Findings From the Four-State Study* (Williamsburg, VA: National Center for State Courts, 1990). See also Victor Flango, "Court Unification and Quality of State Courts," *Just. Sys. J.* 16, no. 3 (1994): 33–55).

4. See, for example, Michael Ignatieff, *The Rights Revolution* (Toronto: House of Anansi, 2000); Charles Epp, *The Rights Revolution: Lawyers, Activists, and Supreme Courts in Comparative Perspective* (Chicago: University of Chicago Press, 1998); Samuel Walker, *The Rights Revolution: Rights and Community in Modern America* (New York: Oxford University Press, 1998); Cass Sunstein, *After The Rights Revolution: Reconceiving the Regulatory State* (Cambridge: Harvard University Press, 1990); and Luc Ferry, *Rights: The New Quarrel Between the Ancients and the Moderns* (Chicago: University of Chicago Press, 1998).

5. In the period immediately after the grant of constitutional status to the Supreme and Superior Courts, there were a heightened number of litigated cases that presented constitutional questions on appeal. From 1967 through 2000, the Supreme Court ruled on challenges to the constitutionality of legislative actions in 69 cases. In 31 (45%) of those cases, the Court found the challenged legislation unconstitutional. This was a dramatic departure from the first 150 years of reported decisions on constitutional questions. Among 182 cases with constitutional decisions between 1816 and 1966, the courts had found legislation unconstitutional in only 33 cases (or 18% of the total).

6. 112 N.H. 99, 289 A. 2d 403 (1972).

7. As the defendant in the case, Mussman had filed a motion to dismiss the petition on the grounds that the Supreme Court had no jurisdiction, claiming that the only remedy available under the constitution was either impeachment or address. The court rejected the argument (112 N.H. at 101). This decision was the second of three involving Mussman. In a case brought a year earlier by the state bar association through a petition for disciplinary action against Mussman on a complaint of professional misconduct as a lawyer, the Supreme Court had asserted its "inherent and statutory (N.H. Rev. Stat. Ann. §311:8) power to supervise the conduct of attorneys for the protection of the public and the maintenance of public confidence in the bar as a whole," and ordered Mussman to be suspended from the practice of law in the state for unethical behavior. Mussman's Case, 111 N.H. 402, 412, 286 A.2d 614 (1971). After its 1972 denial of the defendant's motion to dismiss for want of jurisdiction, the Court then

heard a petition by the attorney general for an inquiry into Mussman's conduct as judge of the District Court of Littleton. The court once again exercised its supervisory power, ordering a suspension of Mussman's authority and duties as a district judge as well. In re Mussman, 113 N.H. 54, 302 A. 2d 822 (1973).

8. Geyh, et al., *Judicial Conduct and Ethics*, 5th ed., 40, 761.

9. Aspirational standard of conduct for American judges were first developed by the ABA in 1924. In 1972, they were replaced with a Model Code of Judicial Conduct intended to both guide the judiciary and serve as a basis for disciplinary actions. Its terms were largely mandatory. See James Alfini, Shailey Gupta-Brietzke, and James McMartin, "Dealing with Judicial Misconduct in the States: Judicial Independence, Accountability and Reform," *S. Tex. L. Rev.* 48 (2007): 890–91. By the 1980s, every state had its own judicial discipline commission. See Cynthia Gray, "Judicial Conduct Commissions: How Judicial Conduct Commissions Work," *Just. Sys. J.* 28, no. 3 (2007): 405–18. See also Kathleen Sampson, *Judicial Conduct Organizations, Governing Provisions*, Vols. 1 and 2 (Chicago: American Judicature Society, 1982, 1984).

10. Four of those nine members had to be active or retired judges of the Supreme Court, Superior Court, a district court, and a probate court; two had to be attorneys in good standing with the bar; and the remaining three were lay persons.

11. State v. LaFrance, 124 N.H. 171, A 2d 340 (1983).

12. N.H. Rev. Stat. Ann. §490:4(a) (1975).

13. Batchelder, "Independence Revisited," 65.

14. In almost all states, the issue of court security is now less a power struggle between the judiciary and other branches than a matter for judicial coordination and collaboration with local, state, and federal funding authorities, and with the officials responsible for actually providing courthouse security. See Timothy Fautsko, Steven Berson, and Steve Swensen, *Status of Court Security in State Courts: A National Perspective* (Williamsburg, VA: National Center for State Courts, 2013).

15. Batchelder, "Independence Revisited," 65.

16. *Constitutional Convention, 1984*, 27. Among the cosponsors was Delegate Martin Gross, who had been assured by Delegate Arthur Nighswander in the 1974 Constitutional Convention that the phrase in Article 73-a that supreme court rules "shall have the force and effect of law" would not change the legislature's traditional participation in court rulemaking. Another cosponsor was Delegate Leo Pepino of Manchester, who as a legislator would later file a proposed constitutional amendment (CACR5) on January 4, 2001, the very first day of the legislative session after the conclusion of the Brock impeachment proceedings, which would make court rulemaking subject to legislative oversight.

17. Ibid, 235. Charles Bass is a non-lawyer Republican who served in the N.H. House of Representatives (1982–1988) and Senate (1988–1992), as well as the U.S. House of Representatives (1994–2006).

18. Delegate Leslie Nixon, an attorney from Manchester, joined Conti in the committee's minority position, arguing that Resolution 100 should not be adopted. Conti was a lawyer admitted to the NJ and N.H. bar, and he had previously been a probation officer and trial court administrator in New Jersey under State Court Administrator Edward McConnell. When McConnell left the New Jersey courts to become the head

of the National Center for State Courts in 1973, he persuaded Conti to follow him and serve as the director of its Northeast Regional Office. Conti was a good friend of Maurice Geiger, who as a delegate to the 1974 convention had sponsored the original resolution that subsequently became Article 73-a. Geiger had sought to be a delegate to the 1984 convention, but he failed to receive enough votes. See N.H., *General Court Manual* (1985), 134 and 156. Among those who worked for Conti in the Northeast Regional Office were James Gainey, who temporarily served as New Hampshire chief justice Kenison's administrative assistant in 1979, and Jeffrey Leidinger, who became the state's full-time director of administrative services in 1980 and first director of its Administrative Office of the Courts in 1984.

19. *Constitutional Convention, 1984*, 235.

20. Ibid, 237.

21. Ibid, 244.

22. Ibid, 246.

23. Ibid, 248.

24. Ibid, 249.

25. See N.H. H.R. Jour. 11 (January 5, 1995), 159.

26. N.H. H.R. Constitutional & Statutory Revision Committee, Public Hearing, CACR5 (January 25, 1995).

27. N.H. H.R. Constitutional & Statutory Revision Committee, Interim Study Report (October 16, 1996).

28. Petition of Mone, 143 N.H. 128, 719 A.2d 626 (1998). For more on this case, see Robert J. Lynn, "Judicial Rulemaking"; Law professor Lawrence Friedman, "On the Justifications for Constitutional Amendment Concurrent Resolution 5," *N.H. Bar J.* 43, no. 3 (2002): 46–49; and New Hampshire Bar Association, "CACR5: Reform Linchpin or Mischief-Maker? A Bar Journal Roundtable Discussion," *N.H. Bar J.* 43, no. 2 (2002): 38–47.

29. The rules would not narrow the admissibility such evidence to instances where it spoke specifically to motive or to some particular aspect of the case. Rather, under Fed. R. Evid. 403 413(a), "The evidence could be considered on any matter to which it is relevant."

30. See Penny White, "The Continuing Evolution of the Federal Rules of Evidence," in Gordon Griller and E. Keith Stott, eds., *Improvement of the Administration of Justice* (Oak Park, IL: American Bar Association, 2002).

31. In support of the constitutionality of HB1549, see Charles Douglas, Memorandum of N.H. House Committee on Corrections and Criminal Justice, and Atty. General Jeffrey Howard and Asst. Attorney General Cynthia White, Memorandum of the Attorney General, both filed with the justices on June 28, 1996, in the matter of the Senate request for an advisory opinion on the bill.

32. N.H. R. Evid. 404(b). The adoption of this rule was seen by the judiciary as no more than the reiteration by rule of a well-established common law provision, as expressed in State v. Lapage, 57 N.H. 245 (1876). Perhaps the best-known expression of the common law rule in American case law was given in People v. Molineux, 168 N.Y. 264 (1901), which formed the basis for Rule 404(b) of the Federal Rules of Evidence. See Appendix E.

33. Chief Appellate Defender James Duggan, Memorandum in Opposition to the Constitutionality of HB1549, filed with the justices in June 1996, in the matter of the Senate request for an advisory opinion on the bill.

34. Opinion of the Judges (Prior Sexual Assault Evidence), 141 N.H. 562, 688 A.2d 1006 (1997). On the aspects of this decision involving due process and rules of evidence, see Danielle Matton, "An Examination of Federal Rules of Evidence 413, 414, and 415 and the Adoption of These Rules by the States," *N.H. Bar J.* 41, no. 3 (2000), 28–35.

35. Quoted by Lynn, "Judicial Rulemaking," 46.

36. Court rulings assuming that distinction in fact went back to the 1960s, in cases such as Garabedian v. William Co., 106 N.H. 156, 207 A. 2d 425 (1965), and Nassif Realty Corporation v. National Fire Insurance Co., 107 N.H. 267, 220 A.2d 748 (1966). See McNamara, "Separation of Powers Principle," 80.

37. Actually, two years before the *PSAE* holding the Court had responded to a similar request by legislators for an advisory opinion on legislation prohibiting the use of evidence related to the victim's manner of dress in sexual assault cases. In that case, they had determined that the statute would indeed pass constitutional muster. McNamara, "Separation of Powers Principle," 81.

At the levels of international, federal and state government, there has been considerable academic and practical exploration of potential conflicts between "substantive law" that creates or defines the rights of citizens (presumably a legislative responsibility) and "procedural law" about effective and efficient means to enforce or protect such rights (more of a judicial responsibility). See, for example, Jeremy Lever, "Why Procedure Is More Important than Substantive Law," *Int'l & Comp. L. Q.* 48, no. 2 (1999): 285–301; Martin Redish and Dennis Murashko, "The Rules Enabling Act and the Procedural-Substantive Tension: A Lesson in Statutory Interpretation," *Minn. L. Rev.* 93, no.1 (2008): 26–95; Simona Grossi, "The Courts and the People in a Democratic System: Against Federal Court Exceptionalism," *Notre Dame L. Rev. Online* 92 (2017): 106–11, http://ndlawreview.org/wp-content/uploads/2017/04/Grossi_Final.pdf; and Minnesota House of Representatives, Research Department, "Separation of Powers: When Statutes and Court Rules Conflict" (2005), http://www.house.leg.state.mn.us/hrd/pubs/ss/ssseppw.pdf.

Part II

TOWARD IMPEACHMENT

Chapter 4

The Fairbanks Scandal and Its Repercussions

By the time of the *Prior Sexual Assault Evidence (PSAE)* holding some legislators were already thinking darker thoughts, not only about the judicial branch of state government but about New Hampshire's entire legal community, including personnel within the attorney general's office (It was an increasingly seamless category to some, especially since the establishment of a unified bar mainly under Court supervision). Precipitating this was a spectacular scandal involving John C. Fairbanks, a Newport lawyer who had served 33 years as a part-time district court judge. On December 28, 1989, Fairbanks was indicted by a Sullivan County grand jury for embezzling $1.8 million from probate clients between 1983 and 1989. He disappeared the very next day, then evaded the law for over four years until he was found dead in a Las Vegas hotel in March 1994.[1]

FAIRBANKS AS PROBATE LAWYER AND DISTRICT COURT JUDGE

Complaints about the integrity of Fairbanks's work as a fiduciary had emerged as early as 1976, when Ms. Diane Trudeau had brought to the Professional Conduct Committee (or PCC, like JCC an appendage of the supreme court) the charge that he had stolen from her father's estate. At the time, Fairbanks himself was a member of the committee, and apparently did not recuse himself from the case. PCC reviewed the matter, concluded that Fairbanks had done nothing inappropriate, and closed the case in 1997 (not, however, before ordering Ms. Trudeau to remain silent about it, out of regard for PCC's own confidentiality regulations).[2] In September 1987, Mrs. Prentice Coonley-Demers filed another formal complaint against Fairbanks with PCC, charging that he had mishandled her mother's estate. This time, PCC did remove Fairbanks as guardian of the estate. But the matter was ended with no further consequences after he paid a settlement of $41,000.[3] In 1988, John Tweedy of Washington, New Hampshire, filed his second complaint with PCC about Fairbanks' mismanagement of the trust fund for Tweedy's mentally disabled brother. In December of that year, Tweedy went beyond PCC, and asked the attorney general's office to investigate Fairbanks actions. But papers from the attorney general indicate that state investigators assigned no more weight to Tweedy's claims than PCC had assigned to any of the charges against Fairbanks it had fielded, and perhaps even less. Eventually, the assistant attorney general heading the inquiry suggested to an investigator that "before you do too much digging, you should interview Fairbanks and see if he has answers to Tweedy's questions. … If he does, that should end the matter."[4]

In fact, concerns about Fairbanks extended beyond his work as a fiduciary; there were longstanding complaints about his performance as a criminal-court judge as well. Claims of disparate sentencing and delays by Fairbanks as a district court judge had been filed with the supreme court's Judicial Conduct Committee (JCC) in the early 1980s; in fact, there were even suspicions that he was a sexual predator taking advantage of young male criminal defendants appearing before him when he sat as a district court judge.[5] But in 1983, JCC had decided that, all things considered, it had grounds to give Fairbanks no more than a private reprimand.[6]

Fairbanks' downfall began with complaints by the children of a client named Helen Meding. Meding died on January 26, 1985, and Fairbanks was appointed executor of the Meding estate the following month. He was required by law to submit an inventory of its assets to the Sullivan County Probate Court within 90 days of his appointment; but he didn't do so until May 6, 1986. Oddly, that delay didn't prevent the Dartmouth National Bank from delivering $265,000 to him for estate taxes, debts, and funeral and administrative expenses (nor, for that matter, did his delay in recording the transaction produce any sanction from the Sullivan County Probate Court).[7] But it did trouble the Meding children, who could not access the account's principal while the inventory was unregistered. Those concerns deepened over the next couple of years, as additional reporting deadlines were missed, taxes went unpaid, and both bank and Probate Court remained unresponsive to their queries.

In January 1989, the AG's investigators informed the Sullivan County Probate Court of John Tweedy's complaints, which merged with and amplified those of the Meding children. At this point, officialdom finally began to bestir itself. Sullivan County Attorney and state Rep. Peter Burling took a public interest in the matter; and the PCC appointed attorney Arthur Nighswander to conduct a special investigation into both Fairbanks' actions and the operations of the probate court entrusted with oversight of them. The resultant publicity led Fairbanks to resign from the New Hampshire state bar on June 6, 1989. That, however, didn't deter Sullivan County Attorney Mark Hathaway from announcing his intent to convene a grand jury to investigate Fairbanks later that month.

Nighswander's report, completed that August, not only expanded the case against Fairbanks, but implicated wider circles of the profession in it. The milieu Nighswander described was one where, by one reckoning, "judges were likely to take the word of a colleague. There was no reason to disbelieve lawyers; you gave your friends the benefit of the doubt."[8] That same month, the supreme court suspended Fairbanks from all practice of law. In September, creditors and victims filed claims amounting to $6 million against Fairbanks in the U.S. Bankruptcy Court.[9] Many would file further complaints with the PCC, and try to reclaim their losses by filing claims with the New Hampshire Bar Association's client protection fund.[10] By the end of 1989, when Fairbanks was indicted and fled the state, the scandal was very public indeed. Over the next four years, as law enforcement agencies proved curiously unable to locate or apprehend him, it would metastasize.

"THE TIP OF THE ICEBERG"

Far more than a single judicial miscreant, after all, seemed to be involved: the affair raised serious questions about the judiciary's capacity, or perhaps willingness, to police itself. Why, after all, had officials not intervened sooner and more decisively to end the ongoing misconduct by Fairbanks? Why had PCC, JCC, even the attorney general's office all seen so little urgency in the matter? Less than a week after Fairbanks' flight, JCC charged Fairbanks' fellow Sullivan County Probate Court Judge Harry Spanos with misconduct for failing to monitor Fairbanks's activities. But by that time, suspicion could hardly be confined to that probate court, or to Sullivan county. Indeed, in some citizens' eyes the entire legal community was now suspect. State Sen. Eleanor Podles observed that "People are doing crazy things with their money now (out of distrust for their lawyers). They don't know what to do." This was scarcely surprising to Podles, since in her view "the Fairbanks case is 'just the tip of the iceberg. There's a lot more to this.'"[11]

The supreme court, acting on the recommendation of a special task force assembled to recommend means of preventing any repetition of the Fairbanks affair, created a special judicial administrator for probate courts, and charged him with bringing accountability and uniformity to all of them. But to many in and out of state government, the court could hardly be trusted to clean up the rot. On the contrary, it seemed a big part of the problem. What was perhaps most distressing, perhaps especially to those already inclined to mistrust the autonomous judiciary that had been evolving under the court's direction, was the difficulty of acquiring information about what had actually happened from the court's own, internal ethical monitors, PCC and JCC. To the increasing exasperation of many, both bodies zealously protected the confidentiality of materials collected during their own inquiries. Critics would make much of the "veil of secrecy" by which, they charged, those supreme court-supervised bodies, purporting to safeguard legal ethics and standards, actually shielded the legal community from proper public scrutiny and accountability.

Rep. Peter Burling was among the first who attempted to pierce that veil. Within a short time after Fairbanks' death 1994, he filed a petition with the supreme court asking it "to release for public inspection 'any and all professional conduct files as may be in existence regarding the late John Fairbanks, whether held by the court or by the Professional Conduct Committee'"[12] Fairbanks, Burling noted, had been under felony indictment, and was now dead. Further, he argued, there was a clear need to assure the public that PCC's handling of the Fairbanks matter was proper; to apprise them of PCC proceedings; and to overcome the perception, fed by the secrecy of those proceedings, that PCC was basically indifferent to public concerns. The court acknowledged that it could, in particular circumstances, override its own written rules on the matter.[13] It acknowledged, as well, the gravity of the concerns Burling articulated. But they were not quite grave enough, it concluded, to trump the need for confidentiality in attorney discipline hearings. Burling's petition was denied.

Public pressure on the state's legal institutions, however, did not abate. By1992, as a result of claims against Fairbanks and a few other bar members, the state bar association's client protection fund was in default. With compensation available from neither that fund nor bankruptcy proceedings, state legislators were growing concerned about the vulnerability of probate courts and the citizens served by them to any repetition of the Fairbanks disaster. The legislative response was twofold, and each entailed deeper public inquiry into the legal community's practices, resources, and level of accountability. The first failed to achieve its goals. The second exceeded them.

INITIAL LEGISLATIVE INVESTIGATIVE EFFORTS

At the start of the January 1996 legislative session, Sen. Beverly Rodeschin introduced a bill requiring all New Hampshire attorneys to be bonded through the state bar association to cover claims of attorney misconduct.[14] By November, a study group commissioned by the Senate's Insurance Committee recommended that the supreme court (since 1968, the bar association's formal supervisor) adopt rules requiring both bonding and an indemnity fund.[15] But the bar and the court's own advisory committee on rules felt that went too far: the cost of surety bonding premiums, they concluded, would be prohibitive, and provide no more protection to clients than an indemnity fund alone could. At that point, the court and state bar effectively deflected the legislature's proposal by generating one of their own. After soliciting counsel from a variety of sources and holding a hearing where oral arguments were presented, the court adopted Rule 55, creating a "Public Protection Fund" to be administered by the state bar.[16]

Court Rule 55 was not exactly what Sen. Rodeschin had had in mind. But on the same day that she had introduced her bill, state Rep. Philip Cobbin had also introduced another bill, this one aimed at adequately compensating citizens victimized by Fairbanks. In its initial form, the bill would establish a commission to decide claims brought by Fairbanks' prey against the State of New Hampshire and provided an appropriation of $6 million to pay those proven sound.[17] Once again, the end result diverged from the initial intent—but this time in a very different direction.

The bill was amended a mere month after its introduction at the instigation of Rep. Cobbin, who wanted its purpose to include a thoroughgoing study of the actions of state officials in the Fairbanks matter. The new version would establish a joint legislative committee to assess the investigation of Fairbanks by the PCC, JCC, and law enforcement agencies, including the attorney general's office—essentially, an investigation of prior investigations. The proceedings of the committee, which came to be called the "Fairbanks I Committee," were to be recorded and transcribed, and all records made public.[18] As the meta-investigators proceeded, they would hear divergent recommendations for avoiding further traumas of this nature. That was quite natural, since there were equally divergent views of what had had happened in the Sullivan County Probate Court.

One understanding emerged from the testimony of Chief Justice Brock when he appeared before the committee on November 12, 1996.[19] Brock defended PCC's and JCC's commitment to confidentiality in cases where potentially libelous accusations had been made but not yet proven, arguing that the public's right to know was recognized through new rules mandating public hearings upon formal determination that probable cause for further investigation did exist. In addition, he offered two proposals for change. The first was ending part-time judgeships, and establishing a fully professionalized, entirely full-time judiciary. The second was replacing elected registers with administratively trained judicial appointees, if necessary by constitutional provision.[20] The latter recommendation referred specifically to the tenure of Sullivan County Register of Probate Bernice MacWilliams.

Voters had first installed MacWilliams in office in 1941, then returned her to it for the next 40 years. Few, apparently, either knew or cared how bad her record-keeping had been through those decades—or that she had effectively, albeit presumably unintentionally, abetted Fairbanks' crimes by making them practically impossible to track or document (it was the Nighswander Report that revealed the administrative chaos in the Sullivan County Probate Court, and its source).[21]

Taken as a whole, what Brock suggested to the committee was that the criminality that had beset Sullivan County was a function of the premodern judicial regime. It reflected the entrenchment, through political clout, of local notables in positions for which they were professionally unsuited and where trusting local authorities left them basically unsupervised.[22] Not surprisingly, Brock's prescription was basically to extend the process of judicial modernization to jurisdictions it had not yet reached. The administration of justice, from judges to clerical staff, should be entirely in the hands of trained professionals without local ties and obligations; the maintenance of professional standards should be entrusted to bodies selected and staffed by those professionals; autonomous local jurisdictions should be ended, and state courts fully de-politicized.

But there was an alternative analysis at hand, from which an alternative set of prescriptions could be gleaned. Both could be drawn from the words of Gov. Steve Merrill, who testified before the committee on the same day as Brock. Merrill, whose public career had begun in the attorney general's office, was fully mindful of the wave of criticism that had been leveled at that office and other law enforcement agencies for failing to bring Fairbanks to justice. Accusations of a deliberate and extensive coverup, he well knew, were publicly bruited about.[23] Not surprisingly, it was law enforcement, not the judicial system, that Merrill stressed. By his reckoning, the problem was not unprofessional or politicized courts but the inadequate financial and statutory resources afforded law enforcement to prosecute white-collar crime.[24] In fact, he directly rejected Brock's agenda, openly endorsing both the system of part-time judges and the election of probate registers.[25] Changing those time-honored features of the state's judicial order, among the last relics of the old ways, would do nothing, Merrill said, to address the problem of white-collar crime. What was needed instead was stronger, better law enforcement.

What was inferrable from Merrill's testimony was that the reforms Brock recommended might well worsen the situation. The problem, according to Merrill, was not that judicial modernization had not yet proceeded far enough, but rather that it had already gone much too far. What that process amounted to was the removal of judges and lawyers from public aaccountability, and the results were now before the state: "professionals" who knew or should have known about Fairbanks' misconduct had engaged in a conspiracy of silence by which law enforcement had been stymied. What was needed was more accountability, more responsiveness to public concerns—not less.

A recent revelation attendant on the Fairbanks investigation did tend to lend weight to the general notion that New Hampshire's legal community was entirely too self-protective. Fairbanks had filed a request to resign from both the bench and the bar in June 1989. Before granting it, the court had entered Fairbanks' request on a distinctive docket established in 1985: a "Special Matters Confidential" docket. The general public and even most legislators had been entirely unaware of it. It had been created "as a designation for bar admissions, requests for subpoenas for professional conduct hearings, appointments of custodians of client files, and judicial discipline cases"—even though all cases that came before PCC or JCC were already confidential.[26] To be sure, when Fairbanks' actions had come before PCC, the court had allowed its disciplinary committee access to the "Special Matters Confidential" docket "for subpoena of records, audit of trust and operating accounts, and appointment of auditor about Fairbanks."[27] But that hardly calmed those who felt that the layers upon layers of protection the court now provided for accused legal professionals suggested a degree of solicitude far in excess of what ordinary citizens could expect.[28]

After the conclusion of all testimony, the "Fairbanks I" committee submitted a report that simultaneously scored the Sullivan County probate system, the PCC, the JCC, and the Attorney General's office for "a systematic failure of government to do its basic duty of protecting citizens from itself."[29] But Rep. Cobbin was not satisfied with that rather amorphous critique, nor persuaded that the committee had really plumbed the depths of the problem. He particularly regretted the committee's lack of subpoena power to compel testimony by additional witnesses. Cobbin was unwilling to let the matter rest quite yet, and he was not alone.

"FAIRBANKS II" AND "FAIRBANKS III" COMMITTEES

In January 1997, Cobbin filed a bill to establish another committee to continue the study of all the Fairbanks investigations, but this time with subpoena power. As amended and passed, the bill basically established the "Fairbanks II" committee Cobbin wanted (save the attorney and professional investigator he had also requested).[30] It was authorized to study not only any actions and all investigations of Fairbanks, but also of other attorneys who may have engaged in serious misconduct. Among the witnesses it deposed were Fairbanks' own lawyers, who testified that they had refused to tell law enforcement officials where they could find him after he absconded because of their ethical responsibilities under his attorney-client privilege. Yet again, the legal community's seemingly sacred commitment to the confidentiality of its denizens' deliberations seemed an obstacle to justice, to accountability, to fulfillment of the public interest. When the Fairbanks II committee delivered its final report in January 1998, Rep. Cobbin found himself again unsatisfied.

There were simply too many questions that remained unanswered. For example, no one had yet uncovered just what had happened to the millions of dollars Fairbanks had stolen (the absence of a professional investigator apparently impeded the committee's inquiry into that).[31] Doggedly, Cobbin put forward another bill, which would create a "Fairbanks III committee" by extending and expanding the powers of the last one. His conviction that the real depth of corruption lying behind Fairbanks' career had yet to be revealed was shared by supporters who testified before the House Judiciary and Family Law Committee that January. They described numerous calls from people with complaints about additional criminal wrongdoing: allegations about failure to turn over state police information; claims that state police "sting" operations had been quashed for unexplained reasons; even the charge that at least four attorneys general had known that Fairbanks was a pedophile but done nothing about it. As introduced, Cobbin's bill was intended to empower the Fairbanks III committee to scrutinize not only Fairbanks' actions and prior investigations of them but, more generally, "the workings of judiciary and enforcement agencies and any other entity which impacts on the ability to identify and investigate criminal wrongdoing by state actors and attorneys in this state."[32] In fact, the bill's sponsors aimed at nothing less than "a permanent legislative committee for oversight of courts and police."[33]

What happened next indicated pretty clearly which interpretation of the lessons of the Fairbanks scandal had won out, at least among legislators.

In keeping with the proposal by Rep. Cobbin, the Judiciary and Family Law Committee proposed the creation of yet another investigative committee, this time a joint House-Senate body fully equipped not only with subpoena power but also the private investigator Fairbanks II had lacked. Fairbanks III was intended to advance beyond the work of its predecessors in other ways, as well. Indeed, the bill's framers had recognized by this time that they needed more than determinations of statutory violations by specific individuals, even specific agencies. The malady they hoped to cure was deeper, more dangerous, and fundamentally constitutional in nature. What had happened, apparently, was an ongoing, systemic betrayal of the New Hampshire's founding, constitutional principles—a betrayal that could be undone only by rededication to those principles. That, in turn, would require that the constitutional revisions of 1966 be revisited. So the legislators who passed the final version of Cobbin's bill in June 1998 directed Fairbanks III members to "examine the adoption of part II, article 41 of the state constitution, relative to the powers of the governor, and the adoption of part II, articles 72-a and 73-a of the state constitution, relative to the judicial powers of the courts and the supreme court and its administration."

In the sixteen meetings that committee chair Alf Jacobson conducted before Fairbanks III submitted its final report to the governor in December 1998, the committee heard from 39 members of the public, as well as Chief Justice Brock, Secretary of State William Gardner, and Attorney Martin Gross, who had been a delegate in the 1974 Constitutional Convention. It decided, in the end, that there was little cause for concern about the powers of the governor. The powers of the Supreme Court and the state judiciary, however, were an entirely different matter.[34]

Longstanding complaints about the absence of the phrase "shall have the force of law" from the voters' guide issued prior to the adoption of Article 73-a were aired yet again. So were questions about the legislature's role in judicial rulemaking since the conferral of administrative responsibility for the entire judiciary on the chief justice in 1978. Apparently to confirm the ill effects of those 1966 and 1978 actions, the report thrust before its readers a wide variety of complaints about the daily operations of courts in New Hampshire's reconfigured judiciary. Divorce and domestic disputes were singled out as particular areas of concern. The rising costs of litigation had expanded the numbers of *pro se* litigants; and these, it was claimed, were often disrespected by judges and ill-served or overtly fleeced by attorneys. Objections were raised to the bar association's intimate association with the bench, and charges were launched that lawyers were overtly intimidated into avoiding or dropping clients.

In fact, there was surprisingly little in the final report about John Fairbanks, or investigations of him. Seen in the light of history and from a national perspective, what Fairbanks' career mainly reflected was weak probate court oversight of fiduciaries in general at the time.[35] But in New Hampshire in the 1990s, far more than probate courts seemed implicated. How far did the rot extend? What was its source? Above all, how was it to be cleansed?

Ominously, the record of testimony in the public hearing on Cobbin's bill contained references to the ill-fated career of John Pickering. Pickering had been Chief Justice of New Hampshire's Superior Court of Judicature in the 1790s, then its highest court. Legislators would contrive to remove him from that office via appointment to the federal bench, where he was impeached in 1804.[36]

NOTES

1. The story of misconduct by Fairbanks and his flight from the law generated considerable public interest. See Royal Ford, "Scandalous Judge's Legacy Won't Die: Rural N.H. town reels from tale of disorder in the court," *Boston Globe,* September 18, 1997, B1, http://www.scribd.com/doc/229520210/John-C-Fairbanks-Scandalous-Judge-s-Legacy-Won-t-Die-Rural-n-h#scribd. Because of his notoriety as a fugitive, Fairbanks was featured on such television crime programs as "Unsolved Mysteries," "America's Most Wanted," and "Hard Copy." See Paul Montgomery, "Small-town Scandal Still Casts a Long, Dark Shadow," *New Hampshire Magazine* (July 1999): 13, available online at http://www.gnbtaxpayers.com/FAIRBANKS,%20JOHN,%20JUDGE%20-%20SCANDAL%20&%20COVER-UP.pdf.

2. Paula Monopoli, *American Probate: Protecting the Public, Improving the Process* (University Press of New England, 2003), 4.

3. Monopoli, *American Probate,* 5.

4. Roger Talbot, "Fairbanks Case Prober Puzzles, then Startles, N.H. Lawmakers," *Manchester Union Leader,* November 14, 1996, http://www.gnbtaxpayers.com/FAIRBANKS,%20JOHN,%20JUDGE%20-%20SCANDAL%20&%20COVER-UP.pdf.

5. Years later, Boston Globe journalist Royal Ford wrote, "No one rose in anger as he led young male defendants who appeared before his bench into his private office, closed the door, and emerged later to find many of them not guilty or give them light sentences. Even the local police chief, when told by young men that they had traded sex for lesser sentences, did not dare take him on directly. He was the judge. … And when reports of the sexual sentence-swapping reached the FBI and State Police, nothing was done. He was, after all, the judge—and a respected lawyer, bank officer, and the scion of a prominent local family" (Royal Ford, "Scandalous Judge's Legacy," *Boston Globe*, September 18, 1997).

6. Those complaints had been referred to the JCC by Gov. John Sununu's legal counsel, Stephen Merrill, who later was elected governor himself, and who was the Attorney General in 1988 when John Tweedy sought a criminal investigation of Fairbanks by Merrill's office. See Monopoli, *American Probate*, 20.

7. Ibid, 6.

8. Ibid., 8.

9. Ibid., 10. In November 1991, Fairbanks' former clients would agree to a settlement of their bankruptcy claims. Although it paid only a small fraction of the amount claimed, the bankruptcy judge later authorized the payment of $232,000 to the bankruptcy trustee for his efforts in securing funds for creditors. Ibid., 17. See also Montgomery, "Small-town Scandal," 13.

10. The American Bar Association (ABA) defines a client protection fund as "a pool of money funded and maintained by a bar association or lawyer regulatory agency, the purpose of which is to reimburse clients who have suffered financial loss due to the dishonest acts of lawyers." The first such fund was created by the organized bar of New Zealand in 1908. In 1959, Vermont became the first American state to establish such a fund. The New Hampshire Bar Association had created its client

protection fund in 1961, building it up with revenues from either a mandatory assessment on all bar members or an allocation from bar dues, to reimburse clients who suffered losses at the hands of a lawyer. See ABA Center for Professional Responsibility, "Client Protection Funds: Lawyers Put Their Money Where Their Mouths Are." http://www.americanbar.org/groups/professional_responsibility/resources/client_protection/tplart02.html. See also, Proposed Public Protection Fund Rule, 142 N.H. 588, 590, 707 A. 2d 125 (1998).

11. Jeff Feingold, "A Legal Black Eye: Cases like the one involving Judge Fairbanks have taken a sizable chunk out of the public's regard for the legal profession," *Spectator* (September 1999), 11.

12. Petition of Burling, 139 N.H. 266, 267, 651 A. 2d 940 (1994).

13. The rule in question was then-Supreme Court Administrative Rule 37 (17), which allowed four exceptions to the confidentiality requirement: (1) when the prosecution of formal charges has been initiated by the PCC itself by filing a petition with the Supreme Court; (2) when an attorney sought reinstatement; (3) when the attorney/respondent requested that the matter be public before the filing of formal charges; and (4) if the PCC investigation was based on the responding attorney's conviction for a crime or being publicly disciplined in another jurisdiction. *Burling*, 139 N.H. at 269. In the current version of the rule governing PCC matters, the exceptions to the confidentiality requirement are much broader and more specific for all disciplinary proceedings begun after April 1, 2000, and they might permit disclosure of PCC records in any future matter such as egregious as that involving Fairbanks. See N.H. S. Ct. R. 37, §§20, 21.

14. See SB513 as introduced, New Hampshire Senate Journal [hereinafter, N.H. S. Jour.] 1 (January 3, 1996), 2. The bill was referred to the Senate Insurance Committee, which held public hearings on January 24. Representatives of the state bar association testified to the complexities Rodeschin's prescription would entail, for both the bar and the Supreme Court under whose rulings it operated. N.H. S. Insurance Committee hearing on SB513 (January 24, 1996).

15. See Proposed Public Protection Fund Rule, 142 N.H. 588, 590.

16. Rule 55 took effect on June 1, 1998. *Id.,* Appendix 2. See also, Nicole Coppes-Gathy, "A Summary of the Public Protection Fund," *N.H. Bar J.* 20, no. 3 (1999): 20–25.

17. HB1593–FN (1996), N.H. H.R. Jour. 4 (January 3, 1996), 140.

18. Ibid. The bill was signed into law in June 1996 as N.H. Laws 1996, Ch. 254. The committee it created was charged to submit its report no later than December 1 of that year.

19. See http://gencourt.state.nh.us/SofS_Archives/1996/house/HB1593H.pdf. The November 12 meeting of the committee is described at 125–26.

20. See N.H. Const. Pt. 2, Art. 71.

21. Mac Williams had first been elected Register of Probate in 1941. In 1976, in her eighties and confined to a nursing home, she had easily won reelection yet again. Arthur Nighswander described her as "very political," noting that "She knew the people of influence, and the ones to whom favor should be given, and she ran the Registry of Probate on a very personal basis." Quoted by Monopoli, *American Probate,* 8.

22. Fairbanks and his family had been trusted, respected members of the community for some time. See, for example, Donna Chiacu, "Ex-Judge's Problems Mystify Newport Neighbors, Associates," *Concord Monitor*, October 30, 1989; and Roger Talbot, "Fairbanks' Delinquency Tolerated; Officials Trusted Ex-Judge," *Manchester Union Leader*, April 30, 1995.

23. John Tweedy was particularly vehement in his accusations. The Attorney General responded to them in some detail in a letter to the Fairbanks I Committee. See Jeffrey Howard, N.H. Atty. General, Letter to Robert Lockwood, Chairman, House Judiciary & Family Law Committee, Re: HB1593, Investigation of John C. Fairbanks (April 25, 1996).

24. See "Meeting of November 12, 1996," in N.H. H.R., Report of House Committee to Study the State Investigation of the John C. Fairbanks Matter (January 1997), 13–14.

25. See Monopoli, *American Probate*, 21.

26. See N.H. Supreme Court, Report on Special Matters Confidential (SMC) Docket (September 29, 2000), Appendix, "Special Matters Confidential Index," docket numbers SMC-89–023 and SMC 89–026.

27. Ibid, SMC-89–026, "In the matter of John C. Fairbanks—PCC petition for subpoena of records, audit of trust and operating accounts, and appointment of auditor."

28. In a December 1996 legislative committee report, Rep. Richard Kennedy called the SMC docket a "system used to shield judicial officers and lawyers from public scrutiny," which he said "should be scrapped entirely or severely restricted by legislative action." On both the exposure of the SMC docket in 2000 and the 1996 comment by Rep. Kennedy about it, see Reporters Committee for Freedom of the Press, "Secret docket for disciplinary cases shocks public, legislators," September 12, 2000, http://www.rcfp.org/browse-media-law-resources/news/secret-docket-disciplinary-cases-shocks-public-legislators. Less than three weeks after the release of the Reporters Committee article of September 12, 2000, the Supreme Court issued a report on the SMC docket, indicating that the Court had reviewed all cases on the SMC docket since its inception in 1985 and had concluded that many cases on the SMC docket need not be kept confidential. Thereupon, the Court announced that it had made those matters public. The report also indicated that the files docketed under SMC 90–015 and SMC-90–016, "Referral of disciplinary matter by Judicial Conduct Committee," must remain confidential under N.H. S. Ct. R. 39(11), even though they had been released to the Fairbanks Investigation Committee. See N.H. Supreme Court, Report on SMC Docket.

29. Ibid, 22–23.

30. The bill granted the committee full power to "take evidence under oath, issue subpoenas for records, and compel testimony." See HB688-FN-A, as introduced, N.H. H.R. Jour. 17 (January 29, 1997), 280, and as amended, N.H. H.R. Cal. 32 (March 4, 1997), 749–50.

31. See Monopoli, *American Probate*, 24.

32. See HB1338-FN-A, as introduced, N.H. H.R. Jour. 3 (January 7, 1998), 104.

33. N.H. H.R. Committee on Judiciary & Family Law, Public Hearing on HB1338-FN-A, Rep. Barbara Richardson testimony (January 27, 1998).

34. N.H. H.R. Final Report, "NH Constitution, Part II, Articles 41, 72-a, 73-a, Adoption Study" (December 1, 1998).

35. As Paula Monopoli has written, the difficulty of overseeing fiduciaries has led to "probate avoidance." She quotes the argument by Norman Dacey in his book, *How to Avoid Probate—Updated*! (New York: Crown, 1980), that the probate system should be avoided because it is now "almost universally corrupt," being "essentially a form of private taxation levied by the legal profession upon the rest of the population. All across the land, both large and small estates are being plundered by lawyers specializing in 'probate practice.'"See Monopoli, *American Probate*, 49.

36. N.H. H.R. Committee on judiciary & Family Law, Public Hearing on HB1338-FN-A (January 27, 1998). The references consisted of excerpts from Charles Bell, *Bench and Bar of New Hampshire* (Boston: Houghton Mifflin, 1894) and Charles Ashman, *Finest Judges Money Can Buy* (Los Angeles: Nash Publishing, 1973).

Chapter 5

Education Funding Litigation

It was perhaps not coincidental that David Brock, author of the *Claremont* decisions that would so roil New Hampshire in the 1990s, had also been one of the first presidential appointees to the State Justice Institute created nearly ten years earlier. The State Justice Institute aimed to facilitate "better coordination between state and federal courts" and "innovative, efficient solutions to common issues faced by all courts," that is, to de-parochialize state courts, open them to exogenous influences, align them with administrative and institutional practices beyond their own borders.[1] In a sense, the *Claremont* rulings represented the jurisprudential correlate of that undertaking. For just as the court's ongoing efforts to professionalize the administration of justice and establish autonomy vis-à-vis the elected branches of government mirrored a national movement of state judiciaries, so too did the substance of the *Claremont* judgments reflect both a general shift in the modes of reasoning other state courts were applying to the particular issue the *Claremont* litigation addressed. Indeed, to the degree that it treated public education as a "right" which public authorities were bound to maintain whatever the inconveniences to themselves, that new thinking on educational funding may itself have reflected a general shift in legal priorities occurring, unevenly but discernibly, across the United States.

THE RIGHTS REVOLUTION AND EDUCATION FUNDING IN NEW HAMPSHIRE

As we have noted previously, the "rights revolution" involved efforts by activists to address conditions in society by turning to the courts rather than to elected officials. Their successes entailed not only new constitutional interpretations, but also what one scholar has described as a dramatic change in the "political economy of litigation" itself: the emergence of advocacy groups committed to particular social causes, backed by "a broad array of funding sources," and fully prepared to undertake long, sometimes circuitous routes to victories in court that were unlikely or even inconceivable in the political arena.[2]

One of those causes was addressing gross inequities in the quality of public education provided by school districts of widely varying financial resources. What plaintiffs have sought here is an enforceable and universal right to a high-quality education, that is, an end to the educational deficits suffered by children in poorer school districts. Scholars have traced three separate waves of litigation in this area.[3]

In the first, lasting from roughly the late 1960s to 1973, plaintiffs mainly brought "equality" suits, arguing that children in poor districts were no less entitled to public resources in the provision of their public education than were students in wealthy districts. In general, that claim rested on the equal-protection clauses in state constitutions and, especially, in the fourteenth amendment to the U.S. Constitution. This first wave of education-funding litigation reached its high-water mark in California in 1971, when John Serrano and a few other parents of children attending a poorly financed public school in Los Angeles brought suit against not particular officials but rather California's very system of public educational finance, which "perpetuated, in their view, a system of educational haves and have-nots."[4] In *Serrano v. Priest*, the California Supreme Court found for the plaintiffs, determining that, by effectively denying educational benefits to a particular category of citizens, California's school-funding arrangements were indeed discriminatory.[5] In its affirmation of the importance of education and insistence on the state's constitutional duty to provide it to all, the finding clearly echoed the Warren Court's epochal *Brown v. Board of Education* decision of 1953. In tandem with *Brown*, it seemed to herald a new constitutional right to an adequate public education.[6]

In that same year in New Hampshire, however, plaintiffs asserting a similar right on similar grounds experienced a very different outcome. The case was *Laconia Board of Education v. City of Laconia*. In it, a local school board tried to compel a city to appropriate funds for services and programs the board considered essential to an adequate educational system. [7] As in *Serrano v. Priest*, plaintiffs claimed that the equal-protection clause of the fourteenth amendment precluded financing public schools by local property taxes alone. But the New Hampshire Supreme Court, faced for the first time with a constitutional claim to educational monies, declined to address that argument, on the grounds that its resolution would require both "the considered attention of all interested persons and agencies" and "a financial and statistical background which is not available in this case or in this record."[8]

Two years later, the U.S. Supreme Court ruled on the matter in *San Antonio School District* case.[9] Its conclusion was that school financing inequities do not, in fact, violate the equal-protection clause of the fourteenth amendment. With that ruling, the first wave of education-funding litigation, based on invocation of equality rights presumed granted by, especially, the federal constitution, essentially came to an end.

But advocates of equal education opportunity were not prepared to concede defeat. Rather, they initiated a second wave of litigation, in which they would focus their attention on state constitutions. All states but Mississippi mandate some sort of system of public education; and most have, if not explicit equal-protection clauses, then language or provisions that have been interpreted as effectively assuring it.[10] Second-wave school-funding litigants, like their first-wave predecessors, pressed "equality" suits, especially on the basis of equal-protection claims derived from states' constitutions. A significant victory was achieved in 1973, when New Jersey's Supreme Court found in *Robinson v. Cahill* that the state's school-funding statute violated its constitutional mandate to provide a "thorough and efficient" education to all. Between then and 1993, the highest courts in 25 states rendered decisions on school-funding cases.[11]

But the results achieved in *Robinson v. Cahill* were equaled only in a handful of other states; far more often, constitutional claims to parity in state educational funding were found wanting.[12] New Hampshire's plaintiffs were no more effective than most other second-wave litigants. In fact, they were rather less so: New Hampshire, plaintiffs would find both the legal and the political path to success effectively blocked, even though the state government had already acknowledged the need for state aid to the poorest of the "property-poor" school districts by special legislative appropriations enacted a decade before the *Robinson v. Cahill* decision.[13]

THE *JESSEMAN* CASE

In New Hampshire, the key case was *Jesseman v. State,* filed in 1982, in which plaintiffs aimed to provide the Supreme Court with the very financial and statistical background it had said it required in the *Laconia School District* case.[14] Those plaintiffs were a group carefully chosen for their stake in the matter, and concomitant standing to sue: seven parents, their children, and their respective property-poor school districts. They initiated their case before the Superior Court for Merrimack County, where they sought a judgment declaring that the state, including the governor, the state department of education, the state board of education, and other state government officials, had a system for funding public education that violated the state constitution.[15]

After 18 months of pretrial discovery, creating a record with thousands of pages, the trial judge allowed an interlocutory appeal to the New Hampshire Supreme Court in September 1983.[16] Once again, the Supreme Court declined to rule on the constitutional question, remanding for further proceedings on whether there is a valid statistical correlation between the educational achievement of students and the real property wealth of the school district or town where those students reside. On remand, the parties engaged in another 18 months of pretrial proceedings.[17] Finally, the case was dropped upon the enactment of legislation providing for state aid to selected school districts under a calculation that came to be known as the "Augenblick Formula."[18]

Since 1920, the state of New Hampshire had generally contributed only 5 percent–10 percent of the total cost of its public schools (the national median between 1920 and 1993 was 50%).[19] This was hardly surprising in the only state in the nation that had never enacted either a state sales or a state income tax, an aversion to state-level taxes that was (and is) described as "the New Hampshire advantage" and a critical component of the "New Hampshire way" by traditionalists. To terminate the *Jesseman* suit without violating that norm, then-Gov. John Sununu and the state legislature offered to create a foundation from which supplemental educational funds could be secured by needy districts. Its aim would be elevating the state's contribution to poor districts to 8 percent, thus increasing its overall contribution to public education to a full 12 percent. This would have still left New Hampshire last in the nation in state support for public education; but the prospect of even modest improvements was enough to turn the *Jesseman* plaintiffs away from further litigation. What they didn't anticipate were the political obstacles to implementing that or, as it turned out, any similar scheme.

CLAREMONT I

From the beginning, Gov. Sununu felt he was bargaining from a position of strength, since in his view the *Jesseman* plaintiffs "didn't have a leg to stand on."[20] The plaintiffs, for their part, lacked the political influence to counter his insistence that the statutory language establishing the foundation contain no reference to "fair," "equitable," or "adequate" funding; that it receive funding only as funds became available; and that no automatic entitlement for poor districts be implied.[21] Those plaintiffs may have been somewhat buoyed by the state's willingness to hire academic and educational consultant John Augenblick to devise a formula for distributing the 8 percent generally intended for poor districts. But the "Augenblick Formula" was never fulfilled; foundation funding never exceeded more than 4 percent. By the early 1990s, the Claremont school district found that, despite discontinuing kindergarten and all sports programs, it could not even finance necessary repairs to its high school's main building. Accreditation was duly withdrawn.

Thus it was that, 10 years after the *Jesseman* suit, "property-poor" school districts again decided they would have to seek legal remedy for what they claimed were ongoing constitutional violations. This time, however, the national trend was more hopeful. A third wave of school-funding litigation had begun around 1989, with plaintiffs securing important victories in state courts in Montana, Texas, and especially Kentucky.

To some degree, these successes reflected a shift in litigants' strategy. For in the third wave of education-funding litigation, the plaintiffs basically eschewed claims to *equal funding* for poor school districts, arguing instead that what states were constitutionally bound to provide was an *adequate education* to even the poorest districts. The aim was requiring states to define what that meant, and to accept fiscal responsibility for seeing that no public-school students were denied it. The remedies chosen might, in fact, entail the same fiscal "leveling" sought in the first and second waves of litigation. But that was secondary (or, perhaps, serendipitous). The fact was, language in the education clauses of most state constitutions seemed firmer on the requirement of effectively educating all citizens than on that of treating all equally.[22]

The Kentucky Supreme Court's finding in *Rose v. Council for Better Education* in 1989 showed just what could be achieved by this strategy.[23] That Court, basing its decision on Kentucky's constitutional mandate to "provide an efficient system of common schools throughout the state," actually found the state's entire common-school system "constitutionally deficient;" determined that "the local school boards' tax effort is not only lacking in uniformity but is also lacking in adequate effort;" and directed the state legislature to provide funding "sufficient to provide each child in Kentucky an adequate education." Perhaps most significantly, the court initiated a consideration of what "adequate education" would mean by articulating seven general learning goals, leaving to the elected branches of state government the responsibility for elaborating them and assisting "each and every child" in Kentucky to reach them.[24]

In 1993, the Supreme Judicial Court of Massachusetts would borrow heavily from *Rose* in a key school-funding decision of its own, *McDuffy v. Secretary of Executive Office of Education.*[25] Noting at the outset that "plaintiffs do not seek a judgment that the Commonwealth has an obligation to provide equal education opportunities to all its students" but rather that the state was constitutionally mandated "to provide every young person in the Commonwealth with an 'adequate' education," the court began by considering the language of the state constitution's education clause. The clause described legislators' and magistrates' duty to "cherish" the cause of learning, and SJC decided that in the late eighteenth century such language could not be construed as merely "aspirational or hortatory." Rather, the duty described was material, and binding.

In fact, the court found that Massachusetts, from colonial times onward, had always assumed responsibility for the education of its citizens, a responsibility partially delegated by the state to towns but never fully abdicated to them. Indeed, with "a law which is credited with beginning the history of public education in America," Massachusetts's state legislature, or General Court, had required towns to maintain a system of public schools as early as 1647, and repeatedly penalized communities that failed to provide proper educational facilities. The education clause of the state constitution was drafted precisely because, in the view of its main author John Adams, "widespread public education was integral to the very existence of a republican government," since "nothing countered political oppression more than 'knowledge diffused generally through the whole body of the people.'" The court concluded that the Commonwealth clearly retained a "duty to provide an education for all its children, rich and poor, in every city and town of the Commonwealth at the public-school level," a duty that "lies squarely on the executive (magistrates) and legislative (Legislatures) branches of this Commonwealth."[26] It concluded by transcribing and endorsing for Massachusetts the seven educational guidelines the Kentucky Supreme Court had set forth in *Rose*.

What was most significant in all this for New Hampshire was the fact that the language of the Massachusetts constitution's education clause was almost the same as the language of the New Hampshire constitution's education clause (the latter had, in fact, been largely copied from the former).[27] So the Masschusetts Supreme Judicial Court's careful analysis of what phrases such as "duty of legislators and magistrates … to cherish the interest of literature and the sciences" and "diffused generally among the body of people" actually meant in the 1780s was entirely transferable to New Hampshire. In fact, New Hampshire, first settled under that name in 1623, had been governed as a part of Massachusetts from 1641 to 1680. So part of the history that Massachusetts's Supreme Judicial Court had drawn on in its *McDuffy* decision was directly relevant to New Hampshire; and New Hampshire's support for education throughout the eighteenth century paralleled Massachusetts's as well. That was why, when the Claremont school district and associated parties finally came before the New Hampshire Supreme Court in 1993, just after the *McDuffy* decision came down, they had reason to expect the same results that plaintiffs in the Massachusetts case had secured.

On December 30, 1993, they got them. The case had originally come before the Superior Court for Merrimack County, where Judge George Manias found no language in the state constitution explicitly mandating a state, rather than local, responsibility for public education; and determined that the local taxes financing it must therefore be consistent only within, not across, school districts.[28] But the New Hampshire Supreme Court reversed and remanded.

Chief Justice Brock, who authored the Supreme Court's unanimous decision, found the linguistic and historical analyses underpinning the recent Massachusetts *McDuffy* decision very persuasive, particularly in light of the two states' interlocking constitutional histories. Brock also noted that the education clause in New Hampshire's constitution had been deliberately located within Part 2, which details the state's "Form of Government." That, he proposed, suggested that the document's framers had meant exactly what they said when they described "knowledge and learning, generally diffused through a community" as "essential to the preservation of a free government." In Brock's view, when those framers confirmed "the duty of the legislators and magistrates, in all future periods of this government, to cherish the interests of literature and all the sciences," they were not expressing a vague aspiration but a solid and reasoned command. What they had in mind, according to their private and public writings, was the impossibility of self-government without an informed citizenry. The sort of education that molded independent, intellectually competent citizens was indeed a constitutional right in New Hampshire, Brock concluded; and any citizen had legal standing to claim it. Providing that education was, therefore, a state duty, to be conscientiously fulfilled by the state's elected officials rather than casually fobbed off to localities.[29] As had the Massachusetts Supreme Judicial Court in its *McDuffy* ruling, Brock's Court concluded that defining the actual requirements of that education and providing the means of meeting them was a "task, in the first instance, for the legislature and the Governor."

But that was where the similarities between Massachusetts' treatment of the issue and New Hampshire's would end.

In Massachusetts, education-funding reform had been gestating well before the *McDuffy* ruling, endorsed by a powerful coalition spearheaded by the formidable Massachusetts Business Alliance for Education, along with organizations of school superintendents and teachers as well as the state chapter of the American Civil Liberties Union.[30] What drove the movement in the Commonwealth was the fact that localities had been forced to curtail their education budgets in response to Proposition 2.5, a ballot initiative that since 1982 had capped property taxes at 2.5 percent of assessed property values. This atypical lack of public funds for schools would be largely rectified by legislation passed within days of the *McDuffy* ruling.[31]

In New Hampshire, by way of contrast, the *Claremont I* plaintiffs had no powerful allies and scant political clout, as the outcome of the *Jesseman* case had demonstrated. Their legal team was heavily reliant on law professors from the state's single law school, and on personnel from New Hampshire Legal Services. In addition, local media were largely hostile or indifferent to their cause.[32] Significantly, the *Claremont I* plaintiffs could not claim to be seeking merely the return of a disrupted *status quo*. Rather, they aimed for a significant revision in the state's traditional approach to public education—with implications for its overall financial arrangements that were, to say the least, disquieting to many.

For unlike Massachusetts's *McDuffy* plaintiffs, New Hampshire's *Claremont I* litigants did not have the luxury of eschewing "equality" claims of questionable constitutional provenance, and confining themselves to the stronger "quality" or "adequacy" arguments that had succeeded in the Commonwealth and other states. There was no way that an "adequate" education could be secured for poor school districts in New Hampshire without challenging longstanding fiscal arrangements. This, in turn, would mean a protracted constitutional battle, because the inescapable fact was that those arrangements were embedded in the state's founding document. Indeed, there was "no other state in the union with the structure of taxing powers and limits comparable to New Hampshire's"—limits that had been limned by the state constitution's authors when, in a significant break with the Massachusetts model, they had elected not to authorize excise or income taxes.[33] The charge delivered by the New Hampshire Supreme Court to the elected branches of state government would have to be fulfilled without recourse to those revenues, or indeed to any except those derived from the one form of taxation on which New Hampshire's constitution smiled: property taxes.

But deployment of those, in turn, would be constrained by language in Part 2, Article of the state constitution stipulating that all "assessments, rates, and taxes" be "proportional and reasonable." New Hampshire's property taxes might perhaps be described as "proportional and reasonable" *within* school districts, but they were hardly that *across* districts. If, as the Brock Court had concluded, public education was ultimately a state responsibility, the state would have to somehow find *statewide* funds that met the "proportional and reasonable" criterion. But it would be very difficult to arrange a "proportional" state levy that did not, to some degree, redistribute monies from wealthy districts to poor ones. For the *Claremont* litigants, then, the "equality" question was simply unavoidable. In a sense, they aspired to a third-wave victory on uncongenial, second-wave terrain.

They had enjoyed a surprising success before the Supreme Court. But success before that body did not mean success within the state. In fact, the court and the judiciary had been moving away from "the New Hampshire way" for some time, if a critical aspect of that traditional way is acknowledged to be judicial subordination to a determinedly "amateur" legislature (i.e., a legislature of plain, unpaid citizens rather than attorneys or trained civil servants). The judiciary had joined numerous other state judiciaries in pursuing the path of professionalization, and in asserting its institutional autonomy vis-à-vis the other branches of state government. But the legislature had remained firmly loyal to the state's original constitutional understanding. Legislative supremacy was, not surprisingly, a sacred principle to New Hampshire legislators, who had remained stubbornly committed to the idea that laws should be made by citizens, not experts. Indeed, the New Hampshire legislature was proudly innocent of the ways of legalists: it was "one of the few legislative forums in this country where lawyers are 'under-represented,'" a circumstance that probably reflected the relative paucity of lawyers themselves within the state's population (compared to their density within that of, for example, Massachusetts).[34]

Claremont I was not the first time New Hampshire's Supreme Court had manifested a new assertiveness since the court's achievement of constitutional status in 1966. But this time, its challenge was to the very core of the "New Hampshire Way:" the conjoined principles of minimal state-level taxation, and maximum devolution of decision-making authority to local levels of government (short of the versions of "home rule" that voters had rejected, of course). The response of New Hampshire's largest newspaper, the conservative *Manchester Union Leader*, was immediate, and predictably fierce: it called the decision "stunning" and forecast a "political tsunami" in response to the "judicial oligarchy" that had issued it.[35] But more ominous, perhaps, was the tone taken by elected officials. Former Gov. Sununu's description of the ruling as "just dumb" was actually comparatively mild.[36] Former Gov. (then Senator) Judd Gregg went much further, decrying the decision as "the grossest despotism" that "directly usurped the authority of the legislature" and carried the "potential … to change the entire way we govern ourselves."[37] Sitting Gov. Steve Merrill made it clear that in his view the case was not about public education at all, which he insisted was perfectly adequate, but about broad-based taxes, which he would fight to the bitter end (his office angrily dismissed a simple proposal by state Sen. Wayne King to form a committee to study how existing school funds might be distributed more equitably as a "Robin Hood plan").[38] Brock had expressed confidence, in his decision, that the state's elected officials "will fulfill their responsibility with respect to defining the specifics of, and the appropriate means to provide through public education, the knowledge and learning essential to the preservation of a free government."[39]

But there seemed to be little enthusiasm for tackling that task in the immediate aftermath of *Claremont I*.

CLAREMONT II AND ITS PROGENY

Some office holders may have hoped for better outcomes in subsequent court battles.[40] When the case went back before the Superior Court for Merrimack

County, the contested issues were the definition of the "adequate" education the court had determined to be a constitutional right; and whether it truly was or could be provided by local school districts using local property-tax revenues. Recently appointed Chairman of the State Board of Education Ovide Lamontagne, a Manchester attorney and future Republican gubernatorial candidate, provided the state's answer to the first question by essentially paraphrasing, without elaboration, the Supreme Court's own, highly general formulation ("An adequate public elementary and secondary education is one which provides each educable child with an opportunity to acquire the knowledge and learning necessary to participate intelligently in the American political, economic, and social systems of a free government."). Regarding the second question, Lamontagne explained that responsibility for further defining and actually providing that adequate education would now simply lie with state and local government jointly—but with the state's role properly confined to establishing the means for school districts to raise their own funds (i.e., with no commitment of state funds).[41]

For their part, the plaintiffs produced testimony by former commissioners of the Department of Education Charles Marston and Jack MacDonald, each of whom tried to counter the state's claim that money had little to do with the quality of education by testifying on the vast discrepancies between the quality of education offered in New Hampshire's richest school districts and its poorest.[42] In his ruling, Judge Manias allowed that the resources available to school districts did indeed vary. But, he explained, his primary concern was whether constitutional duties were or were not fulfilled by the policies Lamontagne projected. Again ruling against the plaintiffs, Manias reasoned that in delegating to the State Board of Education the task of answering the relevant questions, the state had in fact fulfilled the responsibility devolved on it by the Supreme Court in *Claremont I*—whether the plaintiffs (or, for that matter, any court) liked it or not. That argument would remain the core of the anti-*Claremont* viewpoint for the rest of the struggle. Rejection of it by the Supreme Court, in the view of those anti-*Claremont* elements, could be construed only as an unconstitutional violation of the separation of powers, with the Supreme Court assuming a policymaking role constitutionally reserved for the elected branches.[43]

But that, of course, was not how David Brock and most Supreme Court justices saw it when they considered the plaintiffs' appeal of Judge Manias's ruling. Their view would be that what the state called "policy," duly and lawfully formulated by its Board of Education, represented a denial, or even defiance, of the duties the court had issued it; that it had not accepted those duties so long as it skirted any obligation to fund, with statewide revenues, its public schools; and that since the any such revenues would have to be "proportionate and reasonable," they simply could not be derived mainly or even largely from local property taxes. David Brock would say all that and more in the court's *Claremont II* decision of December 17, 1997—probably the single most significant of the court's holdings in the entire education-funding imbroglio.[44]

With Justice Horton dissenting, the court concluded that "The State's duty to provide for an adequate education is constitutionally compelled. The present system selected and crafted by the State to fund public education is, however, unconstitutional."[45] Allowing that "the State may delegate its obligation to provide a constitutionally adequate education to local school districts," the court nonetheless insisted that "it may not do so in a form underscored by unreasonable and inequitable tax burdens." Having thrown out New Hampshire's traditional means of financing public education, the court softened the blow by allowing current arrangements to remain in effect for the 1998 tax year. It also suggested the seven general criteria of educational adequacy articulated by the Kentucky Supreme Court in *Rose* as "benchmarks of a constitutionally adequate public education." "Without intruding on other branches of government," wrote Chief Justice Brock for the majority, "we anticipate that they will promptly develop and adopt specific criteria implementing these guidelines and, in completing this task, will appeal to a broad constituency."

In New Hampshire, supporters of the decision felt "This is how the separation of powers is supposed to work:" a fundamental right had been properly recognized and protected by the governmental body charged with exactly that responsibility, despite the indifference or hostility of current majorities within the electorate or their representatives.[46] But the anti-*Claremont* forces were beside themselves with rage and preparing, at least rhetorically, for an apocalyptic conflict. Sen. Gregg stated that "for a court to usurp the legislative prerogative is to flirt with the threat of despotism that led to the Boston Tea Party and a call for independence that began our nation."[47] Richard Lessner, editorialist for the *Manchester Union-Leader*, announced "Make no mistake: This is a struggle for the very soul of New Hampshire. If the Legislature were to accept this usurpation, then the fundamental nature of the Granite State would forever be changed." But Lessner was apparently not entirely sure that the legislature would rise to the occasion, or that future legislatures might not undo its work even if it did. "What the Legislature can and should do," he opined, "is refer this to the people of New Hampshire in the form of a constitutional question. If the black-robed oligarchs in Concord are offended by the system of taxation the people of New Hampshire have freely chosen as an affront to the constitution—then let us amend the constitution and send the court packing."[48] State Sen. Jim Rubens responded to the call to arms, proposing a constitutional amendment that would allow the legislature to "delegate to the state's political subdivisions in whole or in part, the duty to provide for an adequate education" and confirm that "any tax imposed and levied by any city or town to implement such delegated duty is local, and any such tax which is proportional and reasonable throughout such city or town shall satisfy this article."[49]

Leaders of both parties were, at first, reluctant to endorse so binding and permanent a response to the challenge the court had issued. Rubens's proposal thus failed to secure the three-fifths' vote within both legislative houses needed before a constitutional amendment can proceed to a public ballot in New Hampshire.[50] But that would turn out to be only the first of many attempts to circumvent the *Claremont* rulings by altering the constitution—an unusually strong reaction to a Supreme Court decision.[51] With its holdings on education funding, New Hampshire's Supreme Court was in fact tracking a pattern found in many other state courts across the nation.[52] But nowhere was the opposition deeper or more sustained than here. That opposition would intensify as legislators, and the state's new governor, Democrat Jeanne Shaheen, struggled to meet the court's demands, within the court's time-frame, on the court's terms.

Claremont II represented a special dilemma for Shaheen, who, like every other successful gubernatorial candidate in the state's recent history, had pledged during her campaign never to countenance broad-based taxes. She had defeated Ovide Lamontagne for the office in 1996, and understood full well that her response to the school-funding controversy would have a great deal to do with her prospects for re-election in 1998. At the beginning of that year, she announced her response to *Claremont II*, a proposal she labeled the "ABC (Advancing Better Classrooms) Plan." Key elements of the plan included assembling a working group, including representatives of the local business community as well as educators, to determine "adequacy" standards; and, in lieu of a statewide property tax *per se*, a uniform, statewide rate for local education taxes. The idea was to "lift poorer schools up without dragging others down," and Shaheen was willing to take special pains to reach that latter goal: all taxes beyond those needed for local educational expenses would be rebated to the district that had paid them, meaning that wealthy school districts would actually deliver no funds to poorer ones, or lose any of the advantages they had always enjoyed. The monies with which poorer districts would meet the adequacy criteria were to be provided by a combination of increased cigarette taxes, a portion of the state's lottery revenues, and savings achieved by terminating the foundation that was supposed to administer the "Augenblick formula."[53]

One of the *Claremont* plaintiffs' attorneys, Andru Volinsky, felt that Shaheen's plan promised "reasonable provisions for establishing a state accountability system and for helping to improve schools." But he also felt that "its funding mechanism … was a sham," a concern shared by other supporters of education-funding reform.[54] Conservative legislators, for their part, objected to any assumption of statewide responsibility for public education. On May 21, an odd alliance of pro- and anti-*Claremont* legislators came together to request an advisory opinion by the Supreme Court on the constitutionality of the ABC Plan. The court allowed interested parties to submit comments until June 2, and received no less than 119 of them.[55] In a highly unusual move in such proceedings, the court issued an order for oral argument.

The justices may have hoped that a more public airing of claims and examination of facts might help resolve the issue—by that time, they had certainly recognized the firestorm their *Claremont* holdings had touched off, and the depth of legislative opposition to them. In fact, on May 8 of that year the court had had to rule on a motion to vacate *Claremont II* on a technicality. The case's substance might have been less significant than the resolve it signaled to fight *Claremont* with whatever weapons availed themselves.

One of the justices, Stephen Thayer, had recused himself from both prior *Claremont* cases, because his wife Judith, a member of the Board of Education, had been a defendant in them. In *Claremont II*, Thayer's replacement had been the retired justice William Batchelder. The issue involved in the motion to vacate was the interpretation of a statute permitting retired judges to provide temporary court service when court vacancies arise through recusals or disqualifications, unless those retired judges themselves are "otherwise disqualified" from hearing the case.[56] Plaintiffs argued that the statute should have precluded Batchelder's involvement. Their claim was that since the constitution itself barred judges over the age of 70 from holding judicial office, the "otherwise disqualified" language of the statute should have applied to Batchelder; and if it didn't, then the statute itself was constitutionally deficient. But the court, in a decision to be known as *Claremont III*, found unanimously that the statute's language (permitting the participation of judges "retired from regular active service"), legislative history, and stated intent (to provide a pool of qualified, experienced judges for service in exactly this sort of situation) all weighed against that claim; and that its constitutional provenance was obvious. Notably, however, the motion to vacate had been joined by Senate president Joseph Delahunty. Delahunty, who had opposed Rubens's constitutional amendment, seemed to be serving notice that a reluctance to adopt that particular strategy by no means meant reluctance to continue fighting the *Claremont* rulings.

With *Claremont III* settled, the justices delivered their advisory opinion on the ABC Plan on June 23, 1998.[57] Their decision was unanimous: the plan's proposed abatements would maintain the existing privileges of wealthy school districts and thus violate the constitutional requirement that statewide levies be "proportionate and reasonable." "It should not be forgotten," wrote the justices, "that New Hampshire is not a random collection of isolated cities and towns. The benefits of adequately educated children are shared statewide and are not limited to a particular town or district." But Gov. Shaheen remained convinced that her plan was the only solution on hand that was both constitutionally adequate and politically feasible. With its rejection, she would associate herself with a new effort to amend the constitution, that of House Speaker Donna Sytek.[58]

In fact, the floodgates holding back legislative fury were breaking—a wave of measures would sweep forth throughout the rest of 1998 and into 1999, measures aiming not only to reverse the *Claremont* holdings but to reduce the power and reach of the Supreme Court that had issued them. Each of those years would witness no fewer than 12 such bills, and the subjects they addressed clearly indicated that the legislators who brought them saw the real problem as the independence and administrative autonomy of the court, with the *Claremont* contretemps a festering symptom of that deeper malaise. The bills' ambitions included limiting the court's ability to set rules without legislative oversight; adding a judicial-evaluation dimension to the process of selecting justices; and transferring the supervision of judicial conduct from the court's own Judicial Conduct Committee to a legislative body. Bills transferring responsibility for courts' security arrangements from courts themselves to county sheriffs' offices (excepting the Supreme Court itself) and creating a study committee to review the 1966 constitutional amendment that had given the Supreme Court's administrative rules the force of law were enacted into law.[59] Clearly, the stakes of the conflict between the Supreme Court and the elected branches of government were rising. More than education funding, now, was involved.

But the court would not back down, in part because it clearly shared the conviction that something momentous *was* afoot in New Hampshire. On November 3, 1998, the state moved for a two-year extension of the deadline the court had imposed in *Claremont II*. No legislative effort to resolve the funding crisis had yet secured both sufficient political support and necessary clearance from the court. But the court was unsympathetic to the plight of the elected branches. In its holding denying the motion, known as *Claremont IV*, it articulated its own assessment of the situation. *Claremont IV*, in fact, strongly suggested that justices of the New Hampshire Supreme Court saw themselves, in this particular struggle, as following a path blazed by the U.S. Supreme Court earlier.

They had cited *Brown v. Board of Education* before, echoing in *Claremont II* the Warren Court's point that "In these days, it is doubtful that any child may reasonably be expected to succeed in life if he is denied the opportunity of an education." In *Claremont IV*, they decided to do what the Warren Court had finally done, after its initial hesitations, to reinforce its *Brown* holding, in the *Cooper v. Aaron* decision of 1958.[60] They asserted, in direct and even pugnacious language, the primacy of constitutional rights, whether the prevailing political climate favored them or not. They asserted, no less importantly, the supremacy of the high court in defining and defending those rights. Finally, they asserted their own refusal to stand by idly while the political branches, claiming prerogatives over the formation of social policy, simply denied, obstructed, or evaded responsibilities the court had found constitutionally mandated. It was a decision suggesting that justices of the New Hampshire Supreme Court saw themselves—whether reluctantly or enthusiastically, but quite definitely—as involved in the "rights revolution" that had so shaken both national and state jurisprudence in recent decades:

> Almost five years ago, we held that the New Hampshire Constitution "imposes a duty on the State to provide a constitutionally adequate education to every educable child in the public schools in [this State] and to guarantee adequate funding." … At that time, the court also expressed its "confiden[ce] that the legislature and the Governor w[ould] fulfill their responsibility with respect to defining the specifics of, and the appropriate means to provide through public education, the knowledge and learning essential to the preservation of a free government." … No changes to the current system were made, however, and the State proceeded to defend at trial the adequacy of public education and the constitutionality of school funding in New Hampshire … the legislature has primarily put its efforts into consideration of legislation (the ABC plan) that was determined to contain an unconstitutional funding mechanism … and proposed constitutional amendments designed to nullify in whole or in part this court's decisions in *Claremont I* and *Claremont II*. … There is no indication in the materials before us that the legislature pursued with equal vigor any alternative solutions to remedy the unconstitutional funding system in the event that these avenues failed.
>
> Absent extraordinary circumstances, delay in achieving a constitutional system is inexcusable. The legality of the education funding system in this State has been questioned for at least the past twenty-seven years, and the parties involved in the present action have been engaged in litigation for over seven years. The controlling legal principles are plain. … "[I]t should go without saying that the vitality of these constitutional principles cannot be allowed to yield simply because of disagreement with them." *Brown v. Board of Education*, 349 U.S. 294, 300 (1955). … The constitutional rights of the children in this State to an adequate State-funded education and of all tax-paying citizens in New Hampshire to reasonable and proportional taxation are not to be denied any longer."[61]

But legislators were in no mood to capitulate, either. Less than three months later, on February 11, 1999, the Senate filed another request for the justices to give an advisory opinion on the constitutionality of another senate bill. This one would provide for a referendum enabling the New Hampshire people to choose a tax plan enacted by the legislature to fund a constitutionally adequate public education. In an opinion submitted one month later, the justices held their ground, advising the Senate that the proposed tax plan referendum was yet another unconstitutional measure. In their holding, the court argued that the state constitution does not give the people of the state a right to make decisions by referendum about the creation and collection of general taxes, since such decisions are reserved to the deliberative bodies designed for precisely such purposes. Asking voters to choose between two different education-funding legislative tax plans, the court argued, would represent an unconstitutional delegation of power by the legislature.[62]

Elected officials' next move was passing, with the governor's signature, an act in April 1999 that would finally establish a statewide, uniform education property tax which, along with increases in business-profit taxes and other revenues, would be dedicated to funding public education. As with the ABC Plan, state revenues were to be shared with local school districts, even if they were over and above those local districts' needs. But this time, the districts thus benefited were directed to return particular percentages of the amount they received to the state, with the percentages rising from 10 percent in 1999 to 100 percent by 2004.[63] The *Claremont* plaintiffs challenged various aspects of the plan, especially that gradual phase-in of the tax liability for wealthier districts, a boon not extended to poorer ones. The court addressed only whether the phase-in was constitutional, and decided that it was not ("The practical effect of this phase-in is that in fifty 'property rich' towns across the State, the full rate of $6.60 per thousand is imposed gradually over five years, while taxpayers in the remaining towns pay the full rate immediately."). Quoting its *Claremont II* decision, the court insisted again that "'we were not appointed to establish educational policy, nor to determine the proper way to finance its implementation'" But it asserted yet again that "It is, however, the duty of the judiciary to protect constitutional rights and in doing so to 'support the fundamentals on which the Constitution itself rests'"[64]

That was *Claremont V*, decided on October 15, 1999. Before the year was over, *Claremont VI*, an effort by the state to deny the Claremont plaintiffs' court costs and attorney fees, would be decided. The state claimed that sovereign immunity should preclude those plaintiffs' claim to costs. In the closest it would come to victory in *Claremont* litigation, it secured a unanimous ruling to that effect (although the court did not concede that sovereign immunity also ruled out the award of attorneys' fees).

NOTES

1. See State Justice Institute, "About SJI," http://www.sji.gov/about-sji/.
2. Epp, *Rights Revolution*, 69.

3. William Thro, "Judicial Analysis during the Third Wave of School Finance Litigation: The Massachusetts Decision as a Model," *BC L. Rev.* 35, no. 3 (1994): 597–617.

4. Todd DeMitchell, "School Finance Reform: The Carousel Reform," *School Business Affairs* 65, no. 1 (1999): 42, 43.

5. Serrano v. Priest, 487 P.2d 1241 (1971).

6. See Allen Hubsch, "Note: The Emerging Right to Education Under State Constitutional Law," *Temple L. Rev.* 65 (1992): 1325–48. Hubsch includes an appendix listing each state's primary constitutional section on the provision of an educational system.

7. 111 N.H. 389, 285 A.2d 793 (1971).

8. *Id.*, 285 A.2d at 796.

9. San Antonio Independent School District v. Rodriguez, 411 U.S. 1 (1973).

10. Thro, "Judicial Analysis," 603n. 28, 29.

11. See "Table of School Finance Legal Cases," from Allen Odden and Lawrence Picus, *School Finance: A Policy Perspective* (3rd ed., New York: McGraw-Hill, 2004), http://highered.mheducation.com/sites/0072823186/student_view0/table_of_school_finance_legal_html. In 1993 alone, New Hampshire's was one of five state supreme courts deciding such cases. See also Alexandra Natapoff, "1993: The Year of Living Dangerously: State Courts Expand the Right to Education," *W. Educ. L. Rep.* 3, no. 4 (1994): 639–71.

12. Thro, "Judicial Analysis," 603.

13. Under N.H. Laws 1963, Ch. 199, the legislature provided special aid to the 20 school districts having the "lowest equalized valuation per pupil" by apportioning $102,710 for each year of the coming biennium (1963–1964 and 1964–1965). This approach created some difficulties, however, because there was a question in the next legislative session about whether appropriations for the same purpose under N.H, Laws 1965, Ch. 239, 282, should be in the same amount to the same 20 school districts or to a potentially different set of 20 school districts to be identified under the same criteria as updated by the legislature. In reply to a request from the Governor and Council for an advisory opinion, the justices of the Supreme Court replied that the distribution of aid should be made using the same formula as in 1963, but with each factor updated to reflect the most recently available computation made by the State Board of Education. Opinion of the Justices, 106 N.H. 449, 213 A.2d 915 (1965).

14. Docket No. 82-E-038 (N.H. Superior Court, Merrimack County, filed January 1982).

15. The relevant constitutional text was:

> Knowledge and learning, generally diffused through a community, being essential to the preservation of a free government; and spreading the opportunities and advantages of education through the various parts of the country, being highly conducive to promote this end; it shall be the duty of the legislators and magistrates, in all future periods of this government, to cherish the interest of literature and the sciences, and all seminaries and public schools, to encourage private and public institutions, rewards, and immunities for the promotion of

agriculture, arts, sciences, commerce, trades, manufactures, and natural history of the country; to countenance and inculcate the principles of humanity and general benevolence, public and private charity, industry and economy, honesty and punctuality, sincerity, sobriety, and all social affections, and generous sentiments, among the people: Provided, nevertheless, that no money raised by taxation shall ever be granted or applied for the use of the schools of institutions of any religious sect or denomination. N.H. Const. Pt. 2, Art.83.

16. Jesseman v. State, No. 83–371 (N.H. February 13, 1984). The interlocutory appeal asked whether public education is a "fundamental right" under Article 83; what constitutional test the trial court should use on that question; what constitutional test the trial court should use to determine whether the state's current system for funding public education violated the "equal-protection" clauses of the state constitution; and whether the current funding system violated Part 2, Article 5, which requires that state taxes be "proportional and reasonable."

17. One of the plaintiffs' attorneys in the later *Claremont* cases has argued that the state's weighty discovery demands were intended to exhaust the *Jesseman* plaintiffs' financial resources, and in fact succeeded in doing so. See Andru Volinsky, "New Hampshire's Education-Funding Litigation: Claremont School District v. Governor, 635 A.2d 1375 (N.H. 1993), *modified*, 703 A.2d 1353 (N.H. 1997)," *Neb. L. Rev.* 83, no. 3 (2004): 836–55.

18. For more on the Augenblick Formula, see Douglas Hall, *Plumbing the Numbers #2: Using Per Capita Income in a School Aid Formula: Concerns and Suggestions* (Concord, NH: New Hampshire Center for Public Policy Studies, 2001).

19. Oyebola Olabisi, *New Hampshire's Quest for A Constitutionally Adequate Education: Discussion Paper* (Boston: New England Public Policy Center, Federal Reserve Bank of Boston, 2006), 1.

20. Charles DeGrandpre, "Lex Loci: A Survey of New Hampshire Supreme Court Decisions," *N.H. Bar J.* 35, no. 1 (1994): 69.

21. Volinsky, "Education Funding Litigation," 840.

22. Regina Umpstead, "Determining Adequacy: How Courts Are Redefining State Responsibility for Educational Finance, Goals, and Accountability," *BYU Educ. & L.J.* 2007, no. 2 (2007): 281–320.

23. Rose v. Council for Better Education, 60 Ky. 1289, 790 S.W.2d 186 (1989).

24. The general goals were:

(i) sufficient oral and written communication skills to enable students to function in a complex and rapidly changing civilization;
(ii) sufficient knowledge of economic, social, and political systems to enable the student to make informed choices;
(iii) sufficient understanding of governmental processes to enable the student to understand the issues that affect his or her community, state, and nation;
(iv) sufficient self-knowledge and knowledge of his or her mental and physical well-being;

(v) sufficient grounding in the arts to enable each student to appreciate his or her cultural and historical heritage;
(vi) sufficient training or preparation for advanced training in either academic or vocational fields so as to enable each child to choose and pursue life work intelligently; and
(vii) sufficient levels of academic or vocational skills to enable public-school students to compete favorably with their counterparts in surrounding states, in academics or in the job market.

Id., 790 S.W.2d at 222.

25. McDuffy v. Secretary of the Executive Office of Education, 415 Mass. 545, 615 N.E.2d 516 (1993).

26. *Id.*, 415 Mass. at 606.

27. The language of the Massachusetts constitutional provision on an education system reads as follows:

> Wisdom and knowledge, as well as virtue, diffused generally among the body of the people, being necessary for the preservation of their rights and liberties; and as these depend on spreading the opportunities and advantages of education in the various parts of the country, and among the different orders of the people, it shall be the duty of legislatures and magistrates, in all future periods of this commonwealth, to cherish the interests of literature and the sciences, and all seminaries of them; especially the university at Cambridge, public schools and grammar schools in the towns; to encourage private societies and public institutions, rewards and immunities, for the promotion of agriculture, arts, sciences, commerce, trades, manufactures, and a natural history of the country; to countenance and inculcate the principles of humanity and general benevolence, public and private charity, industry and frugality, honesty and punctuality in their dealings; sincerity, good humor, and all social affections, and generous sentiments, among the people. Mass. Const. Ch. 5, § 2.

28. Order, Motion to Dismiss, Claremont v. Governor, N.H. Super. Ct., Merrimack County, No. 91-#-0306 (August 13, 1992).

29. In fact, in 1789 New Hampshire's legislature had enacted a state-mandated school-tax policy, which it maintained until 1919. The funding mechanism was complex, but the law's most prominent interpreter, the late Walter Backofen, has argued that "the net effect was virtually equivalent to a uniform state-controlled school-rate" that would actually decline during most of its duration as the state's collective tax-wealth expanded. From around the middle of the nineteenth century onward, the arrangement generally "favored equity for the taxpayer over schoolchildren," since schools in towns not expanding their tax base at the same rate and degree as the state in general "were being devastated." Backofen argued that the law and its effects should have figured far more prominently in N.H.'s debates on public-education finances, since "the Law of 1789 cannot avoid being a window on how the State Constitution was interpreted by those closest to its framing, even by the framers

itself." That it didn't, he suggested, might be attributable to the fact that "neither side in the Claremont controversy is served by the framers' intentions as spelled out so unequivocally in the Law of 1789." He noted that, while the 1789 law did codify state responsibility for a threshold of education funding, the absence of any state-mandated definition of "adequacy" suggests that the constitution's framers had been quite prepared to leave that question to localities rather than to the state officials. See Backofen, "Claremont's Achilles' Heel: The Unrecognized Mandatory School-Tax Law of 1789," *N.H. Bar J.* 43, no. 1 (2002): 26–29.

30. See Vivek Rao, "So Ordered? Scrutinizing the Massachusetts Judiciary's Role in the State's Sweeping Education Reform Plan" (2011), https://www.law.berkeley.edu/files/So_Ordered_Rao.pdf.

31. The Education Reform Act had "been in the works since 1991, when the Massachusetts Business Alliance for Education published its report 'Every Child a Winner!'" See Rhoda E. Schneider's "The State Constitutional Mandate for Education: The *McDuffy* and *Hancock* Decisions," published by the Massachusetts Department of Elementary and Secondary Education and available online at http://www.doe.MAedu/lawsregs/litigation/mcduffy_hancock.html.

32. Volinsky, "Education-Funding Litigation," 838–43.

33. Marcus Hurn, "State Constitutional Limits on New Hampshire's Taxing Power," *Pierce L. Rev.* 7, no. 3 (2009): 252–325. Hurn notes that "Despite one significant constitutional amendment and considerable evolution in judicial interpretation, it is still the case that true taxes must be on polls or property. N.H. remains unique among the states in denying the legislature the power to levy excise taxes as such" (Ibid., 253–54). Rather, the state has had recourse to such non-tax levies as fees, penalties, and special-benefit assessments.

34. John D. MacIntosh, "The New Hampshire General Court: A Legislative Primer," *N.H. Bar J.* 42, no. 2 (2001): 19–22. MacIntosh notes that in 2001 "there are fewer than 15 lawyer-members in the House and Senate. In the Senate, 2 of the 5 members of the Judiciary Committee are practicing lawyers, while in the House, 6 of 20 members of the Judiciary Committee are layers." Michele Demary has noted that "Massachusetts has one lawyer for every 132 residents while the ratio is much greater in New Hampshire at one for every 415 persons," adding that "the greater preponderance of attorneys in Massachusetts (not to mention the presence of seven ABA-accredited law schools in the state) may create a greater respect for the role of lawyers, justices, and the court." See Demary "Legislative-Judicial Relations on Contested Issues: Taxes and Same-Sex Marriage," *Judicature* 89, no. 4 (2006): 202, 209.

35. *Manchester Union-Leader*, December 31, 1993, 1. The *Union-Leader*'s reference to a "judicial oligarchy" was cited by a *Boston Globe* journalist. See Laura Kiernan, "Bills Hang on Definition of What Is 'Adequate,'" *Boston Globe*, January 16, 1994.

36. Quoted in the *Manchester Union-Leader*, January 2, 1994, 4. Sununu also announced that the Claremont plaintiffs, "Without a leg, or a pot for that matter," had succeeded "in the face of near unanimous state governmental opposition." Quoted by Charles DeGrandpre, "Lex Loci: A Survey of New Hampshire Supreme Court Decisions," *N.H. Bar J.* 35, no. 1 (1994): 69.

37. Quoted in *Manchester Union-Leader*, January 10, 1994; p. 1.

38. Kiernan, "Bills Hang on Definition of What Is 'Adequate.'"

39. Claremont School District v. Governor (*Claremont I*), 138 N.H. 183, 193 (1993).

40. Gov. Merrill described himself as willing to listen to proposals for a resolution of the issue, but expressed pessimism about the likelihood of a settlement "given the tax-and-spend mentality of the plaintiffs' lawyers." Quoted in the *Manchester Union-Leader*, January 5, 1994, 6.

41. Details of each side's arguments and evidence are recounted by Thomas Hersey, in *The Claremont Education Lawsuit: Bridging the Educational Divide* (Concord, NH: Wiss Institute for Public Policy and Claremont Lawsuit Coalition, 1998).

42. Volinsky, "Education Funding Litigation," 848–49.

43. See, for example, Edward Mosca, "New Hampshire's *Claremont* Case and the Separation of Powers," *Pierce L. Rev.* 4, no. 3 (2006): 409–34.

44. Claremont School District v. Governor, 142 N.H. 462, 702 A.2d 1353 (1997).

45. As the sole dissenter, Justice Sherman Horton wrote that the justices were not appointed to establish educational policy or to determine the proper way to finance its implementation. Under the constitution, he said, such matters must be left to the elected officials in state and local government. Given the legislature's proper delegation, Horton reasoned, its clear designation of the taxing district, the discerned purpose of the tax, and its obvious proportionality within the taxing district, the trial court was correct in deciding that the tests of reasonability and proportionality in Part 2, Article 5 of the state constitution have been met by the current tax system. Horton, in disagreeing that Part 2, Article 83 makes education a "fundamental" right, was challenging what one commentator has called "the higher law vision of state constitutionalism," which "generally holds sway within state supreme courts (at least within school finance law), most likely because such an orientation maximizes judicial power and is consonant with the traditional ability to define the meaning of the U.S. Constitution." 142 N.H. 462, 477–82. See also, Douglas S. Reed, *On Equal Terms: The Constitutional Politics of Educational Opportunity* (Princeton, N.J.: Princeton University Press, 2001), 90.

46. Todd DeMitchell, Joseph Onosko, and Mark Paige, "Amending the N.H. Constitution (CACR12): Education Will No Longer Be Fundamental to the Citizens of New Hampshire," UNH Dept. of Educ. Policy Brief #12–02, March 2012 (www.unh.edu/education).

47. *Manchester Union Leader*, December 19, 1997, A1, A18.

48. *Manchester Union Leader*, December 19, 1997, C1.

49. Quoted by Todd DeMitchell and Barbara Krysiak, "School Finance Reform in the 'Live Free or Die' State: Personal, Legal, and Policy Responses to *Claremont School District v. Governor*," *IJER*. 8, no. 1 (1999): 89, 95.

50. Senate president, Republican Joseph Delahunty, remarked "I'd say that if you play by the rules and the game goes against you, then you can't keep changing the rules … . That's the system. The Supreme Court made a decision and in my opinion we have to address it." The state's Governor, Democrat Jeanne Shaheen, elected in 1996, announced "I reject the notion that this is a simple choice between passing new broad-based taxes or rewriting our constitution to say we have no responsibility to

provide an adequate education to our children." Quoted by DeMitchell and Krysiak, "School Finance Reform," 95.

51. Noting that "Most states have undergone legislative challenges to their system of financing public education," DeMitchell and Krysiak find that "New Hampshire appears to be alone in a response which encompasses a constitutional amendment to overturn a state Supreme Court's decision regarding school finance." They add that "There have been instances of the United States Congress passing legislation in response to Supreme Court decisions, most notably in Establishment Clause and civil rights issues, but none were aimed at changing the constitution as a means of getting around a judicial decision. This appears to be an unprecedented response." Ibid., 95.

52. Since 1971, litigation challenging the validity of public education funding schemes under state constitutions has been filed in 45 states. Regarding the "adequacy" claims within this body of litigation, one analyst finds that "Challengers have emerged victorious in twenty-five states and obtained favorable settlements in four more. In Minnesota, Nebraska, South Dakota, and Wisconsin, courts found that the state constitution guaranteed some level of adequate education but that the state's current system already met the required level. In some cases, defeat in court was not the end of the story. In Oklahoma, the legislature raised taxes to fund smaller class sizes and higher teachers' salaries after education advocates sued in the late 1980s even though the state had prevailed in court. In Florida, after the state supreme court declared that the state constitution did not require educational adequacy, in part because there were no judicially manageable standards, the voters passed an amendment to the state constitution making it very clear just how fundamental a right they thought education was [footnotes omitted]." Sonja Elder, "Enforcing Public Educational Rights via a Private Right of Action," *Duke FL & Soc. Change* 1, no. 1 (2009): 137, 141–42. For more information about each state's decisions and the interpretation of their respective education clauses, see SchoolFunding.Info (formerly the National Education Access Network), "Overview of Litigation History," http://schoolfunding.info/litigation-map/, and Education Law Center, "Summary of School Funding Litigation," http://www.edlawcenter.org/.

53. See Gov. Jeanne Shaheen, "Advancing better classrooms: Governor proposes the ABC Plan to address Claremont decision" (1998), http://www.library.unh.edu/digital/object/claremontpapers:0015.

54. Volinsky, "Education-Funding Litigation," 851.

55. The commentators are listed at the end of the opinion. See Opinion of the Justices (School Financing), 142 N.H. 892, 712 A.2d. 1080 (1998).

56. N.H. Rev. Stat. Ann. §490:3.

57. 142 N.H. 892, 712 A.2d. 1080.

58. Volinsky, "Education-Funding Litigation," 852.

59. See Michele Demary, "Legislative-Judicial Relations."

60. Cooper v. Aaron, 358 U.S. 1 (1958).

61. Claremont School Dist. v. Governor, 143 N.H. 154, 725 A. 2d 648 (1998).

62. The bill in question was SB-FN-A-LOCAL. The supreme court ruled on it in Opinion of the Justices, 143 N.H. 429, 725 A.2d 1082 (1999).

63. N.H. Laws 1999, Ch. 17.

64. Claremont School District v. Governor, 144 N.H. 210, 744 A.2d 1107 (1999).

Chapter 6

Tipping Points

All things considered, it is hardly surprising that the first attempt to remove Justice Brock from office would emerge from the legislature in 1999. That effort was a bill of address cosponsored by Rep. Paul Mirski and Sen. Mary Brown.

MIRSKI-BROWN BILL OF ADDRESS

Mirski had actually decided at the end of 1998 that the chief justice had to go, whereupon he threw down the gauntlet with a personal letter to Brock announcing his intentions and explaining his reasoning. The letter began with a discussion of the principle of legislative supremacy over the judicial branch so clearly laid out in New Hampshire's anti-Federalist constitution of 1784—the experience of British tyranny that had shaped it, the specific constitutional provisions that had embodied it. Mirski concluded his reflections on the proper role and conduct of New Hampshire's courts by noting his own service on the House Judiciary Committee the past two years. It had imbued him, he explained, with deep respect for New Hampshire's legal community as a whole despite the horrid misdeeds of a few. It was not those "honorable men and women" of the state bench and bar who had betrayed the intent of the founders. No, it was David Brock who had led the entire judicial branch down a primrose path. "I have come to the unhappy conclusion," Mirski announced, "that the judiciary, under your leadership, is no longer capable of projecting an interest or even the appearance of an interest in the uniform dispensation of impartial justice."[1]

The rest of the letter set forth Mirski's charges. He began with the claim that Brock's "most egregious act has been to squelch the free speech rights of members of the New Hampshire Bar—as you did in your address to the Bar about a year ago." In January 1998, Brock had told New Hampshire Bar that, while criticism of Court interpretations was entirely healthy, criticism "miscasting the judicial role as tyrannical or illegitimate … is dangerous in a free society, for it will erode public respect for and confidence in the judicial system and the rule of law.[2] Such words, Mirski alleged, carried the implicit threat that "Members of the bar who criticize the courts we now know are destined to be summarily hauled before the court's Professional Conduct Committee for disciplinary action." But there was much more. Brock had been "the principal proponent of an expanded judiciary," Mirski charged, and as such had "asserted for the New Hampshire judiciary the power to tax, the power to field its own police force, and the power to govern without being subject to either the legislature's prerogatives or the people's scrutiny."[3]

In Mirski's view, the first of those offenses—judicial usurpation of "the power to tax"—had occurred with the creation of the Public Protection Fund to compensate victims of John Fairbanks. "Part 1, Article 28 of the Constitution," he lectured, "specifically precludes the establishment of any ' … subsidy, charge, tax, impost, duty … under any pretext whatsoever, without the consent of the people or their representatives in the legislature, or authority derived from that body.'"[4]

Mirski was less specific on the second offense, declining to identify exactly which "recent and self-serving ruling in defense of its right to create and maintain its own police force" he had in mind when launching the charge. But whether he was thinking specifically of the *LaFrance* case, its antecedents, or something else, the general point was clear enough to him: such ruling(s) exemplified the "distance which now separates the Supreme Court's point of view from the substance of the Constitution." And to make matters worse, Brock had actually had the temerity to fire a "warning shot across the legislature's bow in the dicta of that decision in which the court asserts that the legislature has a constitutional obligation to adequately fund the court," which "more than suggests that the court views itself as utterly independent of the public weal."[5]

But it was the third offense, the "power to govern without being subject to either the legislature's prerogatives or the people's scrutiny," which may have most personally exercised Mirski, who had been deeply shaken by the revelations of the Fairbanks scandal. The court's "attempts to conceal records of judicial misbehavior and complaints" was an unmistakable reference to the confidentiality policies of the PCC and JCC, which Brock had vigorously defended before the "Fairbanks III" committee.

It was an extraordinary inventory of grievances, touching directly or indirectly on nearly every effort the court had made regarding the professionalization of law and the independence of the judiciary for decades: supervision of the bar, court unification, state-level finance, judicial rule-making, ethical self-regulation. In fact, what is perhaps most remarkable about the bill Mirski and Sen. Mary Brown actually filed on January 28, 1999, was precisely the scale and generality of the indictment it contained: its five counts accused Brock not of specific actions but of general transgressions, each of which left the judiciary as a whole more tainted than the last.[6] His tenure as chief justice had, in general, "resulted in the destruction of the court's mantle of impartiality by suppressing the right of free speech through the creation of administrative rules which encourage a policy of silencing and punishing the court's critics." He had, in general, "attempted to conceal records of judicial misbehavior and complaints from the legislature and the people." Under his general leadership, "the court has engaged in usurpation of legislative and executive authority." He had even "engaged in attempts to intimidate a legislator who had proposed judicial reform which was repugnant to the self-interest of the court." The legislator was not named, nor was the intimidating action described. Neither, for that matter, was the "pro-active behavior" the court had embarked on under Brock's leadership. Those details, presumably, were to be filled in later.

Not surprisingly, that lack of specificity was highly problematic to the Joint Committee on Address charged with determining what exactly should be done with the Mirski/Brown bill. By March, the committee's chairman, Henry Mock, was explaining to Mirski that the bill's charges would have to be fleshed out with details and supportive evidence before hearings could be conducted. But in Mirski's view, that was to reverse the proper order of things. Production of that evidentiary support and detail would follow those hearings, not precede them. If Mirski and Brown had not provided an airtight case against Brock themselves, it was hardly because there was no case to be made. It was because that case should be made by the legislature as a whole. Brock should not be undone by any individual legislator, nor by any particular legislative committee (certainly not by the Joint Committee on Address, of such recent and ill-advised constitutional provenance). Rather, he should be undone by the people's elected representatives, acting in solemn conclave. The term "legislative supremacy," Mirski would propose, meant exactly that: supremacy of the *legislature*. What might have seemed a fishing expedition to some members of the Joint Committee was adherence to constitutional principle, in Paul Mirski's view.

Mirski explained his thinking in a March 16, 1998 letter responding to Mock's request. He submitted that refusing to advance the bill, open-ended as it properly was at the moment, toward full debate would mean blocking the people's representatives from fulfilling their sacred constitutional duties. That, to Mirski, was almost as objectionable a violation of the founders' intentions as those Brock himself had perpetrated.[7] "I can't provide you with an amended list of reasons fleshed out in the detail you might like," Mirski admitted. "In fact, I don't really have an idea of what would constitute sufficient or insufficient submission from your point of view." But for someone who genuinely believed in legislative supremacy, that was no shortcoming—on the contrary, that was precisely the point. "I think, as with any legislative process, the proper approach would be to initiate hearings on the matter, consider testimony from aggrieved parties and others and then reach a conclusion as to what to recommend to the House and Senate for action."[8]

What must be avoided at all costs, Mirski argued, was a "supplicant" legislature: one willing to yield some of its own constitutional powers to a judicial branch those founders had clearly, and rightly, mistrusted. He had done his part by initiating the indictment; now it was up to legislators, acting jointly and publicly, to do theirs. "If the legislature does not care whether or not its authority is usurped by the judicial branch or if it would rather slough off its responsibility to assert the constitutional rights of its constituents, then House Address #1 will not have a prayer of success," Mirski wrote Mock. "If, however, members of the House and Senate have an interest in defending our constitutional form of government and want to see to it that the interests of the electorate and the power of the electorate always reside within the people's legislature then House Address No. 1 will succeed."[9]

As events would demonstrate, Henry Mock was no admirer of David Brock. But in the end, he and the Joint Committee on Address decided they could not take the action Mirski and Brown were urging. The committee held only one hearing on the bill; and on June 29, members voted unanimously to return an "ought not to pass" recommendation to the legislature, which proceeded to reject the bill by a 256–58 vote.[10]

Yet the Mirski-Brown bill of address against Brock was a highly significant action nonetheless. For whether its charges were fair and accurate or not, they were certainly rooted in a coherent vision of New Hampshire, its civic culture, and the particular model of democracy that culture had long sustained. For some time, that vision had been on a collision course with a newer one incorporating the fully independent judiciary that voters themselves had midwifed with the constitutional amendments of 1966 and 1978.

In that older vision, *all* public officials must be tightly controlled, and kept ever mindful that they are agents, not masters, of the people. In fact, representative government itself was a sort of necessary evil—a retreat from the ideal of direct self-rule made tolerable only by the devolution of as much power as possible to the smallest governing units available. Those local units—towns, districts, counties—were where representatives were most easily monitored, and the political significance of individual citizen maximized. Within this populist vision, state government was to be afforded few functions beyond the protection and facilitation of local government; and measures were in place to make sure that state operatives never forgot the very limited roles voters sent them to Concord to play.

Hence the expectation that each state representative should represent the smallest possible constituency (and if the resulting body, one of the largest legislatures in the Anglophone world, was unwieldy, so much the better); that terms of office for all legislators should be kept short; and that legislative sessions themselves should be comparatively brief. It was, of course, absolutely clear that the legislature itself, where the people were most directly and fully represented, should be the dominant branch of state government—and utterly beyond question that the unelected judiciary, potentially the most dangerous branch of government, should remain at all times subordinate to that legislature's will.[11]

Not everyone in New Hampshire's legislature in 1999 shared Paul Mirski's sense of what was tactically optimal, or even feasible. But legislative-judicial relations in New Hampshire were so deeply fraught by 1999 precisely because so many shared his vision of state government itself, and of a judiciary perverted by developments since the grant of constitutional status. Court unification, administrative autonomy, the various measures taken to fortify judicial independence: all of it represented a departure from the core constitutional principle of legislative supremacy, and all of it was therefore in some sense illicit—whether voters had endorsed the constitutional amendments that had enabled it or not. In fact, to legislators who shared that perspective, *Claremont* was simply the catastrophe that had become inevitable from the moment voters had allowed their judiciary to slip the leash of popular, legislative control.

By 2000, legislative-judicial relations in New Hampshire had changed so substantially that a general public debate, perhaps catalyzed by legislative hearings and occurring not only in Concord but in town halls throughout the state, might have been productive. That sort of broad-gauged, systemic consideration, however, was not undertaken. Instead, the House of Representatives would simply impeach Chief Justice David Brock. *Claremont* would never be very far from the minds of legislators who shared the goal of ousting him—if for no other reason than that it actually remained in litigation throughout the impeachment drama.[12] But by April 2000, they had found entirely new weapons to deploy against the chief justice.

ZIBEL MEMORANDUM AND MCLAUGHLIN REPORT

The actual impeachment charges brought by the House on July 12, 2000, grew out of a memorandum prepared in February of that year by the clerk of the supreme court, Howard Zibel.[13] Zibel was concerned about a number of ethical lapses he believed had been committed by Justice Stephen Thayer—lapses that, Zibel felt, might have elicited stronger responses from Chief Justice Brock. His memorandum detailing those concerns would eventually be delivered to the Judicial Conduct Committee (JCC), itself an office of the supreme court. But the charges brought against Brock would extend well beyond anything Zibel said or implied in that memorandum. The process by which those charges evolved is well worth considering.

Since 1998, Justice Thayer had been enmeshed in peculiarly contentious and complex divorce proceedings.[14] By February 2000, the wrangle had already generated allegations of bank fraud and unreported income against Thayer, and investigations of him by bank authorities and the office of the U.S. Attorney's office. His wife Judith, for her part, had been physically ejected from her house when she tried to block its judge-ordered sale by refusing to vacate.[15] In January 2000, she decided to appeal the divorce itself to the New Hampshire Supreme Court, the only appellate court in the state. Since all five Supreme Court justices would have an obvious conflict hearing a case involving one of their own number, a set of alternates had to be identified and empaneled. That task fell to Chief Justice Brock. His impeachment would rest in no small measure on allegations that in fulfilling it he showed marked favoritism toward his fellow justice, Stephen Thayer.

On February 3, by Zibel's account, Thayer had been in the clerk's office, where he noticed the list of judges who might be eligible to serve on the appeal of *Thayer v. Thayer.* The list itself, compiled in consultation with the chief justice of the Superior Court, was a public document, so Zibel had no grounds for objecting to Thayer's scanning it. But he was taken aback when Thayer verbalized an objection to one of the names on it, Judge George Pappagianis.

Around noon the next day, February 4, Chief Justice Brock told Zibel that he had settled on Pappagianis and Judge Philip Mangones as the final two alternates. Around 1:30 p.m., Brock convened the other justices for case-screenings, to be followed by consultations with supreme court counsel Eileen Fox, whose duties mainly involved liaison work with the elected branches of government. At the beginning of the latter conference, Brock announced his selections of Mangones and Pappagianis. The chief justice would later insist that he had not intended to solicit commentary on his choices; but everyone else in the room would testify that, whatever Brock's intent, they had felt licensed (perhaps implicitly, by word or gesture) to offer their views.[16] At any rate, Justice Thayer immediately and strenuously objected to Judge Pappagianis, as did Justice Sherman Horton. At that point, Brock hastened to Zibel's office to belay his prior instructions, either in deference to those justices' concerns or simply to secure more time to consider the matter.

As it happened, Zibel was on the phone with Pappagianis when Brock entered his office, and had to break off his conversation to respond to the chief justice. Brock disclosed that "Steve and Sherm" had objected to Pappagianis; but, Zibel explained, he had just apprised Pappagianis of his appointment. Brock returned to the conference room and asked Thayer to leave. After determining that Horton's objections were based on the misperception that Pappagianis was to be appointed to a JCC panel rather than to the *Thayer v. Thayer* bench, Brock confirmed his selection of Pappagianis, Thayer's objections notwithstanding. Zibel was unaware of anything that had transpired in the conference room. But he remained gravely troubled by what he saw as an illicit effort by Thayer to directly influence the disposition of his own divorce case—and Brock's apparent willingness to accommodate him.

Over the next few days, Zibel would come to recognize that such behavior might represent not only a violation of the Code of Judicial Conduct but an actual felony under a criminal statute on "Corrupt Practices," involving efforts to exercise unlawful influence on public servants. Zibel deeply respected the chief justice; but he was just as deeply concerned that Brock might not be responding appropriately to Thayer's action. Failure by the public servant in question to report an attempted exertion of improper influence, Zibel realized, could itself constitute a felony under the statute.[17]

Zibel was not the only one disturbed by recent developments involving Thayer. Justice John Broderick and Court Counsel Eileen Fox were similarly upset, and weighing the proper response. Broderick, for his part, would decide that the matter was best handled *in camera*. Over the next few days, he discussed the situation with every other justice, including both Thayer and Brock, satisfying himself that, having raised his colleagues' awareness, the offending behavior was unlikely to be repeated. He also spoke with Eileen Fox; and both spoke with Zibel, who also consulted retired justice William Batchelder and Attorney Charles Doleac, a specialist in ethical issues. Zibel was glad to know that his misgivings regarding the events of February 4 were shared by others. But he was not persuaded that the problem had yet been adequately addressed, or its real scale fully recognized.

That was because Zibel saw the incident as the latest in a string of unethical and even, perhaps, overtly criminal actions by Justice Thayer. The first had occurred the previous year. At the time, it was standard supreme court practice that judges recused from particular cases received, and were permitted to comment on, draft decisions, and sometimes to participate in the conferences finalizing those drafts. Defenders of the policy would insist that the input provided by non-voting justices amounted to little more than stylistic suggestions and occasional insertions of factual points or relevant precedents, all offered only after the decision had been reached and then simply to enhance the quality of the final, written opinion. But Zibel felt that Thayer had seriously abused that policy in 1999, in a conference on a matter from which he had been recused. That was the *Feld* case, when the beleaguered justice had openly advocated for the outcome sought by one of the parties in a case without revealing relevant details of his own relationship with that party.

Thayer was a close friend of Attorney Emile Bussiere, who in the mid-1990s had been involved in a property dispute with Attorney Carolyn Roberge and her father, New Hampshire Bank Commissioner Roland Roberge. The Roberges were represented by Attorney Steven Feld.[18] In 1999, Bussiere formally accused Feld and Carolyn Roberge of willfully dissembling during the discovery phase of the case proceedings. The complaint had been brought to the Professional Conduct Committee, which had duly investigated, found Feld culpable, and recommended the most severe sanction, disbarment (Carolyn was eventually found to be acting not as attorney but as a client in the instances cited). The nature of those sanctions was for the supreme court to decide: it could disbar, as PCC had recommended; it could accept the milder measures, public censure and fine, proposed by the referee the court customarily appointed in such situations to apprise justices of all options; or it could select some other alternative. "The *Feld* case" was that disciplinary matter.

For years, Stephen Thayer had acknowledged a friendship and "financial relationship" with Émile Bussiere, duly recusing himself from any cases involving the latter. Thayer had, however, felt free to participate in the first *Feld* case conference on April 23, 1999, because, technically, the *Feld* case involved not Bussiere himself but only Feld, the JCC, the court, and its referee.[19] But if Thayer's participation in any discussion of the *Feld* case at all raised ethical questions, his actual remarks on the case's resolution raised more: he urged the court to suspend Feld for two years (and Carolyn Roberge for six months). In prescribing the harshness Bussiere favored rather than the moderation the referee had recommended, Thayer was vulnerable to the charge of advancing the agenda of a friend.[20]

Howard Zibel was not present at that conference, or yet aware of Thayer's apparent willingness to promote Bussiere's goal. But Zibel's concern about what had transpired would deepen shortly afterward, when he realized that no one at the conference could have fully understood just how close Thayer's relationship with Bussiere really was. In fact, Thayer had borrowed $50,000 from Bussiere in 1996. That detail had not come to light until Thayer, apprised that his wife's attorney would be requesting the financial disclosure forms mandated by the Code of Judicial Conduct (and aware that the matter would come to the attention of local journalists), had amended his 1996 form to include the information. Zibel's claim was that on May 11, 1999, in the clerk's presence, Thayer had backdated that form to April 15, the filing deadline.[21]

Justice William Johnson, then chairing the JCC, had been at the April 23 discussion of the *Feld* case, and was greatly discomfited by Thayer's remarks: he felt they had gone to the actual resolution of the matter rather than to fine points of the opinion that would eventually express the court's judgment.[22] But Johnson was positively outraged when he learned from Zibel that Thayer had failed to reveal the $50,000 loan until after that conference, and he conveyed his outrage to Chief Justice Brock. Brock, too, hadn't known about the $50,000 until that point, and was upset by the revelation. But, since Thayer had disclosed a financial relationship at least in general terms, the chief justice decided that the confidentiality of the conference room outweighed the transgression; he elected not to report Thayer's behavior to JCC, and advised Johnson to refrain from reporting also. Johnson respected Brock's perspective, and told Zibel he had accepted the chief justice's advice. But he was not prepared to let the matter drop. Instead, he pressed Brock to approach Thayer personally, explain that his failure to report the loan was a facial violation of the Code of Judicial Ethics, and urge Thayer to report himself to JCC. Brock did so, and Thayer had reluctantly agreed, when Brock explained that both Zibel and Johnson were concerned and self-reporting might be best for all concerned.[23]

But that didn't end what Zibel saw as unethical conduct by Thayer in the matter. The justices were then discussing some rule changes for the JCC, and Zibel thought it wrong that Thayer, although scheduled to appear before the JCC himself in July 1999, was nonetheless allowed to participate actively in those discussions of its rules—especially, matters of press releases and media access. Yet again, Howard Zibel felt, Stephen Thayer was effectively lobbying for favorable treatment in his own case.[24]

Through all this, Zibel had been concerned by Chief Justice Brock's failure to effectively rein Thayer in. The Chief, Zibel understood, was quite properly concerned with protecting the confidentiality of court and JCC deliberations, and reluctant to breach it by revealing anything that transpired therein. But Zibel was increasingly inclined to the view that this protocol was carried too far if allowed to outweigh the responsibility to report any of Thayer's several reportable actions—at the very least to the JCC, and perhaps even to the attorney general's office. On February 11, the clerk wrote up a memorandum describing his accumulated misgivings, then spent the next several days considering whether to formally submit the document to the JCC (of which he himself was Executive Secretary).

Zibel again discussed the situation with Justices Broderick and Batchelder, Court Counsel Fox, and Attorney Doleac. He had chosen not to speak personally with Chief Justice Brock, however, later explaining that omission by noting both the firmness of Brock's views on confidentiality and his own belief that, in any event, he had duly communicated his dilemma to representatives of the court.[25] By February 14, Zibel had decided that he would indeed submit his memorandum to the JCC, and settled on February 22 as the date of delivery: he wanted, he would later testify, to give Brock and the court some time to act on their own.[26] To expedite that action, he left a draft of the memorandum for the chief justice, and a note requesting a conversation with him. Brock promptly visited Zibel personally to announce, matter-of-factly, that the matter should be discussed no further outside formal channels.

That day, Justices Broderick, Horton, and Brock decided to seek legal advice regarding their own responsibilities, and to apprise Justice Thayer of Zibel's impending action. All involved understood what could happen if Zibel or anyone else reported Thayer's actions: by law, the JCC itself was bound to report any matter involving possible criminal acts to the attorney general's office. Everyone also understood that Justice Thayer had moved perilously close to prosecutable conduct during his phone conversation with Justice Broderick on the evening of February 14 and in subsequent calls to Chief Justice Brock, with statements like "I'm not going to hang alone;" "If Zibel files this, it'll blow up the Supreme Court;" and "We all do it. We can hang together on this or hang separately."[27] If those words were construed as threats, they would constitute witness tampering and obstruction of government administration.[28]

At that point in time, however, Brock and the other justices elected not to construe Thayer's words that way, but rather less gravely, as intemperate remarks from a colleague under enormous pressure. The court as a body had decided to report Thayer's actions at the February 4 conference on his divorce panel, as well as all *Feld*-related matters, to the JCC; but not those remarks he had made in response to the news about Zibel's plans. Their report was submitted on February 17. Zibel would submit his own memorandum on February 22, as planned. On February 18, Thayer, having refused an invitation to resign from the court, was suspended from it. On February 19, he initiated a suit against Justices Brock, Broderick, and Horton to secure reinstatement.

But by this point, those intra-judicial actions were almost academic, as the matter was about to pass to the executive, and eventually the legislative, branches of state government.

On February 25, Chief Justice Brock's personal attorney delivered Zibel's (unsigned) memorandum to Attorney General Philip McLaughlin. On March 2, legal counsel for the JCC would follow, personally informing McLaughlin that JCC had been apprised of possible criminal acts on the court. The Attorney General's office immediately authorized an investigation, to be conducted under the supervision of Senior Assistant Attorney General Mark Zuckerman. Thayer was to be the focus of the investigation. But criminal investigation of a justice of the New Hampshire Supreme Court was unprecedented in modern times, and Zuckerman's team quickly realized they would have to make important decisions with scant guidance.

The investigators determined fairly quickly that "something terribly wrong had occurred on the court," and would in fact prepare charges against Thayer.[29] Faced with the prospect of a criminal trial, Zuckerman and his team, as representatives of the attorney general's office, felt obliged to anticipate and prepare for the defense Thayer would likely mount. It certainly seemed plausible to assume it would entail insisting that he had never acted outside the supreme court's customary practices on recusal. That, in turn, meant investigators would need as clear and thorough an understanding of those practices as possible—practices hitherto utterly unknown to anyone outside the court. Sitting justices of the New Hampshire Supreme Court understood that they were to be questioned as part of a criminal investigation into one of their own number. What they didn't understand was that "the culture of the court and how it conducted business on a day-to-day basis" were also coming under scrutiny.[30] Nor could anyone know in advance what might come of such probing. No one could have anticipated, for example, Justice Horton's proposing to the AG's investigators that the retired justice Batchelder had been selected by Chief Justice Brock to replace the recused Justice Thayer on the panel that decided *Claremont II* "because the chief justice knew that Justice Batchelder would agree with him."[31]

The three sitting (Brock, Broderick, and Horton) and two retired (Batchelder and Johnson) justices who were interviewed all defended the recusal policy, noting the valuable contributions recused justices could make to final, written opinions. But practices that seemed harmless enough to justices who had engaged in them for years were, in fact, quite troubling to the AG's investigators.[32] More troubling still was the fact that the course of action to be taken regarding them was not yet clear. Since there was no strong criminal case against any justice except Thayer, that determination would not lie with the attorney general's office in any case.

Stephen Thayer's fate, on the other hand, *was* in the AG's hands. Informed in late March that he would be the target of a grand jury investigation, Thayer's attorneys and prosecutors initiated discussions that concluded with his resignation from the court. It was tendered on March 29, "in return for the attorney general's forbearance from presenting criminal charges against him to the grand jury."[33]

The McLaughlin Report was released on March 31. In it, Attorney General McLaughlin explained that he had decided to accept Thayer's offer in part because his investigators had "found that Justice Thayer's comments to the court had, in essence, been invited by the chief justice's demeanor and the court's past practice."[34] In fact, McLaughlin wrote a separate letter to Gov. Shaheen, Senate President Beverly Hollingsworth, and House

Speaker Donna Sytek in which he pointedly noting that the investigation had "revealed institutional practices of the Supreme Court which, in my judgment, as the attorney for the people, should be examined."[35]

Thus had an investigation aimed mainly at possible misdeeds by Stephen Thayer (with other justices implicated only to the degree that they may have wrongly failed to report those specific actions) come to yield not the prosecution of Stephen Thayer but a call by the attorney general for a legislative inquiry into general practices of the supreme court. The McLaughlin Report flatly declared the court's recusal policy "unconstitutional;" announced that "our investigation has discovered conduct and institutional practices at the court at odds with the expectations of the people to whom the court belongs;" and added ominously that "If abuses of process occur in one branch of government then, absent the ability of that branch of government to self-correct, it is the duty of other branches to protect the interests of the people in the integrity of their government."[36] Howard Zibel, who had effectively catalyzed the investigation, immediately dispatched his own missive to Gov. Shaheen, Senate President Hollingsworth, and House Speaker Sytek, protesting that the McLaughlin Report had gone too far.[37]

An outraged Chief Justice Brock, however, was not content to send letters to elected officials. On April 4, he offered the most public rebuttal possible: in an extraordinary action, he conducted a press conference from the well of the supreme court itself.[38] Flanked by Justices Horton and Broderick, as well as retired Justices William Batchelder and William Johnson (current JCC Chair), Brock offered a spirited defense of the court's practices, and an equally vigorous critique of what Attorney General McLaughlin had done and how he had done it.

McLaughlin, Brock argued, had grossly exceeded his charge, using the investigation of Thayer as mere "pretext for an executive branch surprise attack on the judicial branch's internal operating procedures." The court's recusal policy, Brock noted, had been in place for decades, and served the court and the people of New Hampshire well—indeed, the chief justice suggested, had justices known the investigators' real intent, they could and would have explained that far more thoroughly.[39] Despite the report's insinuations, recused justices were certainly not licensed to influence the disposition of cases in which they had a personal interest. In all those years, only one justice had ever tried to. That single offender was Justice Thayer, by his ill-considered remarks on the *Feld* case and on *Thayer v. Thayer*. Those offenses, Brock noted, had been recognized and duly reported to the JCC by the court. In fact, Brock revealed, the justices had already revised their recusal policy, simply to make future transgressions of this sort even less likely. But the McLaughlin Report had neglected to mention that, just as it had neglected to provide any evidence beyond the Thayer matters in support of its suggestion that the court's internal procedures were shady, perhaps even corrupt. "[In] all of the material and in all of the conclusions issued by the attorney general," complained Brock, "there has not been one other example of breach of our sacred duties in screening and deciding cases."

Brock took special aim at McLaughlin's decision not to prosecute Thayer without ever interviewing him.[40] That "immunity from prosecution [gave Thayer] the license to say anything he wants to say in the future," charged Brock. He objected just as vigorously to McLaughlin's release to the legislature of all notes taken and interviews conducted in the course of his investigation, totaling some 120 pages.[41] But what was most striking in Brock's April 4 address was his insistence that what was at stake was nothing less than the independence of the judicial branch of government. "My colleagues and I are profoundly troubled that recent events are intended to compromise your rights to a strong, free and independent judiciary," he stated. Thinking perhaps of *Claremont* and much more, he went on to explain that "There are times that we must make hard decisions in this building and there are decisions made that may not be popular. There are those that would govern by majority will only, against the interest of those in the minority. Without this court, there indeed would be neither minority rights nor minority purposes."[42]

As the McLaughlin Report had gone beyond the terms of the Zibel Memorandum, so too did Brock's rhetoric take the entire matter beyond the terms of the McLaughlin Report—into the far broader questions of judicial independence and the separation of powers. There were, of course, a rather large number of state legislators who had been chafing to consider exactly those questions for quite some time.

NOTES

1. Mirski to Brock, Dec. 16, 1998. Online at http://www.mainstream.net/nhpolitics/mletter.html. Oddly, impeachment inquiries against President Clinton were initiated by the U.S. House of Representatives only three days later, on Dec. 19.
2. See Paul Mirski, Letter to Henry Mock, re: House Address #1, March 16, 1999, http://mainstream.net/nhpolitics/mirski.letter2.html, in which Mirski directly quoted Brock's 1998 address.
3. Mirski to Brock, Dec. 16 1998.
4. Ibid.
5. Ibid.
6. HA1, as introduced and referred to Joint Committee on Address, N.H. H.R. Jour. 18 (January 28, 1999), 272.
7. Mirski to Mock, March 16, 1999. Online at https://mainstream.net/nhpolitics/mirski.letter2.html.
8. Ibid.

9. Ibid.

10. HA1, Roll Call Vote, N.H. H.R. Jour. 77 (July 1, 1999), 2070–72.

11. This was a vision in clear opposition to what political scientist Robert Dahl called the "division of labor" model of democracy, in which those who govern need not be directly responsive to public opinion. See Alan Rosenthal, *The Decline of Representative Democracy: Process, Participation and Power in State Legislatures* (Washington, DC: Congressional Quarterly Press, 1981), 6–7. See also Mark Tushnet's theory of "populist constitutional law," under which "dialogue and democratic self-government" would give the constitution "back to the citizens." See the reference to Tushnet's thinking in Richard Bauman and Tsvi Kahana, *The Least Examined Branch: The Role of the Legislature in the Constitutional State* (NY: Cambridge University Press, 2006), 2.

12. In March 2000, the N.H. Senate filed a request for an advisory opinion on whether the enactment of SB462-FN-A-LOCAL would be constitutional. The funding system proposed under that bill aimed to (1) supplement the existing state-level "baseline assistance for educational adequacy" with aid under alternative formulas for determining "adequacy guarantee assistance;" (2) modify the current formula for determining "baseline assistance for educational adequacy;" (3) reduce the proposed statewide education property tax rate; and (4) appropriate money from the state education trust fund for FY 2000–2001 with which the state education department would make the "adequacy guarantee assistance" distributions. In early December 2000, the justices submitted their advisory opinion that the bill if enacted would require taxpayers to pay real estate taxes at disproportionate and unequal rates to fulfill the state's constitutional duty, so that the proposed plan was unconstitutional under Part 2, Article 5 of the state constitution. Opinion of the Justices (Reformed Public-School Financing System), 145 N.H. 474, 765 A.2d 673 (2000).

13. A draft of the Zibel Memorandum appears in Brown, *Impeachment Trial*, 269–76.

14. Oddly enough, that contentiousness owed quite a lot to a surviving practice of the earlier "populist" era in New Hampshire's legal history: the right of individuals who are not lawyers and not bar-certified to represent clients in state courts. It was non-attorney Theodore Kamasinsky (born Theodore Ratnoff in New York) who, in aggressively defending Thayer's wife Judith, won motions to unseal court records containing details of Stephen Thayer's finances that would greatly embarrass the latter, and help precipitate the entire impeachment drama. Kamasinsky, who had amassed a number of larceny convictions in New York and Connecticut before arriving in New Hampshire, considered himself a crusader for judicial openness and accountability, qualities he found sorely lacking in New Hampshire. His biography, character, role in the impeachment and impact on the state are described by legal analyst Jeffrey Toobin in "The Judge Hunter," *New Yorker*, January 12, 2000, 49–54.

15. Ibid., 53.

16. Brock first offered his disclaimer in his deposition before the House Judiciary Committee. See David Brock deposition (May 18), N.H. H.R. Judiciary Committee, *Investigation by the House Judiciary Committee pursuant to House Resolution 50: Depositions* (Concord, N.H.: The Committee, 2000) [henceforward, HJC

Investigation], 188. Transcripts of all HJC Investigation depositions are available in the N.H. State Library in Concord. Attached to those files are relevant records of Attorney General McLaughlin's prior inquiry (e.g., the "Memoranda of Interviews" conducted by the AG McLaughlin's investigators) and certain materials originally held by the Judicial Conduct Committee.

The impressions of Justices Broderick, Horton, and Thayer, and Court Counsel Eileen Fox, were also conveyed during the HJC investigation. Ibid., see Fox deposition (May 2), 48; Thayer deposition (May 10), 73; Horton deposition (May 16), 139; and Broderick deposition (May 15), 164–65.

17. Zibel was thinking of N.H. Rev. Stat. Ann. §640:3, which provides that persons who privately address to any public servant with "official discretion in a judicial or administrative proceeding any representation, argument, or other communication with the purpose of influencing that discretion on the basis of considerations other than those authorized by law" are guilty of a class B felony. The statute also criminalizes failure by the public servant so addressed to report that behavior to a law enforcement officer.

18. The basic issue was Bussiere's claim to unencumbered ownership of a condominium in a building in Manchester, N.H., that Attorney Carolyn Roberge had formally acquired when its prior owner, Stephen Bronstein, defaulted on a mortgage. Bronstein himself had bought the building from Bussiere and partners, who had originally constructed it. Financing for Roberge's purchase was provided by her father Roland, then N.H. Banking Commissioner. It was the mixed ownership Bussiere claimed to have contractually retained a leasehold on a two-story apartment in the building, free and clear of obligations to all mortgage holders. Roberge disputed that claim, and initiated eviction proceedings against Bussiere. He responded with an equity action (Bussiere v. Roberge, 142 N.H. 905, 714 A.2d 894, 1998). It was Feld's and Roberge's responses to certain discovery requests those actions entailed that led to Bussiere's professional conduct complaint against both.

19. HJC Investigation, Thayer deposition (May 10), 179.

20. That harshness was, of course, also consistent with the recommendation of the PCC, to which Thayer was apparently the Court's informal liaison at the time. Thayer himself hadn't mentioned that function in his own May 10 deposition before HJC, but Chief Justice Brock did in his May 18 deposition (Ibid., 97). Brock explained to HJC Counsel Steinfield that he felt Thayer's remarks had been made in that (semi)official capacity, that is, "that he was talking about the consistency of our opinions." As to the propriety of Thayer's involvement in any conference on the *Feld* case, Brock argued that, technically, such discussion of the case as occurred on that day (April 23, 1999) did not constitute a "conference" at all, since one of the judges who had sat on it (Batchelder) wasn't present, and the two who were Brock himself and Judge Johnson had not read all the materials (Ibid., 89–111).

21. Zibel first claimed in writing that on May 11, 1999, Thayer had amended his financial disclosure forms to reveal a previously concealed loan from Bussiere in the "Zibel Memorandum" (Brown, *Impeachment Trial,* 271). He would repeat the charge to investigators for the attorney general. See State of New Hampshire, Department of Justice, Memorandum of Interview, Howard Zibel (March 3, 2000), by Christopher Domian, Investigator, Criminal Bureau, White Collar Crime and Public Integrity

Unit, 8. That memorandum is attached to the transcript of Zibel's deposition before HJC, in which he again repeated the charge (Zibel deposition, May 4, 180).

22. In fact, Johnson described himself as "livid" over them, and testified that he had expressed his views to Chief Justice Brock personally. HJC Investigation, Johnson deposition (May 9), 107. Johnson, in fact, had been concerned about Thayer's ethics even prior to the *Feld* case. He told the attorney general's investigators that he had also been troubled by Thayer's requests for release from his Court duties so that he could pursue various teaching jobs in order to supplement his income. Memorandum of Interview, William Johnson (March 8), Christopher Domian, Investigator, 7.

23. HJC Investigation, Johnson deposition (May 9), 74–140. Thayer himself adamantly and repeatedly denied any ethical lapse regarding his financial disclosure forms, although his accounts would differ somewhat over time. His earliest written one apparently came in a letter he wrote to Zibel, penned "Out of an abundance of caution" on June 11, 1999. In that letter, Thayer explained that, when filing his 1996 disclosure form, he had unintentionally neglected to mention the loan ("Such omission was not the product of any reflection concerning the loan."). In 1997 and 1998, he wrote, he had been mindful of it, but considered himself in compliance with the terms of the Code of Judicial Conduct since in those years he did acknowledge an "ongoing personal, legal, and *financial* relationship" with Bussiere [emphasis Thayer's]. By 1998, Thayer wrote, "With the help of hindsight" he had come to realize "that it would have been more prudent to have also reviewed my file for 1996 and amended it when I referred to the financial transaction in 1997 or 1998 ... and, therefore, I amended my reports [plural Thayer's] accordingly on May 11, 1999." Thayer closed the letter by insisting that "The spirit and purpose of the rule were never violated," since "The circumstances that I have outlined were the result of human failing and not of any deliberate act." HJC Investigation, William Johnson deposition, May 9, 2000; Exhibit A JC-99-026, copied JCC [Judicial Conduct Committee].

24. On this point, Eileen Fox and Howard Zibel apparently held different views. Fox told the Attorney General's investigators that Thayer would not, in fact, personally benefit by the changes he advocated, since his case had been filed prior to the April 1, 2000, date at which those changes would become effective, if adopted (Memorandum of Interview, Eileen Fox, March 27, by Christopher T. Domian, investigator attached to HJC Investigation, Eileen Fox deposition, May 2, 2000). Zibel, for his part, felt that "Since his case was likely to be pending before the JCC after the effective date of the rules, he was participating in a matter which directly affected his case" (Zibel Memorandum, Appendix 2, Brown, *Impeachment Trial,* 1).

25. HJC Investigation, Zibel deposition (May 4) 144.

26. Zibel testified to that effect before the N.H. Senate. See Brown, *Impeachment Trial*, 49.

27. Justice Broderick would testify that the language Thayer used with him had been considerably stronger. What Thayer told him, Broderick reported, was "'I'm not going to fucking hang out there for that asshole,' meaning Howard Zibel" (HJC Investigation, Broderick deposition, May 15, 216).

28. The statements appeared on p. 19 of the final version of the McLaughlin Report (Brown, *Impeachment Trial,* Appendix 3).

29. HJC Investigation, Mark Zuckerman deposition (June 7, 2000), 29–33.

30. Ibid., 40.

31. Memorandum of Interview, Justice Horton (March 10), by Christopher Domian, Investigator, 2–3. Horton, who dissented on *Claremont II*, acknowledged arguing for the selection of Justice Grimes to that panel precisely because he expected Grimes to agree with *him*. Later, Justice Batchelder would vigorously challenge Horton's claim. Neither his own nor Justice Grimes' views on *Claremont II*, argued Batchelder, were at all predictable, since that was primarily a taxation case involving issues on which each judge had a complex record (HJC Investigation, Batchelder deposition, May 11, 51–58). Horton, for his part, would withdraw his allegation, after the chief justice assured him that the selection of Batchelder over Grimes had been determined by Grimes' failing health and Batchelder's easier access to Concord (Ibid., Horton deposition, May 16, 201).

32. Ibid., 33. Zuckerman himself had suspected almost from the beginning that the investigation might lead to legislative action. That was why he, in consultation with Attorney General McLaughlin, elected to inform legislative leaders, the governor, and Senior Associate Superior Court Justice Linda Dalianis in advance (March 8) that an investigation had been initiated that "might require them to exercise their supervisory or constitutional powers" (McLaughlin Report, 5). Investigators were very mindful of both the difficulty and the importance of maintaining confidentiality in so high level a procedure, and aimed to reduce the likelihood that rumors or inaccuracies would spark actions or utterances that could compromise it and/or any future legislative process.

33. Ibid., 21.

34. Ibid. McLaughlin also noted that Thayer's long record of public service, the nature of the charges against him, and his expressed desire to preserve the honor of the Court made incarceration unlikely even if he should be convicted.

35. The letter is reprinted, along with the McLaughlin Report, in Brown, *Impeachment Trial*, Appendix 3.

36. McLaughlin Report, 1–3, 21.

37. In his letter, dated April 4, 2000, Zibel expressed the view that the McLaughlin Report had "unfairly extrapolate[d]" from specific instances of blameworthy conduct that he had reported. In Zibel's opinion, the Court's shortcomings were administrative rather than ethical ("The real problem of the New Hampshire Supreme Court at present is the crushing case volume of the past decade."). The letter is included among the materials accompanying the transcript of Zibel's May 4 HJC deposition.

38. The text of Brock's entire statement on April 4 appears as Appendix 4 in Brown, *Impeachment Trial,* 305–10.

39. This was a theme that each of the justices would stress when later deposed by the House Judiciary Committee. Had they known that the recusal policy was under scrutiny, testified William Johnson (May 9), William Batchelder (May 12), John Broderick (May 15), Sherman Horton (May 16), and David Brock (May 18), they would have provided far more context, comparisons with other courts' practices, and examples of favorable outcomes. McLaughlin, Zuckerman, and the investigators, for their part, responded with some asperity to the suggestion that they had been deceptive. In his own deposition before HJC, Zuckerman described the claim that justices had been misled "troubling and somewhat remarkable." Nothing about

the investigation had been "shrouded in secrecy," he argued, insisting that his team had simply done what was necessary to conclude an adequate, professional investigation of Thayer. Attorney General McLaughlin, for his part, would publicly state "I assumed in good faith that we had received all the information which they had," adding "Where we go in a criminal investigation is not where someone wants us to go or wishes us to go, it is where the facts take us." "AG Fires Rebuttal at Justices," *Portsmouth Herald*, April 5, 2000.

40. Thayer had declined to be interviewed. Justice Johnson, among other defenders of the Court, would question investigators' willingness to forego prosecuting him without first securing proffer of his testimony, something Johnson said he had never seen before. Had Thayer been required to deliver that proffer in return for immunity from prosecution for the crimes investigated to date, Johnson argued, he would have been precluded from contradicting anything in it, for fear of subsequent prosecution for perjury. Johnson's point, reinforced by Brock on April 4, was that the absence of a proffer left Thayer at complete liberty to make such public utterances as suited him, with no concern about legal liability (HJC Investigation, Johnson deposition, May 9, 2000, 156–57). Mark Zuckerman, in his HJC deposition (June 7, 2000), dismissed concerns about the absence of a proffer at that point in the investigation as groundless. Zuckerman would not acknowledge (unlike McLaughlin himself) that what Thayer had been granted amounted to "immunity." In Zuckerman's view, what had occurred was a "plea negotiation" for particular offenses, nothing more. Thayer could have been prosecuted subsequently, for any offenses that came to light later.

41. Those notes would later be referenced on the floor of the House of Representatives, during delegates' consideration of HR50 authorizing HJC to investigate whether cause existed for the impeachment of David Brock and/or any other Supreme Court Justice. Rep. Hess, one of HR50's sponsors, described himself as "deeply disturbed and dismayed by the revelations that came out of the Attorney General's report just 13 days ago and even more so in the investigation file of some 120 pages." N.H. H.R. Jour. 13 (April 13, 2000), 577.

42. Brown, *Impeachment Trial*, 308.

Part III

THE IMPEACHMENT CRISIS

Chapter 7

The House of Representatives Acts

On April 9, Rep. Mirski and a number of cosponsors submitted to the House of Representatives a resolution, HR50, proposing that the House Judiciary Committee (HJC) be authorized "to investigate whether grounds exist, based on the report of the attorney general, and any information arising out of the judiciary committee investigation, for the house of representatives to exercise its constitutional power to impeach chief justice David A. Brock and/or any other justice of the New Hampshire Supreme Court."[1] The language was deliberately chosen to grant HJC leeway to pursue whatever leads or avenues it might find worth investigating, within or beyond the events described in the McLaughlin Report. It also granted HJC the power "to compel by subpoena the attendance and giving of testimony by any person," and further authority to "compel the production of such things as it deems necessary."

WORK OF HOUSE JUDICIARY COMMITTEE

On April 13, the New Hampshire House approved the resolution by a crushing, 343–7 vote, a tally suggesting the range and depth of legislators' distress about the state's judicial branch. The concern most commonly voiced on the floor that day (in fact, throughout the duration of the crisis) was the "veil of secrecy" the court had allegedly thrown around its practices: secrecy that went well beyond the normal requirements of confidentiality in certain judicial proceedings, secrecy that in fact served only "to shield potential misdeeds."[2] What sorts of malfeasance lurked behind that veil? What were its real wellsprings, and how might they be most effectively addressed? McLaughlin had seemed to suggest that the specific incidents described in his report should be understood as symptoms of something bigger, something entrenched and wrongly normalized. How to proceed?

From the beginning, some representatives wondered whether a focus on Brock and/or particular supreme court justices was really the best way of responding to what many had concluded were entrenched, "systemic" problems within the judiciary. Rep. Marjorie Smith, for example, wanted to know whether there was "anything in this resolution which would permit us to address systemic problems and we can have a long list of what those might be, including how we appoint judges, the judicial conduct committee, a unified bar, a whole series of issues." Whatever HJC was to recommend regarding Brock and the others, asked Smith, "would that mean that everything was taken care of? … Will this resolution in anyway close off the options to deal with systemic problems?" She was not alone in wondering whether the actions directed by HR50 would really bring the state closer to the steps that needed to be taken regarding its judiciary. Rep. Sandra Keans, a member of HJC, pointedly asked whether the committee would retain the subpoena power it had been granted after its recommendations had been delivered. "[I]t is my opinion, and I think it is the opinion across the state, that there are some fundamental problems in the court," offered Keans, "and I don't see how we get at that either with a 'yes' impeach or a 'no' impeach."[3] In response, Rep. Peter Burling pointed to language in HR50 directing HJC to returning to the House "such resolutions, articles of impeachment, or other recommendations as it deems proper." That language, argued Burling, "includes within it the power to make suggestions for legislation, the powers for systemic review, look at all the kinds of things that you as a committee member may feel is in need of work by this legislature."

In fact, supporters of HR50 had to answer questions about HJC's methods, as well as its goals. Rep. Avery, alluding to allegations that the attorney general had entered a plea-bargain with Justice Thayer to secure evidence against Brock and the court itself, asked whether HJC would be similarly empowered to trade for testimony. Rep. Burling replied that HJC was an investigative body, not a prosecutorial one, and had not been granted all the powers of a prosecutor. Significantly, some representatives wondered just how transparent HJC's proceedings should themselves be. After all, reasoned many, HJC could hardly dispel the court's "veil of secrecy" by emulating it—clearly, their own hearings should be fully open and public. Indeed, Rep. Wendelboe not only urged attendance at all HJC hearings by state representatives, but recommended they "encourage the public to attend, history classes, our community TV and so on so that this truly will not be something in secrecy but will be done in the open." Rep. Jacobson, for his part, avowed "My understanding is that every meeting will be held in public … I would be opposed to anything that is done in secret. I think everything should be out in the public."[4]

In the end, those sorts of assurances evidently dispelled whatever misgivings some representatives had about HR50. With the near-unanimous vote in favor of the measure behind them, HJC members immediately set to work formalizing the rules and procedures by which they would conduct their inquiry. Special counsel Joseph Steinfield aided their deliberations by investigating state and national statutes, rules, and cases relevant to impeachment proceedings, recusal policies, improper influence on judicial personnel, and other considerations before the Committee. By April 25, HJC had determined its protocols. One of them authorized Steinfield to "take depositions and engage in other fact-finding efforts," on the understanding that his findings would be presented in an interim report to both the HJC and to House counsel "at the conclusion of that initial phase of the investigation and *before* the taking of evidence at *public* meetings" [italics added].[5]

Rep. Jacobson's assurances notwithstanding, then, the investigation was to begin with a set of closed hearings.[6] Legislators who had expected that HJC proceedings would be absolutely transparent from the outset would soon reveal the depth of their disappointment. But there was another body that felt the committee's proceedings were, on the contrary, all too open.

That was the Judicial Conduct Committee JCC, which sprang into action when Steinfield subpoenaed Howard Zibel, then JCC's executive secretary, and other JCC officers. JCC was initiating its own probe into the matters at hand, and was required by Court-written rules to protect the confidentiality of those proceedings.[7] Represented by William Saturley, it promptly filed a motion asking the supreme court to require the House Judiciary Committee to admit JCC counsel to any depositions of its own personnel, in order to advise witnesses of possible violations of JCC strictures. Steinfield was able to ward off that challenge: on May 13, the court (represented by five alternate justices, of course) accepted his argument that the motion was non-justiciable.[8] Yet many of the witnesses the House Judiciary Committee would depose (and, for that matter, that committee's own counsel) would remain quite mindful of JCC's protocols, often trimming their testimony (questions) and/or the documentation they provided (requested) accordingly.[9]

By May 30, the House Judiciary Committee had taken testimony on all aspects of the *Feld* case; on the events of February 4, 2000 within the supreme court's conference room and elsewhere; on the aftermath of those events; on the court's recusal practices; and on much more. All of it was summarized in the Interim Report that Steinfield submitted on that day. In it, Steinfield also attempted to ascertain the meaning of "bribery, corruption, maladministration or malpractice"—the impeachable offenses specified by the framers of New Hampshire's constitution—as each was likely understood in the late eighteenth century. The first two were clear enough, but not alleged in current proceedings. The latter two were alleged, but no unambiguous definition had been provided when the constitution was written, or since. "Maladministration or malpractice," Steinfield determined, must be broader in meaning than the "other high crimes and misdemeanors" mentioned alongside treason, bribery, and corruption as impeachable offenses in the federal constitution. Yet the term was not so broad that simple negligence, mismanagement, or errors in judgment would fall under it. It had to involve "intentional, or at least reckless, misconduct while serving in a position of public trust."[10]

What standard of proof, then, should HJC members use in determining whether a pattern of such misconduct had in fact occurred? That was another subject on which the state constitution was silent. The lowest standard, Steinfield noted, would be "preponderance of the evidence," as generally applied in civil cases and grand jury deliberations. But a standard connoting simply "more likely than not" seemed rather casual for so momentous an event as the impeachment of the state's highest judicial officer. The most rigorous standard would be "beyond a reasonable doubt." That, however, was ruled out; an impeachment was the equivalent of an indictment, not a conviction, and final determination of guilt or innocence lay with the Senate. What remained was the standard of "clear and convincing" evidence.[11] HJC members would eventually opt for that standard—but only by a 12–9 vote, in part because some members did not believe that any specific burden need be adopted at all.[12]

HJC's members would discuss much more that Steinfield brought to their attention throughout June, amidst public hearings aired relentlessly on New Hampshire's public television station.[13] Most of what those hearings revealed to the state's citizenry, HJC members had already heard in the investigation's initial, closed phase. But no one, within or outside HJC, could be *blasé* about what played out on television screens, and in the state and even national press, throughout June and into July.

There was, for example, the revelation that Brock might have actually conferred personally with Thayer about the staffing of the *Thayer v. Thayer* panel in the hallway of the supreme court building on February 4, after Thayer had been asked to leave the conference room. Thayer, who had declined to be interviewed by the attorney general's investigators, described that scene in his May 10 deposition before HJC.[14]

According to Thayer, he had waited in the hallway after Brock asked him to leave the conference room, until he was fetched back by—Brock himself. In the hallway, Thayer claimed, the two had engaged in a brief discussion of which judges Thayer would and wouldn't find acceptable for appointment to the panel that was to hear his wife's appeal of their divorce ruling. Specifically, Thayer claimed, Brock had told him that Pappagianis would indeed serve on the *Thayer v. Thayer* bench but not on any JCC panel concerned with Thayer's actions; and asked him whether judges Mangones and O'Neill would be acceptable to him.[15] Such an *ex parte* conversation, if it occurred, would constitute a clear and rather egregious violation of New Hampshire's Code of Judicial Conduct. Its specific victim would be Thayer's wife Judith, who had obviously never been granted input into the composition of the panel that would hear her appeal.[16]

Initially, Brock himself couldn't recall whether he had personally gone into the hallway to recall Thayer, or had asked Eileen Fox to do so.[17] But by the time of his own May 18 deposition before HJC, he was certain that "No, I absolutely never went out to get Justice Thayer."[18] The only conversation he acknowledged having with Thayer on the subject occurred later in the day, well after the conference had concluded, when, according to the chief justice, he had tried to explain to Thayer that Pappagianis was a fair-minded judge and that Thayer's outburst in the conference had been "wrong."[19]

To get to the bottom of this, HJC had undertaken a rather close investigation of just who had left the court's conference room on February 4 to summon Justice Thayer from the hallway to which he had been consigned after his outburst, and what might have been said there. Of course, no one could substantiate Thayer's claim about an *ex parte* conversation with Brock; no employee of the court on duty that day recalled seeing the two men together in the hallway. But HJC could and did investigate the question of whether Brock had ever been in the hallway alone with him, leaving the rest to representatives' own assessments of the relative reliability of Thayer's and Brock's accounts. Eileen Fox's testimony was important in this regard, since she recollected that it *had* been Brock who had brought Thayer back. And no one but Broderick was prepared to clearly affirm an alternative rendering of the scene.[20] To Brock's critics on HJC, those were grounds enough to suspect that Brock might well have been in the hallway with Thayer and, *ipso facto*, that the illicit conversation might well have occurred.

But HJC had not confined itself to recent events. On the contrary, it had chosen to scrutinize a legal matter that had arisen 13 years earlier. This was what came to be called "the *Home Gas* case."

The case hardly seemed the stuff of scandal when it first emerged—rather, it began as a fairly routine contractual dispute between two fuel companies.[21] In 1982, Home Gas Corporation, the larger of the two, had come to a distributorship agreement with Strafford Fuels designed to halt competition between the firms in the area around the city of Rochester. The agreement allowed Strafford Fuels to sell propane on behalf of Home Gas in that vicinity, and it remained in effect until 1986. In that year, however, Strafford's founder and president, Edward Dupont, concluded that the arrangement no longer served his company's best interests, and terminated the agreement without cause. The agreement Dupont had signed with Home Gas permitted that termination. But it also contained a stipulation that Strafford could not compete with Home Gas in the Rochester area, either directly or indirectly, for one year after such termination. In 1987, Home Gas sued Strafford and Dupont individually, claiming that, in various ways, they were doing just that.

But the mundane details of that suit were really not what the term "Home Gas" would come to connote in New Hampshire. Mention of it would instead conjure a complex set of charges, countercharges, clashing testimonies, and 13-year-old memories—at the center of which stood allegations of improper, politically motivated behavior by Chief Justice David Brock.[22] According to HJC's own report, those more sensational aspects of the "*Home Gas*" story came to its attention through Zibel's mention of "an old JCC matter regarding Justice Brock" and documentation subsequently supplied by Justice Johnson. In fact, the circumstances surrounding its exposure are not entirely clear.[23] But the affair's seriousness was beyond dispute. The defendant in the original *Home Gas* suit, Edward Dupont, was majority leader of the New Hampshire Senate at the time, with, as would so often be noted, considerable influence on the judiciary's budget in general and judicial salaries in particular. When HJC members, and later the Senate that took up their findings, referred to "the *Home Gas* case," they would be evoking a complex farrago of charges, countercharges, clashing testimonies, and 13-year-old memories.

The supreme court's involvement in the case had actually begun in January 1987. On January 19 of that year, Dupont's company had been ordered by Rockingham County's Superior Court Judge Kenneth McHugh to remove its heating equipment from the homes of customers who, by McHugh's reading of the firms' contractual agreement, should be served by Dupont's rival. Attorney Russell Hilliard, representing Dupont, had petitioned Judge McHugh for a stay of that judgment, arguing that removing the equipment in the dead of winter posed serious logistical difficulties. McHugh had denied the stay, so Hilliard filed a writ of *certiorari* to the supreme court on January 26; and the court had promptly granted it, without a hearing, on January 29. The case had been duly remanded, which was how it came before Judge Douglas Gray. Gray and McHugh both found the alacrity with which the court acted on the matter unusual.[24]

The case was argued before Judge Gray on March 4, 1987; he ruled against Dupont and Strafford Fuels on March 19. By Gray's account, he had not even known that Dupont was a state senator until about March 23 or 25. That, Gray claimed, was when he received a highly unusual phone call from Chief Justice Brock asking about the disposition of the case, informing him of Dupont's position, and noting that the question of judicial pay raises was one on which Dupont would have some input.[25] Such a call was, to say the least, irregular.

But Brock would insist that he never made it. Indeed, his account would diverge quite sharply from Gray's.

In Brock's telling, Senate President William Bartlett, a friend of Dupont, had mentioned the *Home Gas* matter in a meeting with the chief justice on April 24, 1987. Gray had already ruled on the merits; but various motions had been filed since his decision, and the matter remained unsettled. According to Brock, Bartlett pointed to the delay as an example of lassitude he found all too typical of the New Hampshire judiciary.[26] Brock reckoned that the delay did properly concern him, in his capacity as administrative head of the courts.[27] But the fact that rulings related to the case were still pending made any intervention by the chief justice somewhat delicate. So, Brock would later relate, he discussed the matter with his fellow justices, and concluded that he could legitimately check into the status of *Home Gas* by calling the clerk of the Rockingham County Superior Court, Ray Taylor. He would insist adamantly that he had never called Judge Gray.[28] In fact, Brock would claim that it was actually Gray who called *him*, in August, to question him about the Supreme Court's protocols on expedited rulings.[29]

Gray's unwavering rejection of Brock's telling (along with Bartlett's rejection of it, since the senate president denied ever speaking to Brock about Dupont's legal affairs) persuaded a number of HJC members.[30] Their suspicions that Brock had in fact placed the offending call to Gray were reinforced by McHugh, who confirmed that Gray had indeed told him and other colleagues, quite spontaneously, that he had received a call regarding *Home Gas* from the chief justice around March 25. Neither Gray nor anyone else ever suggested that Brock had made any direct effort to influence the judge's decision. But no one denied that such a call would be improper nonetheless, if only out of concern for appearances.[31]

Yet one of the many oddities of the matter is that it was in fact *Gray's* words, not Brock's, that had first raised eyebrows among the judiciary's ethical monitors in 1987. What actually elevated *Home Gas* to notoriety were complaints by Dupont's attorneys (and, apparently, Dupont himself) about comments Gray made in chambers—first in August 1987, again in January 1988—suggesting that Dupont's political status had become a factor in the judicial process. Gray, it was claimed, had suggested that this was first indicated by the rapidity of the Supreme Court's response to Hilliard's request for a stay of Judge McHugh's ruling of January 19, 1987.[32]

According to Brock, Gray's statements were reported to him at different times by Bartlett, Dupont, and Hilliard.[33] In fact, the chief justice was able to produce a letter he had sent Bartlett dated November 19, 1987, in which Brock described himself as "disturbed by what you told me about the alleged remarks of the judge in our mutual friend's case."[34] In that letter, Brock had explained to Bartlett that, with aspects of the case still unresolved, the affected party could either move for the judge's recusal or submit a complaint to the JCC. He had gone on to assure the senate president that, even if neither course was chosen, the matter would nonetheless be fully investigated after the case's resolution. On January 12, 1988, he would say much the same in a letter to Dupont, adding that it would be inappropriate for he himself to meet with a litigant to discuss the case while in process.[35]

Yet Gray's alleged misstatements received no attention until early 1989.[36] By then, the *Home Gas* case was no longer in litigation. But the claims against Gray could not be referred to the JCC, because that body considered cases that came to it only within one year of the incident in question. David Souter, then a member of the New Hampshire Supreme Court, had persuaded his colleagues that allegations regarding prejudicial statements by a judge simply had to be investigated, and if JCC could not do so then the Supreme Court must undertake an inquiry of its own.

The initial phase of that inquiry was delegated to Superior Court Judge Joseph DiClerico, who informed Gray of the complaints against him in a letter of March 27, 1989. Gray had responded indignantly. He claimed that this was the first time he had heard of the charges and, for that matter, the first ethical investigation he had heard of that was not conducted by the JCC—to which no one had reported the (alleged) remarks when they had (allegedly) been made.[37] In an interview with the justices of the supreme court on May 17, 1989, Gray piqued David Souter's attention when he referred to Brock's (alleged) phone call of March 1987 asking about the status of the case. Neither Souter nor anyone else on the court had been aware of such a call. A startled Brock denied having made it, insisting that Gray had instead called him.

But, once again, Souter had insisted that the allegation—this time Gray's, against Brock—must be investigated and reported. The fact that the JCC could take no action after the passage of two years, he argued, did not excuse the court from its own responsibility to investigate. Indeed, in light of a written statement by McHugh and testimony by others confirming that Gray had indeed announced, unprompted, that Brock had placed the call in late March 1987, Brock's four colleagues on the court decided that the call probably had been made, and said so in their report to JCC. That report implicitly allowed that the charge against Brock had in fact deterred the court's investigation of Gray. Whatever the truth of the matter, the appearance of impropriety by the chief justice had disinclined the court to take any further action against Judge Gray, lest that be seen as an attempt to deflect blame from the more powerful jurist.[38]

Yet Brock himself had been quite willing to sign his name to the court's report to JCC, even while maintaining that he had never called Gray.[39] The chief justice apparently considered the matter of who had called whom secondary to the question of prejudicial statements allegedly made by Gray in chambers. But a sizable number of HJC members thought otherwise. After all, Brock's own colleagues on the supreme court, along with a respected superior court judge, had determined that he had in fact made the call, and failed to report it. Indeed, Brock's own claim to have taken elaborate precautions to avoid the appearance of impropriety confirmed the gravity of the matter. Even those not convinced of Brock's maleficence had to grant it some weight in their deliberations.

BROCK TESTIMONY BEFORE HOUSE JUDICIARY COMMITTEE

Unfortunately for Brock, his own testimony in the initial phase of the HJC investigation did nothing to dispel the dark cloud hovering over him. His initial round of questioning by Steinfield on May 18 grew testy on particular points, such as Brock's explanation of how he had come to conclude that actions by Thayer that he had initially found unobjectionable should be reported to JCC, after all.[40] Both sides expressed frustration with what seemed to be ambiguous JCC policies regarding the confidentiality of materials it had collected during the course of its own investigations—policies by which important documents (e.g., the court's missive to JCC) had been rendered inaccessible or redacted.[41] But far worse than any of this for Brock was his subsequent testimony, on May 19 and May 24. A majority of House Judiciary Committee members would conclude that, at various points on those days, the chief justice of the New Hampshire Supreme Court deliberately lied to the HJC.

Like most judges, David Brock was unaccustomed to being deposed, let alone required to defend his integrity in public. An imposing man (he had served in the Marine Corps for three years after graduating from Dartmouth College in 1958), his career had been marked by distinctions and plaudits since earning his law degree at Michigan Law School in just a little more than two years. A member of the New Hampshire Bar since 1963, Brock had been appointed U.S. Attorney for the state by President Nixon in 1969, and held that position until 1972. After an unsuccessful attempt to secure the Republican Party's nomination for the office of U.S. Senator in 1973, a rare failure, his political aspirations were dropped. His judicial career, however, blossomed. In 1976, he was appointed superior court judge; by 1978, he was a supreme court justice; in 1986, he became that body's chief justice. The outcry over *Claremont*, and the 1999 bill of address, had served to remind him that even the most accomplished public figures are not immune from criticism, or personal attack. But nothing had prepared David Brock for the proceedings in which he was now enmeshed.

On May 19, HJC counsel Steinfield pressed Brock on why, given statutory language on public officials' duty to report any attempt to exert "improper influence" on them, he had not reported the threatening statements Thayer had made on February 14 until his first interview with the attorney general's investigators on March 10. After all, by Brock's own account he had actually recognized an obligation to report "pretty soon after it occurred."[42] The chief justice's explanation was that, in addition to the concern both he and Justice Broderick felt for Thayer's mental state, Brock's own attorneys, Michael Ramsdell and Michael Callahan, were advising against filing a report with the AG's office at that time. Thayer, who had refused the court's offer of a voluntary leave of absence, had been suspended on February 23, and sued for wrongful dismissal the very next day. Ramsdell and Callahan feared that, given the ease of interpreting Thayer's remarks as verbalized exasperation rather than serious threats, reporting them to the AG could appear to be retaliation for his civil suit. After some delay, Brock testified, he had nonetheless opted firmly for reporting, and instructed his attorneys to draft a letter describing Thayer's language to the attorney general. On March 3, he approved the letter and authorized his attorneys to deliver it. He said he "assumed that that had been done on March 3."[43]

But the letter had not been sent, as both Brock and Steinfield knew. Shortly after its drafting, Ramsdell and Callahan, whose clients included legislative lobbyists, had elected to withdraw as Brock's counsel. The chief had replaced them with a new team headed by Ralph Lancaster, and both Lancaster and Brock had been shown all materials the attorney general had collected days before Brock's scheduled testimony. They contained no such letter. In fact, Lancaster had checked with the prior legal team, confirmed that it had not been sent, and so informed his client. Yet on March 19, when Steinfield directly asked if he knew whether the letter had ever been sent, Brock answered "Of my personal knowledge, no," and "My assumption is [that] it was filed with the attorney general."[44] Those aware of what was and wasn't in the materials distributed by the AG's office prior to May 19 might have read those remarks charitably (as annoying but minor verbal infelicities, barely relevant to the main points at issue) or uncharitably (as deliberate obfuscations of the truth, perhaps designed to make Brock look more scrupulously law-abiding than he had been). Most HJC members would opt for the latter, in part because of further admissions Steinfield elicited from Brock on May 24.

On that day, under Steinfield's insistent questioning, Brock and Lancaster waived their right to confidential attorney-client communications long enough to publicly acknowledge what Lancaster had established regarding the March 3 letter, and his communication of that information to his client.[45] Steinfield made sure the point was properly underscored ("So you knew that last time? Last time you were here, you knew that this letter had not been sent to the attorney general?"), then moved on to another instance of disingenuousness. This one would prove even more damaging to the chief justice.

Also on May 19, while responding to Steinfield's questions about the *Home Gas* case, Brock had complained "Well, I wish discovery were two-sided here because I'm at a disadvantage. I don't have all the documents to refresh my memory." But Brock actually did have the documents—far more of the *Home Gas* record, in fact, than Steinfield then had. In April, he had located copies of the supreme court's own, comprehensive records on *Home Gas*—the letter by the court to JCC, plus 16 attachments—and sent them on to Lancaster. As of May 19, Steinfield had seen only a few of those materials, some of which (e.g., the court's letter to JCC) were redacted. He had secured that much of the record by subpoenaing the Rockingham County Superior Court, and didn't yet know what more there might be on *Home Gas* to see. But while questioning the chief justice on May 19, Steinfield was struck by the exactitude of Brock's recollection of some aspects of the 13-year-old *Home Gas* case, including rulings and docket entries. He suspected there was more documentation extant than he had yet seen—documentation that Brock must have reviewed it quite recently.

Ralph Lancaster, for his part, had been determined to avoid any violation by Brock of JCC strictures on the confidentiality of investigative materials in its possession. The court's materials on *Home Gas* were now in JCC's hands; and Lancaster (who was in ongoing contact with JCC's own counsel, William Saturley) assumed they were covered by those strictures. He had informed Steinfield as early as May 18 that he was petitioning JCC to waive Rule 40 on confidentiality, so the HJC Counsel would have the entire rage of *Home Gas* documentation. But as of May 19, that waiver had not been confirmed, and Lancaster had publicly and repeatedly counseled his client not to answer questions reflecting familiarity with materials held by JCC. Neither Brock nor Lancaster had stated in so many words that, out of regard for Rule 40, Brock could not reveal the contents of *Home Gas* materials that he had indeed seen; and Steinfield, for his part, did not draw that inference from Lancaster's remarks. By May 22, however, Steinfield had secured access to the entire panoply of *Home Gas* documents: the supreme court, not JCC, had yielded them, in response to yet another subpoena. There was indeed a great deal more there than the Rockingham County Superior Court had delivered—materials that, Steinfield was coming to believe, Brock must have accessed some time ago, then complained on May 19 of not having.

On May 24, in his responses to Steinfield's questions, Brock confirmed that, in fact, he had recently reviewed a wide range of *Home Gas* materials.[46] Not surprisingly, there was a decided edge in the HJC counsel's tone as he pressed Brock to explain why he had wrongly stated on May 19 that he lacked that documentation. Brock responded that, in truth, he hadn't had the materials directly in front of him while testifying then, and couldn't remember exactly when he had actually consulted them although he knew it had been fairly recently. An irritated Steinfield retorted "Well, Mr. Chief Justice, I'm going to calm down, but as you can tell, I am somewhat puzzled to learn today that you had seen all these documents. You knew I hadn't. You turned them over to your lawyer weeks before. … And there's no question that you chose not to tell me about that."[47]

Returning to the unsent March 3 letter, Steinfield read Brock's testimony of May 19 back to him and asked for an explanation. Brock tried to clear himself by proposing that in the relevant testimony, he had actually used the word "was" rather than "is" (i.e., "My assumption *was* that the letter was filed with the attorney general"). When Steinfield asked why he hadn't simply testified that, whatever his earlier belief, he had subsequently learned that the letter hadn't been sent, Lancaster interjected "He wasn't asked the question." At that point, Steinfield grew visibly angry. "I understand. And a completely responsive or completely explanatory response would have been, last week, 'But Mr. Steinfield, I have since learned that it didn't happen, didn't happen.' Isn't that right?" Brock insisted he had no intention to mislead, but Steinfield remained "chagrined to be held to the kind of you-didn't-ask-so-I-didn't-tell kind of circumstance. And I trust we won't have that from here on, okay?"

In normal times, the chief justice's statements regarding the March 3 letter and access to *Home Gas* materials might have seemed simple errors; or, perhaps, lawyerly word-parsing that stopped considerably short of outright, intentional perjury. But these were not normal times. As the HJC investigation proceeded, what became abundantly clear was just how broad and pervasive the mistrust toward Brock really was, and how deeply rooted in recent history.

Attorney General Philip McLaughlin fairly quivered with antipathy toward the chief justice and the entire supreme court when he testified on June 6. Still smarting from Brock's April 4 press conference, McLaughlin was intent on rebutting the charge that his investigation had been politically motivated, or aimed at Brock or the court in general from the beginning. The chief had brought suspicion on himself in several ways, McLaughlin testified, despite investigators' failure to unearth clear and sustainable evidence of criminal wrongdoing. In the first place, Brock had waited far too long before notifying the AG's office of Thayer's possibly criminal actions; had Howard Zibel not prepared his memorandum, McLaughlin felt, it was highly unlikely that the matter would ever have come to light. Brock had testified that, in that first part of February, he had learned that his daughter Tamara had been diagnosed with thyroid cancer; he was, he had explained, somewhat preoccupied with family matters at the time.[48]

But that made scant impression on the attorney general, certainly not enough to mitigate his suspicions of the chief justice's delay in reporting.

What did make a lasting impression on McLaughlin was a remark he said had been attributed to Brock by his attorney Michael Ramsdell when the latter personally delivered the Zibel memorandum to the attorney general on February 25. The remark was "The CJ doesn't think there is anything criminal here." McLaughlin found it highly offensive. "I didn't like that, Mr. Steinfield," he stated testily, adding "Well, the CJ might not have thought this was criminal, but the AG did."[49] No one listening to McLaughlin's explanation of why the remark had so riled him could have failed to think of the Fairbanks affair, with the suspicions it had aroused of JCC coverups and criminal malfeasance concealed by invocations of confidentiality.

> I read into that that if I chose to investigate this and consider it non-criminal and close it, because the JCC would deal with it—the JCC, which exists because the Supreme Court has the power to create a JC. Its rules, in fact, are law. And then, its subsidiary rule is secrecy, and nothing ever comes of it. The public never knows. This is the invitation that I heard. And that is the invitation that I rejected. I thought there was something here that deserved to be looked at.[50]

McLaughlin went much further. Brock, he testified, had been decidedly unhelpful to the AG's investigators, and might even have deliberately obfuscated when questioned by them. He had not even revealed Thayer's threats of February 14–15 until well into the interview. Investigator Christopher Domian had found Brock's responses unsatisfyingly vague, and asked the chief justice whether he ever kept any notes on the matter. "And as it was reported to me," testified McLaughlin, "Judge Brock's response to that was 'You're good. You finally asked the right question.' This isn't a game, Mr. Steinfield. This is a criminal investigation. I didn't like the idea that we had to ask the right question of the chief justice of the New Hampshire Supreme Court in order to get relevant information."[51] If anyone in government had directed the attorney general's investigation from Thayer toward Brock and the court in general, McLaughlin flatly announced, it was David Brock himself.[52] Furthermore, the attorney general was unapologetic about declining to prosecute Thayer. In fact, he stated for the record that he would have been quite prepared to formally immunize Thayer prior to calling him before a grand jury, if that had been necessary to get the testimony needed for the prosecution of "some other judge."[53]

The entire court, McLaughlin felt, had conducted itself poorly throughout the affair. He was particularly irritated by the claim, made by all the justices his investigators had questioned, that they had not been properly informed of the exact nature of the investigation, and would have responded differently to particular questions if they had been. "The judges of the Supreme Court are, from my point of view, citizens of the State of New Hampshire," McLaughlin said. "Every citizen has a duty to give information known to them about criminal misconduct." That was a criticism that Michael Zuckerman amplified when he testified, on June 7. The justices, Zuckerman insisted, had hardly been ambushed. They had all been notified at the outset that the AG's office was investigating the contents of the Zibel memorandum, which in describing Thayer's actions on the *Feld* case clearly implicated the court's general practice of allowing justices to participate in deliberations on cases from which they were recused. "I find it troubling and somewhat remarkable that these comments can be made," Zuckerberg said. "The justices knew, because we told them, that we were conducting a criminal investigation which could well result in a criminal charge. They're justices of the Supreme Court. They know that if a criminal charge is brought, what they told us was going to be discoverable to the defendant, and would be turned over. There was certainly no suggestion in any of these interviews that the information that was being provided to us was in some way going to be shrouded in secrecy."[54]

What the justices had actually said to McLaughlin and his investigators, and what Brock had said on April 4, was that they would have supplied more information about the general benefits of the court's recusal policy if they had known that it had become a focus of the investigation. But what McLaughlin and Zuckerman heard were assertions of privilege by justices persuaded that they, unlike any other witness in a criminal investigation, should be allowed to decide which aspects of the truth were relevant and which should remain confidential. Each side saw in the other's *modus operandi* a rather relaxed attitude toward due process; each put the darkest construction on the other's intentions. But that should have surprised no one. Each's assessment of the other had been souring for quite some time.

Brock, who had probably expended more time and energy lobbying legislators than prior chief justices for the simple reason that so many changes in judicial administration had been proposed or concluded on his watch, freely admitted an abiding dislike of politics and politicians.[55] The world inhabited by judges, he affirmed, was very different from that of politicians, and he would have much preferred to remain within the milieu he understood. "It's very difficult for us to participate in the political arena," Brock testified, since "even when we come over to the legislature to take positions on bills that affect the administration of justice, we're criticized for people—by people as lobbying and we shouldn't be over suggesting what legislators should do; and we'd been under attack for so long."[56]

But if Brock found the ways of legislators distasteful, they were no less put off by his—and had been, long before the McLaughlin Report or the HJC investigation. That, at any rate, was what former Senate President William

Bartlett conveyed during his testimony on June 7. Bartlett claimed that he could remember only one face-to-face conversation with the chief justice, and it hadn't been a pleasant one. "There's no mystery throughout these legislative halls," said Bartlett, "that the chief justice and I weren't on the same terms about how the court operated, and that he wanted his budget passed as was." Bartlett claimed that when he had refused to skirt the usual process of budgetary review, the chief justice had threatened "that he would order us to do his budget, as printed." When Steinfield requested clarification, Bartlett reiterated that Brock had simply announced that "the court had the power to order us to fund the court in the manner that he thought was proper."[57] At that point, Bartlett said, he had simply told Brock that someone with a "different attitude" than the chief justice should serve as the court's liaison to the legislature, and Justice Johnson had eventually been chosen. "I was quite vocal in my thought process regarding pay raises and judges' pay raises in particular," Bartlett continued. Then he elaborated.

> When I first came to the Senate, the unified court system came forth. And I was opposed to the unified court system. And I think—and I really—I assume—this is an assumption—that Dave Brock was pushing for the unified court. … So at that time it was contentious because they were trying to build what I thought was an empire. So that didn't set well with the court system. And so I think that carried on throughout it. You asked me about the Judicial Conduct Committee. I didn't like that part of the—part of the proceedings and I was very vocal about that. I was—objected to judges serving for lifetime. I go back to my youth, and my father was the county commissioner. I saw that I thought my perception of judges were I thought they should spend a little more time on the bench and get things moving. And Dave really thought that his judges were getting underpaid in reflecting the rest of the New England states. … and so we just didn't see eye to eye on those issues.[58]

What all of this had to do with the HJC's investigation into any specific, impeachable actions committed by Brock or any other justice was—nothing, and everything. With the level of mistrust toward Brock personally, and toward the court and judiciary he led, that Bartlett (along with McLaughlin, Zuckerman, and so many others) had evinced, it was hardly surprising that by the time the HJC investigation closed, a clear majority within the committee was strongly inclined toward impeachment.

A minority of HJC members remained opposed. But the most telling split within HJC was not the entirely natural one between majority and minority viewpoints. Rather, it was a split *within* the larger, anti-Brock bloc. That split emerged because the path HJC had taken was not the one that all members would have chosen. In fact, it might not have been the path expected or preferred by representatives who, at the very outset of HJC's investigations, had raised important questions on the floor of the House about the proper focus and purpose of the entire undertaking.

In the view of HJC member Paul Mirski, especially, the committee's investigation had fallen scandalously short of its potential, and a crucial opportunity had been missed. Brock's impeachment, to him, was obviously called for. But the impeachment of this particular jurist should have been only the beginning of HJC's work, not its end point—merely a springboard to the broad, deep, and open examination of the New Hampshire judiciary itself that the committee really should be conducting, and would be if Mirski and his (admittedly, few) allies had their way. The judiciary was a branch of government that, in their view, had clearly run amok, and more than one head would need to roll if it was to be safely returned to what HJC's militants considered its constitutional limits. But Mirski had been disappointed by the leadership provided by Chairman Henry Mock, and frustrated by the reluctance of even the anti-Brock bloc to endorse his own program. Tensions between Mirski and Mock finally boiled over on the floor of the House of Representatives on June 27, the day when Steinfield released his final report to HJC members and House Counsel.[59]

On that day, Mirski took to the rostrum to apologize to friends and supporters in the House at large for having failed to undo HJC's decision to close the initial phase of its investigation to the public, and to secure agreement within the committee to subpoena whoever at least 5 of its 21 members wanted to interrogate. To Mirski, HJC's investigation was a golden opportunity to fully reveal "the true dimension of the court's potential duplicity and corruption" to the people of New Hampshire. But doing that would require deposing, for example, Judith Thayer (who, Mirski proposed, was prepared to reveal that "Stephen Thayer complained regularly of a working majority on the court which predetermined the outcome of cases"); Emile Bussiere (described as "Justice Thayer's mentor and bank," who might well reveal far more than was yet suspected about what his relationship with Thayer had meant to Bussiere's own "friends, clients, and other members of the New Hampshire Bar"); and former gubernatorial aide Michael O'Malley (who might reveal far more than was yet understood about "what truly motivated the particular direction and thrust of the AG's report" and why it had not been issued to the Executive Council, an elected body that monitors certain functions of the governor's office).[60]

Mirski had learned, he explained, the depravity to which the judicial branch had sunk in December 1997, when HJC was attempting to get to the bottom of the Fairbanks scandal. He revealed that HJC had voted to subpoena records of the Judicial Conduct Committee back then, but been thwarted when the majority and minority leaders of the House had joined forces to lobby intensively for a reversal of that vote. That, said Mirski, was when

"I learned the extent to which the New Hampshire Bar's bluebloods were prepared to circle the wagon;" "how aggressive the Judiciary's power elite could be in defense of wrongful behavior by one of their own;" and, above all, "what power and influence the chief justice was able to exert on legislative leadership."

Mock responded both to Mirski's specific charge that the chairman had flatly reneged on a pledge to grant the minority the subpoena latitude Mirski had requested and to the general notion that HJC was taking the path of political expedience. "From the very first inception of HR50," Mock stated, "outside forces have done their damnedest to take over this investigation and it was I who stood in their way and it was 21 other members who stood with me." He didn't specify the "outside forces" referenced, but he did insist that "Henry Mock never, ever made a promise that he would subpoena anyone that a minority of the committee wanted unless he agreed with it." "House Resolution 50 told us to investigate within the confines of the attorney general's report and wherever that might take us," asserted Mock. "It wasn't about Claremont and it wasn't about comments made between a husband and his wife. Sorry." He concluded with the somewhat cryptic remark that "Some people don't know when they are ahead."[61]

Mock's position would prevail. But the decision to eschew the broad, wide-ranging inquiry Mirski wanted in favor of a focus on Brock personally was a pivotal one. It meant that whatever opportunity the proceedings might have provided to seriously air, and perhaps begin healing, the rift that had opened between the legislative and judicial branches of state government would be lost.

HOUSE DEBATE ON JULY 12, 2000

On July 12, 2000, the New Hampshire House of Representatives debated and voted on each of the three articles of impeachment that HJC recommended be brought against Chief Justice Brock. Brock stood accused of "maladministration and malpractice" on the basis of his presumed call to Judge Gray (Article 1); his presumed *ex parte* conversations with recused justices on the Thayer divorce panel, especially those with Thayer himself (Article 2); and his presumed perjury before HJC, apparently delivered "with the intention of hindering the HR50 investigation" on various matters (Article 3).[62] The House would also debate HJC's recommendation that special legislation be passed (HB1500) allowing the chief justice to resign his office between the time of an impeachment by the House and trial by the Senate, so that he could receive the retirement benefits he would have received if he had served until the age of 65.

HJC also noted a few "areas of concern" within the judicial branch itself, "which may fall within the purview of the legislative branch" and "may be considered for judicial reform." These included the appointment process for substitute judges; terms for all judges; the independence of the JCC; and mandatory New Hampshire Bar Association membership for attorneys. No specific recommendations or suggestions on those practices, however, were offered. What was put forth instead was an assertion that "the culture of confidentiality which prevailed in the New Hampshire Supreme Court led to a callousness in the management of our Judiciary, engendering maladministration and malpractice, consequently culminating in these historic impeachment proceedings."[63]

It was a tense, raucous session, remarkable not only for the gravity of the matter under consideration but for the level of passion the debate engendered. For on that historic day, representatives would reveal, in word and deed, just how deep, how widespread—among some, barely containable—their fury really was. The debate had an ebb and flow of its own, which in the end carried representatives well beyond the specific resolutions HJC had brought to the House. In fact, it often flowed well beyond the alleged transgressions of David Brock. What is clear from a study of the day's actions and utterances is how mindful representatives were of the historic shift in the status of the Supreme Court itself, in fact of the state judiciary as a whole, that had been occurring since the 1960s. It was an historic day, and not only because the impeachment of a chief justice was unprecedented. It was an historic day precisely because delegates were consciously reckoning with the state's own history.

At the very outset, Henry Mock, speaking for the pro-impeachment majority on HJC, had to importune Speaker Donna Sytek for order ("Madam Speaker, I can barely hear myself, if we are going to impeach someone I think we ought to be listening").[64] Once he had it, Mock explicitly linked the malfeasance he felt had been uncovered to the court's historic push for independence. "This whole shroud of secrecy in the court began 40 to 50 years ago under the disguise of judicial independence," Mock explained. "Funny things started happening to our Constitution, like little amendments that the people didn't see when they voted. Remember, 73-a again, and then there is Article 4, Part II that got a little parenthesis in there, the voters never saw it. … Slowly the court has become so independent that it has gotten itself into trouble."[65]

Paul Mirski, as usual, went further. In his view, it wasn't some misapplication or exaggeration of the principle of judicial independence that was to blame. The principle itself was to be rejected—as it had been, Mirski argued, by the patriots who had thrown off British rule and framed the state's constitution. Articulating a notably clear and certain vision of state history,

Mirski described "The integration between the merchant class, the judiciary and the power elite" that had prevailed prior to the Revolution, an arrangement that he claimed served to impoverish yeomen by legally blocking their access to hard currency. Those yeomen, Mirski had claimed, had naturally hated the very idea of a judiciary outside popular control, and had deliberately precluded it by constitutional design. "There is no such thing as an institutional separate co-equal branch of government called the judiciary in New Hampshire," Mirski asserted. "The language in Article 37 that says that the separation of powers ought to be kept apart as a free society will admit is an invitation to legislative oversight. It is not language that separates the judiciary from that oversight."[66]

Mirski's notion of judicial independence as a perversion of New Hampshire's founding principles was vigorously contested by, among others, Rep. Cynthia Dokmo, representing HJC's anti-impeachment minority. "It is the Supreme Court and the courts of this land and in this state that guard your individual and minority rights," Dokmo insisted, citing examples she may have hoped would resonate with conservative representatives ("It is the Supreme Court that the *Manchester Union Leader* will go to to preserve the right of freedom of press … It is the Supreme Court that you will go to to uphold your right to bear arms"). Dokmo argued passionately that the charges against Brock, even if true, bore no trace of the ill-intent, calculation, and regularity that, according to Steinfield, characterized genuine "maladministration and malpractice." She maintained that a vote to impeach Brock for the actions in question would "open up the flood gates for impeachment resolution after impeachment resolution." In fact, Rep. Martha Solow (who coauthored with Dokmo the HJC's minority report opposing impeachment) feared that the judicial system had already begun to "melt into turmoil." "No one, I mean almost no one, in this legislature had ever heard of a bill of address before 1999," Solow explained. "Now we talk about how many bills of address we will have for the next session. In one year the monster has grown."[67]

But Solow, Dokmo, and others in their camp knew full well that, to a great many of their colleagues, the prospect of accelerated assaults on particular jurists was hardly disconcerting. There were "some people that might think that is great, because they don't like the court system," acknowledged Dokmo.[68] In fact, the "moans from the audience" she had to endure while making the anti-impeachment case indicated how intense that hostility really was—and how wide its locus. Rep. James Craig, who would vote for each article of impeachment, suggested that it now extended well beyond Brock, beyond the court, even beyond jurists, to practicing lawyers such as himself. "I've taken a lot of grief in newspapers and I've gotten writings from people that say, 'Well, you're a lawyer,'" revealed Craig. "Somebody told me

I looked like a plant for the New Hampshire Bar Association in the hearings. I just want to say here that I resent those remarks."[69]

Rep. Tony Soltani rose to articulate the perceptions that fueled that hostility. What the HJC investigation had confirmed to him was that "there are two classes of people that can resort to courts. One, the disadvantaged, the vulnerable, the poor, the peasants. The other one, the powerful, the invulnerable, the wealthy, the princes." The former, in Soltani's view, included Judith Thayer, who "was perceived as powerless. Therefore, she was preyed upon." Soltani found that "dichotomy … repulsive beyond belief" and argued that it constituted malpractice and maladministration by any common-sense reckoning, no matter what the lawyers in their midst might say ("don't let anybody kid you, malpractice and maladministration is exactly what you think it is. You are as knowledgeable about that as any Harvard or Yale graduate").[70]

Yet despite the force of these background concerns—about either judicial arrogance or judicial independence, either a judiciary or a legislature run amok—representatives constrained themselves to remain focused on the specific misdeeds attributed to David Brock, at least during the debates on each specific article of impeachment that constituted the first part of that day's work. Indeed, opponents of impeachment found themselves at a decided disadvantage whenever Brock's own record reclaimed the spotlight. Even they felt obliged to express frustration with, variously, his administrative practices, his testimony before HJC, and his general relations with the legislature.

"If we could impeach for stupidity, we certainly should," offered anti-impeachment HJC member Robert Rowe, "because without a doubt the Supreme Court was run inefficiently and with stupidity."[71] Rep. Solow labeled Brock's testimony "evasive, weasely … I found him combative. I found him arrogant."[72] Rep. Nancy Ford, another member of HJC's minority, rued the "legendary" battles Brock had had with Senate President Bartlett over nearly every aspect of the court's, and in fact the entire judiciary's, renovated standing ("over the budget, over judicial pay raises, over the policy of the Judicial Conduct Committee, over the independence of the court, over the unified court").[73]

But neither personal dislike, nor administrative complaints, nor even philosophical objections should lead the chamber into an unfair or irrational indictment, insisted Brock's defenders. Rep. Rowe, himself a judge, cautioned the House against scapegoating the chief justice for what were in fact structural problems in need of structural reform. "I do emphatically believe in judicial reform," Rowe said, adding that in the course of its investigation HJC had found "a great number of things that need to be changed and will be changed." But Brock's errors, argued Rowe, simply did not evince the evil or corrupt intent that "malpractice and maladministration" necessarily connoted. The worst of those errors, in fact, were in Rowe's view probably born of nothing but Brock's compassion for Thayer—ill-considered, perhaps, but an understandable misstep to anyone familiar with the interpersonal dynamics at work within an institution like the New Hampshire Supreme Court.[74]

Others in the anti-impeachment camp raised due-process questions throughout the debates on the articles of impeachment. Some regarded investigative practices. At the outset, Dokmo and Solow described the McLaughlin Report that had triggered HJC's investigation as "flawed and incomplete."[75] McLaughlin's investigators, after all, had chosen not to reveal to the three justices they questioned the crucial fact that those justices themselves were under investigation. That omission, according to Dokmo and Solow, reason or opportunity to explain or defend the practices they described.[76] Those representatives found similar flaws in the investigation that had determined that Brock had made an inappropriate phone call to Judge Gray on the *Home Gas* case. HJC had relied heavily on the supreme court's own report on the entire matter, which had indeed concluded that the call had most likely been made. But, Dokmo and Solow noted, the court had reached that conclusion after hearing only from Judges Gray and McHugh (and the latter's testimony, at best, merely confirmed the former's *belief* that the call had been made). No one had actually questioned Raymond Taylor, the clerk whom Brock insisted he had contacted.[77]

Rep. Solow also raised pointed questions about the quality of evidence on Brock's alleged *ex parte* hallway conversation with Thayer. Whether Brock had or hadn't physically summoned Thayer, asked Solow, how could Thayer's claim that the two had improperly discussed court staffing be deemed more credible than Brock's denial—when it was Thayer who had barely escaped criminal indictment; Thayer who alone had a personal interest in discrediting the court as a body; and Thayer who, immunized from prosecution, possessed the means to do so?[78]

None of those points, however, made the slightest difference to the outcome. Procedural and evidentiary concerns were easily deflected by Rep. Mock or another member of HJC's majority by noting that approval of the articles would simply send the matter to the Senate for trial, where the full truth would certainly be ascertained.[79] All three were, in fact, easily approved. But the House was not finished venting its rage on Brock. On the contrary, that rage seemed to intensify. Representatives would decide that the HJC's majority had been entirely too lenient toward the chief justice—an error they did not intend to let stand.

Immediately after passage of Article 3, Rep. Alf Jacobson rose to introduce, as a floor amendment, a fourth article of impeachment indicting Brock for permitting and overseeing the court's recusal practices. Jacobson, a member of HJC, had proposed this article to that body during its deliberations. HJC had voted it down, mainly on the grounds that the policy had been in effect for some time (although no one could confirm exactly when it had been initiated, or by whom). But it was resurfacing at a perfect time, from the point of view of Brock's antagonists—just when the tide of hostility toward the chief justice and all that he represented seemed to be cresting. Rep. Mock, in particular, hammered away at the hypocrisy of the supreme court's recusal policy. He asked the many representatives "who sit on planning boards, school boards, boards of selectmen" to recall "how very, very strict the Supreme Court has been about recused officials sitting on cases" before those sorts of bodies.[80] That was a rigor, Mock noted acidly, from which the justices had chosen, behind closed doors, to exempt themselves.[81] After noting that some 25 other states expressly forbade even the distribution of draft opinions to recused supreme court justices, Jacobson and his amendment's supporters argued that a malignant practice was no less malignant for being long-standing, and that responsibility for all aspects of court administration ultimately lay with the chief justice.

But there was more on those representatives' minds than the recusal policy *per se.* Rep. Leo Pepino, for example, saw in it the court's general inclination to write its own rules, claim force of law for them, then set them beyond statutory renovation ("You must remember that every time they write a rule, for example, Article 73-a of our constitution says this rule is law, even though it might invalidate a state statute … State statutes were disregarded, court rules and state statutes were ignored").[82] Rep. Peter Bergin rose to oppose the Jacobson amendment, arguing that "the recusal policy of the court was abused, but it was abused not by just Chief Justice Brock. It was abused by every member of the court: Justice Broderick, Justice Horton, Justice Johnson, Justice Batchelder, Souter." Bergin cautioned that "if we are going to pass this article of impeachment on Justice Brock, then we might as well impeach all the other justices on the same article."[83] But widening the killing zone, of course, was precisely what a number of representatives had in mind.

The House passed the Jacobson amendment easily (244–108), adding a fourth article of impeachment to the three that HJC had initially submitted. At that point, Paul Mirski offered another floor amendment, simple in nature but profound in consequences. This one would rephrase language in the preamble to HR51, the HJC's resolution containing all three articles of impeachment. The original language formalized, in writing, the "clear and convincing evidence" standard that HJC had decided to adopt, under its own legal counsel's guidance, when it had initiated its investigation. Mirski proposed eliminating that phrase "clear and convincing evidence" from the text.

The explicit purpose, as Rep. Soltani explained at length, was reconfiguring the impeachment action as a fully political action, rather than a quasi-juridical one. Each member of the House, Soltani argued, had the responsibility to represent his constituents as his conscience dictated. "You as individuals decide what the standard of evidence is, what the impeachable conduct is and whether there is sufficient facts to send the case to the Senate for trial," Soltani insisted. "You do that on behalf of your constituents. Any invasion of that right is a derogation of your right and thereby your voters' rights. It just cannot happen." Including the offending phrase "clear and convincing evidence" in the resolution, Soltani claimed, amounted to "turning a political process into a legal process by additional legal mumbo-jumbo which means nothing at all."

Clearly, some representatives did not see the removal of David Brock as the endgame. They had bigger, or at least additional, fish to fry, and excising the "clear and convincing evidence" standard would make it much easier to go after them. Without that standard, for instance, the bar might well be low enough to indict other justices along with Brock. Furthermore, configuring the impeachment of a justice as an openly political act with significantly looser juridical moorings would have a lasting impact, well beyond the matters at hand. The legislature was, after all, establishing historic precedent in this case—letting justices know that impeachment standards could be whatever standards the peoples' elected representatives chose to apply might serve to more effectively restrain future courts, as well as this one.[84] The question was: how far beyond the specific terms of HR51 were representatives willing to go?

By this time, the House had been debating the impeachment of David Brock for seven hours. They had considered each article contained under HR51 separately, under the understanding that "clear and convincing evidence" had indeed been marshaled in support of each, according to HJC's majority, after its own investigation. That is, each of those articles had come to the floor of the House with the endorsement of most of the people who were most familiar with the facts. That had indeed made a difference, and it seemed to many representatives a little late, and arguably more than a little deceptive, to remove that imprimatur now. Rep. Solow stated, plainly and effectively, that "If we adopt this amendment, we will be speaking falsely because the committee did adopt its proposal by clear and convincing evidence."[85] In the end, a majority of representatives (231) would agree with her.

It is notable, however, that no fewer than 113 representatives found themselves unmoved by those compunctions. Rep. Benjamin DePecol, for example, flatly stated "I never used clear and convincing evidence to make my decision. The burden of proof that I used was did it offend me enough that I was willing to impeach a sitting member of the court." DePecol found the "clear and convincing" standard both vague and limiting ("Now this clear and convincing is kind of nefarious. I mean, I can't define it"). He was not alone, nor was this reversal enough to convince Mirski and his associates that they had overreached or that it was time to pull back.[86] In fact, those representatives might have been heartened by the tone of the debate on the next item before the chamber.

This one involved legislation that would have adopted HJC's suggestion that Brock be enabled to resign with a full pension if he voluntarily resigned from the court. The original bill stipulated that the 64-year-old chief justice would begin collecting the pension when he reached the regular retirement age of 65 only if he stepped down *prior* to the initiation of a full Senate trial. Rep. Merton Dyer, however, put forward an amendment removing that stipulation. He did so, he explained, because "it looked like we were driving him or holding a club to his head to get out."[87] Dyer assured the House that the amended measure provided nothing for Brock if he tried and convicted by the Senate; but if acquitted there, his pension was guaranteed if he chose resignation. That, Dyer felt, was a course the legislature should encourage, simply in the interests of restoring normalcy to the court.[88]

In considering the matter, representatives had complex legal and financial implications to weigh (e.g., whether the measure would violate IRS regulations for tax-qualified pension plans, or even remove the state's judicial pension plan from the ranks of tax-qualified plans). They were also aware that any measure passed would require Senate action, which at that point was hardly predictable. But apart from the complexities of tax law and the murkiness of Senators' sentiments, the salient point in the debate was simple: should David Brock be granted a degree of relief from his ordeal? Dyer and others insisted that their main concern was the effective functioning of the court after this prolonged trauma, and that any measure promoting that end was worthwhile. But such was the level of rage at Brock that, to most representatives, it simply wasn't worthwhile enough.

Supporters pointed to Brock's 25 years on the bench, mostly honorable; the tantalizing nearness of his pension; the apparent pettiness of denying it ("Isn't impeachment enough?" asked Rep. William Rose plaintively).[89] But the more common sentiment was voiced by an incredulous Rep. Leo Pepino: "Here is a person we are talking about impeaching and we are going to reward him?"[90] "What do you think your constituents are going to think?" asked Rep. Fran Wendelboe. "I think it would be a pretty hard sell to justify giving him a sweetheart goodbye, a golden handshake." "Give me a break!" exploded an exasperated Rep. Laura Pantelakos. "The House of Representatives is a place where laws are made, not a place that says, 'We know you did wrong, but if you will resign, not cost us any more money or time, or headaches, we will reward you and give you everything you ask for.'"[91] More personally, Rep. Neil Kurk stressed the fact that Brock himself had led the fight against vested, contributory pensions for judges—had they been adopted, the question would be entirely moot. But, no less profligate with public funds than with judicial favors to associates, the chief justice had brought this reversal, too, upon himself.[92] Dyer's amendment was easily voted down, as was another reducing the offer to 80 percent of the pension.

But Brock was not the object of the next floor amendment brought before the House, this one in the context of debate on HR52, which recommended that no article of impeachment be brought against Justice Horton. Paul Mirski's floor amendment would have altered the bill to bring two articles of impeachment against Justice Horton, for participating in an illegitimate recusal policy and for failing to publicly disclose that policy.[93] HJC had already considered that option, and voted by a resounding 19–3 tally not to bring it to the House floor. But that was before the House had decided to add a fourth article of impeachment to the three HJC had recommended. That move, Mirski argued, "changed the dynamic of today's proceedings and this is why. The recusal policy of the court is not a policy for which the chief justice is solely responsible … The majority of the justices on the court were perfectly willing, interested, in having the recusal policy be a part of their daily procedural activities."[94]

Rep. Gregory Carson opposed Mirski's amendment, on the grounds that it represented something uncomfortably close to the retroactive criminalization of a practice presumed legal in the past.[95] "What we don't do," said Gregory, "is to go back and look in hindsight and charge people with crimes, misdemeanors, or sanction penalties against people who have practiced under those practices prior to them being wrong, immoral, illegal." The recusal practice had already been ended, he noted—why the lust to extend the ranks of the culpable? For that matter, even Henry Mock found himself unwilling to endorse Mirski's amendment. "Justice Brock was not impeached on just recusal," he noted (perhaps rankling Mirski a bit when he added that "Whatever Justice Horton did, and he did the recusal bit, whatever he did certainly didn't rise to clear and convincing evidence").[96] Mock further noted that HJC, in considering the range of options open to it, had considered reprimanding both Justices Horton and Broderick, but had found no constitutional provision for such an action ("You can impeach or you can address, and it wasn't a choice we had").[97]

Mirski's amendment was defeated, 190 to 135. But Rep. Robert Boyce, for one, was not prepared to let the matter drop. He registered a formal protest—then rose to express a level of mistrust of the judiciary and even of the legislature itself that would have been even more startling had much of it not already been expressed by Paul Mirski on June 27.[98]

After complaining about the general timidity of HJC's initiatives, Boyce actually went further than Mirski had. Mock's and HJC's decision not to subpoena former Justice Souter, or to in other ways widen its investigatory range, was, Boyce boldly asserted, nothing less than "an attempt to shield from the scrutiny of the Legislature and thereby the public certain current and past members of the Judiciary, the Executive and perhaps the Legislative branches of the state government." Had others been questioned, Boyce wondered, "Would we find collusion between the Governor and members of the court or its staff? Would questioning Justice Souter have exposed further depth of the problems just now being exhumed? Or would the integrity of the U.S. Supreme Court be questioned if it were learned that the flaws in judgment exhibited by members of our Court had parallels and precedents there?" Returning to New Hampshire, Boyce asked "Would a wider investigation reveal as fact what many believe, that those responsible for the cover-up of the corruption of Judge Fairbanks have been elevated to the highest levels in the state and that these people cannot stand scrutiny in the light of day and are in a position to thwart the Legislature's investigation?" Finally, he announced "I for one am not satisfied that this investigation has been thorough nor without bias. That many members of the committee are also members of the Bar and others derive their income from or are married to other members of the Bar leads me to wonder whom these members are serving—their constituents or the Unified Bar."[99]

As Boyce's speech demonstrated, Paul Mirski was not the only representative holding the view that the judicial of branch of New Hampshire state government contained far more rot than could be cleansed by the impeachment of David Brock. Undeterred by the failure of his effort to impeach Justice Horton, Mirski submitted another amendment (4810h) to HR50, aiming now for the impeachment of Justice Broderick ("Same argument, different judge," he explained).[100] At that point, Rep. Steve Vaillancourt made a speech remarkable for its passion and breadth, even on a day that had witnessed so many remarkable speeches.

Vaillancourt began by recollecting a speech made by U.S. Sen. John McCain in which McCain had praised the heroism of a fellow POW in the Hanoi Hilton who had insisted on gathering materials with which to sew an American flag despite the certainty of beating by his captors. The sacrifices these men had made, Vaillancourt said, gave new meaning to the words "liberty and justice for all" in the Pledge of Allegiance, and he had resolved to do everything in his power to see that those words continued to apply in New Hampshire. That, to him, clearly meant indicting Justice Broderick, who, if not as guilty as Chief Justice Brock, had certainly aided and abetted the former's crimes. "But let's compare it to the conspiracy of murder," proposed Vaillancourt, "and I use those words reluctantly, but you know, if somebody drives the get-away car in a murder conspiracy, according to the law, that individual is just as culpable, every bit as culpable, as the man who actually pulled the trigger."[101]

Continuing the analogy to gunplay, the representative argued that post hoc claims by shooters that they hadn't known the gun was loaded should carry no weight—especially in light of the ongoing havoc that New Hampshire's judiciary was wreaking on its citizens. For what made Vaillancourt's speech so memorable was its closing:

> Justice Brock and Justice Broderick both knew the gun was loaded and they didn't want to point it at their friend Justice Thayer, so what they did to that gun is, they pointed it at the judicial system of this state, at every one of us and they fired that gun and if we let them get away with it today, even though Justice Broderick may only be the get-away car driver, then we have failed to do the duty for every other individual in this state, people like Carl Graf who because of the arrogant nature that the court has engendered are languishing in our prisons, because if you read this article in the *Laconia Citizen* recently, this same kind of thing is happening all over because this kind of mentality has been allowed to happen by Broderick, by Brock, and by everybody.[102]

Carl Graf had been convicted in 1996 of sexually assaulting a minor. He had appealed in 1999, claiming that the court had denied his constitutional due-process rights. His argument was that the court had erred by refusing to admit testimony on his own character and history, which would have shown that he was "not the type" to commit a crime of that nature; and by refusing to admit evidence on the victim's character, as well. In addition, Graf had insisted that the judge should have recused himself. The supreme court had rejected his appeal.[103]

In referring to Graf's case, Vaillancourt was clearly shaking his fist at the court *PSAE* opinion—just as speakers throughout the day had shaken rhetorical fists at the constitutional alterations of 1966 and 1977; at the *LaFrance* case, that is, the notion that Court rules could trump legislative statute; at the Fairbanks scandal; at court unification; at Court finances; at the unified bar; indeed, at every tremor that had marked the seismic shift in the state judiciary's institutional role. What had rarely been mentioned, oddly enough, was the *Claremont* case, which representatives had clearly been reluctant to raise lest impeachment be represented as mere payback for an unpopular court ruling.

But if Vaillancourt's reference to Carl Graf and the *PSAE* ruling neatly capped off that litany of complaints, his final words eloquently confirmed the overall vision to which those complaints, taken together, had finally given rise. In his suggestion of judicial malfeasance of near-apocalyptic dimensions ("this same kind of thing is happening all over"), traceable to the court but diffused now throughout the entire system ("this kind of mentality has been allowed to happen by Broderick, by Brock, and by everybody"), Vaillancourt articulated perhaps more sharply than anyone else the deep frustrations, the baffled rage, that so many representatives had felt toward the court for so long.

The House as a whole had already gone far further in expressing that rage than even the pro-impeachment majority on HJC had counseled. It would reject Mirski's attempt to impeach Broderick, as it had rejected his attempt to impeach Horton and his attempt to excise the "clear and convincing evidence" standard from the articles of impeachment themselves. But that didn't mean that passions were in any way cooling. Quite the contrary. It meant that, wisely or not, the House had elected to focus its fury on David Brock, and David Brock alone.

NOTES

1. HR50, as introduced, N.H. H.R. Jour. 13 (April 13, 2000), 571–72.

2. The phrase was used by Rep. Vaillancourt, 1 of the 58 representatives to have voted for the bill of address brought against Brock in 1999. Vaillancourt stated "I don't mean to say I-told-you-so, but I do mean to say that it was an indication a year ago that something was amiss … So here we are now back here with more evidence." Vaillancourt also felt that "Crisis is not too inflammatory a word for what these justices have potentially placed us in. They have placed our society in the danger of reverting to pre-nature, of having respect for the rule of law destroyed and reverting to the state of anarchy." Ibid., 573.

3. Ibid., 573, 575.

4. Ibid., 577.

5. HJC, *Investigation pursuant to House Resolution 50: Interim report of Special Counsel Joseph D. Steinfield* (2000), 4. Steinfield would issue the interim report, including summaries of the testimony he had taken to date, on May 30. He would issue a Memorandum of Law on June 15 and a Final Report on June 27. See HJC, *Investigation pursuant to House Resolution 50: Supplemental memorandum of law by Special Counsel Joseph D. Steinfield* (2000), and HJC, *Investigation pursuant to House Resolution 50: Final report of Special Counsel Joseph D. Steinfield* (2000).

6. In that initial phase of the HJC investigation, HJC Counsel Steinfield routinely informed deponents prior to questioning that, whereas the testimony they would deliver would not be public at that point, he fully expected it to become public at some future point. See, for example, HJC Investigation, Johnson deposition (May 9, 2000), 33.

7. Rule 40 had by instantiated, like all other JCC rules, by the Supreme Court itself. It held that materials relating to a complaint brought to JCC must remain confidential unless and until a decision was made to proceed to a full examination, at which point it would become public.

8. The justices did not accept Steinfield's argument that, since the constitution assigned full responsibility for impeachment to the legislature, supreme court had no authority whatsoever to hear the motion. They did, however, accept the claim that the motion in question did not reflect the grave violation of fundamental rights that would be needed to trigger court intervention into a process that certainly was mainly, if not unqualifiedly, legislative. Petition of Judicial Conduct Committee, 145 N.H. 108, 751 A. 2d 514 (2000).

9. Whereas JCC's own counsel was not present at the depositions taken by HJC, many deponents had their own counsel present, who reminded both investigators and deponents of JCC's confidentiality requirements when they thought it necessary.

10. Interim Report of Special Counsel Joseph Steinfield, 5.

11. Interim Report of Special Counsel Joseph Steinfield, 8.

12. N.H. H.R. Jour. 20 (July 12, 2000), 988.

13. In his Memorandum of Law of June 15, Steinfield discussed various state and federal cases that he hoped HJC members would find helpful in considering the extent to which recused judges might participate in cases (another question on which neither the U.S. nor N.H. Supreme Courts had ever ruled). He also discussed the meaning and application of N.H. Rev. Stat. Ann. §640:3, which held public officials accountable for reporting attempts to exert undue influence; and other legal questions.

14. HJC Investigation, Thayer deposition (May 10), 82–89. Steinfield specifically asked Thayer whether there was any mention of the hallway conversation in the McLaughlin Report or in any of the interview transcripts the attorney general had released. Thayer acknowledged there was no mention of it in any of those materials (87–88).

15. Ibid., 87–90. Judge Mangones would be disqualified, as he had been assigned to deal with a tangential issue in the divorce, involving transcripts.

16. Canon 3, Section B (7) of the Code specifies "A judge shall not initiate, consider, or permit *ex parte* communications or consider other communications made to the judge outside the presence of the parties concerning a pending or impending proceeding."

17. According to the AG's investigators' March 10, 2000 "Memorandum of Interview" with Brock (attached to HJC Investigation, Thayer deposition, May 10), the chief justice indicated then that "he couldn't specifically recall if he had gone to get Justice Thayer personally or if he may have asked Fox to request Justice Thayer's attendance back in the conference room." But during his HJC deposition on May 18, Brock would rule out the first possibility, with the proviso that he might have stepped into the hallway to ask someone else to get Thayer ("Since that interview, I have remembered very clearly that I was sitting at my place at the table, for at least two to three minutes while we waited for Justice Thayer to come back into the room. So that doesn't eliminate the possibility that I stepped out momentarily and asked somebody that I found to go for him and have him come back, but I still think I asked Eileen to do it"). Brock acknowledged the discrepancy between that account and his own March 10 interview, and its contradiction with Eileen Fox's testimony before HJC. Ibid., Brock deposition (May 18), 209.

18. Ibid., 214.

19. Ibid., 216.

20. Ibid., Fox deposition (May 2), 61. Justice Broderick, for his part, had a "very vivid recollection" of Thayer standing near a half-opened conference door and Brock verbally inviting him to return (Broderick deposition, May 15, 175). Justice Horton could recall only that someone had probably left the room to get Thayer, but could not remember who had done so (Horton deposition, May 16, 109–10).

21. Home Gas v. Strafford Fuels, 130 N.H. 74, 534 A. 2d 390 (1987).

22. An overview is provided in the HJC Report Pursuant to HR50, N.H. H.R. Jour. 20 (July 12, 2000), 987–988.

23. At his impeachment trial before the Senate, Brock would testify that, by his understanding, the *Home Gas* case had initially been brought to the attention of investigators from the AG's office by Zibel, in a response to a query about whether Thayer might have any information with which he might embarrass Brock (see Brown, *Impeachment Trial*, 166). HJC Counsel Steinfield, however, would insist during that Senate trial that he himself had learned of *Home Gas* only later, during HJC's own investigation, from Justice Johnson (Ibid., 201). Johnson did not mention the matter during his May 9 deposition. However, one of the documents attached to the transcript of that deposition is a June 29, 1999 memorandum that Johnson wrote to his fellow supreme court justices entitled "Re: W.S.T. [William Stephen Thayer] Filings under Judicial Conduct Code; Rule 38 of the Supreme Court." The memorandum includes an account of a discussion Johnson had with Thayer on June 22, 1999. According to Johnson, Thayer complained bitterly that, in pressuring him to report himself to the JCC regarding his role in the Feld case and failure to report his $50,000 loan from Emile Bussiere, the court had abandoned its "'practice' of bringing complaints against a fellow Supreme Court Justice to the full court before referring them to the JCC.'" Thayer, Johnson recorded, went on to refer to "'the Strafford County dispute involving Ed Dupont and the gas companies' …," insisting that "'The court investigated that matter, heard testimony and did not refer the matter to the JCC.'" But Johnson consulted Zibel, who with the assistance of Donna Craig located the relevant documentation on the case. It revealed that a letter on the matter, signed by all five Justices, had in fact been sent to JCC. Johnson's letter concludes with a clear statement of his own views on the substance of Thayer's complaint: "I firmly believe that it is the role of the JCC, not the members of the Supreme Court, to consider matters which, on their face, appear to be violations of the Code … The Supreme Court should take action only if the JCC concludes that the matter is serious enough to warrant the filing of petition for discipline with the Court. … it is clear to me that the JCC makes the first call and the Supreme Court makes the final call." Exactly when, why, and how that particular memorandum was made available to Steinfield and HJC are not specified in the record.

24. HJC Investigation, Gray deposition (May 23, 2000), 14–16.

25. Ibid., 29–30.

26. As administrative head of the courts, Brock had occasional dealings with Bartlett regarding Senate action on the judicial budget and other matters. Brock described those interactions as "difficult," attributing the tension between himself and Bartlett to the latter's low opinion of the work ethic of state judges (HJC Investigation, Brock deposition, May 19, 2000, 149, 166, 170). At Brock's impeachment trial, Bartlett, in turn, would describe his working relationship with Brock as "less than cordial." Eventually, Justice Johnson would have to replace Brock as the Court's liaison to the Senate Presidents office on budgetary matters. See Brown, *Impeachment Trial*, 108, 164.

27. The state had not yet entrusted oversight of the administrative operations of its 39 courts to an administrative judge. That level of judicial self-oversight would not be established until 1991, by Chief Justice Brock himself.

28. HJC Investigation, Brock deposition (May 19, 2000), 165–69. Brock testified that he made the call in late April. His recollection was that that Taylor could not answer immediately, since he didn't have the case file; but that Taylor did call the Brock the next day to confirm that the case had recently been heard and a decision rendered.

29. Ibid., 162–65.

30. Ibid., Gray deposition (May 23, 2000), 23–25; Bartlett deposition (June 7, 2000), 10–21.

31. Brock tried to account for the discrepancy between his account and Gray's by speculating that Taylor, after fielding the call from the chief justice, might have told Gray about it, and Gray subsequently confused Brock's call to the clerk with a call to himself, then further confused that call with the one he himself had placed to Brock. Ibid., Brock deposition (May 19, 2000), 175–76. But Taylor, in his own June 7 deposition, said that, while he could not be sure, he could not recall having told anyone else about the call (Ibid., Taylor deposition, 12–13).

32. On August 10, 1987, Judge Gray conferenced in his chambers with counsel for *Home Gas* and *Strafford Fuel* on motions for sanctions brought by the plaintiff. Before ruling for the defendant on those particular matters, Gray allegedly suggested that Sen. Dupont's role in the legislature's consideration of judicial pay raises had been at least partially motivated by the way in which the *Home Gas* suit had been adjudicated at trial. Gray's decision was appealed to the Supreme Court, which found in favor of Dupont's firm and remanded to Gray's court for further action. In another conference with counsel, on January 15, 1988, Gray was alleged to have said that "in his view, the decision of the Supreme Court in Senator Dupont's favor was motivated not by the application of legal principles to the facts, but by the identity of Senator Dupont." Ibid., Gray deposition, Exhibit #12: letter from Atty. Russell F. Hilliard to Hon. Joseph DiClerico, Assoc. Justice, N.H. Superior Court, April 17, 1989. Gray would insist in his own testimony before HJC that he hadn't even known Dupont was a senator until Brock's call to him in late March; and that if he had indeed made such statements in chambers, they were made in jest and utterly irrelevant to his decision.

33. Bartlett acknowledged no such communication. Hilliard said he had chatted with Brock about it during a hockey game. Dupont had a record of a call to Brock but no recollection of its substance, and denied asking for any intervention from anyone on his behalf. Brown, *Impeachment Trial,* 108, 152, 112.

34. Ibid., 328.

35. Ibid., 330.

36. Brock would state that the matter "kind of slipped through the cracks." His explanation was that although the supreme court had ruled on certain aspects of the case on November 5, 1987, other parts of it had been remanded to superior court as a result of that decision, and the supreme court was reluctant to initiate any sort of investigation while any aspect of the *Home Gas* case was still pending. HJI Investigation, Brock deposition (May 24, 2000), 136–37.

37. Gray's letter to DiClerico appears as Appendix 13 in Brown, *Impeachment Trial*, 334–36.

38. The court's October13, 1989, letter to JCC (ibid., Appendix 19, 352–355) openly stated that the court had found "clear and convincing evidence" that Judge

Gray had violated Canon 2 of the Code of Judicial Conduct by remarks made to counsel in August, 1987, and "a similar evidentiary basis" for believing that Gray had violated Canon 1 of that code in remarks to counsel in January 1988. Nonetheless, since, despite Brock's own disclaimers, the associate justices did "believe that he [Brock] made a call to Justice Gray," they had concluded that the "possible impression created by the telephone call would be enough to create doubt about the fairness of charging Justice Gray with a violation in this instance," even if the incident had fallen within the JCC's one-year investigatory period.

39. The report reads "The Chief Justice does not have any memory of making a call to Judge Gray as alleged, and believes that he did not. But in light of Justice Gray's comment that he took nothing improper from it, for the purposes of concluding this matter the chief justice otherwise joins in the report." Brown, *Impeachment Trial*, 355.

40. HJC Investigation, Brock deposition (May 18, 2000), 117–44.

41. At the time, JCC was an organ of the supreme court, and the court itself set JCC's rules. These including Rule 40, which provided for the confidentiality of materials related to any pending JCC investigations. One question that emerged during Brock's testimony was whether Rule 40 automatically precluded public access to such materials for the duration of any JCC investigation, or only granted subjects of those investigations a right to petition JCC for that confidentiality. The court's February 17, 2000, letter to JCC reporting Thayer's conduct was one of the documents that had not been made available to HJC Counsel Steinfield, despite his having subpoenaed it from Brock, at the time of Brock's May 18 deposition. Brock and his attorney, Ralph Lancaster, had petitioned JCC to release the letter. But JCC had to weigh the merits of Brock's petition against the merits of Thayer's, who wanted all materials related to JCC's investigation of his own actions protected. In addition, JCC was conducting its own investigation of Brock and the other justices. HJC Investigation, Brock deposition, (May 18), 148–53.

42. Ibid. (May 19), 37. On the statutory requirement to report wrongdoing, see N.H. Rev. Stat. §640:3.

43. HJC Investigation, Brock deposition, (May 18), 39–46.

44. Ibid., 41, 46–47.

45. Ibid. (May 24), 28–29.

46. Ibid., 74–89.

47. Ibid., 89.

48. Brock was able to specify February 7, just a few days after Thayer's explosion at the February 4 conference, as the date when the diagnosis was confirmed, because he recalled discussions with his wife about the latter's need to travel to Texas to be with their daughter.

49. Ibid., McLaughlin deposition (June 6), 83, 80.

50. Ibid., 83–84. Later, during the public hearings conducted by HJC, Brock was apprised of McLaughlin's claim about Ramsdell's remark on February 25. The chief justice denied having ever authorized his attorney to offer any such suggestion to the attorney general (HJC Public Hearings, June 26, 2000, 122–23).

51. HJC Investigation, McLaughlin deposition (June 6), 44. When later apprised of McLaughlin's testimony, Brock firmly denied having bandied words with the AG's

investigators on the cleverness of their questions, or having been anything less than fully forthcoming with them (HJC Public Hearings, June 26, 2000, 126–27).

52. HJC Investigation, ,McLaughlin deposition (June 6), 83–84.

53. Ibid., 85–88.

54. Ibid., Zuckerman deposition (June 7), 39–40, 44.

55. See Brock's speech before the N.H. Bar Association of 1998, in which he described administrative innovations in family, juvenile, and probate courts as well as the court's decision to establish a Public Protection Fund in the wake of the Fairbanks scandal and other matters. The speech is available online at https://web.archive.org/web/20000819013314/http://www.state.nh.us/courts/supreme/speech22.htm.

56. HJC Investigation, Brock deposition (May 19), 107–08. Brock had had to recuse himself from the *Mone* case because he had lobbied legislators so heavily on behalf of the court's position (Ibid., 34).

57. Ibid., Bartlett deposition (June 7), 20–22, 107–08.

58. Ibid., 55–57.

59. N.H. H.R. Jour. 19 (June 27, 2000), 977–79.

60. According to Mirski and other particularly vehement critics of court practices, O'Malley had known details of Zibel's charges before Attorney General McLaughlin himself had seen them. Struck by McLaughlin's subsequent decision not to inform the Executive Council of his investigation, those critics saw the possibility of collusion between the governor's office and representatives of the court, presumably with intent to somehow dilute the McLaughlin Report's charges. Rep. Robert Boyce would reiterate Mirski's suggestions in his own remarks to the House on the day it impeached Brock. N.H. H.R. Jour. 20 (July 12, 2000), 1080).

61. Ibid., Jour. 19 (June 27), 980.

62. Ibid., Jour. 20 (July 12), 988–89.

63. Ibid., 989.

64. Ibid., 993.

65. Ibid., 994.

66. Ibid., 997–98.

67. Ibid., 1033.

68. Ibid., 1004.

69. Ibid., 1012.

70. Ibid., 1018–19.

71. Rowe added, "but we can't impeach for that." Ibid., 1022.

72. Ibid., 1022–23.

73. Ibid., 1032.

74. Rowe, perhaps more than anyone else on HJC, was mindful of the interpersonal dynamics on an institution like the N.H. Supreme Court. "It's like going into a cocoon," he explained. "Nobody calls you. No one talks to you. Your old lawyer friends won't speak to you. It's a very, very lonely job. You have five members there. Sooner or later they become like family and you treat them like family." Ibid., 1018.

75. Reps. Dokmo and Solow formally delivered the minority report of the HJC after Reps. Mock and Janet Wall had delivered the majority report (Ibid., 990).

76. Ibid.

77. This, insisted Dokmo, simply reflected the fact that the Court was investigating the conduct of Judge Gray, not Justice Brock. Brock's alleged call had figured into the Court's report only incidentally, after all. Gray had claimed that the call had been made and, unable to either fully substantiate or dismiss that claim, the Court had chosen to err on the side of caution. But, Dokmo reminded the House, not even Gray, had ever suggested corrupt intent. Indeed, the entire *Home Gas* matter rested on nothing but contested personal testimony, all 13 years old: thin grounds indeed for the removal of the chief justice of the Supreme Court. Ibid., 1003–04.

78. Ibid., 1022.

79. Part II, Article 17 of the state's constitution described the House of Representatives as the "grand inquest" of the state, stipulating that "all impeachments made by them, shall be heard and tried by the senate." Mindful of that, Rep. Solow challenged the idea that approving articles of impeachment represented only confirmation of grounds for trial, or the equivalent of a grand jury action, with the Senate left to determine guilt. Rather, she suggested, it would commit the House as a whole to a finding a guilt, guilt that would then be argued before the Senate by House managers. Solow directly asked pro-impeachment Rep. John Pratt whether "if we vote to impeach, our very vote, if it passes by a majority, will in itself have determined that the actions that are believed to have been taken are so criminal, are so heinous, are so in league with treachery and bribery and corruption, that they rise to the level of an impeachable offense, and thereby won't we in voting to impeach already be passing a judgment and not simply throwing uncertainty to a trial in the Senate?" Pratt replied "The answer to that question, Representative Solow, is a resounding no." His own reading of the state constitution had yielded the view that "Government is messy … For whatever reason, our forefathers thought that the House could do two things: it could serve as the Grand Inquest and if it found an impeachable offense, it could then turn around and prosecute that case before the Senate." Ibid., 1001.

80. Mock and like-minded members of the pro-impeachment camp were apparently thinking of cases such as Winslow v. Holderness Planning Board, 125 N.H. 262, 480 A. 2d 114 (1984), involving an effort to void a decision of the planning board on the grounds that remarks of a board member, made before he assumed his position on the board, indicated prejudgment. The court had decided that the board's decision was indeed void, invoking its own 1908 ruling in Rollins v. Connor, 74 N.H. 456, 69 A. 777, that "mere participation by one disqualified member was sufficient to invalidate" a decision by a city council when sitting in a judicial capacity. In *Rollins*, the Court had specifically held that it was "impossible to estimate the influence one member might have on its associates."

81. N.H. H.R. Jour. 20 (July 12), 1039.

82. Ibid.

83. Ibid., 1040.

84. That was an important concern for Rep. Benjamin DePecol, a member of HJC's pro-impeachment majority, among others. "What we are doing here is an historic precedent thing," he stated. "If this ever happens again, then the next Judiciary Committee and the next body of this House is going to look back at us and say 'What did they use? How did they proceed? … And if we burden them with this kind of

proof, we are effectively making a precedent that will take away some of their leeway and some of their leverage … So I would just say this, clear and convincing, that's up to you. We can't put it on paper. We can't nail it down." Ibid., 1046.

85. Ibid.

86. Ibid., 1047.

87. Ibid., 1053.

88. Dyer's amendment (4813h) was one of two attempts to alter the language of HB1500-FN. The second (4817h) would have granted him 80 percent of his pension, should he choose to retire.

89. N.H., H.R. Jour. 20 (July 12), 1055.

90. Ibid., 1054.

91. Ibid., 1056.

92. Ibid., 1055. Rep. Timothy Robertson, who supported the Dyer amendment, did so in spite of his irritation at its beneficiary: "if he had put in one percent to fund this plan and we had put in 99 percent, after 10 years, 100 percent of it would be his and he would walk away in spite of the fact that in walked in and took a machinegun up there and killed 40 of us." Ibid., 1061.

93. Ibid., 1070–71.

94. "What Article 73-a of the Constitution says," Mirski explained, "is this: that the chief justice, with the concurrence of a majority of the court, sets the policies and procedures for the court." Ibid., 1071.

95. Ibid., 1072.

96. Ibid., 1073.

97. Ibid., 1077.

98. Ibid., 1079.

99. Ibid., 1080.

100. Ibid., 1081.

101. The representative repeatedly decried the sentiment he said he had often heard, to the effect that "We should not take action against Justice Broderick because he is an intellectual, we were told by one member of the committee, because he is a kind person, a sincere person." Ibid., 1082.

102. Ibid., 1083.

103. State v. Graf, 143 N.H. 294, 726 A. 2d 1270 (1999).

Chapter 8

Impeachment Proceedings in the Senate

On July 13, 2000, the House Managers, representatives chosen by their peers to prosecute for the indicting body in the trial to come, marched to the Senate to present their charges. After formal introduction by the Sergeant at Arms, Henry Mock solemnly read the four articles of impeachment and the rest of House resolution. The Senate, Mock concluded, was now called "to exercise its powers … to conduct a full and impartial trial to determine whether David A. Brock, Chief Justice of the Supreme Court of New Hampshire, should be convicted and removed from office if the Senate concludes that he has committed any or all of the acts enumerated in the articles of impeachment below."[1]

PRETRIAL MOTIONS

It was an extraordinary session, and the first ever to be televised gavel to gavel. Senators, minus two who recused themselves, proceeded to duly constitute themselves "a court of impeachment" until the matter was resolved.[2] In so doing, they assumed the responsibilities of both judge and jury. As judges, they would have to first establish, then even-handedly apply, procedural rules; and, in the event of conviction, decide the penalty. As jurors, they would have to ferret the truth from a range of accounts that would certainly be far wider and more divergent than what House had heard, since here Brock would have the right to vigorously challenge the charges against him and submit a full counter-narrative of his own.

Sen. Mark Fernald, a Democrat, was somewhat discomfited by the dual role senators would have to play. "I guess the problem I have is that here we're sort of in a hybrid," he would later remark; "we are a jury, but we're also the judges in the sense that we're potentially going to give instructions to ourselves, and we don't necessarily have that same knowledge of the history and background that a judge would have." Sen. Rick Russman, a Republican, shared Fernald's misgivings. "I have to admit I'm—this really strikes me in an odd way in that, having tried both criminal and civil cases, to actually have the jury making up the rules as it goes along, it's almost hard for me to comprehend."[3]

In fact, the functions of judge and jury are routinely combined in a number of legal settings, from bench trials to state and municipal regulatory actions. But Fernald's and Russman's concerns were quite understandable all the same: the question of trial procedure was an entirely open one, and its resolution might carry the most serious consequences. New Hampshire's senators understood that the trial they were about to conduct would resemble no ordinary civil or criminal trials—neither in the charges to be addressed (not transgressions clearly delineated by law, but assertions that a public official had engaged in something called "maladministration and malpractice") nor in the personnel conducting it (not oracles of the law, but tribunes of the people). Indeed, by some lights an impeachment trial might even be conceptualized as a kind of highly fraught performance review—its entire point, after all, was calling a public servant to public account. But it would be a review conducted under judicial norms, in the form of a trial, not by bureaucratic, electoral, or appointive process. What protocols were most appropriate to adopt? The one thing beyond question from the outset was that "full authority to make, implement, and interpret rules pertaining to impeachment" now fell on them alone.[4] How might they prioritize the interests of their constituents (as had been intended by the constitution's framers when they assigned impeachments to legislators rather than jurists) while maintaining judicial norms of fairness (which those same framers had also mandated when requiring the Senate to "hear, try, and determine" all impeachments as a court)?[5]

That is a difficult task in any impeachment, but perhaps especially in this one. Senators would sit in judgment of a man who had been publicly excoriated for years, not infrequently by senators themselves, for usurping *their own* (i.e., legislative) powers—most recently and egregiously, the formation of tax policy and educational standards in the *Claremont* decisions. Now, the (alleged) usurper would face the (allegedly) usurped. The temptation to configure justice as a wholly, and wholesomely, political act—restoring a cherished mode of governance, by crushing the man who headed the institution eclipsing it—was naturally strong. And New Hampshire's senators were fully mindful of the perils of yielding to it. Sen. Mary Brown, for example, spoke of "the ghost of the *Claremont* Case" as "this invisible presence" hovering over the proceedings from the beginning, and senators' determination not to let that ghost dominate them. "The mere mention of the case brought a collective tension," Brown wrote; "we weren't supposed to go there—this trial wasn't about *Claremont. Be careful*, we all silently warned."[6]

Yet mindfulness of the dangers was not the same as avoiding them. That would require procedural norms duly enacted and rigorously enforced, norms that would be considered morally and constitutionally appropriate by the citizens of the state. To assist them in that task and in the protection of the Senate's own institutional interests, New Hampshire's senators had retained expert, out-of-state counsel: former US Senator George Mitchell, Harold Pachios, and Michael Mahoney, all of Maine. On July 13, a somber Mitchell reminded his new clients of what lay ahead, and offered some advice on navigating it. "Because this is a first, there is no past precedent to guide you," Mitchell said. "But your best guide, in any event, is your own common sense, your personal sense of fairness, and your commitment to public service." It would be vitally important, he added, for the Senate to keep control of the trial. It must be fair, but also "expeditious." Above all, senators must not allow the proceedings to "degenerate into disorderly debate without focus or control."[7]

In fact, a provisional set of trial rules had been prepared in advance of the Senate's July 13 session by a committee of senators chaired by Sen. Caroline McCarley and advised by Senate counsel. They had been hashed out with representatives of the opposing parties, and the full Senate approved them as its next act of that historic July 13 session. Senate President Beverly Hollingworth was designated the trial's presiding officer and empowered to rule on questions of evidence (on the understanding that any questions requiring extended deliberation would be referred to the full Senate); to respond to all requests for subpoenas, writs, and other orders submitted by counsel for both sides; and to otherwise enforce the remaining trial rules. Each senator would be allowed five minutes to question witnesses and/or counsel after testimony was heard, should s/he so choose.

Significantly, Rule XII stipulated that "An article of impeachment shall not be divisible for the purpose of voting." That is: only one vote would be taken on each of the four articles of impeachment, which would simultaneously mark judgment of Brock's culpability *and* judgment of whether the offense itself were grave enough to merit conviction. Brock would stand convicted "If the Senators vote to convict on any article of impeachment;" to survive, he would need "no" votes on all four. That measure seemed a victory for House Managers. It confirmed their own sense of each charge's import; and it eliminated the possibility of senators' concluding that, even if Brock had indeed committed one or more of the acts, he had not been ill-intentioned or irresponsible enough to merit actual conviction.

Another measure, however, might have pleased House Managers less. In his opening statement to the Senate, Henry Mock had expressed the expectation that a "guilty" vote on any article of impeachment would necessarily mean Brock's removal from office ("to determine whether David A. Brock ... should be convicted and removed from office if the Senate concludes that he has committed any or all of the acts enumerated in the articles of impeachment below"). But Rule XII stipulated that if senators found Brock guilty of any charge, "a separate roll call vote shall be taken, on the question of whether the official convicted shall, if removed from office, in addition to such removal, also be disqualified to hold or enjoy any place of honor, trust or profit or profit under this state." The resonant phrase was "if removed from office." With it, senators licensed themselves to fix *either* a milder punishment than removal from office *or* the harsher disqualifications then described. Indeed, retaining a degree of flexibility over the course of the trial was clearly a significant concern: with Rule XIII, they opened the trial rules themselves to modification if that proved advisable ("As necessity may require, the Senate may amend these rules by majority vote").[8]

As it happened, some House representatives were very anxious that some amending take place immediately. Rule V called for another committee of senators to conduct a non-public conference with the parties to develop an explicit trial plan, which would encompass "proposed witnesses, evidence to be taken, motions to be made, and a schedule therefore"—crucial matters all. Rule IX stipulated that, while all trial proceedings would be open to the public, the Senate might enter into closed session to deliberate its votes after all testimony and closing arguments had been heard. It was those provisions for discussions and decisions outside the public eye that triggered the first open protest against the Senate's conduct of the trial.

It was the work not of the House Managers, who had helped negotiate the rules, but rather a set of militants in the impeachment movement now insisting that "To allow these secret hearings [sic] to go forward will cause permanent and irreversible harm to the public at large and to the petitioners specifically."[9] The petitioners were Reps. Soltani, Mirski, Christiansen, Alger, and Quant, springing into action on July 14 with a request for *ex parte* injunctive relief against Presiding Officer Hollingworth in the Superior Court for Merrimack County. Their argument was that the confidential deliberations authorized by the trial rules violated the "Right-to-Know" Law,[10] as well as two articles of the state constitution (Article 8, in both Part 1 and Part 2). The petition came to Judge Manias, and his July 17 ruling effectively underscored what was at stake.

"Rule V," Manias wrote, "promotes the vital public interest in taking politics out of the establishment of a trial schedule which, in turn, will help to insure the justness of the outcome of the trial."[11] Manias did credit a part of the petitioners' case, rejecting the respondent's argument that the petitioners' claim represented a nonjusticiable, political agenda. The "petitioners in this case have raised statutory and constitutional rights that are cognizable by this

Court," he wrote, "and it cannot be the case that the Senate has the authority to fashion rules of procedure that violate the New Hampshire Constitution." But he went on to note that, while the open-meetings provisions of the Right to Know law contained a long list of bodies to which the rule must apply, the state's courts were notably absent from it—and the Senate, now, was sitting as a court. On the constitutional argument, Manias observed that both Articles 8 forbade "unreasonable" restrictions of public access. The confidentiality of the deliberations in question was hardly unreasonable, he felt, since it would enable members to "express their positions free of any need for public posturing" and "allow the parties to step outside their adversarial roles and work toward a reasonable, practical, and fair procedure for the trial."[12]

When the Senate met again, on July 25, it approved the trial plan that had been prepared since its prior session (by essentially the same group that had prepared the trial rules, also chaired by Sen. McCarley).[13] Depositions were to be completed by September 25, and conducted according to the rules of the Superior Court of New Hampshire. In general, the standard New Hampshire Rules of Evidence, as interpreted by the presiding officer, were to provide guidance on evidentiary questions. Those rules would preclude hearsay, unless an exception to them was authorized. That drew commentary from Sen. Gary Francoeur, who noted that much of the evidence considered by the House might have been labeled hearsay. Francoeur's point was, in fact, well taken. The ban on hearsay, generally applied to jury trials, is often loosened in other sorts of proceedings, e.g., those adjudicated by people trained to properly process such evidence. Indeed, there is considerable scholarly support for the idea that impeachment trials ought to be considered one of them.[14] Other aspects of the plan, however, were accepted without demurral, including its stipulation that "the use of expert witnesses is generally disfavored," as would be "the inclusion in witness lists of Members of the House of Representatives." Arrangements were made for senators to visit the supreme court building, where they could view for themselves the conference room and hallway where significant events were held to have occurred on February 4. The starting date for the trial was moved back from August 21 to September 18 ("we can't pretend that we're not facing things like Labor Day and a primary election," observed Sen. McCarley), and August 21 and 22 were set aside for rulings on pre-trial motions submitted by both sides.[15]

It was hardly surprising that those motions would be numerous, and weighty. In fact, the resolution of those motions actually went a long way toward determining the final outcome of the impeachment. With the overall procedural shape of the trial to be determined by senators themselves, each side aimed to win approval for motions that would configure it in the most advantageous way possible. There was a wide spectrum of possibilities, and each side preferred a location nearer one of its poles.

On one pole stood a highly rule-bound and punctiliously legalistic proceeding, guided by established state or national legal precedent, templated whenever possible by the protocols of criminal trials. Generally speaking, Brock and his attorneys hoped that senators would opt for something nearer that model. The closer these proceedings were to a conventional trial, preferably a criminal trial, the easier it would be to keep senators focused on the specific allegations of recognizable wrongdoing at hand: tangible manifestations of a closely defined "maladministration," rather than some general aura of it. That would leave the burden of proof squarely on the prosecution, where Brock's team naturally felt it belonged.

On the other end of the spectrum stood a considerably more open-ended process: less encumbered by procedural rules intended for other types of proceedings; leaving key decisions to senators' own consciences and sense of the public interest, rather than pre-determined by legalistic formalisms; guided when guidance was needed at least as much by legislative statute as by legal precedent. In general, the House Managers sought something closer to that arrangement. From their perspective, the less formalized and constraining trial procedures were, the more space and weight might be granted those broader considerations of the public interest they felt should be at work. "Politics" in that sense, they would argue, should and must be honored here.

The debates on pre-trial motions constituted nothing less than an extended struggle over which model would prevail. The first clash involved the defense's motion to dismiss each of the four articles of impeachment outright.[16] That motion was less quixotic, and the debate on it less *pro forma,* than might have been expected. It enabled the defense to present itself at the outset as the guardians of established legal norms and practices, champions of fundamental due-process principles long enshrined in U.S. and New Hampshire legal history. And in so doing, it foregrounded the question of elemental fairness to the man whose fate now lay in senators' hands.

Brock's counsel (Michael Madigan, assisted by Steven Ross and Leslie Turner) found glaring violations of time-tested legal values in each of the four articles of impeachment, and several that spanned all of them. Article 1, involving the *Home Gas* matter (Brock's alleged phone call to Gray, and his failure to inform his fellow justices that he had made it), should be "barred by the statute of limitations and the doctrine of laches," argued Madigan and his team. The events in question, after all, had occurred some 13 years earlier, and no proper court allowed prosecutors to ransack as much of the past as they pleased in search of charges in non-capital cases. Granted, New Hampshire had neither statutory nor constitutional means of setting a time limit to impeachment charges; there was no statute of limitations, technically speaking. But basic legal principle required the Senate to set its own—specifically, the well-established equity principle of *laches,* expressing the eminently reasonable notion that extended delays in bringing claims deprived both defendants and courts of reliable evidence. In fact, while no time-limiting statute existed, there was precedent for determining how much time must elapse before ethical charges of the sort now brought against Brock could be considered beyond truthful reckoning. It was found within the judicial system itself: the one-year statute of limitations employed by JCC.[17]

On both Article 2 and Article 3, the defense team charged the House with a significant procedural error, technically termed "duplicity," in its indictment. In setting its trial rules, the Senate had committed itself to single votes on each article of impeachment. But Article 2 contained two offenses (Brock's *ex parte* discussion of the Thayer divorce panel with recused justices in conference, and his similarly *ex parte* conversation with Thayer about it in the hallway). Article 3 contained four (Brock's testimony regarding the March 3 letter to the attorney general; his access to documentation on *Home Gas*; his hallway conversation with Thayer; and his phone call to Judge Gray). Since separate offenses would not receive separate votes, it was entirely possible that "guilty" votes could be rendered on either article overall, even amidst deep divergences of opinion on which of the alleged offenses had actually been proven. Indeed, it was entirely possible that Brock could be convicted on either article even though only a minority of senators actually thought him guilty of any one of the specific offenses listed within it.[18]

Centuries of legal experience had taught judicial bodies to preclude that sort of miscarriage of justice with various procedural barriers against "duplicitous," multicount indictments. Brock's defense team urged the New Hampshire Senate to do the same. After all, argued Madigan and his associates, the "designation of the Senate as a court carries with it the strong implication that the Senate should apply well-recognized judicial principles of due process," with cues taken from prior court decisions because "that jurisprudence embodies the values of fairness and justice that ought to be the polestar of our determinations."[19] In particular, the claims of perjury set forth in Article 3 should be held to those rigorous standards of proof customarily enforced in court—the House should be required to prove that they were simultaneously conscious lies uttered under oath, and tangibly material to the HJC investigation.[20]

Article 4, regarding Brock's administration of the recusal policy, represented nothing less than the outright negation of law, according to the defense. It "fails to identify a single law, regulation, canon of judicial conduct, or any other recognized standard of conduct that the chief justice purportedly violated," charged Madigan. In fact, it "fails to identify a single specific instance of alleged misconduct. It does not even describe any specific acts of which the chief justice is accused."[21] But, continued the defense team, it was hardly surprising that the House Managers would be confused on just how the recusal policy constituted "maladministration," since they were clearly confused on what "maladministration" meant in the first place. Noting that the actual language of the New Hampshire constitution authorized impeachment only for "bribery, corruption, malpractice or maladministration in office," Madigan and his colleagues claimed a rough consensus among legal commentators "that this standard permits impeachment only for serious acts of willful misconduct." Indeed, they submitted, scholar Joseph Isenbergh had clearly demonstrated that words such as maladministration "may not sound like crimes to modern ears, [but] they are in fact terms for various types of misdemeanors treated as criminal offenses" at the time of the framing.[22]

In their retort, Steinfield and co-counsel Peter Ball denied the defense's interpretation of the juridical principles it had invoked even while insisting that legal norms intended to protect defendants in criminal trials were not applicable to an impeachment trial in the first place. This proceeding, they insisted, should advance the broad public interest in an impartial judiciary. Configuring it as a criminal trial would mean elevating the defendant's interests over those of the public—a fundamental misunderstanding of the entire *raison d'etre* of impeachment itself.

Steinfield began his rebuttal by addressing the defense claim that Article 1 was vitiated by the principle underlying statutes of limitation. That was "completely without substance," he asserted, since "Statutes of limitations are exactly that—*statutes,*" which neither the New Hampshire legislature nor the US Congress had seen fit to apply to "impeachment proceedings against judges who are accused of wrongdoing and who otherwise hold their office for life."[23] If senators sought guidance here, they should look to actual legislative enactments, and the nearest relevant one in New Hampshire was a statute[24] dealing with the prosecution of public officials. According to Steinfield, it authorized prosecutions either while the suspect official was in office, or within two years of leaving it. And defense counsel's suggestion that the Senate emulate JCC and dismiss charges more than a year old was, Steinfield felt, downright risible. It would be a "supreme irony" if the Senate, in trying the chief justice of the Supreme Court, were to bind itself to procedural rules the court itself had fashioned.[25] Why not simply let Brock try himself?

As for the doctrine of *laches*, it was not at all relevant to these proceedings.[26] Its application, Steinfield explained, ordinarily required proof of both unreasonable delay and prejudice.[27] The delay in investigating the *Home Gas* case could hardly be described as unreasonable: thanks to the JCC's confidentiality policies, no one outside the court and its own committee had known of it until now. Nor was there any hint of prejudice against Brock. On the contrary, he had been exonerated of any wrongdoing—by an investigation conducted by his own court, an investigation that cried out for reconsideration.[28]

In fact, by Steinfield's lights defense counsel's repeated invocation of criminal-trial procedures was both simplistic and oddly selective. Madigan's insistence that the impeachment articles were inadmissibly vague was a case in point. "Chief Brock is not seeking the particulars of his alleged conduct, but rather the House's theory of why his conduct was wrongful—information which no criminal prosecutor would be required to provide" at the stage the proceedings had thus far reached (confirmation by the full House, acting as grand jury, of an indictment prepared by HJC, acting as prosecutors).[29] In fact, Brock had already been given far more information than most criminal defendants have at this stage, having seen every bit of evidence the House had seen.

As to the claim of "duplicity" in Articles 2 and 3, Steinfield insisted that Brock's team "confuses the impeachable offense alleged with the specifications of that alleged offense." An indictment is improperly "duplicitous," Steinfield explained, when it charges two or more offenses in one count. But the impeachment articles charged single offenses, with multiple instances specified. Article 2 charged Brock with "the impeachable offense of maladministration or malpractice in connection with the case of *Thayer v. Thayer*," with two distinct *ex parte* communications specified. Similarly, Article 3 charged him with maladministration or malpractice for testifying falsely in the HJC investigation. There were four instances specified, but it didn't matter which of them senators concurred on, or even whether a majority concurred on any single one. What mattered was simply that a majority conclude that he lied about *something*—that would, and should, be enough to convict.[30] In any case, "duplicitous indictment" was a term borrowed from criminal law, and "because of the numerous differences between a criminal case and an impeachment … criminal law precedents are of little value here."[31]

As to Article 4, senators shouldn't allow Brock to hide behind the claim that he was simply continuing a practice that some predecessor, at some undetermined point in the past, had initiated. The *Feld* case, and Justice Johnson's strenuous objections to Thayer's interventions on it, should have pointed up the policy's wrongness—and indeed would have, to anyone less wed to the notion that judicial confidentiality trumps all. "The Chief Justice allowed the culture of confidentiality to trump the constitutional imperative of impartiality," Steinfield argued, and that most definitely constituted "maladministration" if the term were construed as broadly as it should be.[32]

The understanding of that term, of course, was a crucial question. According to Thomas Sheridan's *General Dictionary of the English Language* (London, 1780), the word "maladministration" was understood in the late eighteenth century to mean "bad management of affairs" (and after all, Steinfield pointedly reminded senators, Brock and his court had used that same dictionary's definition of "cherish" when considering its constitutional implications for the funding of public education, in their *Claremont* holdings). Granted, "maladministration" clearly implied more than mere negligence or poor judgment; it must connote "willful or reckless conduct in violation of the public trust." But the offense need not be as egregious as the bribery and corruption with which it was linked—indeed, the framers of New Hampshire's constitution, in deliberately including a term the federal constitution's authors eschewed, clearly signaled that they wanted a wider understanding of what was impeachable. Obviously, the court's recusal policy "seriously misled the citizens of New Hampshire," who had been promised judicial impartiality.[33]

Of course, Steinfield recognized, adherence to the principles of a criminal trial might incline senators toward a more stringent definition of maladministration. In a criminal trial, after all, a great many obstacles are put in the path of the prosecution, all designed to strengthen defendants' position. That was right and proper, since what was at stake there was the liberty all Americans cherish. But that was precisely why it was so wrong to liken an impeachment trial to a criminal trial, and to surround the defendant with a similar web of protections. "A criminal procedure is designed to be punitive, whereas an impeachment conviction is designed to be remedial," Steinfield submitted, citing Justice Joseph Story's observation of 1833 that impeachment is "a proceeding purely of a political nature. It is not so much designed to punish an offender as to secure the state against gross official misdemeanors. It touches neither his person nor his party, but simply divests him of his political capacity."[34]

Those last points were made in reference to the defense's August 4 motion for adoption of "beyond a reasonable doubt" as the standard for conviction.[35] On that day, the defense had also filed motions to require a two-thirds vote to convict, and to permit penalties short of removal from office in the event of conviction.[36] Steinfield and the House Managers had no objections to the last of those. But they had very strenuous objections to the first two.

Both motions, and much more, were debated vigorously before the entire Senate on August 21. Madigan began that day's deliberations by elaborating the litany of infirmities he had found in each article of impeachment—before dropping the rather surprising announcement that he was now requesting formal dismissal of only Articles 1 and 4. He concluded by reiterating the defense's fundamental war cry: an impeachment trial is not a political but a juridical act. "It's been written that a charge of impeachment is in many ways a political act," he said. "But not so for the trial of impeachment." The Senate, he insisted, was now sitting "not as a legislative body but as a court of impeachment, where facts must be proven … a far different proceeding than that of the House."[37] Defense attorney Leslie Turner returned to that theme in her defense of the "beyond a reasonable doubt" standard. The House had adopted only a "clear and convincing evidence" criterion in its assessment of the evidence against Brock. Surely the Senate, the higher deliberative body, should adopt a more rigorous one.[38] In fact, anything less than the full, public endorsement of "beyond a reasonable doubt" would invite charges that senators' judgments were unanchored, malleable, or even personal—"political" in the worst, most narrow sense.[39]

But "political" in the best sense—acting in defense of the public interest—was precisely what the prosecuting team wanted senators to be. Steinfield began his own opening statement by reminding senators just how overwhelmingly the House had voted each of the four articles, as if such broad bipartisan support amply refuted any suggestion that the case against Brock rested on bias or personal animus. "Beyond a reasonable doubt," he would explain, is a standard reserved mainly to criminal cases—but an impeachment trial is a very different kettle of fish. Its main purpose was less ascertaining whether an individual had transgressed a specific law in specific way than protecting the public from the broad and general dangers presented by any "mal-administering" official. Senators, in fact, need publicly tie themselves to no specific standard of proof at all; once they fully understood the stakes, they would surely do what needed to be done on behalf of their constituents.

The idea that a two-thirds vote should be required to convict was, in Steinfield's view, a particularly egregious error.[40] That "would put the interests of the person who is impeached above the public interest that is protected by the constitutional process of impeachment," he intoned. Defense counsel had implored senators to consider the "stigma" David Brock would carry if convicted. Such harsh punishment, they had contended, could be imposed only in recognition of palpable, proven crimes. But Steinfield insisted repeatedly that talk of "stigmas" and "punishments" was overdone. True, Brock would be pained by a conviction. He had already been pained by the act of impeachment, which could not be undone. But he was not facing imprisonment, or even a fine. The real injured parties were the citizens of New Hampshire—who sought not retribution, but simply relief from an official who had betrayed their trust.

Having heard these opening arguments, the Senate met the next day to settle the many procedural questions before it. It was quite clear from the beginning that the prosecution's perspective on the properly political nature of impeachment had secured considerable support. At one point in the discussion of standards of evidence, Sen. Gary Francoeur rose to offer a full-throated endorsement of it. The entire discussion of evidentiary standards, he felt, "assumes that the matter before this body is a case, a judicial proceeding. It's not a judicial proceeding. If the framers had intended it that way, the constitution would have bestowed this duty upon a judge and jury." Senators, Francoeur felt, should reserve the right to judge Brock as they and the citizens they represented saw fit, rather than binding themselves to courthouse conventions that were never meant to regulate an event of this nature. "This is a unique proceeding, one that hasn't been initiated in 200 years," he continued.

"By declining to adopt a single standard of proof, this body would allow each senator the opportunity to vote his or her conscience."[41]

Francoeur was not the only senator who felt that ordinary courtroom practices would only impede a full manifestation of the peoples' will and judgment. Sen. Richard Trombly, for one, was determined that private jury deliberations, standard operating procedure in most courts, be eschewed here. On July 31, he had submitted to President Hollingworth a motion which essentially brought to the full Senate the crux of the proposal that Reps. Soltani, Mirski, and others had brought to Judge Manias's court. If passed, the proposal would amend Rule IX of the trial rules the Senate had already adopted so that nothing whatsoever that was about to transpire would be concealed from television cameras, or the public. In fact, the Senate would now vote publicly on several other procedural questions that had seemed settled earlier, including single votes on each article of impeachment. Whatever the outcome of prior considerations, in court or in Sen. McCarley's planning committee or even in the Senate, it was important that open, roll-call votes on individual items be held now.

For much of the day, the pendulum seemed to be swinging in favor of the less rule-bound, more "political" proceeding favored by prosecutors. Regarding standards of evidence, both the "beyond a reasonable doubt" and the "clear and convincing evidence" criteria were voted down, leaving senators free to judge as the peoples' chosen spokesmen rather than as jurors at a criminal trial.[42] "Maladministration," senators decided, was a term that neither could nor should be defined precisely; each senator would construe that as he or she saw fit, as well. A single vote on each article of impeachment, already endorsed by both the McCarley committee and the prosecution, was reaffirmed (after the Senate had duly rejected Madigan's motion for dismissal).[43]

But when the senators took up the question of the vote count needed to convict, a somewhat different sentiment seemed to settle over them. Sen. Pignatelli noted that "essentially, we are challenging another branch of government. I don't believe a bare-majority vote is sufficient. It does not pay the proper respect to the judiciary, an equal branch of government."[44] Sen. Fraser referred to the "agonized" deliberations on this question the McCarley committee had conducted, before finally recommending conviction only by vote of two-thirds of the Senate.[45] "In my view," Fraser continued, "of all the things we're doing today, this is the most important one. … I think it's a linchpin of everything we're going to do."[46]

In the end, the two-thirds rule was adopted—an enormous boon to the defense, and a victory for the principle that political judgment should be qualified by juridical norms in an impeachment process.[47] It also represented an affirmation of the institutional independence of the judiciary. Absent such a requirement, the 1966 constitutional grant of independence might have been fatally compromised, in that judges making decisions disapproved by a simple majority of representatives and senators might thereby be more easily removed by impeachment.

At last, the Senate came to Sen. Trombly's motion, and the debate on that may have been the day's most telling. "The public must be invested in our decision," argued Trombly. "They must understand why we did what we did." Sen. Diane Krueger agreed. Especially now that no specific standard of proof had been adopted, she said, it was vital that the public see for themselves exactly how and why senators would reach their conclusions. Senators Fraser, Below, D'Alessandro, and Brown all spoke in favor of the Trombly motion.[48]

But Sen. Fred King led the charge against it. "Make no mistake about it, what we're doing here, we're having a trial. ... If we're going to have a free give-and-take a few weeks before a major election, I think it will be best accomplished where we can talk behind closed doors." Sen. Squires joined him. "I do agree that justice is served to some extent by the deliberation of a jury outside of the public eye. This is a trial. ... Every trial that I'm aware of, the jury does have an opportunity to deliberate as they see fit." Sen. McCarley took that side, as well. The federal constitution itself had been debated behind closed doors in Philadelphia in 1787, she observed, adding "I believe that full and frank discussion cannot occur under the spotlight of the cameras and the radios."[49]

The Senate divided down the middle on the Trombly motion, 11–11. That was not enough to pass, leaving the privacy of jury deliberations intact. It was perhaps the most fitting conclusion to the day, since the Senate as a body was indeed of a mixed mind not only on the Trombly motion but on the entire nature of what it was about to do. The day's votes had revealed the persuasive force of the prosecution's claim that the trial was "political" in the sense that it asserted the sovereignty of the citizenry over their officials, with senators fully licensed to channel that sovereign public's will. Yet there were also significant victories for the defense's claim that the imperatives of justice pointed elsewhere: toward the notion that expressions of the sovereign will must be contained within chosen legal forms, lest "the people" devolve into "the mob" so feared by the framers.

As a result of the August 22 decisions, the trial's overall procedures would delicately balance those political and juridical modalities. Taken as a whole, those procedures might even be understood to comprise a third way—that of "natural equity" or even, perhaps, "common sense justice." Senators might prioritize neither the public clamor that had brought them to this moment, nor a rigid legal formalism, but rather simple fairness and balance, as each's conscience illumined them. That, after all, had been the essence of Senator George Mitchell's counsel on July 13, when they had first accepted the House's charge to impeach.

But whatever equilibrium the Senate was reaching would be sorely tested over the next few weeks, as each side filed motions aimed at securing some sort of tactical advantage for itself. Madigan would repeatedly ask for more specificity on Article 2. Which specific statements by Brock, in response to the thousands of queries by two different investigating bodies he had answered over a two-month period when he was facing not only professional but family crises, were the House Managers labeling perjurious? Prosecutors' responses would call forth only demands for further specificity.[50] Steinfield and his team, for their part, demanded fuller rationales for the names appearing on the defense's witness list, early versions of which had included court administrators and justices representing the Louisiana, California, Connecticut, Maine, and Rhode Island Supreme Courts.[51] That represented "nothing more than an attempt to call high-ranking jurists and a court administrator to the witness stand to say nice things about the chief justice," argued prosecutors. Brock's team had their own complaints about the prosecution's intention to call Steven Lubet, a professor at Northwestern University and recognized authority on judicial ethics ("Such testimony seeks to instruct the Senate on matters of law and will not assist the Senate to understand the evidence or determine any facts at issue in the case").[52]

Each side had lawyers it wanted to subpoena. The prosecution wanted Brock's prior counsel Michael Ramsdell; the defense wanted Thayer's counsel William Brennan (and even Steinfield himself, to produce notes taken during the HJC investigation). Each side, naturally, attempted to deny the other side that testimony by invoking lawyer-client privilege. Each side insisted the principle was inapplicable in current circumstances (i.e., when the other side deployed it).[53] The sparring went on right to the eve of the trial, with each side winning and losing its fair share of those tactical motions.

But the strange political-juridical hybrid that had been created on August 22 would stand; and if the proceedings were not structured as most civil or criminal trials are, they would nonetheless constitute a recognizably "real" trial. As would be expected in any trial, each allegation and counter-allegation, each charge and each rebuttal, would be forced through a fine-mesh sieve of critical scrutiny. As in other trials, a jury would finally decide what to make of what remained. This particular jury was acutely aware of the stakes.[54]

"THE CRUCIBLE OF CROSS-EXAMINATION"

Over the 15-day course of the trial, neither side's attorneys produced any stunning revelations. There were no dramatic new admissions or exhibits, no entirely unanticipated twists and turns. Senators heard few facts that hadn't been known, at least in basic form, to HJC investigators, or accessible to the House (and, by then, to the public) as a whole. Yet the trial in its entirety did generate substantially more nuanced, detailed, and contextualized accounts of the events in question than either the attorney general's report or the HJC investigation. That was attributable mainly to procedural features that had been lacking in those prior inquiries. One was the adversarial format—especially what at one attorney called the "crucible of cross-examination"—deployed in any trial.[55] The other was specific to this one: the ability of jurors/senators to pose questions of their own to each witness. By trial's end, those jurors/senators' understandings of what likely had and hadn't transpired, along with its gravity and implications, were broader and deeper than any other kind of proceeding could probably have yielded.

Before it could proceed, though, senators would have settle some *in limine* (from Latin for "at the threshold") motions before them. Once again, counsel for each side framed the underlying issue as the degree to which the impeachment could and should be understood as the equivalent of a criminal trial: still a fundamental category error to the House Managers, still the only fair and reasonable modality to the defense. These debates—not the outcomes, but the debates themselves—may have foreshadowed the way senators would approach the largest question before them.

The day began with a return to the matter of "hearsay" evidence, that is, a skirmish over a defense motion to preclude, in advance, the solicitation of hearsay evidence by counsel for the House Managers. Defense attorney Leslie Turner argued that, while hearsay testimony might have a place in an investigative processes, ordinary rules of evidence required courts to exercise great caution in its use at trial; and its inherent unreliability should utterly rule out its deployment in so grave a proceeding as the one the Senate was about to undertake.[56] In his response, House counsel Steinfield stressed the oddity of the defense's effort to represent their motion as an act of fidelity to conventional trial procedures. "And what happens at trial, what happens under the rules of evidence," noted Steinfield, "is that a question is asked. And if there is an objection, then there is a ruling." A blanket attempt to exclude "hearsay" at the outset ignored protocols by which trials are actually conducted, he continued, protocols that fully recognized the difficulty of trying to determine in advance what might constitute irrelevant or unreliable testimony. "Let counsel ask their questions and trust the presiding officer to make appropriate rulings on a specific question-by-question basis," Steinfield concluded. He won the skirmish.[57]

Yet the defense might have scored another sort of victory simply by raising the question. "And frankly, I'm pleased that my colleagues who are non-lawyers are having this opportunity to hear about … the value and the questions about hearsay evidence," declared Sen. Russman, "because it's long been a concern of mine that people are routinely indicted on hearsay evidence and have to face trial just by somebody saying for them that 'Well, this is what I heard. This is what I understand.'"[58] If the intent was to remind senators of the perils of reliance on second-hand testimony, especially from long ago, the defense had made its point.

They appeared to secure benefit from the next skirmish as well, this one on their motion to preclude testimony by legal ethicist Steven Lubet, who would be one of the few witnesses who had not already been heard during the HJC investigation.[59] Steinfield would present the Code of Judicial Conduct as a guide to what might, at least, constitute judicial "maladministration and malpractice." He expected Lubet to provide valuable commentary on whether the acts with which Brock was charged did constitute serious violations of it, given the intent of the Code's authors and other states' historical experience enforcing it since its revision in 1972. The House counsel responded to defense efforts to bar Lubet with the argument that expert testimony on that subject was sorely needed, since judicial ethical codes weren't something with which most laymen, even senators, were particularly conversant. "How many of us have ever read the Code of Judicial Conduct?" asked Steinfield. "Well, perhaps judges read it. They are supposed to .... I have never read it before. I don't know if any of you have ever read it before. ... Professor Lubet is a student of the Code of Judicial Conduct, which I suggest to you is not a document that is so self-evidently clear on its face that none of us would benefit from some help from someone who would bring to the table a national and informed perspective regarding judicial conduct."[60]

Unsurprisingly, defense counsel argued that Lubet's opinion on whether Brock's alleged actions constituted grave violations of the Code could have scant value so long as the actual truth of those claims was contested, that is, for the duration of the trial. Nor, proposed the defense, could Lubet tell senators whether any of those violations, even if proven, constituted "maladministration and malpractice," since the meaning of those terms had been deliberately left to senators to decide for themselves.

The prosecution won this skirmish, too—in part because, as Sen. Fraser put it, "the more I can learn about the process and the more I can learn from whoever is testifying, it's important to me to make an informed decision."[61] Once again, however, what was happening within senators' minds may have been as important as the final, 14–8 vote to reject the defense's motion. Sen. Fred King and others made the point that Lubet, a prosecution witness, would be testifying on the basis of what he had learned from HJC depositions alone, claims not yet submitted to cross-examination or determined to be true; and that senators would therefore need to assess his testimony with a particularly critical eye.[62] Sen. Russman went so far as to briefly put forth an amendment permitting Lubet to testify only on judicial conduct issues in general, excluding any opinions he might have on whether the violations alleged here would constitute maladministration.[63] Concern with avoiding any hint of prejudice toward the defendant was such that senators' vote to admit Lubet's testimony was accompanied by a provision specifically authorizing Brock, too, to call such expert witnesses as he felt necessary.

But it was the question of "character" witnesses that revealed the degree to which senators had been influenced by defense counsel's repeated attempts to secure for their client the level of protection generally granted to defendants in a criminal trial—whether the impeachment proceedings were publicly acknowledged as such or not. Madigan and his colleagues proposed to call a corporate president, a court administrator, and a number of judges from various jurisdictions across the country to testify to "the level of care used by Chief Justice Brock in safeguarding the integrity and reputation of the New Hampshire Supreme Court and judiciary."[64] Speaking for the House Managers, Peter Ball quoted the federal rules of evidence on which New Hampshire's were based ("Character evidence is of slight probative value and may be very prejudicial"). It was reluctantly allowed in criminal cases, Ball conceded, despite doubts about its relevance and reliability, simply because "so much is at stake in criminal cases." But such testimony had no place here. "Now, it's a little bit of *déjà vu* all over again," declared Ball with some exasperation; "but we've discussed during this case and when we were before you the last time, that this is not a criminal trial, that there are many differences." The Senate had already accepted that point, Ball observed, by rejecting "beyond a reasonable doubt" as the standard of evidence. It should continue to resist defense efforts to elevate the protection of the chief justice over the well-being of the citizenry that, through its representatives, had called him to account.[65]

But Leslie Turner, speaking for Brock, had citations of her own to deploy. One was taken from Steinfield's own motion to compel the testimony of Brock's former attorney Michael Ramsdell, in which House counsel had bluntly declared that "Chief Justice Brock's credibility is a subject at the very heart of these proceedings." Another was Rule 608 of the New Hampshire Rules of Evidence, which stipulated that "evidence of a truthful character is admissible only after the character of the witness for truthfulness has been attacked by opinion, reputation, evidence or otherwise." Above all, Turner insisted that there was surely as much at stake here as the fines and jail terms at issue in most criminal trails: nothing less than historic precedent, alongside the legacy of David Brock's entire life as a judge ("Well, here this is the first impeachment trial in the history of New Hampshire. What's at stake is a man's professional career").[66]

That position scored heavily with a number of senators. Sen. Fernald felt that "even though this isn't a criminal proceeding, the chief justice is being accused of lying, and so I think he is the accused here, that it is equivalent to a criminal matter on perjury." Sen. Trombly, too, felt that " while this may not be a criminal matter specifically, most certainly it rises much more than a fender-bender … I think that impeachment is considerably more serious than a civil trial." Indeed, the debate on Brock's character witnesses was one of the few procedural questions on which Senate President Hollingworth publicly committed herself. "I had a little bit of concern about this motion because I was concerned about whether in fact it was criminal or civil, and since we're here it's neither. It's another animal," she stated for the record. Yet, she added, her study of impeachment left her with a clear view that the defendant in these proceedings "should be allowed the fullest extent to defend himself."[67] The vote to permit Brock's character witnesses was a lopsided 20–2. As it happened, the defense would never even call those character witnesses. The debate, perhaps, yielded benefit enough.

At any rate, whether Brock's team had or had not succeeded in establishing a "presumption of innocence" toward Brock by the time of opening statements, they had made it clear that the prosecution would need to do more than simply recapitulate evidence already presented before HJC. Now, at trial, all prior claims would be aggressively challenged by the defense; and the narratives that House Managers' counsel would put forward on each of the four articles of impeachment would be assessed for plausibility alongside alternative, Brock-friendly narratives offered by the defense. This meant that, ironically, the prosecution's posture over the course of the trial would often enough be markedly "defensive," in that it had to be geared to fending off attacks by Brock's team on the credibility of key prosecution witnesses and the overall stories their accounts presented.

Prosecutors and defenders all strove mightily to achieve their respective aims, and the results were tangible: a few new facts but, more often, new interpretive possibilities, sometimes favoring the defense, sometimes the prosecution. By the end of 14 days of testimony and counsel summations, senators would find themselves dealing with far more granular, complex, and perhaps confusing versions of events than had been yet disclosed.

Article I and the entire *Home Gas* matter was a case in point. By the end of the trial, the jury of senators heard a great deal to support the prosecution's claim that Brock had called Judge Gray on or about March 25, 1987—dropping the unsolicited information that one of the litigants was a state senator with a significant role to play in judicial pay raises into what was ostensibly a query about where the *Home Gas* litigation currently stood. Senators would have before them a substantial body of documentation on the case, most importantly the entirety of the supreme court's report to JCC on the matter, complete with all addenda. That 1989 report on the case, which Judge

DiClerico had prepared and the court as a whole had approved and forwarded to JCC, was probably the single most damning piece of evidence against Brock on the *Home Gas* charges. There was no way around the fact that all four of Brock's colleagues had concluded, on the basis of written statements by Superior Court Judges Gray and McHugh as well as Gray's oral testimony, that, despite the chief justice's disclaimers, he must have called Gray. Nor was there any way around the justices' open admission in that report, repeated at trial, that they would have been more prompt in bringing the complaints to JCC about Gray's in-chambers comments, which had first triggered ethical concerns on the adjudication of *Home Gas,* had they known about Brock's call earlier.[68] True, in light of the fact that Gray himself had taken nothing untoward from the call, the justices had found no wrongdoing on Brock's part. But it had, nonetheless, resulted in both Gray's and Brock's avoiding direct JCC scrutiny.

In his opening remarks and thereafter, Steinfield attacked the notion that the call was a harmless and indeed proper administrative inquiry, prompted by a constituent. The constituent who had prompted this particular call, House counsel stressed, was Senate President William Bartlett ("I wonder whether anyone believes that if the average citizen called the chief justice that would prompt a call of the type that Article 1 alleges"); and if either Bartlett or Dupont really had grounds for complaint about the pace of judicial decision-making, there were other means of addressing them.[69] In fact, testimony that Steinfield elicited would suggest that the *Home Gas* matter might actually be worse than it seemed in the specific charges contained in Article I. For Judges Gray and McHugh not only stood firmly by their earlier accounts of Brock's call to Gray, but also raised questions about whether there might have been something malodorous in the Supreme Court's overall role in the case from beginning to end.

McHugh, whose initial ruling favoring Home Gas over Dupont's company had been overturned by the court, testified that in 1987 he had indeed wondered about the alacrity with which the justices had granted Dupont's lawyers' writ of *certiorari* without so much as a hearing—then promptly acted in his favor. "And I don't know the statistics for you," said McHugh, "but you can ask any lawyer, and there are some in your group which will tell you that to have the supreme court consider interlocutory appeals is very, very rare in and of itself."[70] At the time, McHugh said, "I felt this case was not being handled procedurally like other cases were handled," adding that "Curious is a mild word" to describe his feelings about the path *Home Gas* was taking through the judiciary.[71]

Gray, too, testified to real surprise at the way the court had handled *Home Gas* litigation whenever it reached them. In fact, said Gray, in 1989, when the justices had called on him to answer charges about improper remarks in chambers two years earlier, he had not only revealed Brock's highly unusual call but had wondered aloud about the entirety of the supreme court's involvement in the case. "I get a call from the chief justice and this case goes from start to finish in the Supreme Court—from filing, I mean to a final decision in the Supreme Court in less than a year," he recalled telling the court in 1989. "What would you think?"[72]

But under cross-examination, McHugh revealed that he himself had not known until that very day that the judge who had overturned him on *Home Gas* was none other than David Souter. In response to a direct question from Sen. Fred King, McHugh promptly disavowed any suggestion that Souter's decision might have been in some way "tainted" ("see, I don't even know what he knew ... I don't want to use the word 'tainted' because I've never believed that that was the case").[73] The next day, the defense questioned Howard Zibel about how unusual a court order such as the one that had raised McHugh's eyebrows really was. Not very, Zibel said; in fact, the court's willingness to counter McHugh's ruling had conformed to a time-honored principle of maintaining the *status quo* while a contractual matter was in litigation, since that ruling would have altered it.[74]

Judge Gray's testimony, too, would lose some of its sting under defense counsel's challenges. He had continued to maintain that he hadn't even known that one of the litigants in *Home Gas* was a state senator until Brock told him. But he proved unaware that he himself had been a member of the supreme court/superior court liaison committee in those days—service that, defense counsel Leslie Turner suggested, would surely have made him aware of legislators, including Dupont, involved in judicial appropriations.[75] Further, his description of his relationship with McHugh was markedly warmer than McHugh's own.[76] Overall, Gray's responses and demeanor on the stand led Sen. Krueger to characterize him as "someone who sort of delights in humor, in a little bit of sarcasm and irony," someone who "could make jocular something that really has no meaning to him." She would bluntly ask McHugh "Did it ever cross your mind that maybe Judge Gray, when he told you about that phone call, was using what we used to call in Catholic school a poetic license?"[77]

McHugh thought no such thing ("I'm just telling you that for now a 15-year relationship, for him to joke about it or exaggerate a call would be totally out of his character"). But in the end, senators would have to weigh the House Managers' general account of Brock's *Home Gas* involvement as a grave and impeachable offense with the two-pronged attack on it mounted over the course of the trial by the defense. What Madigan and his colleagues stressed was that (a) memories of events so long ago, and especially of their origins and meaning, were anything but reliable; and (b) the phone call, if it was placed at all, was neither sinister nor inexplicable.

The first of those points was demonstrated by both William Bartlett and Edward Dupont, whose alleged conversations with Brock figured so importantly in the *Home Gas* matter. Neither could recall discussing the case with Brock, or even with each other. But documentation on the case included letters Brock had penned to each of them (to Bartlett on November 10, 1987 and to Dupont on January 12, 1988) acknowledging complaints from them about the Rockingham County Superior Court's handling of *Home Gas*; describing the options available to litigants with such concerns (e.g., motions for the sitting judge's recusal, complaints to JCC); and pledging personal attention to the matter when the case had fully concluded.[78] Both former senators would acknowledge now, as they had to HJC, that the letters must have been prompted by conversations they simply could not remember.

The degree of dissonance among various peoples' memories of *Home Gas* matters was further underscored by the testimony of Judge Philip Hollman, one of the few trial witnesses who had not been heard by HJC. Judge Gray had no recollection of any conversation with Hollman on *Home Gas*. But Hollman recalled Gray's telling him not only that Brock had called but also that he, Gray, intended to call Brock—and, a short while later, that he had indeed done so, to ask about whether the court planned to expedite its deliberations on an aspect of *Home Gas* litigation remaining before it.[79]

Hollman was actually called as a prosecution witness, for obvious reasons: Steinfield needed to stress the part of Hollman's testimony that reinforced Gray's claim that he had taken a call from Brock on *Home Gas* rather than the part that reinforced Brock's claim that the call had been made by Gray *to* Brock, and at a later date. But the defense's general strategy on the entire *Home Gas* matter was not to buttress Brock's claim that he had never called anyone at Rockingham County Superior Court except its clerk, Ray Taylor. Rather, Madigan and his team aimed to persuade senators that no one's memory of those events, or even understanding of them while they were underway, was truly solid; and that even if Brock had indeed called Gray, he had not committed anything resembling "maladministration and malpractice," as House Managers charged. Steinfield might have minimized the support Hollman rendered Brock on the first of those claims. But he couldn't prevent Hollman from burnishing defense claims on the second.

Hollman's impression, he said, was that Brock's call had been prompted by "some sort of complaint about Judge Gray," and

> If that is the case, then it is within the realm of the—in my mind anyway—it's within the realm of the administrative responsibilities of the chief justice … the chief justice of the supreme court is the highest judicial official in the state who's also ultimately responsible for the administration of the courts. And that's certainly a very legitimate reason for him to have called, in my mind.[80]

Hollman also undercut the House Managers' claim that a call from the chief justice to a trial judge on a case in process was all but unprecedented. He himself, Hollman testified on cross-examination, had fielded a call from Brock some years ago, regarding a ruling he had made on the reach of a criminal defendant's right to counsel. Brock had apparently been confronted by an angry legislator on the matter, and had called Hollman simply so that he could provide an informed response. "And I felt," Hollman stated clearly, "that that was a very legitimate thing for the chief justice to do."[81]

From his opening statement onward, Steinfield would insist on the flimsiness of these exculpatory claims. If Brock really had grounds to question the efficiency or even the propriety of Gray's actions on *Home Gas*, he had other options for dealing with the problem. "One might well call the administrator or the chief justice of the trial court," Steinfield had said then. But a direct intervention to the trial judge by the chief justice of the supreme court was not only unnecessary, it should have been unthinkable—especially in light of the fact that the case had already come before the court once, and might well return there on appeal. "But the moment the chief justice places a phone call directly to a trial judge about a pending case, you have a corrosive effect on the requirement of impartiality," Steinfield had pleaded. "It can't be allowed."[82] The fact that there had been no effort to influence Judge Gray's actual decision, argued Steinfield, was irrelevant. The Code of Judicial Ethics did not manifest a "no harm, no foul" sensibility on such matters.[83]

But Judge Edwin Kelly, administrative judge of the state's district court, would vigorously challenge the prosecution's claim that Brock's call represented maladministration. Kelly's position entailed administrative oversight of all 39 district court locations and their judges. Brock indeed might have directed his inquiry about the progress of *Home Gas* to the chief justice of the statewide superior court, Kelly noted, rather than to the specific trial judge hearing the case—if the former office had existed in 1987. But, he explained, it wasn't until 1990 that the Supreme Court had created an administrative judgeship for each statewide court within the judiciary (at the time, superior, district, and probate); and not until 1991 that the measure, Rule 54, was fully implemented.[84] JCC was clearly the proper venue for complaints regarding actual adjudication, Kelly pointed out. But administrative problems were an entirely different order of business, and direct communications by a judge in a statewide supervisory role to the individual judge in question was a perfectly valid, indeed indispensable, way of handling them. He himself, Kelly said, did it routinely when citizens, including litigants or even elected officials, brought complaints. Furthermore, he continued, it would be perfectly appropriate for the chief justice, whose administrative duties encompassed the entirety of the judiciary and superseded Kelly's own, to do the same. To Kelly, such actions should be seen "in the context of New Hampshire expectations. And those are not going to be the expectations in Chicago or Boston or even Washington, D.C." The State of New Hampshire, Kelly declared, "has been clear, its people through its constitution, that they expect that their government—all three branches—are going to be very close, accessible and responsive to people."[85]

Rhetorically, Kelly's attempt to represent Brock's phone call to Gray not as a violation of the state's civic ethos but as a kind of fulfillment of it provided one of the trial's more interesting moments. Asked his overall impression of Brock as an administrator, he began with an observation that few, by then, could have denied. "New Hampshire has undergone a huge change, and so certainly has the judiciary," Kelly noted, in reference to the changes wrought by the constitutional amendments that went into effect in 1966–1978. "This has not been a time of quiet."[86] In that context, Kelly felt Brock should be seen as "someone who has had to navigate some very, very difficult changes in the expectations of the public toward the judiciary." In Kelly's view, Brock had navigated those changes supremely well—in fact, he should be understood not as transgressor but as embodiment of New Hampshire values. "I think that he will be looked back upon as someone who has advocated vigorously for the courts," he declared, "and not the courts as an institution, but the courts as a means of serving the interests of the people of the state."[87]

But it might have been Judge William Batchelder who offered the most provocative rejoinder to the House Managers' case on *Home Gas*. Batchelder had been a supreme court justice in 1989, and a signatory of the letter the court sent to JCC after its own inquiry into both Gray's and Brock's alleged actions had been concluded. But Batchelder tended to minimize even the light reproof the justices had directed to Brock. They had had nothing to go on, he stressed, except Gray's claim that Brock had called; Brock's insistence that he had called only the clerk Ray Taylor; and McHugh's written statement confirming that Gray *believed* Brock had called. "Always remember this," Batchelder cautioned, "your judgment is never any better than your information," and in this instance, information had been sketchy at best.[88] The determination that Brock had called, Batchelder suggested, should be taken "in the context of the way Judge Gray might take it and I guess, for purposes of reporting to the conduct committee, this would have some palliative effect concerning Judge Gray's violations."[89] That is, according to Batchelder, the justices had never seen Brock's call to Gray as the serious transgression that HJC had interpreted their letter as confirming ("It was not something that really excited us that much at that moment"), since it had been a purely administrative action with no adjudicative import. Rather, they had included it in their report to the JCC at least in part to soften the blow that the body of that report would deliver to Judge Gray by taking his word more or less at face value on this particular point, even over the chief justice's. Brock's own willingness to sign the report while demurring on that point suggests that he himself had seen no great damage to his own stature in it.[90]

Senators could make what they would of the notion that, in criticizing Brock, his fellow justices had hoped for "some palliative effect" on Judge Gray, the main subject of their inquiry. But after two weeks of testimony, the *Home Gas* case and Article I could reasonably be described as a tangle. Article II, involving events on February 4, would be no less thoroughly problematic.

The first part of Article II scored Brock for inviting a consideration of Thayer's divorce panel with Thayer himself and other judges, all of them recused from the case, at the February 4 conference. Over the course of the trial, the defense team barely contested that charge. Everyone at that conference had already testified before HJC, and would again before the Senate, to feeling that Brock did signal, intentionally or unintentionally, a willingness to entertain feedback on the substitute judges he had chosen. Brock himself, while insisting that he had never meant to elicit commentary, acknowledged that even mentioning the appointments in that setting had been a mistake.[91] But such an error, taken alone, could hardly constitute grounds for impeachment. The weightier charge in Article II was clearly its second part. That was the claim that, after the by-now notorious February 4 case conference, Brock had engaged in an *ex parte* hallway conversation on the divorce panel with Thayer, all but granting the latter a potential veto power over appointments to it. It was one of the most shocking and damaging of the impeachment allegations. But to substantiate it, prosecutors had to convince senators not only that Brock had definitely spent at least a few moments alone in the hallway with Thayer, but that Thayer's own account of what was said was entirely credible. Brock's team, naturally, contested each point quite vigorously.

By the end of the trial, senators were left with much to ponder on those points. Among the participants in that February 4 conference, only Eileen Fox had been willing to tell both the AG's team and HJC that it had been Brock who had gone into the hallway where Thayer had been exiled to summon him back to the conference room. Under Steinfield's questioning at trial, she basically stood by her prior account. But on cross-examination, she had conceded that, while she was certain that she herself did not leave the room to get Thayer, she couldn't be quite as sure that Brock himself did ("I'd say it's less clear. I'm more certain of my own actions than I am of other people's actions").[92] Justice Horton told a similar story. He too was sure he didn't fetch Thayer from the hallway; but he had no recollection of exactly who did. Justice Broderick now went further, explicitly reneging on earlier statements that Brock might have left the conference room and affirming now, with certainty, that he had not. Now, he explained, having had time to reflect carefully on the incident, he clearly recalled that Thayer had simply appeared at the conference-room door to ask whether he could come back.[93] Broderick openly acknowledged that this account diverged from his initial rendering to the attorney general's investigators. But Broderick really wasn't the prosecution's main challenge on the hallway conversation.

Thayer was. For the prosecution to succeed, senators would have to believe Thayer's story, that is, prosecutors would have to find ways to repel the defense's sustained assault on his credibility. Over the course of the trial, Justices Horton, Broderick, and later Johnson provided a great deal of ammunition for that assault, by relating the various grievances Thayer had accumulated during his years on the court.

Horton explained that those grievances went as far back as 1990, when Thayer had been appointed to replace David Souter, recently elevated to the U.S. Supreme Court, on the U.S. Court of Appeals for the First Circuit. The appointment had fallen through when the American Bar Association declined to endorse him. According to Horton, Thayer was convinced that Brock and Johnson, in particular, had "done him in on" when questioned by ABA representatives on his suitability for the job. That ill-will had been deepened, explained Horton and other justices, by a variety of incidents: Brock's insistence that Thayer curtail the time he spent, and the income he earned, on teaching, when it had seemed to interfere with his duties on the court; the pressure that Brock and Johnson had exerted on him to self-report his role in the *Feld* case to JCC; and the decision by Brock, Horton, and Broderick to place him on administrative leave from the court. All in all, senators were given considerable reason to view Stephen Thayer as a man with ample reason to lash out at David Brock with a false story—a man both aggrieved and desperate enough to accuse the chief justice of an *ex parte* conversation that never occurred, in exchange for the attorney general's willingness to forego prosecution for his own, all-too-real offenses.

Steinfield needed to buff Thayer's credibility when the beleaguered justice testified on September 21. But to do that, the witness would have to flatly deny a number of the assertions made publicly and repeatedly by a number of others. Among the most telling was Howard Zibel's claim that Thayer had tampered with his financial-disclosure forms. Thayer said he simply could not understand Zibel's charges. First of all, he had never "backdated" anything ("and if I were to do something like that, I certainly wouldn't have done it in front of Mr. Zibel").[94] In November 1997, he explained, Zibel had told him his 1996 form was missing, and he had naturally assumed it had been somehow misplaced. But he knew he had filed it at the April 1997 deadline, so he quite innocently used that date on his November re-filing. Yes, Thayer admitted, he should have specifically noted his $50,000 loan from Emile Bussiere earlier than he did. But, he claimed, "it wasn't an intentional desire not to put it down. I just—it's just a mistake"—a mistake he fully rectified on May 11, 1999, when he appended statements to his 1997, 1998, and 1999 disclosures acknowledging the loan.[95] Thayer also denied that he had ever taken from Zibel's desk a list of substitute judges for his divorce panel. Rather, it was Zibel who had mentioned Pappagianis (and it remained Thayer's view that Pappagianis should *not* have been eligible, because Thayer had once reversed one of his opinions and Pappagianis had responded with an indignant letter).[96]

Thayer also had to counter the general impression Justice Johnson had left in his HJC testimony, to be repeated before the Senate, regarding Thayer's remarks at the April 23, 1999 discussion of the *Feld* case. Those remarks, Thayer argued, were not out of order. As supreme court liaison to the Professional Conduct Committee, he was simply noting that the stern judgment that body had recommended was actually in line with precedent on similar cases, even though the court-appointed referee had rejected it. He had not pressed any particular action on his colleagues, Thayer insisted, but simply apprised them of something he knew—precisely the sort of contribution from non-voting justices that had always been welcomed in conference.[97] Finally, Thayer had to counter the notion that he had threatened anyone in his phone conversations with Broderick and Brock on February 14 and 15. When he said that Zibel's memo would "blow up the court" and that he would "not hang alone," he was simply speaking the truth, he claimed. Public scandal would surely follow, and it could hardly be confined to himself. It was the New Hampshire Supreme Court, Thayer said, that he was worried about.[98]

He had been upset by his suspension from it and filed suit for readmission because he had been denied any sort of hearing or opportunity to defend himself.[99] But despite all that had happened, Thayer claimed he bore Brock no grudge. On the contrary, he had nothing but praise for the chief justice—indeed, prosecutors might have wished that Thayer had been a little less extravagant in his praise for the man they were trying to convict of serious wrongdoing.[100] Brock had been right about those teaching jobs, Thayer now acknowledged. It was not lack of support by Brock or any other colleague that had cost him the federal appointment, he explained, but antagonisms he had aroused within the defense bar during his days as a zealous prosecutor and Reaganite Republican (and as it turned out, losing out on that appointment had turned out to be "one of the best thing that ever happened" to him anyway, as it marked the beginning of his turn toward teaching). Brock was an exceptional administrator, a consensus-builder. He had been sympathetic and understanding throughout Thayer's personal ordeal. Thayer, himself a Vietnam veteran, went so far as to say "if the chief justice was the 'CO' and he said fix bayonets and go up that hill, I'd do it. I'd follow him. That is not something an old infantry officer says lightly."[101]

But Steinfield knew that none of that would rehabilitate his only witness to the February 4 hallway conversation if Thayer couldn't provide a convincing account of just how, despite being the original focus of both the Zibel memo and the McLaughlin Report, he had managed to avoid indictment—unless it had been to offer testimony implicating Brock to an attorney general who had grown to deeply dislike the chief justice. The story Thayer told was complex, and not entirely clear.

He had received a letter from Attorney General McLaughlin dated March 27 announcing that he would be the subject of a grand jury investigation and possible criminal charges based on his outburst at the February 4 conference and statements he made in his February 14–15 phone conversations with Broderick and Brock. At that point, Thayer had decided to resign—not, he insisted, in return for any promise by the AG to forego prosecution, but simply out of exhaustion and the realization that, with actual criminal proceedings in the offing, he could not possibly function effectively as a Supreme Court justice. McLaughlin, in turn, had elected to cancel those criminal proceedings for reasons of *his* own, fully explained in the McLaughlin Report (e.g., the potential difficulty of securing a conviction and Thayer's long record of distinguished service).[102] True, Thayer's attorneys did discuss his resigning in relation to the grand-jury investigation. But he had never authorized any sort of deal, and in fact had no prior knowledge that such discussions were underway.[103]

Unfortunately for Thayer, the McLaughlin Report had specifically described a negotiation between attorney general's office office and Thayer's attorneys by which Thayer *had* resigned "in return for the attorney general's forbearance from presenting criminal charges against him to the grand jury."[104] That claim of a *quid pro quo*, Thayer insisted, was simply wrong—or, at least, *he* had never interpreted what transpired in those terms. He never thought he needed immunity, he claimed, because he never believed he had committed any crime. Yet he also acknowledged that "there's no doubt that my understanding was that if I'd resign, they probably weren't going to prosecute."[105]

Thayer's explanation of just how he had come to resign may or may not have enhanced his credibility to senators. But the most important part of his testimony involved when, why, and to whom he had revealed the story of the hallway conversation. According to Thayer, he had confided the story of the hallway conversation to his attorney William Brennan in February, soon after it occurred. It had not appeared in the McLaughlin Report, released at the end of March, and was presumably not yet known to the AG. But Brennan had recognized that an *ex parte* conversation on his divorce panel would expose Thayer to at least as much legal risk as Brock, if and when it was made known. In Thayer's telling, he had reluctantly concluded that an immunity arrangement with the AG would be necessary after all only when he was called to testify before HJC. By April 21, Brennan had disclosed the hallway conversation to the AG, while preparing an "offer of proof" to secure his client's immunity for anything he might say to HJC. A second immunity arrangement was made to cover Thayer's interviews with the AG's own office. Both were made, Thayer stressed, on the understanding that if he committed perjury at any point, his immunity would be voided and he would be prosecuted for that offense as well as all prior ones. That's why, he insisted, he had every reason to be honest on these questions. On May 3, Thayer received a letter confirming the arrangement, and on that same day he personally told the AG's investigators all about the hallway conversation.[106]

Defense attorney Madigan conducted the cross-examination, and it was tense.[107] Was it really plausible that Thayer had never authorized his lawyers to trade his resignation for the end of grand jury proceedings? That Attorney General McLaughlin and his investigators were all falsifying matters? Why would they? Thayer claimed that he had confided the story of the hallway conversation to Brennan in February, and that Brennan had revealed it to the AG's investigators a few weeks later. But the earliest *recorded* account of it was May 3, precisely when he had received his immunity letter. Was that not suspicious? Thayer's account of his engagement in the *Feld* case differed markedly from Johnson's: Thayer represented it as a mild and conventional interpellation, while Johnson found it so forceful and egregious a breach of protocol that he twice complained to the chief justice himself. What to make of that discrepancy? What to make of the myriad contradictions between Thayer's testimony and Howard Zibel's? Why would Zibel repeatedly misrepresent Thayer's handling of his financial disclosure firms? Had Zibel, McLaughlin, and Johnson *all* grossly misread Thayer's actual actions? What about Thayer's relationship with Brock? The chief justice had testified to HJC that he and Thayer had never had a particularly close relationship; he would reiterate that at trial. Was it really plausible that, despite their various collisions over the years, Thayer was as unencumbered by ill will toward Brock as he now let on?

At the very end of the trial, as his next-to-last witness, Steinfield would bring William Brennan before the Senate, to back up Thayer's account of how the hallway conversation had come to the attention of investigators.[108] Brennan testified that a very upset Thayer had called him on the evening of February 14, after reading the copy of the Zibel memo that Brock had sent him. He had no notes of that conversation, but Brennan did remember Thayer's mentioning that he had spoken with Brock about his divorce panel on February 4. The next morning, Brennan claimed, Thayer had gone on to provide a detailed account of the entire *ex parte* hallway conversation the next morning. He had absolutely no reason to lie about that conversation, since it actually worsened his own legal position. Thayer had indeed authorized him to offer his resignation to the attorney general, Brennan acknowledged on cross-examination; but not in return for dropping the grand jury action.

Thayer, claimed Brennan, simply *hoped* the AG would take that course. But nothing had been traded—no matter what the McLaughlin Report said ("I am saying to you that as far as Stephen Thayer was concerned, that statement is not accurate").[109]

What were senators to make of it all? Had Thayer earned their confidence? Could his account of the hallway conversation be trusted? Could they even be sure, with only Eileen Fox's now-qualified testimony, that Brock had ever gone into the hallway to fetch him? Was there really enough evidence to support a "Yes" vote to impeach on Article 1?

Consideration of Article III, alleging that Brock had twice lied to HJC in order to impede its investigation, would produce some of the sharpest exchange of the trial. That was hardly surprising. Several senators had openly stated during pretrial procedural debates that they considered these claims tantamount to criminal perjury, which meant that the House Managers' counsel would have to demonstrate that Brock had willingly, maliciously, and repeatedly lied to legislators. In short, Steinfield and his team would have to show that the chief justice was practically beyond trust, even beyond respect. That was sure to cause a stir.

Steinfield brought Brock's former lawyers, Michael Callahan and Michael Ramsdell, to the stand, and each witness explicitly contradicted Brock's account of what had transpired on the morning of March 3. According to them, they had drafted a letter to the attorney general describing Thayer's threats to "blow up the court," in deference to their client's wishes but against their own better judgment. Callahan and Ramsdell both insisted that, while they had indeed faxed Brock the draft, they had continued to oppose sending it. In fact, they said, they were sure they had received Brock's grudging but clear assent to their perspective on the morning of March 3. Certainly, each claimed, nothing had been said to the chief justice indicating that the letter was actually *en route* to Attorney General McLaughlin.[110]

That Brock had thought otherwise at first was no more than a misunderstanding. But Ralph Lancaster, who had replaced Ramsdell and Callahan as Brock's counsel after their withdrawal, had directly informed his client that the letter had not been sent; and that was well before Brock's May 19 testimony before HJC. On that day, Steinfield argued, Brock's responses to queries about whether he knew the letter's fate—a letter Steinfield had placed directly before him—could hardly be put down to confusion or faulty memory or anything but deliberate deception. "Of my personal knowledge, no," the chief justice had said; and "My assumption is [*that*] it was filed with the attorney general." Why, Steinfield would demand, had he not simply stated that he had thought the letter had been sent, but now realized it hadn't? Why had he not simply told the truth? Before the Senate, Brock would defend his replies in a variety of ways. "I—I don't recall ever having seen the draft of that letter on the letterhead of Gallagher, Callahan," he said at one point, under Steinfield's questioning. At another, he offered "What I was doing at that point in time was saying, my personal knowledge base all along had been that that March 3 letter—or that the threats had been reported on March 3 by the counsel to the attorney general. That's what I intended by that."[111] But Steinfield dismantled those explanations mercilessly. If Brock's lawyer had told him that he would not be able to accompany the chief justice at his HJC deposition, Steinfield would ask, "would you then have personal knowledge of that fact?" If he came to the courthouse and a clerk told him that an appeal had been filed in a case, "you'd have a personal knowledge of that fact, would you not?" Well, Steinfield continued, Brock's lawyer *had* told him that the March 3 letter had never been sent, and claiming that he had no "personal knowledge" of what had happened to it simply wouldn't wash.

In his concluding remarks, Steinfield tried to address the points that he knew, from the queries senators had addressed to Ramsdell and Callahan, were troubling a number of them. Perjury, after all, entails both intent and materiality. What exactly was the materiality of Brock's denial of knowledge about the disposition of that letter to the HJC's investigation? What had been his motivation to lie on May 19? What was the significance of the entire matter, since Brock had personally informed the AG himself of Thayer's threats on March 10 anyway? Steinfield's explanation was simple. The McLaughlin Report made no ruling, offered no finding, on whether Brock had complied with his duty to report Thayer's threats—even though both the threats themselves and Brock's awareness of them *as* threats were mentioned in it. Why not? HJC had wanted to know, and it was entitled to investigate under the terms of HR50. Brock's lies had deflected that investigation.[112]

But it was the misstatements about his familiarity with the *Home Gas* documentation that really angered Steinfield, because they involved what he considered even more egregious dissimulation—abetted by Ralph Lancaster, and entailing a veiled insult to Steinfield's own professionalism.

Senators already knew that on May 19, when responding to Steinfield's questions about *Home Gas*, Brock had complained he didn't have the relevant documents in front of him to refresh his memory. They also knew that Brock's memory had in fact been amply refreshed by an extensive review of those documents, which he had secured from the supreme court's own archives and sent on to Lancaster in April. But they wouldn't know the full backstory until the very end of the impeachment trial, when Steinfield explained it.

He and his team hadn't known about the *Home Gas* affair, Steinfield said in his closing remarks, until May 14, when former Justice Johnson had given them a heavily redacted copy of the report the supreme court had sent to JCC on the matter, and a very few of the addenda. The House Managers' lawyers had "agonized" over what to do; the matter, after all, was 13 years old. Yet, in the end, they had decided it couldn't be ignored, and served subpoenas to JCC, to Rockingham County Superior Court, and to the New Hampshire Supreme Court itself to secure any and all documentation the case might have generated. Steinfield had proceeded ethically, informing Lancaster and his client that Brock would be questioned on *Home Gas* but promising not to raise the question until the defense had a chance to go over all written materials relative to the case. What he hadn't known, and what no one chose to tell him, was that the defense had been in possession of all that documentation all along—most of which Steinfield himself had never seen, and didn't even know existed.[113]

But the actions of Lancaster, whom Steinfield considered a friend and mentor, were to the House Managers' counsel almost as objectionable as Brock's.[114] Lancaster had advised his client to exercise extreme caution in answering questions on *Home Gas* before HJC, publicly interrupting exchanges between Brock and his questioners. He said his reasoning was that, once the court had deposited the materials it had collected with JCC, those materials might well fall under that body's rules of confidentiality. But to Steinfield, those scruples were simply bogus. The *Home Gas* investigation had been conducted by the supreme court, not JCC, and Steinfield insisted that the documentation produced therefore fell outside the purview of Rule 40. And then, Steinfield felt, Lancaster had quite literally added insult to injury.

On September 28, Lancaster told senators that when he was first retained by Brock and gone over the relevant documents in his client's possession, he had not thought that so old a matter as *Home Gas* would interest HJC investigators, and had casually set the documents aside. When he learned otherwise, he felt he had cause to worry: even though the documents Brock had shown him had come from the supreme court's own archives, copies were in JCC's possession—and the actual wording of Rule 40 held confidential "all information, communications, materials, papers, files and transcripts, written or oral, received or developed by the committee in the course of its work." He simply wasn't sure, Lancaster said, whether information on *Home Gas* was privileged or not, and advised his counsel to err on the side of caution lest he incur censure from yet another quarter. He had also, he explained, frantically petitioned JCC counsel William Saturley to waive confidentiality on the *Home Gas* materials, and convey them all to Steinfield at once. That Saturley had not secured all JCC members' approval of that waiver by Jay 19 was neither his nor Brock's fault. Nor, Lancaster had suggested, was it their fault that, when Brock had declined to answer questions drawing on his knowledge of *Home Gas* materials, Steinfield had failed to ask the obvious follow-up question: "Is it the case that you have the documents in your possession but can't divulge their contents because of JCC confidentiality?" Lancaster explained that, like any good attorney, he had advised his client to answer the question that was asked, no more and no less. It was opposing counsel's job to ask the right questions.[115] In fact, Lancaster said, Steinfield had missed the obvious follow-up question regarding that March 3 letter to the AG, as well. When Brock had said he had no "personal knowledge" that the letter had not been sent, Lancaster proposed, "The next logical question is, 'From any source, Justice Brock, not just from your own personal knowledge.'"[116]

Relations between Steinfield and Lancaster seemed to undergo visible change over the course of Lancaster's testimony (Sen. Squires would remark that their exchanges "alternated rapidly between discussion between friends, suddenly between adversaries, suddenly first name and then a formal name, and most astonishingly, the mentor-student relationship, all happening within seconds, which is disconcerting, frankly").[117] Lancaster would acknowledge to Sen. Brown that he could and should have just given Steinfield the materials that he and Brock had, and explained that they simply didn't yet know whether they comprised the totality of JCC's holdings on *Home Gas*.[118] Steinfield, however, was unforgiving. In fact, in his closing statement he would suggest that the defense had played even dirtier pool than he had initially described. What Brock and his defender had undertaken was a kind of "legalistic alchemy," Steinfield argued. "You take something that is not entitled to Rule 40 and you say, 'We'll send it over to the JCC and then nobody will know about it.' That just can't be right."[119] At the very least, declared Steinfield, Brock's refusal to simply acknowledge that he had indeed seen the *Home Gas* documents but couldn't reveal their contents constituted "the kind of hairsplitting, the kind of excuse-making that nobody can permit of any witness, much less a justice of the court."[120]

Senators, however, would also have to consider the testimony of JCC counsel William Saturley, who firmly supported Lancaster's side of the story. First of all, Saturley explained, there were good reasons why JCC was so scrupulous about confidentiality. In any sort of investigation, investigators don't want witnesses to know what information other witnesses have imparted, since they can then tailor their own answers accordingly. In addition, one or another party is usually unhappy with the end result of litigation, and claims that a particular judge has been unfair are, unsurprisingly, common. Should those charges be made public prior to serious vetting by JCC, public confidence in judges, including blameless ones, would certainly be affected (to say nothing of the risk of libel action by an unfairly maligned judge).[121] So seriously did JCC take the confidentiality requirement, according to Saturley, that its reading of Rule 40 might well license it to charge violators with contempt of the supreme court itself (JCC's linkage to the court was thus defended as a kind of enforcement mechanism).

From the point of view of Saturley and the JCC, then, Lancaster's concerns were entirely proper. In fact, JCC'S counsel acknowledged, the specific reason why the *Home Gas* materials couldn't be released without waivers from all JCC members was that Brock was currently the subject of a JCC investigation, which had been stayed pending the outcome of the impeachment. Despite repeated efforts, House Managers' counsel Ball simply could not get Saturley to concede that JCC rules did not prevent the supreme court or Brock himself from releasing the *Home Gas* materials even if JCC couldn't. The furthest JCC's representative would go was to acknowledge that if a case were outside JCC's own, one-year time limit on investigations, a complainant might be empowered to reveal that a complaint had been filed.[122] He concluded by stressing how strenuously Lancaster had sought the waiver from JCC, and transfer of all *Home Gas* materials to Steinfield.[123]

That left Article IV, on the recusal policy. In his opening statement, Steinfield had described Article IV as "the most profound of the four articles," since it was the only one that "addresses institutional misconduct."[124] Granted, the policy had been in place prior to Brock's elevation to chief justice, and even prior to his appointment to the supreme court. But Brock had headed the institution for fourteen years. He had clearly chosen to continue the practice, and must be held personally accountable for its abuse in the *Feld* case and, perhaps, others. Over the course of the trial, Steinfield would establish just how carefully each court opinion was read and checked, then re-read and re-checked, by justices themselves; by their individual law clerks; by the court's own clerks, Howard Zibel and David Peck; by executive secretary Margaret Haskett. The claim that recused justices' input was needed to somehow maintain grammatical standards or enhance the quality of the final "product," he would propose, was absurd. Indeed, most of the judges who testified (Johnson, Batchelder, Hollman, Gray, McHugh) would reveal that, when recused, they themselves never considered such involvement.

Yet every supreme court justice, past and present, who testified would insist that, in all their time on the court, they had never witnessed a single abuse of the practice until Thayer's action on the *Feld* case—and even that was debatable. To confirm the gravity of what had been done for all those years, on Brock's watch, Steinfield would rely on Prof. Steven Lubet. It would be Lubet's first testimony at the impeachment trial of a state justice.

He began by describing the background of the Model Code of Judicial Conduct produced by the American Bar Association in 1972, replacing its 1924 version. One crucial principle embodied in the old Code, Lubet explained, had been judges' "duty to sit." Questions about possible judicial bias had to be persuasive before a judge could be relieved of his role in any particular case; the judge, that is, enjoyed a presumption of innocence. But by 1972, the ABA had undergone what Lubet called "a sea change in attitude" on the question of bias. With Canon 3 (C and D), the authors of the new Code consciously rejected the old norm, and required judges to step aside should there be any credible *appearance* of impartiality. The 1972 Model Code had won acceptance throughout the judicial universe, Lubet explained. It had been promptly adopted by the Judicial Conference of the United States, which set policy for U.S. district and appellate courts; and by the year 2000, 49 of 51 jurisdictions, including New Hampshire, had adopted it either in whole or part. Indeed, said Lubet, New Hampshire had distinguished itself by prioritizing the principle of judicial impartiality 200 years earlier than the ABA had. Its constitutional language calling for judges to hold themselves "as impartial as the lot of humanity will admit" was, in his view, "the single most elegant iteration of that concept that I've come across."[125]

Lubet acknowledged that he could offer senators no guidance on the veracity of the charges leveled against Brock; only on whether, if true, they represented serious violations of the state's Code. That said, his conclusion was clear. They did.

Regarding Article I and *Home Gas*, Lubet said, he did not mean to imply that any communication between the chief justice, as administrative head of the judiciary, and a trial judge would be unethical. But Brock's call to Judge Gray was, because it was prompted by a powerful politician (Bartlett) on behalf of another powerful politician (Dupont). The point wasn't whether Brock intended to influence Gray's ruling, or whether Gray inferred any such intent. The point, rather, was not the reality but the appearance of partiality, since the call was wholly unknown to one of the parties in the case. The offense was worsened by the fact that in March 1987 the case had already come before the supreme court once, and might well do so again.[126] Regarding Article II, Lubet said that Brock should not even have announced his appointments to Thayer's divorce panel in that conference of February 4, let alone invited comment on them. His leaving the room to ask Zibel to put Pappagianis's invitation on hold indicated responsiveness to Thayer's *ex parte* importuning, thus aggravating the offense.[127]

But Lubet reserved his strongest language for Article IV. He was quite sure that Brock's maintenance of the recusal policy was "not consistent with the requirements of the Code of Judicial Conduct." After all, Lubet noted, Canon 3C of the 1972 Code clearly stated that "A judge should disqualify himself in a proceeding in which his impartiality might reasonably be questioned." That should be read in tandem with Canon 3D, which further stipulated that "A judge who is disqualified, must withdraw from the proceeding." "Not must refrain from voting," Lubet emphasized, "but 'must withdraw.'"[128] Of course, the 1972 Model Code had provided for exceptions. If a judge were to disclose, on the record, the basis of the disqualification, and if the parties to the case and their respective counsel were to agree, in writing and with no participation from the judge, that the latter might continue, then the disqualification was lifted. But that, Lubet said, was precisely his point. The language chosen illustrated "the bright line, the complete separation that's expected. A judge who is disqualified can't even be present when the parties to the case are discussing whether or not to remit the disqualification. That's how thorough it is."[129] There was only conclusion: "Disqualification means disqualification."[130]

Lubet had little regard for the argument that recused justices' might legitimately contribute to the wording, annotation, or stylistic quality of the final opinion. Suggestions on "grammar and style," he explained, could not be "hermetically sealed from outcome:" however innocuous such input might seem at first glance, it might very well affect the scope of the opinion or how it would be applied in the future. The main point was that public perceptions of judicial integrity were hardly enhanced by the vision of judges very publicly walking off the bench when certain cases came before them, them walking back into the conference room as the decision was being formulated. The thinking behind the new Code was very clear: the days of a somewhat relaxed approach to judicial disqualifications were over. But Brock had ignored it.[131]

Defense counsel Ross's cross-examination was aggressive, even confrontational.[132] Yes, he induced Lubet to admit, the Code had never been intended to provide a basis of civil liability or criminal prosecution. Yes, the Code did specifically state that not every transgression need result in disciplinary action; that should depend on "the seriousness of the transgression, whether there is a pattern of improper activity and the effect of the improper activity on others or on the judicial system." Yes, disciplinary action, if appropriate, might take a variety of forms (such as private reprimand, public reprimand, or suspension). Yes, Lubet's testimony was offered on the understanding, but not the certainty, that the facts Steinfield had provided him were true. Yes, Lubet had already expressed some opinions regarding the impeachment on public radio.[133]

But Lubet seemed prepared for Ross's attempts to undermine the value of his testimony. His comments on public radio, the witness insisted, had in no way incurred the "appearance of partiality" for which he now so sternly criticized Brock. He had simply explained how he believed the charges should be assessed *if* true (and, to be sure, he had been shown "five of six volumes of sworn testimony from Justice Brock, as well as other documents that had been produced," so his views were not exactly groundless).[134] Steinfield, on re-direct, took pains to assure senators that Lubet in no way aimed to usurp their own responsibility to determine the consequences of Brock's actions, if proven; or the penalties he would incur, if convicted. Most disciplinary proceedings, Lubet explained, have two phases, one on culpable conduct and one on consequences, and he had never presumed to comment on anything but the latter.[135]

Yet senators' questions suggested that doubts remained. Sen. Fred King raised the question of whether *all* supreme court justices should be liable to disciplinary action alongside Brock, since all of them had been just as aware as he of the new strictures regarding disqualification that Lubet had cited, and just as indifferent to them. It was a difficult question for Lubet—he declined to offer an opinion on any other justice's culpability. "I have not thought through" that point, Lubet said, "and therefore I am reluctant to give you an opinion that I thought the justices personally violated the code … I do think, as I've said before, that the policy is wrong."[136] But Sen. Squires pressed him hard. Were all the other justices just "weak-kneed ethicists and couldn't see what you believe to be obvious, or did they simply fall in lock-step with the chief justice and do what he told them?" Squires demanded. "3C says a judge should disqualify … And it appears that these judges did this. And yet you're unable to conclude that they're in violation of the code ... How is it possible that they can retreat behind this policy?" Lubet replied "Well, I didn't say that they could, actually. I said that I don't know because I haven't considered that issue in the context of this proceeding … you know, there's a limit to what I undertook to do in reaching and opinion, and what you've asked me for is beyond that. And the reason it's beyond it is because there's an additional consideration between the associates and the chief."[137]

But Squires would not relent. "If that's true," he concluded, "then your statement—or Mr. Steinfield's statement—that you came here only to share the truth with us and talk about ethics in some general manner fails, because I've asked you a fundamental ethical question, 'Did the actions of the associate justices violate the code of conduct,' and you can't answer it." A few moments later, Lubet would acknowledge to Sen. Brown that, just as the associate justices might merit forbearance since they had been following the lead of their Chief, so might the chief justice merit a degree of it since he was following a policy that his predecessors had set in place.[138]

Lubet's testimony would be challenged by Judges Kelly, Johnson, and Batchelder, as well. Kelly, referring to Lubet's conclusions regarding Articles I and II, explained that Canon 3 of the Code of Judicial Conduct is divided into Part A on adjudicative matters and Part B on administrative matters. That was deliberate, as there were ethical considerations specific to each sphere; and Kelly felt that Lubet had wrongly conflated them.[139] Johnson, while vigorously denying that his complaints to Brock about Thayer's actions on the *Feld* case involved any critique at all of the recusal policy itself, bluntly declared that "There wasn't even a thought in my mind that we were in violation of the Code of Ethics … and I think Mr. Lubet was just plain, flat wrong when he told this committee and this Senate that it was a violation as he did, and I was here at the time of his testimony."[140] Batchelder, testifying near the end of the trial, told Sen. Brown that, with the release of the McLaughlin Report, "I expected that there would be an entire array of cases for the State to consider where lines had been crossed. I have yet to see such a list. Two cases have been mentioned and each of the cases that we talked about have been dealt with by the court and by the attorney general."[141]

Chief Justice David Brock followed Batchelder to the stand, and stayed there the better part of two days. After nearly two weeks of exhaustive testimony on each article of impeachment, senators might have been forgiven the expectation that Brock's own testimony might be somewhat anticlimactic. But they would have been wrong.

By that time, they had heard numerous witnesses praise the chief justice, both personally and professionally. Stephen Thayer, of all people, had spoken of the compassion Brock had shown him in his time of troubles, prior to the events of February 4. "The Chief knew the stress I was under," Thayer testified, "and he'd come in and he'd talk to me about it … my estrangement from my son has been very, very difficult for me. He's a father. … He told me it was going to get better; that wait a few years and my son would come back."[142] David Peck, Supreme Court Deputy Clerk, echoed that description. "David Brock is as fine a man as I've ever met and ever worked for," Peck said. "I could tell you stories of times when I've had troubles at the court, when he has recognized my problem he's brought me into his office, talked to me for 15, 20 minutes and listened to me, really helped me through."[143] Howard Zibel described him as "one of the great justices … he calls them as he sees them and [is] fearless for the consequences in the press, and I think you can't ask more of a jurist than that." Explicitly countering the notion that the chief justice had sealed the judiciary off from public accountability, Zibel explained that, on the contrary, it was Brock who had changed the composition of the JCC so that laypersons would constitute a plurality, and who had made its process *less* confidential by insisting that any proceedings against judges that JCC actually brought to the supreme court would be public (New Hampshire's process, Zibel claimed, was "the most open in the nation").[144]

In lauding Brock's jurisprudence, Judge Batchelder chose the somewhat risky path of addressing the *Claremont* litigation directly. "Now, you have to know that David Brock is an unrepentant, card-carrying Nixon Republican," Batchelder began. "He has been counsel to [former Republican governors] Meldrim Thompson and John Sununu. These are not the criteria of a bomb-throwing Bolshevik. And I watched him work out the first Claremont case. And it would have been so easy to turn our backs on that. … And I saw him really turn aside from every political fiber in his body and mind and turn away from it and author an opinion that he thought—and we agreed with him, along with Judge Grimes—was right on the law and a correct interpretation of the Constitution and the oath which he took to support. Is that enough?"[145]

It was enough for Steinfield to openly acknowledge to senators that "if a person exists out there who thinks ill of Chief Justice Brock as a person, I'm not aware of it." But that was not the point, he said. "This is not a case about character," Steinfield explained. "It is a case about conduct."[146] And Brock, for all his many fine qualities, had engaged in conduct that merited impeachment and conviction. In grilling Brock on October 2 and 3, Steinfield made sure senators fully understood why he felt Brock simply could not be trusted, and his account of events not believed.

Under Madigan's questions, Brock had reiterated in considerable detail his own accounts of the events behind each article of impeachment. That lasted half of October 2 and well into October 3, whereupon Steinfield began his cross-examination. He opened with an intriguing exchange on Anglo-American trial procedures. "Chief Justice Brock," Steinfield asked, "would you agree with me that a trial is a search for the truth?" Yes, Brock replied. Steinfield continued, "Now, one of the features of the Anglo-American system of trials is cross-examination, am I right?" Brock affirmed that, too. Steinfield then asked for the chief justice's understanding of the function of cross-examination, and Brock answered that it is "to test the truth of testimony that's come out on direct examination," adding "This is something that is unique to this proceeding." This particular cross-examination would test Brock's testimony as severely as it had been tested to date. In fact, from that opening colloquy on, Steinfield would reveal discrepancy after discrepancy between the accounts Brock had just elaborated to the Senate, and the accounts of nearly everyone else who had participated in the events in question. He would reveal, as well, internal inconsistencies within Brock's own testimony, delivered now to three different investigating bodies. The question was: how would senators assess them?

Some of those discrepancies were arguably inconsequential. For example, Brock had testified to both HJC and the Senate that at some point well after that eventful February 4 case conference, he had sought out Thayer in an office in the law clerks' wing of the court building to explain that he had been compelled to exile him from the meeting because "what you did was wrong." Subsequently, Brock said, he had briefly chatted with Justices Horton and Broderick, noting that Thayer's outburst was "something we were going to have to deal with next week."[147] But neither Broderick nor Horton recalled any such chat on that highly memorable day. On March 10, Brock had told the attorney general's investigators that he couldn't remember whether he had gone out into the hallway to fetch Thayer, or had asked Eileen Fox to do it. Yet by the time of his testimony to HJC, he was positive he had never left the conference room.

But the examples kept coming, and it may have been the accumulation of inconsistencies, rather than the gravity of any one or two, that the House Managers' counsel hoped would trouble senators. For example, Brock had testified to HJC that he had recognized a duty to report Thayer's threats of February 14 and 15 "pretty soon after they occurred." Indeed, on March 19 he stated unambiguously that a statute (N.H. Rev. Stat. Ann. §640:3) "imposed a duty on me and others who were threatened."[148] Why, then, hadn't he reported to law-enforcement agents immediately?[149] Brock tried to correct himself. What he had meant, he said, was that the statute "raised an issue as to whether I was" obliged to report Thayer's words, but "I didn't immediately think of [§640:3] and analyze whether what he said that night, that the next day I had an obligation to report the threats." Rather, he and his fellow justices "discussed this in a calm and deliberative way with our counsel and received some advice concerning that at that time."[150] But why did his lawyers' accounts of those deliberations, on matters so vital to so many careers, diverge so widely from Brock's own?

Steinfield read back to him his own testimony of May 19, when Brock had told HJC that by March 3 Callahan and Ramsdell had more or less come to agree with him that Thayer should be reported to the AG for February 14–15 remarks. When asked who told him so, he replied "That would have been Mr. Callahan." But when shown the letter again, Brock had to acknowledge "When I look at this, I can't remember that he expressly said 'We will now file this with the attorney general.'" Steinfield then read relevant portions of the testimony by Ramsdell and Callahan; the latter, in particular, clearly recalled that on March 3 Brock had acquiesced to his attorneys' view that reporting Thayer's words as threats would be unwise. "Was that testimony correct?" Steinfield asked. "That was not correct," Brock replied.[151] In that case, asked Steinfield, "can we agree that your testimony and Mr. Callahan's testimony on this point is 180 degrees opposite?" "I guess I don't think of it in geometric terms," Brock replied.[152]

Steinfield reminded the chief justice that he had also testified to informing Horton and Broderick that he had reported Thayer to the attorney general. Brock was no longer sure whether that had been after March 3, or after his March 10 interview with the AG's team. "But I did at some point," he insisted. Yet neither Horton nor Broderick could remember that conversation, either. "Mr. Steinfield, our memories are different," Brock said.[153]

But why should Brock's memories be trusted, when they so often clashed with others'? The *Feld* case conference provided another illustration. According to both Horton's and Johnson's testimony, Thayer's intervention had catalyzed an extensive and substantive debate (Horton had called it "brilliant" and said it had changed his own thinking on the matter, even though he was not voting on it). Brock, who had recently undergone prostate surgery, said he had briefly left the conference room and must have missed that discussion. But participants described the discussion as lasting at least 15 minutes—quite a long absence for the conference's convener.[154]

Regarding *Home Gas*, Steinfield raised questions about the odd time-lapse between Brock's awareness of complaints against Judge Gray, and the inception of the investigation. Gray had allegedly made biased remarks in conference in August 1987 (which Brock must have learned about that November, as indicated by his letter to Bartlett) and again in January 1988 (which Brock also knew, as indicated by his letter to Dupont that month). Brock had professed concerns about addressing the complaints while *Home Gas*-related matters were still in Gray's court. But the case had concluded there in January 1988, yet no investigation was initiated until March 1989. This was well past the JCC's one-year limit on investigations. Steinfield made sure senators knew that Brock himself had chaired JCC from October 1981 until April 1989, and was well aware of the time limit. He himself had no explanation for the delay ("it had somehow fallen through the cracks"). Might he have wanted to keep the matter from JCC in order to make sure his phone call to Gray never came to light? Brock had always insisted that his call had been to Ray Taylor, and that it had been in 1987. Yet phone records had confirmed a call from Taylor to Brock in February 1989, not 1987.[155] And of course, Steinfield's view that Brock had perpetrated obvious falsehoods regarding his familiarity with the *Home Gas* documentation itself, as well as what he knew about that un-mailed March 3 letter, was perfectly clear.

The House Managers' chief counsel began his closing statement by allowing that "no one can have sat through these proceedings without feeling compassion for Chief Justice Brock and his family."[156] No one, he insisted, had ever claimed Brock was a bad man.[157] But maladministration was maladministration all the same, Steinfield insisted, and in this case "it reaches a level of such seriousness that it needs to be addressed."[158] The point, he reminded senators, was the protection of the public interest, which must always be their first priority.[159]

Counsel for each side made much of historical precedent in their closing statements. For the defense, Steven Ross quoted William Wirt, longest-serving attorney general in US history, who while defending impeached federal judge James Peck in 1830 had affirmed that "an impeachment is not a mere inquiry, in the nature of an inquest of office, whether an officer be qualified for his place, or whether some reason of policy or expediency may not demand his removal, but a criminal prosecution, for the support of which the proof of some willful violation of a known law of the land is known to be indispensably required."[160] Ross didn't refer to more modern impeachments, when the notion that the practice should be reserved for criminal offenses was fully rejected. He did, however, make an attempt to address concerns senators might have about inconsistencies in testimony. When justices contradicted each other or even themselves, proposed Ross, "It's not that either justice was lying or trying to mislead the Senate. It's not even in that instance that their memories were all that different ... It was that the way they understood what they were being called to talk about differed." Head defense counsel Michael Madigan, for his part, would reiterate the notion that senators should maintain a high burden of proof in an impeachment trial, which he insisted the House Managers had not met.[161]

Finally, Henry Mock spoke briefly on behalf of the House of Representatives. "Compassion," he said, "must be tempered by our duty to uphold our Constitution and to protect the constitutional rights of citizens of this state." *Claremont* had played no role at all in the impeachment of the chief justice, Mock insisted. Nor had the House been "overzealous." Rather, Mock said, "We are here because of what we saw as bad management of the court administration including a recusal policy gone awry, a policy when finally revealed to sunlight that was met with astonished disbelief by lawyers and non-lawyers alike." In conclusion, he returned to the themes he had emphasized throughout the House's impeachment. "And perhaps the most important reason that we are here is because the administration of justice, cloaked in secrecy, faulted; in fact, it failed, hidden under the disguise of judicial privilege and confidentiality ... There is no right of secrecy at the Supreme Court." And finally: "The trial has been similar to other legal proceedings but it is, in fact, constitutionally designed to be a political process. The real clients of the House and the Senate are the people of New Hampshire. Or first consideration in acting on this impeachment has been and must continue to be the best interest of the citizens of this state."[162]

SENATE JUDGMENT

Senators would articulate their own understanding of what they had witnessed and its significance on October 10, the fifteenth day of the trial. It was a day of both eloquence and careful thought. It was certainly a day of high drama. Senators' remarks revealed not only attentiveness to the granular details of the evidence they heard for and against Brock, but also mindfulness of the broader civic questions the impeachment had raised.

These latter included the question of what, exactly, should be prioritized in an impeachment trial, and its essential purpose. Sen. Francoeur endorsed Steinfield's and Mock's view that "The function of an impeachment trial is to protect the public," and determined that the public's right to an impartial judiciary in peril had indeed been jeopardized by Brock's actions.[163] Sen. Brown went further, proposing that the problem stretched beyond Brock to the entire institutional culture of New Hampshire's judiciary, and that the point of the impeachment was a kind of institutional cleansing. "I think secrecy is what brought us here," Brown said; "I think the notion that secrecy is somehow necessary has led to a lot of the public distrust and suspicion, and I think the Chief primarily is responsible to that." Brown faulted "the institutional reluctance to understand the vital necessity for public confidence," and asked senators to recognize that "To a certain extent it is our responsibility, as the last resort for the public, to restore confidence in the supreme court." That, she said, "can be accomplished only one way, and that is with a new Chief and new rules followed by close public scrutiny ... Sunlight is the best elixir."[164]

But the trial's presiding officer, Sen. Hollingworth, thought differently. Impeachment, she argued, "is not intended as a process to which the House and Senate would restore confidence in another branch of government." Senators, Hollingworth felt, "should not attempt to restore confidence in a judicial practice or if there is less confidence in that process, we trample on the rights of an individual who is not guilty."[165] Others shared her discomfort with the notion that the fate of the individual before them should be secondary to a responsibility to monitor the internal affairs of another branch of government. "The House of Representatives has asked us to consider our clients to be the people of New Hampshire," said Sen. Squires, "implying that failure to adopt these four articles of impeachments puts at great risk the most basic rights of all of us. I must, with great respect, disagree. An institution is not on trial and we do not have a client. A man is on trial, and we are constituted as a jury to—as the House counsel reminded us—to base our judgments, and ultimately our vote, on the evidence that we have heard in this room concerning the conduct of one man."[166]

Even Sen. Trombly, whose motion to keep all proceedings open had been based on his conviction that "The public must be invested in our decision," proved unwilling in the end to endorse Mock's emphasis on the political dimension of impeachment. "Representative Mock also said that this was a political process, and I have to disagree," said Trombly. "I've not weighed or based any of my decisions on any of these articles of impeachment on how they resonate with my constituents. They'll make up their own minds, and I'll accept their decision, because that's how this process works."[167] "We have to look at the conduct in all this, not the public perception," agreed Sen. Cohen.[168] Sen. Russman, too, confided that he had deliberately approached the proceedings as an attorney rather than a tribune of the people. "I am a lawyer by profession," he said, "and I'm prouder than ever, frankly, to be that." With a lawyerly concern for precedent, Russman reminded his colleagues that "Both defense and prosecution in this case have noted the lack of substantive case law in judicial impeachment nationally." That, Russman felt, suggested that "Either the conduct of the judges throughout the nation is generally above reproach, or more states have viewed that the implementation of committees such as the JCC are effective in investigating, safeguarding, and maintaining the integrity of the judiciary." New Hampshire, Russman implied, should do the same.[169]

There were numerous expressions of support for judicial reform—most often framed as hope that the judiciary would heal itself. Sen. Wheeler felt that "The JCC, not the legislature, enforces the judicial canon of ethics. Perhaps some changes need to be considered for the JCC, but not through the process of impeachment."[170] Sen. John King felt that "a good result is, if there is such a thing, would be the judicial branch to review, create and implement more effective and specific rules and methods to handle judicial information with the public …" [171] Indeed, a deep commitment to the separation of powers, and serious misgivings about what the impeachment portended for it, was expressed by several senators. "I hope as the legislature contemplates change," said Sen. Fred King, "it does not lose sight of Article 37 in the constitution, and I quote, 'The legislative, executive and judicial ought to be kept as separate from and independent of each as the nature of our free government will admit.'"[172] "My fervent hope, after passions have cooled and reason once again prevails," said Sen. Wheeler, "is that the legislature will recognize and affirm a central doctrine of our constitution: the separation of powers. … Impeachment is an awesome weapon which should be used extremely sparingly. A mistake, an error in judgment, cannot be an impeachable offense."[173]

Finally, a majority of senators would find themselves unable to conclude that the allegations against Brock, even if true, reached that higher level of malfeasance—however indeterminate it would remain. "We are all 'of the lot of humanity,'" said Sen. Larsen, paraphrasing the state constitution, "and therefore imperfect creatures prone to error." Brock, Larsen believed, did have "episodes of questionable judgment and commissions of error," and the senator took those lapses seriously ("I believe the legislature and the Judicial Conduct Committee may review other options"). But he simply could not condone conviction. Neither could Sen. Pignatelli, who declared "For Justice Brock in particular, but also for the other justices who have seen their integrity attacked in recent months, I want to say this. You are human beings who make human errors, but you have served us well."[174]

"The fact that we are here today," Sen. Wheeler said, "is proof that no life follows a five-year plan."[175] Brock may have been guilty of errors of judgment, but after 14 days of testimony Wheeler couldn't help "thinking how tricky our memories are and how little we remember," adding "The evidence here, because it is conflicting, is not convincing."[176] That was a viewpoint shared by most of her colleagues. Sen. Francoeur and some others would remain angry at what they perceived as Brock's sanctimony regarding the ethical mote in other judges' eyes and indifference toward the beam in his own. But on the whole, the House Managers had failed to convince most of their colleagues in the Senate that David Brock represented the looming threat to the public interest that the House of Representatives feared he was when they had so overwhelmingly voted to impeach back on July 12. Sen. Krueger supplied an eloquent summation of what she personally had experienced between them and October 10—feelings that were likely not confined to herself:

> I did not come to this trial unbiased. I came very biased. I came from the House. I was not just friends with, but I was certainly cohorts, co-sponsors with the conservatives in the House that were wishing, hoping and sensing the need for judicial reform. I came to this trial almost convinced, Madam President, that in fact I would find huge injustices within the court system; that I would find at its helm a tyrannical master who in fact sought to cover over policies and procedures that would harm the people of the State of New Hampshire and my people. My District 16 people. I didn't find it.
>
> I can't tell you whose 13-year memory is correct. I can't tell you what happened. … I do know the public's information, unless they have watched every solitary moment of this trial, has been filtered through people with other agendas. We would be naïve to think anything else. … I have not heard a history of tyranny at the court. What I have heard has been testimony of appreciation of him as a man and as a justice by all who testified here, including his chief adversary, Steve Thayer. I'm not convinced that the judicial system has not worked, that it has been injured."[177]

Neither were most of Krueger's colleagues, as the final vote counts demonstrated. On the first three articles of impeachment, Brock was acquitted by resounding majorities: 18–4, 17–5, and 18–4. On the fourth article, the vote was only nominally closer, at 14–8. Sen. Krueger said, "I know what's ahead of me after this trial is over. I know that I will be looked at as a traitor to conservatives."[178] By some, perhaps. But not all conservatives—or, for that matter, liberals—would feel that the outcome of the trial was a crushing disappointment.

Coda to Impeachment

On November 21, 2000, just weeks after the conclusion of the Brock impeachment proceedings, the New Hampshire Committee on Judicial Conduct rendered an informal decision on ethics complaints against former Justice Stephen Thayer. Proceedings against him had begun before his resignation from the supreme court on March 31, 2000, after which he filed a petition in the supreme court for a writ of prohibition against any further disciplinary proceedings. With a panel of replacement judges sitting by appointment in place of the justices who had all been obliged to recuse themselves, the court denied Thayer's petition. They ruled in August 2000 that his resignation had not extinguished the disciplinary committee's authority to continue investigating his conduct as a sitting justice.[179]

At the conclusion of its investigation, the committee found that Thayer had failed to make a required public disclosure of loans he had received from attorney Émile Bussiere. The committee also found it likely that Thayer's performance of judicial duties had been impaired by his independent teaching activities at two law schools in Boston, and that his participation in cases from which he been recused was a violation of the code of judicial conduct. Yet the committee decided that there would be little benefit in holding a public hearing on those issues.[180]

Meanwhile, the Committee on Judicial Conduct had also begun an investigation of Chief Justice Brock in March 2000, based on the events with Thayer that had led to the Zibel memorandum, the report by Attorney General McLaughlin, and the April 2000 impeachment inquiry by the House Judicial Committee. The committee invited Chief Justice Brock to respond to the inquiry, and it resumed its discussions with him after the presentation of evidence and Senate decision in the impeachment proceedings. In April 2001, the committee concluded its investigation and issued an admonishment against him rather than holding further public hearings.[181] The committee found that Brock's conduct had violated the code of judicial conduct in three aspects of his handling of Thayer: (1) Thayer's participation in discussions concerning the rules of the conduct committee: (2) Thayer's objection to one of the members of the replacement judges to hear the appeal of his own divorce case; (3) the extent of employment and income generated by Thayer's outside teaching activities in 1999–2000.[182]

The conclusion of judicial disciplinary proceedings against Thayer and Brock brought an end to the institutional investigations of their behavior. Yet the passing of the impeachment crisis did not bring an end to concerns about the relative powers of the judiciary and the legislature. In fact, it was still clear in early 2001 that neither the Brock impeachment nor the judicial disciplinary proceedings against him had resolved the tension between the legislature and the judiciary.

NOTES

1. N.H. General Court, *Impeachment of David A. Brock, Chief Justice of the New Hampshire Supreme Court: before the New Hampshire Senate sitting as a Court of Impeachment* (Concord, N.H.: The Senate, 2000), Impeachment Trial Transcript (July 13, 2000), 5–6. In addition to Mock, the House Managers consisted of Reps.

Phyllis Woods, Loren Jean, Jane Wall, James Craig, and John Pratt. Betsy Miller served as legal counsel to the House itself. The State Library of N.H. in Concord contains full transcripts of each of the trial's 15 sessions, as well as full documentation of all pre-trial motions and decisions on them, and copies of all documents submitted as exhibits by each side and accepted by the Senate.

2. Those were Sen. Gordon, who had served as a law clerk under Brock; and Sen. Roberge, whose family had been involved in the litigation that had given rise to the *Feld* case.

3. Trial Transcript (August 22), 414–15.

4. See Horton v. McLaughlin, 149 N.H. 141, 821 A. 2d 947 (2003). In this case, the state's Supreme Court would reject an effort by Justices Horton, Brock, and Broderick to secure reimbursement for the legal fees they had incurred in the impeachment. The plaintiffs' action resulted from the Attorney General's refusal to provide the legal representation they had initially claimed, on the basis of N.H. Rev. Stat. Ann. §99-D:2. But the Court ruled that the Attorney General had correctly determined that the statute was inapplicable in impeachment cases; that the controlling principle in the case was separation of powers doctrine; and that granting the plaintiffs' request would amount to a judicial incursion into the prerogatives of another branch of government. In its ruling, the Court invoked Part 2, Articles 17 and 38 of the N.H. constitution. Article 17 requires the House of Representatives to serve as the "the grand inquest of the state" in impeachment cases; while Article 38 requires the Senate to function as "court, with full power and authority to hear, try and determine all impeachments made by the house of representatives." That latter responsibility, the Court confirmed, entailed final control of all procedural matters.

5. Both constitutional theory and recent history demonstrate the range of procedural choices open to legislators conducting an impeachment. For the federal model, see Floyd M. Riddick and Robert B. Dove, *Procedure and Guidelines for Impeachment Trials in the United States Senate: Prepared Pursuant to Senate Resolution 439, 99th Congress, 2d Session* (Washington: U.S. G.P.O., 1986), 2–7. For an example of one conducted as an explicitly civil proceeding, see Nebraska Legislature ex. rel. State v. Hergert, 271 Neb. 976, 720 N.W.2d 372 (2006).

6. Brown, *Impeachment Trial*, 259.

7. Trial Transcript (July 13), 14–16.

8. Trial Document No. 15, Final Rules of Procedure and Practice for Impeachment Trials (amended July 25).

9. Trial Document No. 6, Soltani, *et. al.*, Petition for Injunctive Relief with Request for Temporary Restraining Order, filed July 14, N.H. Superior Court, Merrimack County.

10. N.H. Rev. Stat. Ann. Ch. 91-A.

11. Trial Document No. 10, Notice of Decision and Order, Soltani, et al., v. Hollingworth (00-E-240, N.H. Superior Court, Merrimack County, July 17), 6–10.

12. Ibid., 5–6. It is worth noting that federal courts, too, have held that suits by defendants to interrupt impeachment proceedings are non-justiciable. A leading case is Nixon v. United States, 506 U.S. 224 (1993), where Judge Walter Nixon sought a declaratory judgment in federal district court that his impeachment conviction was

void, and that his judicial salary and privileges should be reinstated. The District Court held that his claim was nonjusticiable, 744 F. Supp. 9 (DC 1990), and the Court of Appeals for the District of Columbia Circuit agreed. 290 U.S. App. D. C. 420, 938 F. 2d 239 (1991). When the case reached the Supreme Court, it confirmed that decision. Specifically, it concluded that because the U.S. Constitution gives the "sole" power of impeachment to the Congress, the judiciary has no role in the impeachment process and may not intervene. In his opinion for the Supreme Court, Chief Justice Rehnquist wrote: "A controversy is nonjusticiable—*i.e.,* involves a political question—where there is "a textually demonstrable constitutional commitment of the issue to a coordinate political department; or a lack of judicially discoverable and manageable standards for resolving it." Baker v. Carr, 369 U.S. 186, 217 (1962). But the courts must, in the first instance, interpret the text in question and determine whether and to what extent the issue is textually committed. See *Baker v. Carr;* see also, Powell v. McCormack, 395 U.S. 486, 519 (1969). As the discussion that follows makes clear, the concept of a textual commitment to a coordinate political department is not completely separate from the concept of a lack of judicially discoverable and manageable standards for resolving it; the lack of judicially manageable standards may strengthen the conclusion that there is a textually demonstrable commitment to a coordinate branch." 506 US at 228–229. The New Hampshire petition filed by Soltani and his colleagues was not one by an impeachment defendant to challenge the validity of legislative impeachment proceedings, but was instead a dispute brought by legislative participants in the Brock impeachment, and the Superior Court judge concluded that there were "judicially discoverable and manageable standards for resolving it."

13. Trial Transcript (July 25).

14. Roger Park notes that "the hearsay ban is often loosened when adjudicators sit without a jury, for example, in administrative law adjudications, in arbitration, or in courts of limited jurisdiction." Roger Park, "Exporting the Hearsay Provisions of the Federal Rules of Evidence," *BU Int'l L.J.* 33, no. 2 (2015): 327–42. At 330n. 14, Park quotes Frederick Schauer, who wrote "It is ubiquitous that judges, magistrates, arbitrators, masters, and diverse other adjudicators, when sitting without a jury, will typically … allow hearsay evidence to be offered, announcing that such evidence will be given exactly the weight its intrinsic probative value deserves." Schauer, "On the Supposed Jury-Dependence of Evidence Law," *U. Pa. L. Rev.* 155, no. 1 (2006): 165, 177. Applying this line of thinking on hearsay to impeachment trials, Alan Hirsch writes: "The Senate would presumably be more flexible in allowing in evidence than would be the judge in a regular trial. Much evidence is kept out of trials because jurors, as laypeople, might find it confusing or prejudicial. Arguably, the Senators, many of whom are lawyers, would be able to assess the value of such evidence. Take the hearsay rule, which (absent various circumstances) excludes a witness's testimony about what someone else told the witness. The theory is that, if the person who allegedly made the statement does not take the stand, there's no opportunity for the other side to cross-examine and show that the statement was false. However, senators may recognize this problem and give the evidence less weight—hence there's no need to exclude the evidence altogether." Hirsch, "What Rules Govern Impeachment Trials?" *A Citizen's Guide to Impeachment* (Washington, DC: Essential Books, 1998), §14.

See also Charles Black, *Impeachment: A Handbook* (New Haven, Ct.: Yale University Press, 1998). "Both the House and the Senate ought to hear and consider all evidence which seems relevant, without regard to technical rules," writes Black; "Senators are in any case continually exposed to 'hearsay' evidence; they cannot be sequestered and kept away from newspapers, like a jury. If they cannot be trusted to weigh evidence, appropriately discounting for all the factors of unreliability that have led to our keeping some evidence away from juries, then they are not in any way up to the job, and 'rules of evidence' will not help" (Black, 18). See also Michael Gerhardt, *The Federal Impeachment Process: A Constitutional and Historical Analysis* (Chicago: University of Chicago Press, 2000). Gerhardt cites Black's handbook and adds "An impeachment trial is not the usual kind of trial, nor does it involve a typical jury. Rather, impeachments are extraordinary hearings administered by a sophisticated and politically savvy body—the Congress of the United States" (Gerhardt, 115).

15. Trial Transcript (July 25), 8.

16. Trial Document No. 47, "Brock Motion to Dismiss the Articles of Impeachment and for a More Definite Statement with Supporting Memorandum" (August 4).

17. Ibid., 2–7.

18. Ibid., 10–11.

19. Ibid., 11.

20. Ibid., 12–13.

21. Ibid., 14–15.

22. Ibid., 15–16. The quotation is from Isenbergh, "Impeachment and Presidential Immunity from Judicial Process," *Yale L. & Pol'y Rev.* 18, no. 1 (1999): 53, 75. In the ensuing debate, both the defense and prosecution would also make repeated references to Hoffer and Hull, *Impeachment in America*.

23. Trial Document No. 69, "Memorandum of the House of Representatives in Response to Pre-Trial Motions Filed by Chief Justice Brock," 2.

24. N.H. Rev. Stat. Ann. §625:8.

25. Trial Document No. 69, 5.

26. Ibid., 4. Steinfield noted that Brock himself had held that "where no civil statute of limitations exists a court may not borrow the criminal statute but may only consider whether the action is barred by the doctrine of laches." The case he cited was Appeal of Naswa Motor Inn, 144 N.H. 89, 738 A.2d 349 (1999).

27. "Laches" arises when there has been unreasonable delay that could prejudice the opposing party. The question figured into the federal impeachment proceedings brought against both Judge Alcee Hastings in 1988–1989 and Judge Thomas Porteous in 2009. In Hastings's appeal of his conviction by the Senate, the judge wrote that impeachments are rare, and because of their grave significance the legislature must be given adequate time to verify that an impeachment is warranted. While there was delay in the impeachment proceedings against Judge Alcee Hastings, it was deemed reasonable under the extraordinary circumstances of the case (See Hastings v. U.S., 802 F. Supp. 490 (US D.D.C, 1992). When Judge Thomas Porteous sought injunctive relief against impeachment proceedings in Congress, the lawyers for Special Counsel Alan Baron (the impeachment prosecutor) argued that "Judge Porteous' suit is barred by the doctrine of laches inasmuch as he has inexcusably delayed, until the very eve

of the Committee's first public hearing, asserting his Fifth Amendment claim, and the Committee would be unduly prejudiced by this delay." See Defendants' Opposition to Motion for Temporary Restraining Order and Preliminary Injunction, and Memorandum of Points and Authorities in Support of their Motion to Dismiss, Porteous v. Baron, U.S. District Court for the District of Columbia, Case No. 1:09-cv-2131 (RJL) (November 13, 2009).

28. Trial Document No. 69, "Memorandum of the House of Representatives in Response to Pre-Trial Motions Filed by Chief Justice Brock," 6–7.

29. Ibid., 8–10.

30. Ibid., 16–20.

31. Ibid., 20. On the other hand, argued Steinfield, the actions of, for example, the U.S. Senate, which had refused a motion to dismiss the proposed impeachment of Judge Walter Nixon in 1989 on similar grounds, were very relevant indeed.

32. Ibid., 24–25.

33. Ibid., 24–26.

34. Ibid., 34–35. The quote was from Vol. 2, § 801 of Story, *Commentaries*. Part I, Article 39 of the N.H. constitution, by limiting the consequences of conviction in an impeachment trial to removal from office and disqualification from holding future office, contains language similar to that in the federal constitution.

35. Trial Document No. 48.

36. Trial Document Nos. 49, 50.

37. Trial Transcript (August 21), 5–39.

38. Charles Black writes "Weighing the standards, I would be sure that one ought not to be satisfied with the mere 'preponderance' of an ordinary civil trial, but perhaps must be satisfied with something less than the 'beyond reasonable doubt' standard of the ordinary criminal trial, in the full literal meaning of that standard. 'Overwhelming preponderance of the evidence' comes perhaps as close as present legal language can to denoting the desired standard." Black, *Impeachment Handbook*, 17). In *Federal Impeachment Process,* at 113, Michael Gerhardt cites Black when proposing that "the standard of proof in an impeachment proceeding should be a hybrid of the standards of proof in civil and criminal trials to accommodate the hybrid nature of impeachment trials."

39. Trial Transcript (August 21), 70–73.

40. In fact, among states with constitutional provisions for impeachment trials, only N.H. and Massachusetts failed to require a supermajority to convict. Not surprisingly, each side had its own interpretation of that omission. "I think a fair conclusion is that the Constitution itself contemplates a simple majority in order to impeach," argued Steinfield. Steven Ross, for the defense, proposed that the framers' silence on the subject signaled an invitation to senators tasked with this responsibility to trust to their own best judgment. Ibid.

41. Ibid. (August 22), 443–44.

42. Ibid., 446–449. There had been no support for a "preponderance of the evidence" standard.

43. Ibid., 265–449.

44. Ibid., 409.

45. The New Hampshire constitution does not have an provision specifying the vote required for conviction on articles of impeachment. See N.H. Const. Pt. 2, Art. 38, which at its adoption in 1784 was virtually identical to a similar provision in the 1780 Massachusetts Constitution. Marshall, *State Constitution*, 169.

Six officials have been impeached in Massachusetts history (a sheriff, a probate judge, and four justices of the peace), all between 1788 and 1826. Historical records of the impeachment proceedings for those officials suggest that a simple majority vote is sufficient for conviction. See Octavius Pickering and William Gardiner, *Report of the Trial by Impeachment of James Prescott, Esquire, Judge of the Probate of Wills . . . with an Appendix, Containing an Account of Former Impeachments in the Same State* (Boston, MA: Daily Advertiser, 1821), 207, 214–19; and Abel Bowen and Jerome Smith, *The Boston News-letter, and City Record, Volume 1* (Boston, MA: Abel Bowen, 1826), 92.

Yet only two other states (Alabama and Iowa) expressly allow for conviction by a simple majority, while 45 states require at least a two-thirds majority. See Council of State Governments, *Book of the States, Vol. 42*, Table 4.8.

Before 2000, the only previous impeachment under the 1784 New Hampshire Constitution was that of Justice Woodbury Langdon. Articles of impeachment were filed against Langdon, but he resigned his position before a trial was held. See John Phillip Reid, *Legislating the Courts*, 35–39. As a result, the Langdon impeachment proceedings could provide no historical guidance on what vote would be required to convict Brock. The New Hampshire Senate's deliberations on requiring a two-thirds supermajority to convict were reminiscent of the deliberations by the framers of the US Constitution in 1787 resulting in a federal requirement for a two-thirds vote. See Hoffer and Hull, *Impeachment in America*, 101.

46. Trial Transcript (August 22), 422.

47. It would also withstand an effort by Rep. Alf Jacobson to secure a restraining order preventing its implementation, on the grounds that it violated the state constitution. Trial Document Nos. 83, 188.

48. Trial Transcript (August 22), 465–76.

49. Ibid., 467–72.

50. See, for example, Trial Document Nos. 94, 96, 120.

51. E.g., Trial Document Nos. 97, 116, 118.

52. E.g., Trial Document Nos. 127, 138, 142, 143.

53. E.g., Trial Document Nos. 96, 102, 124, 130.

54. After the trial, House Manager Phyllis Woods would argue that the Senate arrived at the wrong conclusion precisely because the process was configured legalistically rather than politically. "I sincerely hope," she wrote, "that, if in the future, the Legislature is ever in this situation again that they will learn from what happened here and perhaps consider not getting so hung up on making the impeachment proceeding a legal 'trial' but more of an investigation, communication, and hearing of the facts. In this way, the people can be truly represented by their elected officials and our legal system can be protected on their behalf in a fair and impartial manner." In her view, the trial was "just bizarre and not a trial at all but what I viewed as a travesty of justice." She expressed that view in one of the several letters that Senators and other

participants in the impeachment wrote to Sen. Mary Brown after its conclusion, which Brown included at the end of her book on it. Brown, *Impeachment Trial*, 254–55.

55. Defense counsel Michael Madigan used the phrase in his closing statement. Trial Transcript (October 5), 3862. Even if Madigan was not making any intentional reference to "The Crucible," a 1953 play by Arthur Miller about the Salem witch trials of 1692, he surely might have claimed as an advocate for Brock that there were similarities.

56. "House counsel pursued the Articles of impeachment without the protections of the rules of evidence," said Turner, "and we seek only to ensure that such actions do not occur during these proceedings." Trial Transcript (September 28), 14.

57. Ibid., 21.

58. Ibid., 66.

59. Lubet's expertise had been utilized by numerous state judicial-conduct committees, and he had advised the Judiciary Committee of the U.S. House of Representatives in the trial of Judge Walter Nixon.

60. Trial Transcript (September 18), 33–34.

61. Ibid., 77.

62. Sen. King said "I am concerned about allowing this high-powered law professor to come in here and teach us law. I prefer to not have that imposed on me. I think I'm capable of making the decision as a layperson." Ibid., 70.

63. Ibid., 80.

64. Ibid., 53–54.

65. Ibid., 42–45.

66. Ibid., 49–53.

67. Ibid., 112–19.

68. The justices, in their report to JCC, explained their decision not to inquire into allegations, by Sen. Dupont and his attorney Russell Hilliard, of prejudicial in-chamber remarks by Gray thusly: "Despite concern at the thought of taking no action, the court believed it would be better not to interfere in a pending case on the basis of information that had come through political channels than to risk the impression that this court was allowing itself to be used to bring politics to bear upon the selection of the trial judge as a result of dissatisfaction with his actions to date." But, the justices continued, "If the associate justices had known that Chief Justice Brock had already spoken with the trial judge as described above, they would undoubtedly have brought the matter to your attention immediately." Brown, *Impeachment Trial,* 352–55.

69. Trial Transcript (September 18), 139. Steinfield noted that "If a party to a lawsuit is not receiving the kind of prompt attention that the party thinks he or she should have, then the law provides for remedies. You can file a motion to expedite. You can file some other type of motion. And this is not a mere technicality … If the trial judge isn't moving fast enough, it may be that some kind of rights of due process are at risk and there are remedies that the law provides but one of them is not a unilateral phone call from an appellate judge to the trial judge in which the other party in this case, *Home Gas*, is excluded." Ibid., 140–41.

70. Ibid. (September 26), 1863.

71. Ibid., 1828, 1837.

72. Ibid. (September 25), 1710. Zibel would be called to the stand by both the House Managers (on September 19) and by Brock's counsel (on September 25).

73. Ibid. (September 26), 1872–73.

74. Ibid. (September 27), 153–59.

75. Ibid. (September 25), 1727–32. Gray would also concede that he might have learned of Dupont's office from McHugh, who by his own account had initiated their conversation on *Home Gas* after the case had passed into Gray's hands.

76. Judge Gray mentioned fishing outings and occasional dinners but Judge McHugh said "I never fished with him," explaining that the two were "probably best friends amongst judges in the courthouse" but that "outside the courthouse, I mean, I did not regularly call him." Ibid. (September 26), 1870.

77. Sen. Diane Krueger also noted that Gray "certainly seemed someone concerned with pay raises, that's for sure." Ibid., 1853–54.

78. Brown, *Impeachment Trial*, 330, 332.

79. Trial Transcript (September 26), 1887–1900.

80. Ibid., 1926–27.

81. Ibid., 1937–39.

82. Ibid. (September 18), 140–41.

83. Ibid., 144.

84. Ibid. (September 29), 2885. Kelly explicitly testified that "there was no format for the chief justice to hand that complaint off to anybody in the district court" in 1987.

85. Ibid., 2900.

86. Ibid., 2907.

87. Ibid., 2908.

88. Ibid. (October 2), 41.

89. Ibid., 34–41.

90. Brown, *Impeachment Trial*, 157.

91. Trial Transcript (October 3), 12.

92. Ibid. (September 19), 315–16.

93. Ibid. (September 20), 602, 692–93, 699–700.

94. Ibid. (September 21), 953.

95. Ibid., 952. For Thayer's general account of this question under Steinfield's examination, see 949–56. Thayer's 1997 and 1998 financial-disclosure forms, with the attachment, were Brock Exhibits 3 and 344. His 1999 form was House Exhibit 29.

96. Ibid. (September 21), 962–64.

97. Thayer provided this account of his involvement in the *Feld* case under defense attorney Madigan's cross-examination. Ibid., 1019–32.

98. Ibid., 957–59, 981–88.

99. Ibid., 986–87.

100. Ibid., 936–48.

101. Ibid., 942.

102. Ibid., 1032–46.

103. Ibid., 1042.

104. What the McLaughlin Report says (at 21) is: "On March 28, 2000, Justice Thayer's attorneys approached members of the investigative team and asked the

Attorney General's Office to consider alternative dispositions of the investigation. On March 29, 2000, Justice Thayer offered to submit his resignation from the Supreme Court in return for the Attorney General's forbearance from presenting criminal charges against him to the grand jury." Brown, *Impeachment Trial*, 301.

105. Trial Transcript (September 21), 1044–45.

106. Ibid., 881–86; 1033–45. Thayer's conversation with the Attorney General's office was tape-recorded, and admitted as an exhibit (Brock 86) at the impeachment trial.

107. Ibid., 992–1072; Ibid. (September 22), 1148–57.

108. It appears that the question of which aspects of lawyer-client confidentiality Thayer and Brennan could and would waive hadn't been settled until then.

109. Ibid. (October 4), 3702–45.

110. Ibid. (September 26), 2041–84 (Callahan testimony); ibid. (September 27), 8–51 (Ramsdell testimony).

111. Ibid. (October 30), 165, 168.

112. Ibid. (October 4), 3760–64.

113. Ibid., 3782–87.

114. Ibid. (September 28), 2580, 2608.

115. Ibid., 2569–2608.

116. Ibid., 2625–27.

117. Ibid., 2640.

118. Ibid., 2633.

119. Ibid. (October 5), 3791.

120. Ibid., 3777.

121. Ibid. (September 29), 2679.

122. Ibid., 2750–52.

123. Ibid., 2754.

124. Ibid. (September 18), 168.

125. Ibid. (September 22), 1226.

126. Ibid., 1263–76.

127. Ibid., 1248–57.

128. Ibid., 1240–42. The principle articulated in those provisions of the 1972 Model Code, Lubet felt, was echoed in N.H. Rule 38, Canon 2.1, on "Disqualification."

129. Trial Transcript (September 22), 1241–42.

130. Ibid., 1241.

131. Ibid., 1232–33.

132. In an exchange, over whether Lubet had ever said that the call from Brock to Judge Gray had been made at Sen. Bartlett's "behest," Lubet ventured "Now, your next question for me, I suppose, is what if it wasn't made at the behest?" Ross, who had stressed the compensation Lubet would receive for his testimony, snapped, "Well, why don't you do your job that you're being paid for and let me do mine, if that's all right with you." Ibid., 1313.

133. Ibid., 1290–97.

134. Ibid., 1340–62.

135. Ibid., 1363–70.

136. Ibid., 1381–82.

137. Ibid., 1381–83.
138. Ibid., 1390–91.
139. Ibid. (September 29), 2885.
140. Ibid. (September 25), 1541.
141. Ibid. (October 2), 119.
142. Ibid. (September 21), 937.
143. Ibid. (September 28), 2437.
144. Ibid. (September 20), 510–12.
145. Ibid. (October 2), 51–52.
146. Ibid. (October 5), 3756.
147. Ibid. (October 3), 21–25.
148. Ibid., 141.
149. Ibid., 141–42.
150. Ibid., 138–39.
151. Ibid., 147–48.
152. Ibid., 157.
153. Ibid., 160.
154. Ibid., 196–206.
155. That had been established by the testimony of Margaret Haskett, Brock's executive secretary, on September 26. Trial Transcript (September 26, 2000), 1962–68. Taylor could not remember which year it was. Ibid. (September 26), 2001.
156. Ibid. (October 5), 3754.
157. Ibid., 3756.
158. Ibid.
159. "Are we talking about punishing or are we talking about protecting? And all of the authorities tell us that the function of impeachment is to protect the public" Ibid., 3957.
160. Ibid., 3858–59.
161. Ibid., 3889–90.
162. Ibid., 3981–90.
163. Ibid. (October 10), 4029.
164. Ibid., 4045–47, 4052.
165. Ibid., 4160–61.
166. Ibid., 4041.
167. Ibid., 4063.
168. Ibid., 4065.
169. Ibid., 4077–81.
170. Ibid., 4109.
171. Ibid., 4057.
172. Ibid., 4009.
173. Ibid., 4106–07.
174. Ibid., 4022.
175. Ibid., 4095.
176. Ibid., 4097–98.
177. Ibid., 4069–73.

178. Ibid., 4070.

179. Petition of Thayer, 145 N.H. 177, 761 A.2d 1052 (2000).

180. Cynthia Gray, "Controversy and Reform in New Hampshire," *Judicial Conduct Reporter* 23, no. 1 (2001): 1, 6.

181. Ibid.

182. In re Brock, Docket No. JC-00–010A (JCC, April 20, 2001).

Part IV

AFTERMATH

Chapter 9

Populist Efforts to Constrain Judicial Power

In view of the events after 1966 that led to the Brock impeachment, there was general agreement among stakeholders that further changes must be made. Yet there were differing views about the best course of action to follow. In the wake of the Brock impeachment, would it be necessary to revert to the pre-1966 state of affairs, with the legislature authorized by the people to ensure that judicial power would be exercised in a manner serving the rights of citizens? Or would it be more appropriate to view the institutional independence and judicial administration of a unified court system, all resulting from the 1966–1978 constitutional amendments, as the foundation for the "next reform phase," involving "more serious reforms that could only be effected by a mature, self-confident judiciary"?[1]

Some legislative advocates of what they called "judicial reform" were asserting that the judiciary had gone too far after the court modernization efforts embodied in the constitutional amendments of 1964–1978. They argued that the judiciary had so far exceeded the limits on its legitimate power as set forth in the 1784 New Hampshire constitution that the people of the state were now subject to not just "judicial activism," but "judicial arrogance." This chapter explores the efforts by some proponents of that civic populism, so integral to New Hampshire's governing ethos throughout its history, to restore the judiciary to what they felt was its proper constitutional role. Those efforts involved the adoption of means that echoed those at play in the debate over separation of powers in New Hampshire in the early nineteenth century.

New Hampshire's civic populists, of course, had long been marked by mistrust of professionals, overt antipathy to elites, and commitment to the fullest possible involvement in government of citizens falling into neither category. The logical corollary of those norms has always been a strong preference for the most local, accessible, and modest levels of government whenever possible. Hence the state's special attractiveness to libertarians, convinced as they are that the more distant a governing agency, and the broader its mandate, the more dire a threat it poses to personal liberty. In recent years, elements of the libertarian community nationwide have come to view the "Live Free or Die" state as uniquely congenial to their values and agendas.[2]

Libertarianism, to be sure, should not be casually conflated with populism: the polestar of libertarians is individual liberty, that of populists the sovereignty of "plain folk." Nonetheless, the overlap between some libertarian and populist priorities has been clear enough to both—especially regarding an unelected, independent judiciary. Those anxieties, and the measures that would be required to allay them, have been very effectively articulated by, for example, Rep. Daniel Itse.[3] His concerns and those of like-minded citizens of the state go beyond the judicial elitism that all civic populists dislike; beyond even the judicial autonomy that many deem dangerous. They reach the very idea that the administration of justice and the defense of core constitutional values should be the purview of a distinct and essentially unbeholden branch of government, however it is organized. That vision is manifest in a number of the more radical proposals that have been put forward since the Brock impeachment.

Such proposals have been accompanied by other, less ambitious populist measures, designed to mitigate or partially reverse the professionalization of judicial functions rather than to undercut the judiciary's status as a separate, explicitly non-political branch of government. In fact, the overall range and diversity of reform measures since 2001 has been remarkable and merits detailed consideration.

CHALLENGING PROFESSIONALISM IN THE LAW

The view that justice should not be left exclusively to unelected judges and credentialed attorneys but rather be the work, wherever practicable, of "the people themselves" is not confined to New Hampshire.[4] Yet it is deeply rooted there, enjoying bipartisan support for most of the state's history. In recent years, that support seems to have shifted somewhat: Republicans have shown far more zeal in promoting this principle than Democrats. In the decade after impeachment, divided government has generally made realization of this particular feature of the populist agenda difficult. Yet supporters have shown remarkable tenacity, persisting in their efforts to this day.

In the 2000 session of the legislature, a Republican representative cosponsored a bill that would require the governor to appoint non-attorneys as judges until non-attorneys would make up half of all judges in the state, with that ratio retained thereafter.[5] Deemed "inexpedient to legislate" in the House, it was followed in 2003 by a House resolution proposed by Republicans and urging the governor and executive council to consider appointing a non-lawyer to the supreme court.[6] That failed, as well. But in 2006, Republican House members filed yet another bill aimed at increasing laymen's role on the bench itself. This one proposed the creation of a "a superior court of common law," with all judges being non-lawyers "deemed to have common sense;" with all matters tried before a jury; and with plea bargains or settlements prohibited. That bill did proceed to a floor vote, where it was overwhelmingly rejected.[7]

Populists also aimed to end the dominance of trained lawyers in courtroom practice, and could point to clear historical precedent for their efforts.[8] Since 1842, statutory law in New Hampshire has indeed provided that any litigant or party to a case may self-represent, or be represented "by any citizen of good character" (a 1999 statutory amendment provided that "a citizen shall be presumed to be of good character unless demonstrated otherwise)."[9] In 2006, however, Republican representatives went considerably further by submitting a bill calling for a committee to study the effects of rescinding the charter of the New Hampshire Bar Association; replacing the supreme court's inherent power to regulate attorneys with statutory authority; and providing that any citizen of good character could be a member of the bar.[10] That bill passed by a comfortable margin in the Republican-controlled House. It died in the Senate, but only a year later a Republican introduced another bill to repeal the corporate status of the Bar Association.[11] The new bill called the Bar Association "a constitutionally prohibited monopoly and conspiracy of power in the practice of law," with an unlawful accumulation of assets that should on its dissolution "escheat to the state."[12] That too was unsuccessful, but its sponsor would try again in the 2011–2012 legislative session. At that point, his prospects seemed much improved.

Republicans enjoyed overwhelming legislative majorities in those years, first secured in the general election of November 2010.[13] In January 2011, soon after those remarks, Republican Rep. Daniel Itse introduced two bills giving voice to populist urges to roll back judicial power and expand that of the people, and the people's elected legislators. The first, HCR 17, repudiated the New Hampshire Supreme Court's 1875 decision in *Copp v. Henniker*. That decision had reaffirmed the constitutional right to a jury trial in civil cases except in those varieties adjudicated by referees rather than juries prior to 1784.[14] Itse's objection lay mainly in his claim that the case's confirmation of those exceptions had been wrongly used to deny proper jury trials in what he called "the new class of civil cases … between the government and the people," for example, cases involving parental rights.[15] His second bill, HCR 18, would have similarly voided the historic *Merrill v. Sherburne* decision rejecting the practice of "restoration to law" as an unconstitutional exercise by the legislature of judicial powers. The House Judiciary Committee rejected both of Itse's bills as "inexpedient to legislate." But efforts to expand the power of elected officials at the expense of unelected judges, and that of laymen over trained lawyers, were not over.

A Republican submitted a bill calling for the elimination of supreme court control over the legal profession. Instead, a corporate body called "The Bar Association of the State of New Hampshire would be led by the governor, the executive councilors, and the majority and minority leaders of the House and Senate judiciary commttees."[16] The bill failed, but in November 2011 several Republican legislators filed another that would eliminate the mandatory requirement that lawyers be members of a bar association or other professional organization as a condition for practicing law in the state.[17] That bill passed easily in the House. It was stymied in the Senate due in part to Democrats' stronger showing in the November 2012 elections.[18]

SPONSORING PETITIONS FOR REDRESS OF GRIEVANCES AGAINST THE JUDICIARY

There were other fronts, however, in populists' struggle against legal professionalism and professionals. As early as 2008, five Republicans in the then-Democratic controlled House had sponsored a bill to establish a procedure whereby members of the legislature could introduce citizens' petitions for redress of grievances. It had been rejected by a roll call vote, with only 16 Democrats voting for it.[19]

Then in December 2010, after Republicans had regained control of the legislature, House Speaker William O'Brien announced the establishment and membership of what was to be a new standing committee to be named the "Committee on Redress of Grievances," evoking the right of petition long enshrined in British, American, and New Hampshire jurisprudence.[20] Formally bipartisan, the committee's composition (11 Republicans, 4 Democrats) actually reflected the strong Republican majority in the House.[21] Moreover, every single one of the petitions that the committee considered would be sponsored by Republican representatives.[22]

Theoretically, the committee could consider grievances against any state official. But in fact three-fourths involved court-related matters, of which all but three were family cases. About two-thirds of all grievances brought to the committee were against judges or marital masters, as opposed to non-judicial state officials.[23]

Among them were six requests that a bill of address be filed against the judiciary; five requests that a judge be impeached; and three requests for other disciplinary action.[24] No petition requested such removal action against any non-judicial government official. In the end, no member of the judiciary would actually be removed by either address or impeachment, and the Grievance Committee itself would be dissolved shortly after Democrats regained control of the House that November.[25]

Yet the idea of having a formal process for bringing grievances against courts to the legislature persists. As recently as 2014, legislators filed a bill proposing to reinstate the redress procedure by statute, with an appropriation for compensation of petitioners. It was rejected by nearly a three-to-one margin, with only one Democrat voting in favor of it.[26]

NARROWING THE EQUITY JURISDICTION OF COURTS IN FAMILY MATTERS

Historically, the function of equity has been to correct the law where it is deficient because of its tendency to establish rules without exceptions.[27] It has been said that "the common-law courts chained the hands of liberal judges with iron bonds of intricate rules of procedure," requiring the application of rules with "arbitrary and technical severity, often thereby frustrating the ends of justice."[28]

In most American states, including New Hampshire, divorce is traditionally a statutory matter, with rules that are "strictly legal," in that they "define the capacities and incapacities of persons to acquire rights or to be subject to duties." Despite the fact that divorce and related proceedings are wholly statutory, they are nonetheless always heard by a court or a judge with equity jurisdiction, because the relief granted is not primarily monetary but instead involves the equitable remedy of changing a person's official status.[29]

As one law professor has observed, judges today have more discretion in divorce cases than in any other field of law involving the relations between individuals, as distinguished from their relations with the government:

> Divorce law has traditionally relied on judicial wisdom to achieve fair results. Instead of bright-line rules, legislatures have typically given judges in the divorce court almost unlimited discretion, bounded only by indeterminate standards or lists of factors that may be considered. Judicial discretion has also been enhanced by the rarity of jury trials in divorce cases; in almost all divorce actions the judge both determines the facts and interprets the law.[30]

In recent years, the scope of judicial discretion exercised by judges in family matters has come under criticism because it is perceived by some to cause a lack of predictability in the fairness of decisions. Critics have argued that there is a need for fixed rules to guide the discretion of judges in family matters.[31]

Criticism of judicial discretion in family matters by law professors and lawyers has had an echo in the complaints by some citizens in New Hampshire that the range of discretion exercised in family matters was unfair and corrupt.[32] In fact, claims of abuse of discretion were the basis for three bills filed in the New Hampshire legislature to have marital masters and a judge removed by address.

In January 2010, Republican representatives (including three members of the House Redress of Grievances Committee) filed three bills in January 2010 to have marital master Philip Cross removed by address along with Michael Garner, another marital master, and Lucinda Sadler, a district court judge.[33] The two marital masters were accused of exceeding their constitutional authority and abusing their discretion: Garner by his recommended orders in a divorce dispute that a child attend public school because of religious issues associated with the prospect of her being homeschooled;[34] and Cross by his recommended orders in three hotly contested divorce cases.[35] The bill against Judge Sadler accused her of abusing her discretion, or being negligent or incompetent, by approving the orders as recommended by Masters Cross and Garner in those cases.[36]

All three bills were referred to the Joint Legislative Committee on Address, with six members appointed by the Speaker of the House and six appointed by the President of the Senate. After meetings and public hearings, a majority of the joint committee concluded that none of the three bills stated a reasonable cause for removal.[37] The full house voted in favor of the committee majority's "ought not to pass" recommendations on the bills against Garner and Cross. It voted to lay the bill it voted to lay the bill against Sadler on the table, where it died.[38]

Though they found that the alleged actions by Master Cross were not sufficient cause for removal by address, the majority of the Joint Committee nonetheless observed that the offenses of which he was accused might be impeachable, since his actions were in the course of his regular duties in his official position and may have fallen under the plain meaning of the word "malpractice."[39] That prospect was soon taken up by Republican members of the Redress of Grievances Committee. In 2011, they filed a resolution calling for an investigation of whether there were grounds to impeach Cross or any justice of the New Hampshire superior court.[40] Yet by a vote of 14–1, the House Judiciary Committee concluded in April 2012 that no further action should be taken. They reasoned that Cross, as a marital master appointed by the judiciary rather than by governor and council, was not an "official" legitimately subject to impeachment under the state constitution. In addition, because the resolution named no specific judge, they concluded that there was no specific person to investigate for actions that might be considered impeachable.[41]

The mixed law-and-equity status of court proceedings in family cases in New Hampshire is reflected in a statutory grant of equity jurisdiction to the courts in the judicial branch's family division. Dissatisfied with the outcome of their efforts to have marital masters or judges removed for what they considered abuse of discretion in family cases, some of the Republican representatives who had been members of the House Redress of Grievances Committee took a different approach.

Joined by other Republicans, they filed bills in 2013, 2014, and 2015 to "clarify" the equity jurisdiction granted by statute to the courts in family cases.[42] Each bill proposed that the statutory grant of equity jurisdiction be amended so that the powers of a court of equity could no longer be exercised regardless of any contrary statute, but instead could be exercised only in the absence of any special statutory provision.[43] Each of these bills was found "inexpedient to legislate."

In 2017, they filed the same bill yet another time, and this time they were successful in the House. Speaking in favor of its passage on behalf of a majority of the Judiciary Committee, Rep. Michael Sylvia said that statute granting equity jurisdiction, as currently written, "leaves open an overly broad reach as it relates to other statutes. This existing language allows the court to disregard statutes which have been put in place to narrow the courts' jurisdiction in equity cases."[44] The House then passed the bill by a vote of 192–161, sending it to the Senate for consideration.[45] But the Senate Judiciary Committee's unanimous recommendation was that the bill was "inexpedient to legislate." That recommendation was approved by voice vote in May 2017.[46]

PROMOTING JURY NULLIFICATION

In addition to the measures described above, partisan populists in the legislature pursued a measure aimed at enhancing the power of laymen in adjudication. It had to do with jury nullification, or the intentional refusal by a jury to render a verdict, usually in a criminal trial, consistent with the instructions on relevant law by the trial judge.[47]

In the history of American jurisprudence, jury nullification has been deployed by a variety of groups pursuing different agendas (including freedom of the press, in the celebrated *Zenger* case of the colonial era).[48] Today, however, it is most often seen in libertarian terms, as a way for juries to serve as a check on government enforcement of what are seen as unjust, immoral, or oppressive laws.[49] That was the likely sentiment of Republican legislators who, in January 2011, filed a bill that would allow juries "to judge the application of the law in relationship to the facts in controversy."[50] Passed in both chambers and signed into law in June 2012, it empowered juries in New Hampshire to override the rulings of judges who they believed were misinterpreting or misapplying the relevant law.[51] Supporters felt that the law also authorized defense attorneys to openly inform juries of this power, even over the objections of judges.[52]

That understanding of the statute soon came under question, however. After being convicted of drug trafficking, a criminal defendant asserted on appeal that the trial judge had failed to comply with the new statute by declining to apprise the jury of its nullification powers, effectively contravening his right to a "jury nullification defense."[53] In a unanimous opinion, the supreme court upheld the trial judge and affirmed the conviction, insisting that "jury nullification is neither a right of the defendant nor a defense recognized by law" and denying that the law invoked was in any sense "a jury nullification statute." Writing for the court, Justice Robert Lynn acknowledged that the statute requires the trial judge to allow a jury nullification defense, but concluded that "it does not require the court to allow the defendant to inform the jury that it has the right to judge the law or the right to ignore the law."[54] One conservative national commentator asserted that the supreme court's ruling had "eviscerated a law that was openly intended and widely interpreted as a shot in the arm for the right of jurors to consider the law as well as the facts in criminal cases."[55]

Since that decision was entered, Republican legislators have filed five bills in the House that would require a trial court to instruct jurors that it is the province of the jury, and not the judge, to determine the applicability of the law to the facts of a case. In the 2013–2014 legislative sessions, three such bills failed in the House.[56]

With Republicans regaining a House majority again in the November 2014 and 2016 elections, however, Republican proponents of jury nullification inched closer to victory. A 2016 bill requiring the trial court to give the "jury nullification" instruction to jurors passed the House, only to be rejected in the Senate.[57] In 2017, House Republicans filed yet another jury nullification bill, which again passed the House in a narrow vote. It was opposed by all but three Democrats. Passage was secured despite a minority report by a Democratic member of the House Judiciary Committee noting that "The philosophy behind this bill has been uniformly rejected in the United States and has failed to pass at least 12 times in the past 23 years in New Hampshire."[58] With such a narrow vote in the House, the bill did not fare well in the Senate. In May 2017, based on a unanimous Senate Judiciary Committee report that it was "inexpedient to legislate," the bill was killed by a 17–6 roll call vote.[59]

NOTES

1. See Robert Tobin, *Judicial Branch*, 195.

2. The Free State Project was formed in 2001 to facilitate the migration of a projected 20,000 libertarians to the state which they, through involvement in local politics, might most plausibly convert to a genuine outpost of libertarian practice. In 2003, New Hampshire was chosen as their destination. While the migration hasn't yet reached anything like the numbers originally projected, it has sustained the New Hampshire Liberty Alliance, which promotes the Project's basic goals. Thus far, organized libertarianism has sent a small but active contingent to the House of Representatives, and tangibly reinforced the power of populists in particular political undertakings. Both the Free State Project and the Liberty Alliance maintain websites describing their activities and agendas (https://freestateproject.org, and https://www.nhliberty.org), as does the state's Libertarian Party (https://www.lpnh.org).

3. Rep. Itse, first elected to the House in 2001, wrote an article-by-article analysis of the state constitution, *The People's Liberty: A Commentary on the Constitution of the State of New Hampshire,* 4th ed. (Concord, NH: House Republican Alliance, 2007). He argues that Article 35, customarily thought to establish a separate, though not yet independent, judicial power, has been seriously misinterpreted. When the document in its entirety is surveyed, Itse finds, its basic purposes are obviously establishing legislative supremacy within state government and, simultaneously, protecting citizens' personal and property rights from encroachments by that government. Observing that "[T]he Constitution constrains government" overall, he reasons "therefore, the judiciary as a power of government can violate the Constitution" and concludes that "It would be absurd to leave the interpretation of the Constitution solely to a power of government over which the people, the sovereigns, have no direct power" (Ibid., 32). Itse goes on to propose that, since "Government is by its nature political, the embodiment of the will of the people," then "any perceived wrongs, oppression, must be addressed by a political body;" and, "as Article 1 and 37 make the people the final arbiters of constitutionality, the Legislature is the only governmental power for the redress of grievances, including the constitutionality of law. It is a right of the people that their constitutional rights which they have defined be adjudicated only by a governmental power over which they have direct control" (Ibid., 28). Further, Itse finds considerable evidence in the language and organization of the constitution to support the idea that bench trials ought to be replaced by jury trials whenever possible, and especially in "new types of civil cases" such as those involving parental rights (Ibid., 22). He insists that *Merrill v. Sherburne* was wrongly decided in 1819, and that the legislature's Redress of Grievance function was therefore wrongly curtailed (Ibid., 29–30). Those proposals, taken together, would substantially diminish the functions assigned to a separate judicial branch of government. In addition, Itse argues that the state constitution grants a right to life for the unborn (at 4); specifically authorizes capital punishment (Ibid., 20, 31); clearly rules out programs such as Social Security or any other measure for the relief of poverty (Ibid., 32); and sustains a theoretical right of secession (Ibid., 11). Above all, Itse feels that the constitution of New Hampshire assumes that the polity will be guided by "Evangelical principles of personal

accountability and responsibility" (Ibid., 5; see also 4, 6, 9, and others). He received the New Hampshire Liberty Alliance's "Legislator of the Year" Award in 2015.

4. See Larry Kramer, *People Themselves*; Elizabeth Beaumont, *Civic Constitution*; John Finn, *Peopling Constitution*; and Corey Brettschneider, "Popular Constitutionalism and the Argument for Judicial Review," *Pol. Theory* 34, no. 4 (2006): 516–21.

5. HB1408 (2000).

6. HR8 (2003), sponsored by five Republicans.

7. HB1641 (2006). When two of its cosponsors offered an identical bill in 2007 (HB245, 2007), it was again rejected, this time by voice vote.

8. Legal historian Lawrence M. Friedman writes that admission to practice in New Hampshire courts required both experience and education between 1805 and 1833, but that all education or training requirements were abolished between 1842 and 1872. Friedman, *A History of American Law* (New York: Simon & Schuster, 1973), 276, 566.

9. See N.H. Rev. Stats. Ann. 311:1, as most recently amended by N.H. Laws 1999, 251:1, eff. January 1, 2000.

10. HB1768 (2006), sponsored by seven Republicans. Authority to regulate the bar had long been claimed by the New Hampshire judiciary as a reasonable exercise of its inherent power. See, for example, Bryant's Case, 24 N.H. 149 (1851); Ricker's Petition, 66 N.H. 207, 29 A. 559 (1890); and Unification of Bar, 109 N.H. 260, 248 A.2d 709 (1968).

11. See N.H. H. R. Jour. 26, Roll Call (March 9, 2006), 1545–1549, and N.H. S. Jour. 10 (April 6, 2006), 324.

12. See HB670 (2007), found "inexpedient to legislate" in the House.

13. Newly elected House Speaker William O'Brien described the Republican triumph in distinctly populist tones, as a mandate for "government of public servants and not elite rulers" that "stands with citizens and not over them." N.H. H.R. Jour. 1 (December 1, 2010).

14. 55 N.H. 179 (1875). That constitutional right to a jury trial had been defended by New Hampshire courts as early as the *Ten Pounds Act* cases of 1786–87. As in that earlier litigation, the point at issue in *Copp v. Henniker* was whether the legislature had the power to establish tribunals and conduct adjudication under its own aegis, apart from judicial institutions.

15. Itse, *People's Liberty*. New Hampshire courts currently assign certain cases in family law to quasi-judicial officers called "marital masters."

16. HB346 (2011), voted "inexpedient to legislate."

17. HB1474 (2012), cosponsored by seven Republicans.

18. N.H. H.R. Jour. 23 (March 8, 2012), 1443–1445; N.H. S. Cal. 19 (May 8, 2012).

19. See N.H. H.R. Jour. 24 (March 12, 2008), 1323–25.

20. See Gregory Mark, "The Vestigial Constitution: The History and Significance of the Right to Petition." *Fordham L. Rev.* 66, no. 6 (1998), 2153–2231. See also, Stephen A. Higginson, "A Short History of the Right to Petition Government for the Redress of Grievances," *Yale L. J.* 96, no. 1 (1986): 142–66. In the New Hampshire

Constitution, the Bill of Rights has two separate articles relating to redress of grievances. Article 31 describes the entire purpose of the legislature as "the redress of public grievances and for making such laws as the public good may require;" while Article 32 states that the public has a right of assembly, a right to instruct their representatives, and a right to petition the legislative body for "redress of the wrongs done to them, and of the grievances they suffer."

21. N.H. H.R. Jour. 1 (December 1, 2010).

22. Source: analysis (on file with the authors) of data and information on petitions for redress of grievances, as reported by Rep. Timothy Horrigan, Democratic member of the House Committee on Redress of Grievances. According to Horrigan, there were 65 petitions in all, dated 2009–2015, that were considered by legislators involved in the redress process of the committee. Of those, 45 were new, 15 were "repeats" from a prior year, 1 was removed, and 4 were missing from committee records altogether. See Horrigan, Home Page, "My [session year] Legislative Session page," http://www.timothyhorrigan.com/index.002.html.

23. Ibid. These calculations reflect adjustments for missing, removed, or re-filed petitions.

24. Source: analysis (on file with the authors) of data and information reported by Rep. Timothy Horrigan, "My Legislation Session Page."

25. For criticism of that legislative decision, see Darryl W. Perry, "NH House Removes the Grievance Committee," *Free Keene,* January 2, 2013, http://freekeene.com/2013/01/02/nh-house-removes-the-grievance-committee/:

> Rep. Gary Richardson, who motioned for the rule change, said the New Hampshire House is one of the most representative bodies, and any outstanding or pressing issue could be raised via legislation, on a case-by-case basis. The main problem with that claim is that legislation can only be proposed during a brief period between Legislative Sessions. Secondly, the claim assumes that someone's Representative will actually introduce the requested legislation.

26. HB1165 (2014), sponsored by four Republicans and one Democrat, was rejected by a House roll call vote, with its Democratic cosponsor being the only member of his party voting for it.

27. Howard Oleck, "Historical Nature of Equity Jurisprudence," *Fordham L. Rev.* 20, no. 1 (1951): 23.

28. Aaron Friedberg, "The Merger of Law and Equity." *St. John's L. Rev.* 12, no. 2 (1938): 317–18.

29. John Pomeroy, *Pomeroy's Equity Jurisprudence and Equitable Remedies* (San Francisco, CA: Bancroft-Whitney, 1905), Vol. 1, §98.

30. Marsha Garrison, "How Do Judges Decide Divorce Cases—an Empirical Analysis of Discretionary Decision Making," *N.C. L. Rev.* 74, no. 2 (1996): 401, 403–04.

31. Ibid. See also, Jane Murphy, "Eroding the Myth of Discretionary Justice in Family Law: The Child Support Experiment," *N.C. L. Rev.* 70, no. 1 (1991): 209–42;

and Carl Schneider, "The Tension Between Rules and Discretion in Family Law: A Report and Reflection," *Fam. L. Q.* 27, no. 2 (1993): 229–45.

32. See, for example, Dot Knightly, "New Hampshire's Corrupt Family Courts: Be amazed at the abuses NH Families suffer in NH Family Courts!" *Merrimack, NH Patch,* June 13, 2014, https://patch.com/new-hampshire/merrimack/be-amazed-at-the-abuses-nh-families-suffer-in-nh-family-courts.

33. N.H. H.R. Jour. 6 (January 6, 2010), 248.

34. HA1, as introduced, N.H. H.R. Jour. 6 (January 6, 2010) 248.

35. Ibid., HA3, as introduced.

36. Ibid., HA2, as introduced.

37. N.H. H.R. Cal. 39 (May 14, 2010), Report by Joint Committee of Address under HA1, HA2, HA3.

38. N.H. H.R. Jour. 51 (June 2, 2010), 2301–10.

39. Report by Joint Committee of Address, note 37 above.

40. N.H. H.R. Jour. 3 (January 6, 2011), 195.

41. N.H. H.R. Cal. 34, Majority Report Pursuant to HR7 (April 27, 2012), 1971–72.

42. The 2013 bill in the House of Representatives (HB611) was sponsored by 12 Republicans, including five representatives who had been members of the House Redress of Grievances Committee. N.H. H.R. Jour. 12 (January 3, 2013), 202. In 2014, a virtually identical statutory amendment was proposed in a Senate bill (SB352) sponsored by Republican senator. N.H. S. Jour. 1 (January 8, 2014), 12. The 2015 version of the bill (HB443) had 13 sponsors, all Republican, including four former members of the House Grievances Committee. N.H. H.R. Jour. 12 (January 8, 2013), 223.

43. Each bill would amend RSA 490-D:3 in the following fashion:

> 490-D:3 Equity Jurisdiction. The judicial branch family division shall have the powers of a court of equity in cases where subject matter jurisdiction lies with the judicial branch family division *and where no other special provision has been made by law*. Suits in equity where subject matter jurisdiction lies with the judicial branch family division including, but not limited to, petitions for divorce, nullity of marriage, alimony, custody of children, support, and other similar proceedings may be heard upon oral testimony or depositions, or both, or when both parties consent, or service having been made and a notice of the time and place of the hearing having been given, when both parties appear. Such suits may be heard by any justice of the judicial branch family division at any time, but nothing contained in this section shall be construed as limiting the power of the judicial branch family division to have issues of fact framed and tried by a jury, according to the rules in equity, or the course of such proceedings at common law.

44. N.H. H.R. Jour. 10 (March 9, 2017), 16.

45. Ibid.

46. N.H. S. Jour. 16 (May 11, 2017).

47. Paula Hannaford-Agor, "Judicial Nullification? Judicial Compliance and Noncompliance with Jury Improvement Efforts," *N. Ill. U. L. Rev.* 28 (2008): 407, 421.

48. See Clay Conrad, *Jury Nullification: The Evolution of a Doctrine* (Washington, DC: Cato Institute, 2013); Stanton D. Krauss, "An Inquiry into the Right of Criminal Juries to Determine the Law in Colonial America," *J. Criminal Law & Criminology* 89, no. 1 (1998): 111–214; and Alan Scheflin and Jon M. Van Dyke, "Merciful Juries: The Resilience of Jury Nullification," *Wash. & Lee L. Rev.* 48, no. 1 (1996): 165–83.

49. For example, the official 2016 national political platform of the Libertarian Party states, "We assert the common-law right of juries to judge not only the facts but also the justice of the law." Libertarian Party, "2016 Platform" (adopted by convention, May 2016), https://www.lp.org/platform/.

50. HB146 (2012), cosponsored by five Republicans.

51. N.H. Laws 2012, Ch. 243, codified as N.H. Rev. Stat. Ann. § 519:23-a.

52. See Tim Lynch, "Jury Nullification Law Signed by New Hampshire Governor," *PoliceMisconduct.net,* June 27, 2012, https://www.policemisconduct.net/jury-nullification-law-signed-new-hampshire-governor/?+Policemisconductnet+%28PoliceMisconduct.net%29.

53. State v. Paul,—NH—, 104 A. 3d 1058, 1059 (2014).

54. *Id.*, 1062, 1063.

55. J.D. Tuccille, "Hit and Run Blog: Jury Nullification Law Gutted by New Hampshire Supreme Court, *Reason.com,* October 24, 2014, http://reason.com/blog/2014/10/24/jury-nullification-law-gutted-by-new-ham.

56. HB1452 (2014), HB246 (2015), and HB470 (2015), all rejected, with opposition from almost all Democrats.

57. HB1270 (2016), passed in the House with support from only five Democrats, and rejected in the Senate.

58. N.H. H.R. Cal. 10 (February 3, 2017), 10.

59. N.H. S. Jour. 16 (May 11, 2017), 419.

Chapter 10

Restoring Interbranch Comity

The recent record of New Hampshire's populists is one of both remarkable persistence and, thus far, consistent failure. The persistence is easily explained: the values lying behind these measures can be traced to the state's founding, and its earliest understanding of the judicial function in state government. To explain the failure, however, more recent history must be invoked. For if most legislators proved unreceptive to populist calls for a de-professionalized judiciary re-subordinated to legislative will, it may well have been because after the Brock impeachment—and precisely while radical proposals were emanating from populist quarters—representatives of that judiciary and responsible legislators were seeking out, and eventually finding, ways to bridge the gulf that had opened between elected officials and the judicial branch.

The central, and thorniest, issue has been legislative involvement in court rulemaking, that is, in the actual processes by which justice would be determined and delivered in New Hampshire. Finding a solution that maintained the independent judiciary the state had finally achieved without rendering it utterly impervious to any input whatsoever from the people's elected representatives would be a halting, difficult process lasting well over a decade. Yet it appears to have succeeded, in no small measure because the state's voters, by their actions on crucial ballot questions, essentially compelled both branches to reforge, on new grounds, the comity that had been lost.

SHARING CONSTITUTIONAL AUTHORITY TO PROMULGATE COURT RULES

On January 4, 2001, two bills were filed for constitutional amendments challenging the court's rulemaking power under Article 73-a. The first, which proposed repealing Article 73-a altogether, was more dramatic; and the second, while allowing court rules adopted by the judiciary to have the force of law, called for legislative override of there was any conflict with a statute.[1] Since "legislative override" seemed to have better prospects, the more dramatic bill's sponsor agreed to its dismissal.[2] Rep. Alf Jacobson, a legislator supporting legislative override, claimed that most of the criticism of Article 73-a was focused on one issue: the veil of secrecy thrown over internal judicial operations, pierced only lightly by the Fairbanks scandal. "I have looked at the Constitution," he said, "and I can't find anything in it that says that one branch of government shall operate in secrecy."[3]

Lawyers who argued in support of legislative override included Martin Gross, a former mayor of Concord.[4] Gross noted the many times in New Hampshire history when "the legislature has stepped in to reform the judicial process because the judges either would not or could not do it." He also recounted the concerns he had had as a delegate to the 1974 Constitutional Convention, when he had pointedly questioned fellow delegate Arthur Nighswander about whether the sentence giving court-promulgated rules "the force and effect of law" would affect legislative "ability to provide by statute for court procedures in the future."[5] His worst fears were realized, Gross explained, by the assertion in the *Prior Sexual Assault Evidence* advisory opinion that matters of procedure were under the "exclusive jurisdiction of the courts."[6] "I don't think it's appropriate in light of our history," he said, "for the court to have done what it's seen to have done in *PSAE* to say that they are the only ones who know what's best."

The legislative-override bill came out of committee with a 3-1 vote in favor of passage in January 2002, and final passage by the Senate came in February 2002.[7] But when it appeared on the general election ballot in November 2002, a majority of voters (50.9%) rejected it.[8] That tally must have surprised the bill's supporters, who had appeared convinced that the pubic fully supported a wider legislative, and reduced judicial, role in regulating courts. Yet when tested at the ballot box, the proposal failed to earn even majority support, let alone the two-thirds vote required to amend the constitution.

Legislative critics of exclusive judicial authority over court rulemaking, however, were not deterred by their defeat. Just two months later, in January 2003, Rep. Henry Mock filed the legislative-override bill again, arguing that the public had been misled by the wording of the earlier version that voters had rejected in November. Mock testified in a hearing on the bill that many voters had been confused because the ballot question asked whether "the General Court shall have the same powers as the Supreme Court" over court rulemaking. Those voters, Mock claimed, did not realize that the words "General Court" refer to the legislature and not to anything in the judicial branch. The legislature concurred, and a new ballot question was prepared with the term "General Court" replaced by "Legislature."[9] In January 2004, the full House of Representatives approved it by roll-call vote, with Republican legislators in favor by an overwhelming margin.[10]

In April 2004, the Senate approved the bill, breaking along strict party lines.[11] In November 2004, it appeared again in the general election ballot. This time, it received a "yes" vote from 56.9 percent of the voters. But that did not represent the two-thirds majority required for the adoption of a constitutional amendment, so it failed again.[12] In fact, the 2004 vote would turn out to be the high-water mark of efforts to constitutionally reassert clear legislative supervision of judicial administration. Legislative efforts in 2006 and 2010 to introduce similar constitutional amendments would be found "inexpedient to legislate."[13]

Then in 2011, a bill was filed that involved a highly partisan political matter by calling for the attorney general to join other states in mounting a legal challenge to the federal "Patient Protection and Affordable Care Act" ("Obamacare"). It was passed by the House of Representatives in March 2011, with Democrats voting 93–0 against it.[14] In May 2011, the Senate tabled the bill and adopted a resolution requesting a supreme court advisory opinion on whether the bill would violate the state constitution. In June 2011, the justices answered that the bill would indeed violate constitutional separation of powers, in that it assumed legislative capacities beyond those set forth in the constitution.[15]

In September 2011, the Senate allowed the bill to "die on the table." But in the next month, over unanimous opposition from Democrats, the House passed a resolution repudiating the advisory opinion.[16] When the Senate ignored the resolution, a new bill was filed in the House. As originally introduced, the bill proposed that Article 73-a should be repealed altogether, thereby eliminating the constitutional authority of the chief justice to make rules governing the administration of the courts.[17] In March 2012, the House passed the bill, with Democrats voting 94–0 against it.[18]

Testifying on behalf of the Supreme Court in a Senate hearing on the new bill, Justices Gary Hicks and Robert Lynn both expressed opposition to its initial form. Yet they also favored appropriate legislative authority in the court rulemaking process. Soon after the conclusion of the hearing, the Senate Judiciary Committee adopted an amended version of the bill, giving the legislature concurrent power over court rulemaking with the chief justice, with statute superseding court-issued rule in the case of any conflict but only if the statute were "not contrary to the constitution."[19] The full Senate voted in support of the committee report.[20] In the House of Representatives in early June, the House approved the Senate's amended version of the bill by a vote meeting the three-fifths margin required for inclusion in the general election ballot in November 2012.[21] But it failed to gain the support of a majority of the voters.[22]

Even though the ballot question was rejected by voters in November 2012, the supreme court itself would nonetheless endorse the essence of it. In fact, just days before that popular vote, the court had rendered a decision that went a long way toward rendering this issue, too, moot. This outcome had been presaged in an article written soon after the conclusion of the Brock impeachment. In March 2001, when he was an associate justice of the New Hampshire Superior Court, Robert Lynn wrote a bar journal article addressing "the role which the legislative and judicial branches of government should properly play in establishing procedural and evidentiary rules for New Hampshire courts."[23] He gave particular attention to the supreme court's 1997 advisory opinion that a proposed statute on the admissibility of prior sexual assault evidence (*PSAE*) would violate the separation of powers provision of the state constitution. This decision was based on the court's conclusion that rules of evidence are largely "procedural" rather than "substantive," so that they are within the exclusive rulemaking power of the courts, and beyond the power of the legislature to change.[24] Lynn argued that judicial supremacy over procedural law (a) is fundamentally inconsistent with the separation-of-powers doctrine; (b) can stifle efforts at reform; and (c) is not necessary to protect judicial independence.[25] This reasoning had made him a vocal supporter of the failed efforts to amend Article 73-a that were reflected in the 2002, 2004 and 2012 bills.

As a supreme court justice, however, Lynn, along with his colleagues, would be provided an opportunity to determine the scope of the *PSAE* decision as precedent for decisions on the law of evidence. In 2011, in *State v. Ploof*, the supreme court rejected an argument based on the *PSAE* decision, that a statute on the involuntary commitment of sexually violent predators violated constitutional separation of powers principles by regulating evidence in such cases and "thereby usurping the judicial function of making relevancy determinations in sexual predator cases without regard for the particular facts or circumstances involved in such a case."[26] Writing for a unanimous court, Justice Carole Ann Conboy explained that, as an advisory opinion rather than a litigated case, the *PSAE* decision did not constitute binding precedent. Moreover, she wrote, "the circumstances of this case are different and the State does not ask us to reexamine *Opinion of the Justices*."[27]

Then in 2012, just days before the ballot question would be voted on by citizens as "Question 2" on the November general election ballot, the court rendered a unanimous decision in the *Southern New Hampshire Medical Center* case, concluding that the assertion of exclusive judicial authority over evidentiary rules in the *PSAE* advisory opinion "is inconsistent with prior precedent," and "that th[is] area ... is one in which the Judiciary and Legislature share concurrent authority, absent constitutional considerations, such as impairment of the court's ability to function."[28]

As submitted to voters in November 2012, the wording of the ballot question was that Article 73-a should be amended to give priority to a statute over a conflicting rule, but only if the judiciary found the statute constitutional. In its *Southern New Hampshire Medical Center* decision, the supreme court interpreted Article 73-a as adopted in 1974, and without the need for further amendment, to mean that the legislature fully retained its traditional concurrent authority over court procedure.[29] It is difficult to overstate the import of this ruling. In a spirit of both comity and prudence, the court itself was seeking to remove authority over court rulemaking as a source of legislative-judicial tension.

The new understanding on rulemaking authority had not been hammered out in a vacuum. Rather, it had developed alongside parallel, similarly difficult negotiations on the delineation and enforcement of judicial ethics.

CHANGING JUDICIAL DISCIPLINE STRUCTURE AND PROCEDURES

The Brock Court itself had decided to abandon its longstanding practice of allowing recused judges a non-voting role in drafting opinions even before the McLaughlin Report had brought it to light.[30] In fact, in September 2000, just after the House had voted to impeach the chief justice, the supreme court had commissioned a "Task Force for the Renewal of Judicial Conduct Procedures." Its assignment was to study judicial conduct procedures in New Hampshire, and make recommendations for changes to assure that judges would comply with them. It delivered its report in January 2001, and in August of that year the supreme court decided to accept its recommendation to replace the existing code of judicial ethics with a new one modeled largely on the ABA's 1990 version. As in the ABA code, compliance would be mandatory. Failure by a judge to comply with its canons could be the basis for disciplinary action.[31]

Another critical feature of the January 2001 report by the task force was its recommendations on the nature and membership of the body that would enforce that code.[32] The judges, lawyers, and laypersons who had composed the JCC after it was established in 1977 had all been appointees of the supreme court, following court-set rules.[33] The task force's report, however, recommended that the JCC be replaced by a new Conduct Commission that would be independent of the supreme court, with membership to include appointees not only of the New Hampshire Supreme Court but also of the Governor, the President of the Senate, the Speaker of the House, and the President of the New Hampshire Bar Association. Moreover, the new commission should not be physically located at the supreme court, but should have its own separate office and should hold its meetings off court premises; should not be staffed by court personnel; and should have separate funding, not included in the budget of the supreme court.

In May 2001, the supreme court issued an administrative order creating the new Commission under a new Code of Judicial Conduct and providing that the new body would be totally independent of the court system, with its own staff, office space, and funding as suggested by the task force.[34] The order included transition provisions calling for the "Court JCC" (i.e., the pre-Commission JCC) to remain temporarily in existence to complete action on all matters pending before it on the effective date of the new code.

All "Court JCC" proceedings in those matters were to be governed by the pre-task force code of conduct, which would be supplanted by the new 2001 code when all pending "Court JCC" cases were completed.[35] The new code of conduct would go into effect 60 days after funds were first appropriated by the legislature for its implementation.

Those arrangements, however, ran counter to the expectation of the legislature that the JCC would be fully and immediately replaced by the new Commission.[36] Perhaps to reassert legislators' role in the process, the Senate promptly passed a bill endorsing the new disciplinary body envisioned by the task force report but increasing the number of legislative appointees, at the expense of those allotted the governor and the supreme court.[37] That bill was referred to a conference committee, which elected to retain many of its original features, including expanded legislative authority to appoint citizen members and a further amendment requiring that attorneys appointed by the state bar president be subject to approval by the governor and the legislative leaders. The bill was ultimately passed in both chambers, funded, and signed into law by Gov. Shaheen in July 2001.[38] It stipulated that the new 2001 Supreme Court Code of Judicial Conduct would provide interim rules for the new Commission, to the extent that those rules were not inconsistent with the new statute. It also emphatically rejected the idea of close ties between the disciplinary body and the supreme court, providing as well that the new commission must adopt its own rules to replace the 2001 supreme court code of conduct.[39]

When the new statute became effective as of January 1, 2002, the state thus had two judicial conduct bodies—the new, independent Commission and the (preexisting) Court JCC. The two bodies sought to communicate informally in 2002 to avoid overlap in their efforts.[40] But in September 2003, matters were further complicated by a new bill, passed by both legislative chambers, and signed into law by Gov. Craig Benson, all on the very same day. It included a provision, requiring that all complaints against judges and clerks under the 2001 statute be directed to the new Commission.[41] Faced with this unexpected development, the Court JCC filed a petition in the supreme court in December 2003, seeking instructions about its own duties and challenging the constitutionality of the new judicial conduct statute.

In a decision rendered on June 14, 2004, the supreme court held the statute unconstitutional.[42] Justices argued that the regulation of court proceedings and officers, including the power to discipline judges, is an inherent and exclusive power of the judicial branch; the state, they held, therefore violated the separation of powers doctrine. The decision was an important one. The court had already demonstrated readiness to strengthen judicial ethics, to distance the enforcement body from itself, and to grant wider input by the elected branches into it. By voiding the September 2003 statute, however, it also demonstrated that final approval of the terms by which judicial ethics would be monitored belonged to the New Hampshire Supreme Court, not the legislature.

After that 2004 decision, the Supreme Court's Advisory Committee on Rules began work on revisions to the Code of Judicial Conduct and, in the spirit of the task force's recommendations, amending the membership structure of the disciplinary body In January 2005, the court approved those recommendations. The new State JCC (differently composed and institutionally situated than the Court JCC, with a different code to enforce) would have 11 members: (a) three trial judges and a court clerk appointed by the supreme court; (b) one attorney appointed by the state bar president; and (c) six public members, none of whom could be a judge, attorney, clerk of court, or elected or appointed public official: one appointed by the state bar president; one appointed by the supreme court; two appointed by the Governor; one appointed by the President of the Senate; and one appointed by the Speaker of the House.[43] The new code provisions also followed task force recommendations by providing that the State JCC would have a committee address determined by the committee; and, subject to the availability of funds, it would select its own office space, which should not be in the facilities of any branch of government. It would hire its own staff and prepare its own budget request, as a separate program accounting unit ("PAU") within the judicial branch budget.[44]

In February 2005, the supreme court requested legislation regarding the State JCC's access to confidential information, for example, hearings in child abuse and other cases not open to the public. In what might be seen as a legislative acknowledgment of the constitutional legitimacy of the State JCC, a statute was passed and signed into law by Gov. John Lynch in June 2005 allowing State JCC members to review such confidential information in closed sessions, and without need to disclose details to the public. Balancing proper public or legislative access to sensitive court materials with proper due-process protections had been difficult in New Hampshire, especially since the Fairbanks scandal. The June 2005 legislation seemed to accomplish the task. Then, in September of that year, an important symbolic step was taken to emphasize the organizational independence of the State JCC from the supreme court. State JCC members voted, with the approval of the supreme court, to strike the words "Supreme Court" from its name, so that the official name of the body would be "The State of New Hampshire Judicial Conduct Committee."[45]

In all of these developments, the judicial branch's leaders showed a willingness to work with the legislature to implement the recommendations of the task force. Yet they also insisted on compliance with the separation of powers, and continued to defend judicial prerogatives.

In 2008, a matter arose that could be seen to demonstrate the new relationship between the judiciary and the legislature with regard to judicial discipline. A bipartisan bill of address was filed by Reps. David Bettencourt, Laura Pantelakos, Bob Odell, Martha Fuller Clark, Lucy Weber, and Maureen Mooney, calling for the removal of Patricia C. Coffey from her position as a superior court justice.[46] The bill asserted that Justice Coffey had aided in a 2003 transfer of some of her lawyer-husband's real property to a trust, of which she was the sole trustee, so that the transferred property would be less accessible to the husband's creditors. At the time of the transfers, her husband was under investigation by the Bar Association's Professional Conduct Committee, and in 2005 he was disbarred. In 2007 Justice Coffey was censured and given a three-month suspension without pay by the Judicial Conduct Committee because her participation in the fraudulent transfer of assets amounted to a violation of the Code of Judicial Conduct.[47]

The bill was referred to a Joint Legislative Committee on Address, with members appointed from both the House and the Senate. While the deliberations of the Joint Committee were beginning, however, the supreme court ruled on Justice Coffey's appeal from the JCC decision against her.[48] After the court decision not only affirmed the JCC ruling, but also concluded that the three-month suspension without pay must be increased to three years, Justice Coffey resigned from the bench.[49] As a result, the bill of address was tabled on a voice vote by the entire House, after which it subsequently died.[50]

FAVORING MERIT SELECTION OF JUDGES OVER OTHER ALTERNATIVES

The New Hampshire Constitution of 1784 was like those in most of the other original states in its provisions to select judges by appointment, often with measures to prevent the governor from controlling the judiciary. Soon, however, most other states began to choose judges by popular election. Yet between 1784 and 1966 in New Hampshire, there was only one time (1850) that the popular election of judges was ever reviewed by constitutional convention delegates and offered as a ballot question for citizen consideration.[51]

In 1966, the amendment granting constitutional status to the New Hampshire Supreme Court and Superior Court created a different situation by placing those levels of court beyond the power of the legislature to create and abolish courts. Almost immediately, there were efforts to change the selection and tenure of judges. The 1974 Constitutional Convention had three of them,[52] and the 1984 Constitutional Convention had nine.[53] None of them were approved by delegates. Meanwhile, 21 legislative proposals for constitutional amendments to change judicial selection and tenure were filed between 1973 and 2000, but all were unsuccessful.[54] After the end of the Brock impeachment proceedings, efforts by legislators continued, with 19 constitutional amendment proposals filed to change judicial selection and tenure were filed. But all of them failed,[55]

Yet if all those efforts were unsuccessful, there were two others that followed a different course after the Brock impeachment. One involved enacted legislation for the position of chief justice to rotate every five years among the justices of the supreme court. The second, with more long-lasting effect, has involved the use of a "judicial selection commission" to apply merit criteria in the consideration of nominees for judicial positions.

After his acquittal of impeachment charges, David Brock returned to service as the chief justice of the supreme court. He would continue in office until he retired on December 31, 2003. Yet the legislative focus on his position as part of the tension between the New Hampshire judiciary and the legislature did not go away after his impeachment acquittal. Indeed, in a move that one commentator saw as evidence of the continuing "toxic effect" of the *Claremont* decisions on the structure of New Hampshire government,[56] the New Hampshire legislature soon sought to assure that nobody would ever again achieve Brock's longevity as chief justice.[57] The story of that effort, however, might indicate that the impeachment proceedings against Brock were most significantly about the institutional stress associated with the role of Brock and his immediate predecessors as chief justices during the decades of change since the 1960s, whatever feelings there might be against Brock personally, and however much feeling there was in favor of "payback" against him and the supreme court for the *Claremont* decisions.

On January 4, 2001, the very first day of the legislative session beginning right after Chief Justice Brock's impeachment acquittal, Sen. Ned Gordon filed a bill that would change statutory law on the justices of the supreme court by establishing a five-year rotating term based on seniority for the chief justice of the supreme court, thereby eliminating lifetime tenure in that position. The bill was passed by both the Senate and the House and sent to Gov. Jeanne Shaheen, who signed it into law on June 11, 2001.[58]

Yet as Chief Justice Brock's retirement date approached as of the end of December 2003, Shaheen's successor Gov. Craig Benson challenged the automatic five-year rotation of the office of chief justice. Benson's contention was that it represented an incursion into the executive branch's appointment power, a viewpoint shared by the executive council. On December 9, 2003, he and the executive council requested an advisory opinion, asking the justices to give answers on whether the statute violated state constitutional provisions on judicial selection and separation of powers.[59] Just 10 days later, the justices asked on constitutional grounds to be excused from answering the questions posed, claiming a lack of authority under the state constitution to issue advisory opinions about already-existing legislation.[60]

In place of an advisory opinion, the governor and council then sought the same relief by filing a petition on December 24, 2003, asking the supreme court to issue a declaratory judgment on the very same questions.[61] The court accepted the petition and named replacements for all of the sitting supreme court justices, and oral argument was held on March 1, 2004.[62] In a unanimous decision issued at the end of April 2004, the court characterized the statute in question as one that "for the first time purports to 'unbundle' the administrative functions traditionally attributed to the chief justice from his or her underlying judicial functions." The court rejected the notion advanced in the statute, writing that "The administrative and legislative powers and duties assigned to the chief justice by the constitution are inextricably bound together with those adjudicatory duties and are incidents of and inherent in that office."[63] Citing its decision in *Petition of Mone*, the court also found that the statute violated the separation of powers doctrine.[64]

It is important to understand the import of the court's decision in that case. On the surface, the court was resolving a conflict between the executive and legislative branches of government, and it ruled in favor of governor and council. Yet the consequences of the decision were broader than that. First, the decision reinforced the status of the supreme court and the judicial branch as having the final word on the meaning and interpretation of the New Hampshire constitution. Moreover, the acceptance of the ruling by both of the other branches of government reinforced the notion that the courts must be accorded decisional independence, free of political interference. Finally, the ruling nullified a legislative attempt by statute to alter the continuity of leadership over the judicial branch, thereby reaffirming the institutional independence of the judiciary. By upholding the constitutional power of the executive branch, the supreme court was thus able to uphold separation of powers and protect the institutional status of the judiciary.

At the beginning of December 2003, Chief Justice Brock announced his retirement.[65] Since the 2001 statute was still in force at the time, the most senior associate justice, John Broderick, was consequently sworn in on January 2, 2004, to begin a five-year term as chief justice. When the replacement justices sitting as the supreme court found that statute unconstitutional, it was necessary for Gov. Benson to propose a new chief justice for approval by the executive council. Benson nominated Broderick. After a hearing on May 5, 2004, the councilors voted 4–1 to confirm him.[66]

After the Brock impeachment, the selection and tenure of judges had thus drawn considerable legislative attention in New Hampshire. But the election of judges was consistently rejected, and five-year tenure for the chief justice was declared unconstitutional. Yet a more modest attempt to bring greater rigor to the process of judicial selection has enjoyed a measure of success. It involves use of a "judicial-selection commission" to apply specified merit criteria in the consideration of judicial nominees, and represents another effort to enhance judicial accountability without compromising judicial independence.[67]

The proposed judicial-selection commission was to consist of a mix of respected lawyers and citizens, which would then vet all judicial candidates; governors would select judges from the pool of qualified candidates thus assembled.[68] The idea was adopted by Gov. Jeanne Shaheen, who gave it life by executive order in June 2000, a full month before the House of Representatives voted to impeach Brock.[69] One of the judicial appointments Shaheen made through the new "merit selection" process was that of Linda Stewart Dalianis, who in 2000 became the first woman ever named to sit on New Hampshire's five-member Supreme Court.

Efforts to render the new merit-selection process permanent, however, have been unsuccessful. In January 2001, just two months after the conclusion of the Brock impeachment, a bipartisan bill was introduced in the New Hampshire Senate to establish a judicial nominating commission by statute.[70] Three weeks later, a bipartisan bill was introduced in the House proposing a virtually identical judicial nominating commission.[71] But both bills were deemed "inexpedient to legislate" by virtue of a1977 advisory opinion of the supreme court suggesting that statutory creation of a judicial-selection commission would unconstitutionally infringe on the appointive powers of the governor and executive council.[72] Recognizing that only a constitutional amendment would resolve the matter, one was filed in 2002. But it failed as well, for fear that it might unduly politicize the selection process.[73] So did another bipartisan legislative effort of 2003, again as an encroachment on executive-branch powers of appointment.[74] Merit selection has lasted, for the most part, from that day to this—but only through gubernatorial executive actions.[75]

MEASURING PERFORMANCE OF SITTING JUDGES AND MARITAL MASTERS

In 1987, the New Hampshire Supreme Court had introduced a judicial performance evaluation program patterned on national guidelines promulgated by the ABA.[76] One legislator, however, considered the operation of the evaluation process "sporadic at best."[77] In April 2000, Gov. Jeanne Shaheen signed legislation requiring the judiciary to design and implement a new evaluation program, by which the performance of all superior, district, and probate courts would be evaluated at least every three years. The program was to be in effect no later than the end of March 2001. At that time, the court adopted a new rule, setting provisional evaluation program procedures and performance criteria pending approval of a final plan.[78]

The law might have raised legitimate questions about whether the legislature had the constitutional authority to require such a program by statute. The supreme court, however, rendered the issue moot by adopting a rule that directly followed the statutory language.[79] In March 2001, it formally established the evaluation program in all state courts.

The enhanced program would measure the performance of judges against benchmarks jointly established by the N.H. Supreme Court and the Administrative Council for the Judicial Branch (a body consisting of the chief justice, the administrative judge for each trial court, and the state court administrator), and shared with the leaders of the other branches of state government.[80] Trial court judges and marital masters were now to be evaluated by uniform, carefully considered standards.[81] Although all records and information obtained during the evaluation process were generally to be kept confidential, a judge or marital master who failed two consecutive performance evaluations or purposely failed to complete prescribed performance improvement would be deemed to have waived any right to confidentiality, and the results of his or her evaluations would be made public.[82]

In January 2011, new legislation was proposed for the establishment of a judicial performance review commission that would work with the judicial branch of government but not be organizationally dependent on it. In 2012, an amended version of the bill was approved by both chambers and signed into law.[83] In a cooperative effort to meet the new requirements by the effective date of the amended statute, the supreme court then revised its rules to create a judicial performance advisory committee to make recommendations for strengthening the design and implementation of the evaluation process.[84] The committee would consist of the administrative judges of the superior court and circuit court, the chairs of the Senate and House Judiciary Committees, the executive director of the New Hampshire Public Defender Program, the executive director of the Judicial Council (or a designee), a deputy attorney general, and the chair of the Bar Association's Committee on Cooperation with the courts (or a designee).[85] An article in the state bar news indicated that the purpose of the committee would be "to make the evaluation process more accurate and fair, while improving the performance of judges and the judicial system as a whole."[86]

The collaboration between the New Hampshire legislature and judiciary since 2000 in the enhancement of the performance evaluation program begun in 1987 shows a gratifying degree of interbranch consensus about this approach to promoting judicial accountability. The adoption of standards to measure the performance of trial and appellate court judges in an ongoing manner is highly relevant to citizens' perception of the integrity and competence of state judges. Indeed, the provisions in the new supreme court rules on judicial performance, and especially those for purposeful failure to complete prescribed improvement steps, can serve as important criteria for deciding whether the actual removal of a judge or marital master by address or impeachment is warranted.

REQUESTING AND RENDERING ADVISORY OPINIONS

Since 2001, there may have been a potentially significant shift in the way that the justices of the supreme court and elected officials in the legislative and executive branches of state government view advisory opinions. The evidence is mixed, and there may not be a settled pattern after only 16 years since the conclusion of impeachment proceedings against Chief Justice Brock. Yet it is worthwhile to identify some specific developments that may warrant future scrutiny.

Perhaps most significant is the fact that there have been only eight requests for advisory opinions during that period, or an average of only one every two years. In the period from 1901 through 1966, by comparison, there was an average of more than two per year; and from 1967 through 2000, more than four per year were requested. The incidence of such requests since 2001 is in fact close to that in the last third of the nineteenth century, after the end of the Civil War.

The frequency of advisory opinions is driven by the legislature and by governor and council, most often a result of debate and conflict within or between the elected branches of government.[87] The lower frequency of advisory opinion requests since 2001 may be a consequence of a reduced level of debate and conflict. On the other hand, it may reflect an inclination in the elected branches (whether explicit or not) to rely less on prior constitutional interpretation by the judiciary, and to assert their own authority and capacity to interpret constitutional requirements.[88]

Reluctance to request advisory opinions may reflect an expectation that, after the 1966 constitutional amendment granting institutional judicial independence, the judiciary may be more willing to find proposed executive or legislative actions unconstitutional. This may be an explanation for the fact that the justices responding to advisory opinion requests on constitutional questions in 1967–2000 indicated they considered less than half of the proposed actions under consideration to be constitutional. This inclination has continued: in advisory opinions on constitutionality since 2001, the justices responded that they considered four of six proposed legislative actions unconstitutional. See Appendix C for more information.

The justices themselves declined to respond to two of the eight requests for advisory opinions that had been made since 2001. Although this may simply have been a result of the specific features of those two requests,[89] it might also have reflected a desire on the part of the justices to avoid entanglement when possible in matters they might consider more properly resolved through litigation.[90]

RULING ON STATE EDUCATION FUNDING CHALLENGES

The supreme court's deliberations over education funding did not end when the *Claremont VI* decision was rendered in 1999, before the commencement of the Brock impeachment proceedings. But the membership of the supreme court bench was changing, with Justices Sherman Horton and Stephen Thayer replaced by Justices Joseph Nadeau and Linda Dalianis in 2000. In December 2000, just after the conclusion of the impeachment trial, four of the justices (with Nadeau and Dalianis joining Brock and Broderick) rendered an advisory opinion that a reformed public-school financing system proposed by the Senate would not "satisfy the requirements of part II, articles 5, 6, and 83 of the New Hampshire constitution."[91] After that, the fifth position on the bench was filled by the appointment of James Duggan to the court.

With three new justices on the court, its mix of judicial perspectives began to change on whether the state was meeting its education funding obligations under the state constitution. This change was evident in the *Sirrell* case, involving a statewide property tax for education funding.[92] In *Sirrell*, the justices reversed a trial court decision finding the statewide property tax unconstitutional as applied, which would have required the state to repay the $880 million that had been collected under the tax to date. David Brock and John Broderick, the last two justices whose involvement in education-funding litigation stretched back to *Claremont I*, would for the first time find themselves in the minority on a case regarding state action in this area. Brock and Broderick felt that the plaintiffs in the case had met their burden of proof in demonstrating that the tax as applied did not sufficiently alter the financial disparities among school districts that had always lain at the root of the controversy. The three new justices, on the other hand, saw no constitutional infirmity in the tax or in its implementation.

In September 2001, the *Claremont* plaintiffs then asked the supreme court to declare that the legislature's newest education funding program was "unconstitutional on its face." This time, Brock and Broderick found a third justice to support their view, Justice Duggan. The majority view was that the state's duty to provide a constitutionally adequate education must include measures of accountability, and that, since the new statutory program provided no actual mandate for either the local school district or the state education department to do anything, it did not fulfill the state's constitutional duty.[93] In their dissent, Justices Nadeau and Dalianis explicitly argued that the existing laws, rules, and regulations on the state's duty to provide a constitutionally adequate education are sufficient, and that the majority's definition of accountability exceeds what is constitutionally required.[94]

The *Claremont VII* decision was the last to be rendered in that long-running set of cases. After that, judicial involvement in school funding eventually reached a degree of closure, through decisions in two cases involving the Londonderry School District.

In *Londonderry I*,[95] the plaintiffs filed a trial court complaint in 2005 that the state had failed to comply with the supreme court's 1997 order in *Claremont II* to define a constitutionally adequate education. When the matter was appealed, Brock and Nadeau had retired, so that the supreme court now had two more justices who had not participated in any of the earlier *Claremont* decisions. In its decision, the supreme court affirmed the trial court's ruling for the plaintiffs. It also retained jurisdiction over the core issue of what defines a "constitutionally adequate education," pending legislative response to the ruling. However, it withheld a ruling on the remaining issues of cost, accountability, and taxation because "the definition of a constitutionally adequate education is essential to all other issues."

The legislature responded by enacting a statute defining a constitutionally "adequate" education.[96] Before the supreme court in 2008, the *Londonderry II* petitioners did not challenge the constitutional sufficiency of the new definition of a constitutionally adequate education. Moreover, while they did claim that there were several infirmities in the new statutes, they nonetheless informed the court that they would assent to a dismissal of this case without prejudice "if the state would commit to making a good faith effort to fulfill, by June 30, 2008, the remaining three mandates of its constitutional duty to provide an adequate education to every child in the state."[97]

In response, the state claimed that the action was now moot. They maintained that, with the enactment of the new laws in 2007 and 2008, the state had now taken sufficient steps toward satisfying its constitutional duty to render the issue moot by establishing state education costing and funding legislation and creating a legislative oversight committee as an affirmative first step toward ensuring accountability. In a majority opinion written by Justice Hicks, with Justices Dalianis and Galway concurring, the court agreed with the respondents, finding that the action was now moot. On that basis, it dismissed the case.[98]

EXERCISING JUDICIAL REVIEW OF LEGISLATIVE ACTIONS IN GENERAL

A second critical consideration in terms of perceived "judicial arrogance" has to do with judicial decisions involving challenges to the constitutionality of legislative actions. Despite a history of populist concern about the exercise of judicial power, it appears that no effort was ever made between 1784 and 2000 to impose limits on the power of the judiciary to review the constitutionality of legislation in New Hampshire.[99] Even after the Brock impeachment, and despite the continued incidence of court rulings invalidating legislation on constitutional grounds at a much higher rate than before 1966, there has still been no strong effort to constrain the power of judicial review in general. Although legislators filed four bills between 2003 and 2012 proposing constitutional limits on judicial review in general, each of them was rather summarily disposed as "inexpedient to legislate."[100]

Table 10.1 shows judicial review outcomes in 2001–2016, comparing those in 2001–2010 under Chief Justices Brock and Broderick with those in 2011–2016 under Chief Justice Dalianis. After the conclusion of the impeachment proceedings, when David Brock returned as chief justice and was then succeeded by John Broderick, the percent of judicial review cases with statutes found unconstitutional was almost as high in 2001–2010 (41.7%) as it had been in 1967–2000 (44.9%). A significant majority of the judicial review cases decided in 2001–2010 involved claims of such "rights revolution" issues as state or federal due process and such state constitutional grounds as equal protection, access to justice, and education adequacy. Separation of powers issues, which ranked high in 1967–2000, continued to be grounds for challenges to legislation in 2001–2016.

Perhaps the outcomes of judicial review cases after Linda Dalianis became chief justice in 2011 are every bit as striking as those in the three decades right after the Supreme Court was granted constitutional status in 1966. There were 18 judicial review cases decided between 2011 and the end of December 2016, and the percentage of them with decisions that legislative action was unconstitutional

Table 10.1 New Hampshire Judicial Review Outcomes, 2001–2016

		2001–2010			*2011–2016*		
Rank 1967–2000	*Constitutional Issue*	*Rank 2001–2010*	*Cases*[a]	*Held Unconstitutional*	*Rank 2011–2016*	*Cases*[a]	*Held Unconstitutional*
3	NH Separation of Powers	1	6	3	1t	3	0
2	NH Due Process	2t	4	1	5t	2	0
11	*US 14th Am Due Process*	*2t*	*4*	*1*	*8t*	*1*	*0*
5	NH Exercise of Leg. Power	4t	2	0	8t	1	0
13	NH Retrospective Laws	"	2	1	1t	3	2
6	NH Access to Justice	"	2	0	5t	2	0
1	NH Equal Protection	"	2	0	8t	1	0
[b]	NH Education Adequacy	"	2	1	N/A	0	0
[c]	NH Natural Rights	9t	1	1	N/A	0	0
7	NH Police Power	"	1	0	N/A	0	0
[c]	NH Free Speech	"	1	1	N/A	0	0
[b]	NH Right to Jury Trial	"	1	1	8t	1	1
9	NH Ex Post Facto Laws	"	1	0	N/A	0	0
[c]	NH Voting Rights	"	1	1	5t	2	1
15	NH Unfunded Mandates	"	1	0	8t	1	0
[c]	NH "Money Bill" Origin	"	1	0	N/A	0	0
6	NH Access to Government	"	1	0	8t	1	0
[c]	NH Right to Bear Arms	"	1	0	N/A	0	0
4	*US 14th Am Equal Protection*	"	*1*	*1*	*8t*	*1*	*0*

(Continued)

Table 10.1 (*Continued*)

		2001–2010			2011–2016		
Rank 1967–2000	*Constitutional Issue*	*Rank 2001–2010*	*Cases*[a]	*Held Unconstitutional*	*Rank 2011–2016*	*Cases*[a]	*Held Unconstitutional*
c	*US Free Speech*	"	*1*	*1*	*N/A*	*0*	*0*
b	NH Contract Rights	N/A	0	0	1t	3	0
c	NH Adv. Opinion Standing	N/A	0	0	8t	1	1
c	*US Impairment of Contracts*	*N/A*	*0*	*0*	*1t*	*3*	*0*
	Total Issues		36	13		26	5
	Judicial Review Cases, 2001–2016		24	10		18	5
	Percent Held Unconstitutional (%)			41.7			27.8
	Judicial Review Cases, 1817–2016					293	79
	Percent Held Unconstitutional (%)						27.0

Source: Case-by-case analysis (on file with authors) of 293 reported New Hampshire decisions involving judicial review of the constitutionality of legislative actions, as published from 1817 through 2016. For further information, see Appendix B.

[a] In many cases, more than one constitutional issue may have been presented, so that the cumulative total of cases with specific constitutional issues is greater than the actual number of judicial review cases.

[b] This was among the issues presented only once in 1967–2000 judicial review cases.

[c] This was one of the issues not raised in any judicial review cases in 1967–2000.

(27.8%) was considerably lower than from the levels in 1967–2000 and 2001–2010. In fact, the percent of rulings against the constitutionality of legislation in 2011–2016 was virtually identical to the overall total average (27.0%) for the entire historical period of reported judicial decisions from 1817 through 2016.

The reduction in judicial review decisions holding legislation unconstitutional might be explained in part by there being a somewhat-different case mix, involving relatively fewer due process, equal protection, or other cases presenting "rights revolution" issues. It may also be a consequence of a changeover in the membership of the high court, perhaps with justices who have a different jurisprudential approach to the kinds of constitutional issues presented in judicial review cases. There may also be another important possible explanation—that the number of judicial review cases to date is simply too small to reflect much more than the effects of pure chance.

NOTES

1. Constitutional Amendment Concurrent Resolutions (CACR) 4 and 5, as introduced, N.H.H.R. Jour. 15 (January 4, 2001), 172, 173.
2. CACR4 (2002), N.H. H.R. Jour. 5 (January 2, 2002), 192.
3. Jacobsen testimony, N.H. S. Committee on Judiciary, Hearing on CACR5 (2002) (May 23, 2001), 7, 8.
4. Ibid., 46–47.
5. *Constitutional Convention, 1974*, 261–62.
6. 141 N.H. 562, 688 A.2d 1006 (1997).
7. See N.H. S. Jour. 6 (February 20, 2002), 165.
8. See N.H., General Ct. Manual 2003, 366.
9. See CACR5 (2004), House Judiciary Committee, Public Hearing (February 14, 2003), http://gencourt.state.nh.us/SofS_Archives/2004/house/CACR5H.pdf.
10. Democrats voted against the measure by a margin of 62–42. CACR5 (2004), House Roll Call (January 15, 2004), http://www.gencourt.state.N.H..us/bill_status/Roll_Calls/billstatus_rcdetails.aspx?vs=17&sy=2004&lb=H&eb=CACR0005&sortoption=&txtsessionyear=2004&ddlsponsors=&lsr=298. One independent representative voted against the bill.
11. CACR5 (2004), Senate Roll Call (April 29, 2004), http://www.gencourt.state.N.H..us/bill_status/Roll_Calls/billstatus_rcdetails.aspx?vs=46&sy=2004&lb=S&eb=CACR0005&sortoption=&txtsessionyear=2004&ddlsponsors=&lsr=298.
12. N.H. Gen. Ct. Manual 2005, 450, https://archive.org/stream/manualforgeneral59newh#page/450/mode/2up.
13. CACR36 (2006) and CACR20 (2010).
14. HB89 (2011), Roll Call Vote #60 (March 15, 2011), http://www.gencourt.state.N.H..us/bill_status/Roll_calls/billstatus_rcdetails.aspx?vs=60&sy=2011&lb=H&eb=HB0089&sortoption=billnumber&txtsessionyear=2011&txtbillnumber=hb89&ddlsponsors=&lsr=335.

15. Opinion of the Justices (Requiring Attorney General to Join Lawsuit), 162 N.H. 160, 27 A.3d 859 (2011).

16. With that resolution [HR13 (2011)], wrote Andrew Cohen, the Republican members of the House sought as legislators to "defend the power delegated to them in the Constitution by the people" rather than "let it be wrongfully handed over to unelected officials." Cohen, "In New Hampshire, a GOP-Led Assault on the State Judiciary," *Atlantic* (October 13, 2011), https://www.theatlantic.com/politics/archive/2011/10/in-new-hampshire-a-gop-led-assault-on-the-state-judiciary/246535/.

17. CACR26, as introduced, N.H. H. Jour. 7 (January 4, 2012), 366.

18. CACR26, House Roll Call Vote, N.H. H. Jour. 28 (March 21, 2012), 1689–1691. That May, Rep. Paul Mirski testified before a Senate committee that his appointment in 1997 to a committee investigating the Fairbanks scandal had left him with a dark view of the judiciary, troubled by both administrative problems in the courts and corruption in the legal community. For a newspaper account of the hearing, see John DiStaso, "Separation-of-powers: N.H. Supreme Court offers compromise on rule-making constitutional amendment plan," *N.H. Union Leader,* May 3, 2012, http://www.unionleader.com/article/20120503/NEWS06/120509947&template=mobileart.

19. CACR26, Senate Judiciary Amendment No. 2012–2041S (May 7, 2012).

20. CACR26, Senate Roll Call Vote, N.H. S. Cal. 19 (May 16, 2012).

21. CACR26, House Roll Call Vote, N.H. H. Jour. 51 (June 6, 2012), 2587–2589.

22. N.H. Secretary of State, Constitutional Amendment Questions—2012 General Election, http://sos.N.H..gov/2012ConConGen.aspx.

23. See Lynn, "Judicial Rule-Making and the Separation of Powers in New Hampshire: The Need for Constitutional Reform," *N.H. Bar J.* 42, no. 1 (2001): 44–69.

24. *PSAE,* 141 N.H. 562, 688 A.2d 1006 (1997).

25. Lynn, "Judicial Rule-Making." On separation of powers, he wrote:

> The historical record both in N.H. and elsewhere plainly shows that there had never been a serious question as to the power of the legislature to make rules governing court practice and procedure; the central point in debates over court rule-making generally concerned the wisdom of extending this power to the judiciary, not removing it from the legislature. Yet … the court has completely shifted the focus of the rule-making analysis. Instead of the substance-procedure dichotomy serving as a limitation on judicial power (i.e., by prohibiting the courts from making rules of substantive law) as had been understood by prior case law and by the drafters of article 73-a, it has now become a limitation on legislative power (by prohibiting the legislature from making procedural law).

26. State v. Ploof, 162 N.H. 609, 34 A.3d 563, 577 (2011).

27. *Id.*

28. Petition of Southern N.H. Medical Center, 164 N.H. 319, 55 A.3d 988 (October 30, 2012).

29. *Id.*, 55 A.3d at 996–97. Chief Justice Dalianis quoted the 1974 exchange between constitutional convention delegates Martin Gross and Arthur Nighswander, in which Nighswander assured Gross that the adoption of the resolution that became

Article 73-a would not deprive the legislature of its concurrent power to regulate court procedure by statute, including laws concerning evidentiary rules. See *Constitutional Convention, 1974*, 261–62.

30. At the time, national judicial ethics models did not emphasize the risk of such a practice. The focus of the ABA Canon on disqualification of judges was overwhelmingly on trial judges, and the circumstances in which litigants and lawyers might question their impartiality. See Richard Flamm, *Judicial Disqualification: Recusal and Disqualification of Judges*, 2d ed. (Berkeley, CA: Banks & Jordan, 2007), §29.4 (2015 cumulative supplement). It was not until 2007, when the ABA adopted a revised model code, that the national canons addressed the impropriety or appearance of impropriety of any *ex parte* communication by the judge deciding a case at the trial or appellate levels with a judge who has been disqualified from hearing the matter. ABA Model Code (2007), Canon 2.9 (A) (3), Comment 5.

31. The 1990 revision to the ABA model code that the Task Force referred to was significant for its substitution of the word "shall" for "should" throughout the document to make clear that its provisions were no longer just hortatory or prescriptive suggestions, but instead must be understood as rules that were mandatory and enforceable in their application to judge behavior. See James Alfini, Shailey Gupta-Brietzke, and James McMartin, "Dealing with Judicial Misconduct in the States: Judicial Independence, Accountability and Reform," *S. Tex. L. Rev.* 48 (2007): 889–1135. See also Cynthia Gray, "Controversy and Reform in New Hampshire," *Judicial Conduct Reporter* 23, no. 1 (2001): 1, 5.

32. Jonathan DeFelice and Wilfred Sanders, *Task Force for the Renewal of Judicial Conduct Procedures, Report to Supreme Court of New Hampshire* (Concord, NH: Supreme Court, 2001).

33. See Virginia Garrell-Michaud, *An Evaluation of the Supreme Court of New Hampshire Committee on Judicial Conduct and Professional Conduct Committee* (Concord, NH: Governor's Commission on Crime and Delinquency, Grant No. 78-I-A2001 E07, 1979), 2–3.

34. N.H. Supreme Court Order, May 7, 2001.

35. The text of the order of May 7, 2001, did not include any new procedural rules for judicial disciplinary proceedings. As the new CC was being formed, David Hodges and John Newsom both resigned from being members of the JCC. A public radio report at the time indicated that Newsom was zealous in his defense of the JCC's rules of confidentiality, arguing that they were a necessary due process protection in judicial disciplinary proceedings. See New Hampshire Public Radio, "JCC Members Quit Committee and Sound Off," http://info.nhpr.org/node/1197.

36. See the comments in the commission's annual report for FY 2002:

> The Judicial Conduct Commission was created with the expectation that the Supreme Court Commission on Judicial Conduct, which has the same duties, would be disbanded. That has not happened. Thus, two similarly named panels are operating in parallel, costing taxpayers' money, and causing much confusion for the public.

Judicial Conduct Commission, Report, 2002, 2, http://wermenh.com/courts/annual_2002.html.

37. SB197 (2001), adopted by voice vote, N.H. S. Jour. 19 (June 26, 2001), 687–692.

38. N.H. Rev. Stat. Ann. § 494-A:12, enacted by N.H. Laws 2001, Ch. 267.

39. Under the statute, new rules to govern all proceedings before the new commission were approved and effective on May 10, 2002. See *Procedural Rules of Judicial Conduct Commission* (2002), as reproduced at http://wermenh.com/courts/proceduralrules.html.

40. JCC, Annual Report 2002.

41. N.H. Laws 2003, Ch. 319.

42. In re: Petition of the Judicial Conduct Committee, 151 N.H. 123, 855 A.2d 535 (2004).

43. This membership provision was thus much closer to that provided by the July 2001 bill than to the 2003 bill.

44. Supreme Court Order R-2004–004, In re December 2004 Report of the Advisory Committee on Rules, January 25, 2005.

45. See JCC, Annual Report, 2008, 5.

46. N.H. H.R. Jour. 29 (March 19, 2008), 1603.

47. HA1, as introduced, N.H. H.R. Jour. 29 (March 19, 2008), 1603.

48. Coffey's Case, 157 N.H. 156, 949 A. 2d 102 (2008).

49. See Norma Love, "Judge Coffey resigns," *Seacoast Online,* April 21, 2008, http://www.seacoastonline.com/article/20080421/NEWS/80421015.

50. N.H. H.R. Jour. 33 (April 23, 2008), 1745.

51. See Marshall, State Constitution, 233.

52. See Rinden and Lyman, *Constitutional Amendment Proposals*, 86.

53. See summaries of committee reports and delegate votes, *Constitutional Convention, 1984.*

54. See Rinden and Lyman, *Constitutional Amendment Proposals*, 16, 17, 90, and 91; N.H. H.R. Jour., Numerical Index of Bills (1985), 940; N.H. S. Jour., vol.2, Constitutional Amendment Concurrent Resolutions (1987), 2066; and N.H. General Court, Bill Status System, Constitutional Amendment Concurrent Resolutions, Session Years 1989–2000, HYPERLINK "http://www.gencourt.state.nh.us/bill_status/" http://www.gencourt.state.N.H..us/bill_status/.

55. N.H. General Court, Bill Status System, Session Years 2001–2016, http://www.gencourt.state.N.H..us/bill_status/.

56. See Charles DeGrandpre, "Lex Loci: A Survey of N.H. Supreme Court Decisions," *N.H. Bar J.* 45, no. 1 (2004): 91.

57. In a tribute to Brock at his retirement, Justice William Batchelder observed that Brock had served as chief justice for more than 17 years, a term longer than any of the preceding 32 chief justices with the exceptions of Frank Kenison (1952–1977), Frank Parsons (1902–1924), William Richardson (1816–1838), and Charles Doe (1876–1896). Batchelder, "The Judicial Journey of David A. Brock," *N.H. Bar J.* 47, no. 4 (2007): 5–9.

58. SB35 (2001), repealing and reenacting N.H. Rev. Stat. Ann. § 490:1, as amended and passed, N.H. S. Jour. 9 (April 12, 2001), 106–107, and N.H. H.R. Jour. 47 (May 17, 2001), 1440 and 1442. Signed into law as N.H. Laws 2001, Ch. 50.

59. See Opinion of the Justices (Appointment of Chief Justice of the Supreme Court), 150 N.H. 355, 842 A.2d 816 (December 19, 2003).

60. *Id.*, 150 N.H. at 356.

61. See Petition of Governor and Executive Council, 151 N.H. 1, 846 A. 2d 1148 (2004).

62. *Id.,* 151 N.H. at 10. All of the sitting Supreme Court justices had to recuse themselves. Instead, retired Supreme Court Justice Johnson sat by special assignment under N.H. Rev. Stat. Ann. §490:3; in addition, Superior Court Chief Justice Murphy and retired Superior Court Justices Temple, Gray, and Hollman also sat by special assignment under that statute.

63. 151 N.H. at 6–9.

64. *Id.*, 9–10.

65. N.H. Judicial Branch, "News Release: Chief Justice Brock Announces Retirement, Effective December 31" (December 1, 2003).

66. N.H. Governor and Council Minutes, June 2, 2004, 2.

67. In 1940, Missouri had become the first state to use a nominating commission to aid in the selection of judges. Today, the practice has been adopted in more than 20 states, and is widely recognized as a viable alternative to both the election and the unassisted appointment of judges. See Ryan Owens, Alexander Tahk, Patrick Wohlfarth, and Amanda Bryan, "Nominating Commissions, Judicial Retention, and Forward-Looking Behavior on State Supreme Courts: An Empirical Examination of Selection and Retention Methods," 15 *St. Pol. & Pol'y Q*. 15, no. 2 (2015): 211, 213.

68. Ibid.

69. Shaheen, Executive Order 2000–9, "An order establishing a Judicial Selection Commission" (June 30, 2000).

70. SB24 (2002), N.H. S. Jour. 2 (January 4, 2001), 24.

71. HB582 (2002), N.H. H.R. Jour. 18 (January 25, 2001), 252.

72. Opinion of the Justices, 117 N.H 398, 374 A.2d 638 (1977).

73. CACR33 (2002), passed by Senate, but rejected by House. N.H. S. Jour. 6 (February 20, 2002), 165–166; N.H. H.R. Jour. 34 (April 17, 2002), 1318–1319.

74. HB130 (2003), voted inexpedient to legislate, N.H. H.R. Jour. 14 (February 6, 2003), 288.

75. In December 2003, Gov. Craig Benson issued an executive order abolishing the merit selection commission that Shaheen had created. Benson, Executive Order 2003–10, "An Order Abolishing the Judicial Selection Commission," December 9, 2003. Then in February 2005, soon after he won the governorship, John Lynch reversed Benson's action with another executive order recreating the commission. Lynch, Executive Order 2005–2, "An Order Establishing a Judicial Selection Commission" (February 5, 2005). In 2013 Lynch's successor, Margaret Hassan, renewed it with an executive order of her own. Hassan, Executive Order 2013–06, "an order establishing a Judicial Selection Commission" (April 23, 2013). In November 2016, Christopher Sununu was elected governor, and he issued an order continuing the use of a judicial selection commission. Sununu, Executive Order 2017–01, "an order establishing a Judicial Selection Commission" (February 6, 2017).

76. Institute for the Advancement of the American Legal System [IAALS], "Judicial Performance Evaluation>New Hampshire," http://iaals.du.edu/sites/default/files/documents/publications/newhampshirejpe.pdf.

77. See N.H. S. Judiciary Committee, Hearing on HB568, Rep. Henry Mock testimony, N.H. S. Cal. 17 (March 22, 2000), 28.

78. N.H. Supreme Court, Order (March 27, 2001). The kind of JPE program that the statute required would follow the model of one first created in Alaska in 1975 to provide voters with information about individual judges facing retention elections. Sharon Paynter and Richard Kearney, "Who Watches the Watchmen: Evaluating Judicial Performance in American States," *Admin. & Soc'y* 41, no. 8 (2010), 933.

79. See N.H. S. Judiciary Committee, Hearing on SB249, Howard Zibel testimony for Supreme Court, N.H. S. Cal. 3 (January 21, 2014).

80. N.H. Supreme Court, Report on Judicial Performance Evaluation Program (2001), 2.

81. See N.H. S. Ct. R. 56 (II)(D)(2, 3) and (IV)(B)(3).

82. Ibid. In the event that the evaluation results for a judge or marital master were made public, the rule provides that the identity of persons furnishing evaluation information about him or her under the JPE process would remain confidential. It did not take long for judicial leaders to find a performance problem and show their responsiveness by reporting it to the leaders of the other branches of government. The JPE report for 2004 indicated that results for one of the superior court judges evaluated in 2003 were significantly below the norm. The results of a follow-up evaluation for that judge showed a very significant improvement in every one of the component categories of the evaluation. See Report on JPE Program (June 30, 2006), 6.

83. See N.H. Laws 2012, Ch. 72.

84. N.H. S. Ct. R. 56 (I)(B), as added July 17, 2012, effective July 22, 2012.

85. IAALS, "Judicial Performance Evaluation>New Hampshire."

86. Kristen Senz, "Measuring Judicial Performance," *N.H. Bar News* (February 19, 2014), https://www.nhbar.org/publications/display-news-issue.asp?id=7197.

87. See Topf, *Doubtful Experiment*, 181–84.

88. See Tushnet, *Taking Constitution Away from Courts,* 33–71.

89. In each of the two controversies where the justices declined to render an advisory opinion, the Court subsequently held the legislation in question to be unconstitutional when it was before them as a litigated matter. In Opinion of the Justices (Appointment of Chief Justice of Supreme Court), 150 NH 355, 842 A.2d 816 (2003), the justices declined to respond to a request from Governor and Council on whether a statute that would establish a five-year rotation by seniority in the position of chief justice would violate constitutional requirements. When the same issues were presented to the Court in a request for a declaratory judgment, a panel of replacement judges sitting as the Court declared the five-year rotation statute unconstitutional. Petition of Governor & Council, 151 N.H. 1, 846 A. 2d 1148 (2004).Later, in Opinion of the Justices (Domicile for Voting Purposes), 167 N.H. 539, 115 A.3d 257 (2015), the justices declined to respond because similar or identical questions were posed in a case then pending before the Court. See Guare v. State, 117 A. 3d 731 (N.H. 2015), for the Court's decision in that case on appeal, declaring the domicile statute in question to be unconstitutional.

90. For a discussion of judicial animosity toward advisory opinions, see Topf, *Doubtful Experiment*, 69–83.

91. Opinion of the Justices (Reformed Public-School Financing System), 145 N.H. 474, 765 A.2d 673 (2000).

92. Sirrell v. State, 146 N.H. 364, 780 A.2d 494 (2001).

93. *Id.*, 147 N.H. at 519.

94. *Id.*, 524.

95. Londonderry School District v. State, 154 N.H. 153, 907 A.2d 988 (2006).

96. N.H. Laws 2007, Ch. 270, codified at N.H. Rev. Stat. Ann. Ch. 193-E.

97. Londonderry School District v. State, 157 N.H. 734, 958 A. 2d 930 (2008).

98. *Id.*, 958 A.2d at 933. Chief Justice Broderick and Justice Duggan each filed separate dissenting opinions, however. As the last remaining member of the pre-impeachment "Claremont" court, Broderick expressed disagreement that the action was now moot, writing that the State had still not met its acknowledged obligation, "despite its near decade long assurances that our public education system would contain the requisite controls to ensure the delivery of a constitutionally adequate education." In Justice Duggan's dissent, he noted the parties' memoranda showed considerable factual disagreements best addressed by a trial court, so that the appeal should be dismissed without prejudice and the case remanded to superior court.

99. See Marshall, *State Constitution*, 233.

100. These bills were CACR11 (2003), CACR16 (2005), CACR2 (2008), and CACR28 (2012).

Conclusion

Some aspects of this story clearly reflect New Hampshire's own, distinctive history and civic culture. None of them, individually, is unique; but their confluence has arguably created a peculiar political and judicial environment in the state, from which the impeachment of David Brock eventually issued.

Perhaps most significant was the oddity of citizens' approving changes in the constitutional status of the judicial branch of government in 1966, thereby breaking with traditions dating from 1784, while at the same time rejecting proposed changes of a comparable magnitude in the constitutional status of the legislative and executive branches.

New Hampshire is not the only state where legislators, especially, must remain closely attuned to every shift in public opinion by virtue of biannual elections, small electoral districts, and similar measures. Nor is it the only state where a corollary of that firm commitment to citizen rule is suspicion of government by experts. But in New Hampshire, voters' relentless rejections of any and all attempts to elevate the role of those experts by professionalizing the operations of the elected branches—whether by extending terms, expanding staffs, raising salaries, or anything else—is special. Clearly, the state's citizens want those officials to remain amateurs in the classic Athenian sense: they are to be ordinary citizens acting on the daily concerns of their peers, and not on what might be considered esoteric visions, or agendas hatched by governmental technocrats.

Judicial officials, on the other hand, had promoted the professionalization of their own branch almost since statehood, through the gradual transfer of responsibility in court proceedings from laymen to trained and credentialed legal specialists. That had been tolerated, even encouraged, so long as the judiciary itself remained institutionally subordinate to the people's elected representatives and, as a rule, unwilling to openly challenge them. But in

1966, the state's highest courts secured a wholly unprecedented institutional independence from the elected branches; and in 1978, the Supreme Court secured a similarly novel degree of concentrated administrative authority over a newly unified statewide court system. In traditionalists' eyes, New Hampshire's judiciary was announcing that, henceforth, justice would be handled entirely by professionals, while elected representatives simply provided the funding.

That kind of structural dysfunction—civic populism reaffirmed in two branches of state government, purged from the third—might have been easier to manage but for features of that third branch that set it off not only from the rest of the state's government, but from other state judiciaries as well. The near-absence in New Hampshire prior to 2001 of any of the mechanisms by which most other states maintain judicial accountability—periodic popular election of judges, specific terms of office as opposed to good-behavior tenure, mechanisms for merit selection of judicial candidates—rendered inter-branch relations in the state peculiarly tense. That tenseness, in turn, gave a special edge, in New Hampshire, to issues involving the judiciary in the 1990s.

New Hampshire was hardly the only state in the nation to experience the sort of judicial misconduct that John Fairbanks perpetrated (the case of Justice Rolf Larsen in Pennsylvania, for example, comes to mind). But the Fairbanks scandal occurred in a state where, for structural reasons, mistrust of the judiciary was already deepening; thanks to Fairbanks and his enablers, what had been generalized concerns about inter-branch relations were clouded with new fears regarding the personal probity of individual judges. Nor was New Hampshire alone in the conflicts engendered by judicial involvement in the funding of public schools. The issues were exactly the same in, for instance, California (where the state supreme court's actions helped pave the way for the removal from office, by retention election, of Chief Justice Rose Bird).[1] In fact, those issues were nothing other than state-level extensions of the rights revolution associated with the Warren Court and felt across the nation.[2] But given recent developments in New Hampshire, the entire matter there could be cast not as an errant decision or even set of decisions, but as symptom of a judiciary that had shed all vestiges of popular control and must be brought to heel.

Given this alignment of circumstances, something like the Brock impeachment may well have been unavoidable. In fact, it may even have been healthy: not because Chief Justice Brock was himself the malefactor his antagonists portrayed, which most now agree he was not, but because the structural dysfunction we describe simply had to be resolved. The system required something cathartic, something by which the gravity of the issues could be burned into public awareness and restorative action catalyzed.

Alternative methods of producing one may have existed, in theory. The practicality of each, however, remains questionable. A blue-ribbon panel examining the state of legislative-judicial relations might have been assembled; but the state had summoned them up before, yet serious problems remained. New legislation reconfiguring those relations, driven by an aroused electorate, is similarly easy to imagine. But the contours of legislation that could have passed constitutional muster at the time are, at best, unclear. Impeachment was dramatic, painful, and quite arguably unjust to David Brock. Yet in the end, it was also effective.

And it is precisely that effectiveness that makes our story so much more than a parochial one.

For New Hampshire now provides nothing less than an ongoing test of whether judicial independence *can* be sustained *within* a populist civic culture, and whether citizens can indeed expect their state courts to be free of both corrupting external influences *and* the arrogance of the unbeholden. We hope that the results of what New Hampshire has undertaken since 2000 will be monitored widely and closely. What is happening there is an experiment, and the implications for state judiciaries elsewhere are significant.

In a provocative 1998 article, Paul Carrington argued that judicial indifference to widely held norms and public priorities had generated a potentially disastrous backlash. The stakes of state-level judicial elections had massively expanded, with the predictable result that they had become partisan warzones. In the increasingly venomous political climate of the times, Carrington argued, the optimal ways of assuring judicial accountability had become, by and large, unsaleable. Neither merit selection nor any other form of appointment granting significant roles to bar or bench, he felt, could escape public scorn as "a masquerade to put political power in the hands of the organized bar and other members of the elite."[3] For that reason, Carrington concluded that "In some form, judicial elections are here to stay."[4] But, given the new consequentiality of those contests, along with the power and ubiquity of new communications technologies, judges engaged in those elections would inevitably undergo campaigns of de-legitimation so relentless and unprincipled that public confidence in the judiciary itself must continue to erode.[5]

At the end of 2017, it is difficult to argue that the political climate is in any way less partisan or less vicious than the one Carrington surveyed nearly twenty years ago. Yet New Hampshire has attempted exactly what he felt such a climate rendered unlikely to succeed. It has continued to reject judicial elections in any form (and, for that matter, more aggressive attempts to elevate the judicial role of laymen over that of professionals), endorsing merit selection and routine performance review of judges instead. So far, the experiment seems to be working—if, that is, the absence of the sort of sustained assault on the integrity of the judiciary that Carrington feared and that some states, including New Hampshire, have indeed experienced is any indication. That success, it would seem, traces to the willingness of both judicial and elected officials to find measures around which all but overtly anti-juridical militants could eventually coalesce. The center, we hope, will hold.

If it does, New Hampshire's experience might shed considerable light on a key question raised by recent scholarship on the role of state-level judiciaries. That scholarship has advanced the proposition that there is, in fact, a coherent tradition of sub-national constitutional reasoning in the United States, reflecting the fact that state constitutions issue from different polities and promote different aims than the federal one.[6] Questions of judicial independence and accountability are approached differently on the state level simply because state constitutions generally grant more direct and extensive powers to voters than does the federal. That principle appears to apply, in particular, to the judicial branch. Judges in most states' high courts, after all, are constitutionally required to participate in some sort of elective process. In addition, most state constitutions are both much easier to amend than the federal constitution (thus extending voters' ability to reverse undesirable judicial actions) and far more detailed (thus constricting the interpretive latitude judges can assume).

One might reasonably expect that the general thrust of state-level constitutional interpretation would favor the principle of accountability over independence in regard to judicial matters. But the historical record is open to debate. In fact, one reading of that record indicates the opposite—that over the course of American history, voters have consistently pushed for fully depoliticized, independent state courts.[7] By another reading, what voters have sought is an overall balance between independence with accountability, with one or the other priority elevated at different times, in different places, for different reasons.[8]

The New Hampshire experience seems to support the latter interpretation. In fact, it seems to support Robert Tobin's suggestion that the achievement of institutional independence by state-level judiciaries must and should be followed by enhanced measures to assure the accountability of state courts, that the latter is essentially the necessary second phase of judicial reform within states.[9] If the measures New Hampshire has taken do yield long-term stability in legislative-judicial relations, and a citizenry content with the quality of its judicial institutions, Tobin's prescriptions might be reinforced.

That can happen, of course, only if citizens and officials maintain their awareness of the competing yet equally legitimate claims of law and politics; and, above all, the ability to balance them wisely. Those are not simple tasks. We propose that the New Hampshire legislature carried them out with skill and integrity during the impeachment of Chief Justice Brock. We believe that achievement should be noted by all concerned with judicial integrity and state governance.

NOTES

1. Paul Carrington, "Judicial Independence and Democratic Accountability in Highest State Courts," *Law & Contemp. Probs.* 61, no. 3 (1999): 79, 81–87.

2. Ibid.

3. Ibid., 106,

4. Ibid., 107.

5. Ibid., 107–127. Carrington found few ways of mitigating the "crisis of politically generated mistrust" that he found afflicting most state judiciaries. In the end, he favored measures such as extending the terms of state supreme court justices (to render them less vulnerable to political attack) and tort law reform (i.e., legislation restoring liability for outright defamation in judicial elections). Aware of the political difficulties involved in securing these and other reforms, he invested his main hope in adoption of the Japanese practice of a merit-based appointive process complemented by a single confirmation election.

6. Relevant works include John Dinan, *American State Constitutional Tradition*; Jed Shugerman, *People's Courts;* and Tarr, *Without Fear or Favor.*

7. Shugerman, *People's Courts.*

8. For an extended book review of Shugerman, *People's Courts*, see John Dinan, "Independence and Accountability in State Judicial Selection," *Tex. L. Rev.* 91, no. 3 (2013): 633–49.

9. See Tobin, *Judicial Branch*, 195.

Appendix A

State Chief Justices Who Have Been Impeached

In the words of one historian American constitutional culture since 1960 might properly be called an "age of impeachment." David Kyvig argues that impeachment has been transformed from a procedure to be used sparingly, and then only as a last resort, to much more frequently used political weapon.[1] Yet it is important to understand that highly publicized calls to impeach a public official seldom lead to anything more. As defined here, an official has been "impeached" only when formal articles of impeachment have been filed against him or her. This definition therefore excludes circumstances in which an impeachment inquiry has been proposed, an impeachment inquiry has been made, or any other step in which the process has come to an end (including when an official resigns his or her position) before the formal filing of articles of impeachment.

Although the number of justices in the highest court of any state is only a small fraction of its trial court judges, the chief justices of a state are among the most visible officials in state government, and they are responsible for hearing matters that may have long-term and statewide significance. The impeachment of David Brock was only the seventh time in American history that a state court chief justice has been impeached. Before Brock's impeachment in 2000, five state court chief justices had formal articles of impeachment filed against them and faced the prospect of an impeachment trial. (One of them, John McClure, was impeached twice.)

EDWARD SHIPPEN

In 1803, Pennsylvania chief justice Shippen was impeached with two associate justices in the midst of the struggle over politics and judicial independence between Federalists under John Adams and Republicans under Thomas Jefferson.[2] Shippen was one of three Federalist justices accused of acting oppressively by punishing Thomas Passmore, a Philadelphia businessman and active Republican, for contempt of court.[3] After a Senate trial, Shippen was acquitted when the Senate vote fell short of required two-thirds majority.[4]

JOHN MCCLURE (1871)

In Reconstruction-era Arkansas in 1871,[5] Chief Justice John McClure was suspected of taking part in an alleged conspiracy with Gov. Powell Clayton and others, and he was tried on a single article of impeachment charging him with having unlawfully issued an order restraining the lieutenant governor from exercising the duties of the office of governor while Governor Clayton was suspended from office pending the conclusion of impeachment proceedings against him.[6] At the commencement of trial in the Senate, McClure filed a demurrer, asserting that his issuance of a temporary restraining order was lawful because the House of Representatives had not given formal notice to the Senate that it had impeached Clayton. After extended debate, the Senate agreed with McClure's argument that the Clayton impeachment had thus not yet been consummated when he had issued what was an otherwise legitimate temporary restraining order; and the Senate then voted unanimously to accept McClure's demurrer motion.

JOHN MCCLURE (1874)

In 1874, Arkansas Democrats impeached Chief Justice McClure a second time. In May 1874, the Supreme Court of Arkansas granted a writ of *quo warranto* challenging the gubernatorial election of Elisha Baxter. The six articles of impeachment alleged that McClure was guilty of treason for having contrived the case as part of what some called an attempted "coup d'état" to oust Baxter from office in favor of his gubernatorial opponent. That Arkansas Supreme Court decision was ignored by US president Ulysses Grant, who had declared Baxter to be the legitimate governor of Arkansas, and it was subsequently overturned. Legislation was enacted that authorized the immediate suspension and pro tempore replacement of McClure and others upon impeachment.[7] Then the impeachment trial was mooted and the justices' terms of office were ended by the adoption of the Arkansas Constitution of 1874 and section 21 of its schedule for implementation.[8]

DAVID FURCHES

A Republican candidate for governor of North Carolina in 1892, David Furches was impeached amid partisan conflict with white-supremacist Democrats over a recent suffrage amendment disfranchising black citizens.[9] In 1899, the Democrat-controlled legislature transferred the responsibilities of a minor state official to an agency controlled by Democrats. In 1901, not long becoming Chief Justice upon the death of his predecessor, Furches and Associate Justice Robert Douglas were impeached and accused of a constitutional violation for upholding a trial court order that the state auditor and state treasurer must compensate the person dismissed from office as result of that legislative action.[10] After trial, the Senate vote fell short of two-thirds majority required for conviction.[11]

FREDERICK BRANSON

In 1927, after Gov. Henry Johnston sought to prohibit the legislature from meeting in extraordinary session, the House of Representatives impeached Oklahoma Johnston.[12] Chief Justice Branson was impeached as well for his court's confirmation of a trial decision enjoining legislature from convening in extraordinary session, holding that legislature possessed no inherent power to convene on its own motion, and that legislators could exercise no official functions until either called into extraordinary session by the governor or until the next regular session convened in January 1929.[13] There was no trial, for the Senate found that the articles of impeachment were void as having been prepared and filed without lawful authority.[14]

CHARLES MASON

In 1929, the same year as Gov. Henry Johnston was impeached a second time and removed from office for "general incompetence," the last impeachment of a state chief justice before David Brock was also in Oklahoma. Chief Justice Mason and two associate justices, all Republicans, were impeached by a Democrat-controlled House or Representatives on claims that they showed a lack of integrity in certain court decisions and were under undue influence of some lawyers appearing before the court. One of the articles against each justice had to do with the Supreme Court's decision in the case of *Simpson v. Hill*, on the basis of which Chief Justice Branson had previously been impeached.[15] Without trial, the Senate dismissed charges against Mason after the impeachment trial acquittal of Justice J. W. Clark.[16]

NOTES

1. See David Kyvig, *The Age of Impeachment: American Constitutional Culture since 1960* (Lawrence, KS: University Press of Kansas, 2008).

2. See Richard Ellis, *The Jeffersonian Crisis: Courts and Politics in the Young Republic* (New York: W.W. Norton, 1974), 164–70.

3. Passmore had been involved in a dispute over insurance for a ship lost at sea and was accused of libel for calling his opponent a "liar, rascal, and coward." When he refused to retract his words, he was found in contempt of court, fined, and sent to jail. See Hoffer and Hull, *Impeachment in America*, 221.

4. See William Hamilton, *Report of the Trial and Acquittal of Edward Shippen, Esq., Chief Justice, and Jasper Yeates and Thomas Smith, Esquires, Assistant Justices of the Supreme Court of Pennsylvania, on an Impeachment before the Senate of the Commonwealth, January 1805* (Lancaster, PA: Lancaster Journal, 1805).

5. To assess the impeachment of McClure in the context of Reconstruction-era Arkansas, see Thomas DeBlack, *With Fire and Sword: Arkansas, 1861–1874* (Fayetteville, AR: University of Arkansas Press, 2003); J.W. Looney, *Distinguishing the Righteous from the Roguish: The Arkansas Supreme Court, 1836–1874* (Fayetteville, AR: University of Arkansas Press, 2016); and Carl Moneyhon, *The Impact of the Civil War and Reconstruction on Arkansas: Persistence in the Midst of Ruin* (Fayetteville, AR: University of Arkansas Press, 2002).

6. Cortez Ewing, "Arkansas Reconstruction Impeachments," *Ark. Historical Q.* 13, no. 2 (1954): 149–53.

7. Steven Smith, "Impeachment, Address, and the Removal of Judges in Arkansas: An Historical Perspective," *Ark. L. Rev.* 32 (1978): 253, 267; Logan Stafford, "Judicial Coup D'état: Mandamus, Quo Warranto and the Original Jurisdiction of the Supreme Court of Arkansas," *U. Ark. Little Rock L. J.* 20, no. 4 (1998): 891, 973–74; see also Stafford, "The Arkansas Supreme Court and the Aftermath of the Civil War," *U. Ark. Little Rock L. J.* 23, no. 2 (2001): 355, 365–66.

8. See Arkansas, *Journal of the House of Representatives of the Twentieth General Assembly of Arkansas* (1874), 224, 229.

9. See William Powell (ed.), *Dictionary of North Carolina Biography: Volume 2* (Chapel Hill, NC: University of North Carolina Press, 2000), 255.

10. William Powell, *North Carolina through Four Centuries* (Chapel Hill, NC: University of North Carolina Press, 2010), 445.

11. See North Carolina, *Trial of David M. Furches, Now Chief Justice and Formerly Associate Justice and Robert M. Douglas, Associate Justice of the Supreme Court of North Carolina, on Impeachment by the House of Representatives for High Crimes and Misdemeanors* (Raleigh, NC: Edwards & Broughton, and E.M. Uzzell, 1901).

12. Frank Creel, "Court in Peril: The Legislative-Judicial Struggle," in Oklahoma Historical Society, *Chronicles of Oklahoma* 52 (1974): 220, 229–30.

13. Simpson v. Hill, 128 Okl. 269, 263 P. 635, 56 A.L.R. 706 (1927).

14. See Oklahoma, *Journal of the Proceedings of the State Senate Sitting as a Court of Impeachment* (Oklahoma City, OK, 1927), 55–57, 103.

15. Creel, "Court in Peril," 234–235.

16. See Oklahoma, *Transcript of Proceedings of the Senate of the Twelfth Legislature, State of Oklahoma*, by Fletcher Riley (Oklahoma City, OK: Leader Press, 1929).

Appendix B

Constitutional Issues in N.H. Judicial Review Cases

In the official reports of decisions by New Hampshire's court of last resort between the earliest reports published and those through 2016, the authors have found 293 decisions on challenges to the constitutionality of legislation.[1] Presented here is a brief consideration of some pertinent case aspects, including features distinguishing those in which legislation was found constitutional from those in which it was found unconstitutional.[2]

MOST FREQUENTLY RAISED ISSUES UNDER STATE CONSTITUTION

Valid Exercise of Legislative Power (46 cases)
Police Power (46)
Separation of Powers (35)
Due Process (28)
Equal Protection (27)
Retrospective Laws (25)
Valid Delegation of Legislative Power (17)
Right to Trial by Jury (15)
Contract Rights (10)
Access to Justice (10)
Eminent Domain (9)
Natural Rights (7)
Freedom of Religion (5)
Elections and Elective Franchise (5)
Free Speech (4)
Excessive Punishment (4)

Ex Post Facto Laws (4)
Reciprocity–Fair Tax Share (4)
Unfunded Mandates (4)
Education Adequacy (3)
Access to Government (2)
All Other (9)[3]

MOST FREQUENT GROUNDS FOR FINDING LEGISLATION TO VIOLATE STATE CONSTITUTION

Separation of Powers (11 cases)
Equal Protection (11)
Valid Exercise of Legislative Power (10)
Due Process (9)
Retrospective Laws (5)
Right to Trial by Jury (5)
Access to Justice (4)
Valid Delegation of Legislative Power (4)
Police Power (3)
Contract Rights (2)
Natural Rights (2)
Elections and Elective Franchise (2)
Reciprocity—Fair Tax Share (2)
Education Adequacy (2)
All Other (5)[4]

MOST FREQUENTLY RAISED ISSUES UNDER U.S. CONSTITUTION

14th Amendment Equal Protection (16 cases)
14th Amendment Due Process (11)
  Both Due Process and Equal Protection (4)[5]
Interstate Commerce (9)
Privileges and Immunities (5)
Ex Post Facto Laws (3)
Impairment of Contracts (3)
Cruel and Unusual Punishment (2)
Free Speech (2)
All Other (2)[6]

MOST FREQUENT GROUNDS FOR FINDING LEGISLATION TO VIOLATE U.S. CONSTITUTION

14th Amendment Equal Protection (7 cases)
Interstate Commerce (6)
Privileges and Immunities (4)
14th Am Due Process (2)
Free Speech (2)
All Other (0)[7]

NOTES

1. The detailed case-by-case data on which this appendix is based are on file with the authors.

2. In a number of cases, more than one constitutional claim was raised, and some involved claims under both state and federal constitutions.

3. Each of the following issues came up once in a judicial review case: judicial disqualification; legislative compensation; "money bill" origin; protection of competition; right to bear arms; senate elections; standing to request an advisory opinion; state government framework; and valid exercise of governor's power.

4. A violation of the state constitution was found once each for the following issues: eminent domain; free speech; legislative compensation; unfunded mandates; and standing to request an advisory opinion. For the following issues, a constitutional violation was never found: freedom of religion; excessive punishment; ex post facto laws; framework of state government; protection of competition; senate elections; valid exercise of governor's power; judicial disqualification; "money bill" origin; access to government; and right to bear arms.

5. In addition to cases involving alleged violations of either the due process clause or the equal protection clause of the 14th Amendment, there were four separate cases with claimed violations of both clauses.

6. Other grounds for violations of the U.S. Constitution were reapportionment (1 case) and involuntary servitude (1 case).

7. No violations were found on any of the following U.S. Constitutional grounds: reapportionment; involuntary servitude; 14th Amendment due process and equal protection together; cruel and unusual punishment; ex post facto laws, or impairment of contracts.

Appendix C

New Hampshire Advisory Opinion Requests and Outcomes

The very first request for an advisory opinion in New Hampshire appears to have been made in 1816. The Governor and Council asked whether the Legislature had authority under the state constitution to amend the charter granted by the British King to the Trustees of Dartmouth College, by increasing the number of trustees, and whether the Governor and Council would have authority under June 1816 legislation to fill any vacancies in the Boards of Trustees of Dartmouth College. The justices responded that the constitutional provision authorizing requests for advisory opinions[1] does not permit such requests on a question affecting private rights alone, on which interested persons are entitled to be heard. They replied further that the Governor and Council had no authority to fill vacancies occurring after the date of the first scheduled meeting of the trustees.[2]

From the very beginning, the justices were thus defining the scope of their obligation under the constitutional provision allowing requests for advisory opinions. One aspect of this has to do with decisions about who is authorized to make such requests. In 1877, when the mayor and aldermen of the City of Manchester requested advice on who has the power to appoint and remove members of the fire department of Manchester, they declined to respond, stating that the state constitution does not authorize local government officials to ask for advisory opinions.[3]

Much more recently, the justices took a further step to define who is authorized to seek an advisory opinion. In a 2014 decision on appeal in a question involving the constitutionality of a statute that would allow taxpayers to establish standing to sue in a civil matter without showing that their personal rights had been impaired of prejudiced, the court held the statute unconstitutional. They reasoned that the statute had the effect of requiring the justices to render advisory opinions to private citizens, and they held that this would violate the constitutional provision on advisory opinions.[4]

Authority to request advisory opinions is thus limited to the Governor and Council, the Senate, and the House of Representatives. Requests from each of those bodies have yielded the following responses from the justices.

GOVERNOR AND COUNCIL (84 REQUESTS)

Proposed action found constitutional: 37 cases
Proposed action found only partially constitutional: 0 cases
Proposed action found not constitutional: 31 cases
Justices declined to render opinion: 6 cases
Statutory interpretation only: 10 cases

SENATE (85 REQUESTS)

Proposed action found constitutional: 37 cases
Proposed action found only partially constitutional: 5 cases
Proposed action found not constitutional: 29 cases
Justices declined to render opinion: 10 cases
Statutory interpretation only: 4 cases

HOUSE OF REPRESENTATIVES (152 REQUESTS)

Proposed action found constitutional: 79 cases
Proposed action found only partially constitutional: 14 cases
Proposed action found not constitutional: 48 cases
Justices declined to render opinion: 11 cases
Statutory interpretation only: 0 cases

NOTES

1. N.H. Const. Pt. 2, Art. 74.
2. Opinion of the Justices (1816), not officially published until 67 years later, at 62 N.H. 704 (1883).
3. Opinion of the Justices, 62 N.H. 706 (1877).
4. Duncan v. State, 166 N.H. 630, 102 A.3d 913 (2014).

Appendix D

Evidence of Other Crimes, Including Prior Sexual Assault

To promote fairness and meet due process requirements, English and American case law has traditionally called for great care to be exercised by a trial court in deciding whether a judge should allow jury members to consider evidence that a criminal defendant may previously have been charged with the commission of other crimes that might suggest a propensity for criminal behavior. Maintaining that a defendant should be tried only for the crime for which he or she is now being charged, courts have held that evidence tending to show character or propensity is generally inadmissible. As stated in the early twentieth-century *Molineux* case, such evidence may be considered admissible for more limited purposes other than proving the guilt of the defendant, but only after the court has balanced the potential relevance and probative value of such evidence against the risk that it will unduly prejudice jurors against a defendant.[1]

Presented below in Table D.1 is a comparison of the federal rules of evidence on the admissibility of other crimes, including evidence of prior sexual assaults, with comparable state court evidence rules. New Hampshire and most other states have adopted rules of evidence modeled on the federal rules. The evidence code in California is extensive but organized differently from the federal rules. Yet the table also shows that 36 states (including New Hampshire) have chosen not to adopt additional evidence rules that are similar or analogous to Fed. R. Evid. 413 and 414. In other words, New Hampshire and most other states have decided not to carve out a sex crimes/child molestation exception to the general evidentiary rule.

Table D.1 Rules on Admissibility of Prior Sexual Assault Evidence, as Exception to General Prohibition against Character or Propensity Evidence

Relation of State & Federal Propensity Evidence Rules[a]	*Court Rules or Case Law in Specific States*
The state *has* adopted rule(s) like the federal rules on admissibility of prior sexual assault evidence[b] or prior child molestation evidence[c]	AK, AZ, CA, FL, GA, IL, KS, LA, NE, WI
The state allows propensity evidence *only* in child molestation cases	MO[d], UT
The state has *not* adopted rule(s) like the federal rules on either prior sexual assault evidence or prior child molestation evidence	AL, AR, CO, CT, DE, HI, ID, IN, IA, KY, ME, MD, MA, MI, MN, MS, MT, NV, *NH*, NJ, NM, NY, NC, ND, OH, OK, OR, PA, RI, SC, SD, TN, TX, VT, VA, WA, WV, WY

Source: federal and state rules of evidence, as inspected in September 2014, with March 2016 update on Missouri (see note "d" below).

[a] On the admissibility of character or propensity evidence, the courts in all states follow a common-law rule or court rule identical or similar to Rule 404(b) of the Federal Rules of Evidence (F.R. Evid.), which provides the following:

> Evidence of a crime, wrong, or other act is not admissible to prove a person's character in order to show that on a particular occasion the person acted in accordance with the character. This evidence may be admissible for another purpose, such as proving motive, opportunity, intent, preparation, plan, knowledge, identity, absence of mistake, or lack of accident. On request by a defendant in a criminal case, the prosecutor must provide reasonable notice of the general nature of any such evidence that the prosecutor intends to offer at trial; and do so before trial — or during trial if the court, for good cause, excuses lack of pretrial notice.

[b] In the prosecution of an adult criminal defendant for sexual assault, F.R. Evid. 413(a) creates an exception to F.R. Evid. 404(b), providing as follows:

> In a criminal case in which a defendant is accused of a sexual assault, the court may admit evidence that the defendant committed any other sexual assault. The evidence may be considered on any matter to which it is relevant.

[c] In the prosecution of an adult criminal defendant for child molestation, F. R. Evid. 414(a) creates another exception to F. R. Evid. 404(b), providing that:

> In a criminal case in which a defendant is accused of a sexual assault, the court may admit evidence that the defendant committed any other sexual assault. The evidence may be considered on any matter to which it is relevant.

[d] In State v. Ellison, 239 S.W.3d 603 (Mo. 2007), on appeal from a conviction for child molestation, the Missouri Supreme Court invalidated a statute providing for the admissibility of prior sexual abuse evidence to show a defendant's propensity to commit the acts of which he or she was accused, holding that it violated state constitutional provisions that a criminal defendant has "the right to be tried only on the offense charged." In the wake of that decision, the state legislature proposed a constitutional amendment designed to allow relevant propensity evidence to be admissible in court in prosecutions of sexual crimes against child victims. In November 2014, voters overwhelmingly approved that measure. See Missouri Secretary of State, "2014 Ballot Measures," http://www.sos.mo.gov/elections/2014ballot/.

NOTE

1. People v. Molineux, 168 N.Y. 264, 62 L.R.A. 193 (1901), is considered a classic American statement of this evidentiary rule.

Appendix E

Involvement of State Legislatures in Court Rulemaking

Historically, it was common in American states for there to be a shared legislative-judicial power over court practice and procedure. By the early twentieth century, however, such prominent legal scholars as Roscoe Pound[1] and John Henry Wigmore[2] argued against any legislative involvement whatsoever in matters of court practice and procedure. The New Hampshire constitutional amendment expressly granting rulemaking power to the judiciary made it one of many states taking such a step in the decades after the end of World War II. In place of the almost universal historical "concurrent jurisdiction" between legislative and judicial branches over court practice and procedure, states have now adopted several different solutions to the problem of how to allocate responsibility for court rules between legislatures and courts. The range of different approaches is suggested in Table E.1.

The greatest variance among the states is in the extent to which the oversight of practice and procedure by judicial leaders is subject to any degree of popular involvement or control through elected legislators. Although a majority of state constitutions now specifically address questions of legislative and judicial power over court practice and procedure, there are still a number of states where the allocation of power is a matter of either legislation or the expression of inherent judicial power, or a mix of both. While judicial authority over court rules is still subject to legislative power in a majority of states, Table E.1 shows that a significant number of states appear to give primacy to the judicial branch.

Table E.1. Court Rulemaking Power of State Legislatures in New Hampshire and Other States

	States Shown by Source of Authority to Make Court Rules [a]					
Legislative Power Relative to Judicial Power in Terms of Court Rulemaking Authority	*Constitution*	*Inherent Court Power*	*Constitution/Statutes*	*Constitution/Inherent/Statutes*	*Inherent Power/ Statute*	*Statute*
Exclusive Judicial Authority	AZ, DE, HI, KY, MI, *NH* [c], NJ [e], ND, WV	MN, NM			AR, ID, IN, MS, OK, WA, WY	
Broad Judicial Authority, with Limited Exceptions	CO [f], GA [g], PA [h]					
Judicial Power Shared with Legislative Power	*NH* [d]	CT [i]		*NH* [b]	KS [j]	WI [k]
Change or repeal requires super majority vote in legislature	AK, FL, SC, UT					
Full legislative power to approve, change, or repeal	AL, MO, MT, OH, SD, VT		MD		TN	IA
Rules must be consistent with or not in conflict with statutes	CA [l], LA, NE, TX, VA			IL	MA, NV	OR

Court rulemaking authority by legislative grant or subject to reserved legislative powers	NC [m]	NY [n]	ME, RI

Source: With notes added for this table, and with additional information added about New Hampshire and Connecticut, basic information here is from Connecticut General Assembly, Office of Legal Research, "Court Rules in Other States – Legislative Approval" (2008), https://www.cga.ct.gov/2008/rpt/2008-R-0430.htm.

[a] Unless otherwise indicated, initial power to adopt court rules in each state is expressly vested in the judiciary. For all states except NH, legislative power relative to judicial power in terms of court rulemaking authority is shown as it is currently understood by the authors. NH is highlighted here to show historical changes in legislative and judicial authority over court rulemaking.

[b] In NH, the relation between courts and legislature in terms of court practice and procedure from 1784 to 1966 was well within a common state pattern of shared legislative-judicial power over court practice and procedure. See Robert Lynn, "Judicial Rule-Making and the Separation of Powers in New Hampshire: The Need for Constitutional Reform," *New Hampshire Bar Journal*, Vol. 44, No. 1 (2001), 44-69.

[c] In *Opinion of the Justices (Prior Sexual Assault Evidence)*, 141 N.H. 562, 688 A.2d 1006 (1997) [*PSAE*], the NH Supreme Court held that a proposed statute on admissibility of prior sexual assaults by an adult criminal defendant would be an unconstitutional violation of separation of powers, because the legislation would intrude on exclusive judicial authority to regulate evidence in such matters.

[d] In *Petition of Southern New Hampshire Medical* Center, 164 N.H. 319, 55 A.3d 988 (2012), the NH Supreme Court ruled that language used in the *PSAE* opinion was unnecessarily broad, and that the judiciary and legislature share concurrent authority over court rulemaking, except that the legislature may not enact procedural statutes that the Supreme Court would find unconstitutional.[e] In NJ, the state supreme court has interpreted the constitutional provision on court rulemaking to confer exclusive authority on the judicial branch. *Winberry v. Salisbury*, 5 N.J. 240, 74 A. 2d 406 (1950). *Winberry* was cited by the NH Supreme Court in its *PSAE* advisory opinion (see note c above).

[f] In CO, the legislature can adopt rules only for misdemeanor trials in limited-jurisdiction courts.

[g] In GA, legislative power is limited to creation of certain kinds of pilot programs.

[h] In PA, the constitution has been interpreted to allow legislation only in the narrow area of protecting child witnesses.

[i] On court rulemaking in CT, see Thomas Bishop, "Evidence Rulemaking: Balancing the Separation of Powers," *Connecticut Law Review*, Vol. 43, No. 1 (2010), 265-302.

[j] In KS, separation of powers has been interpreted to allow procedural statutes unless they conflict with a court rule.

[k] WI statutes provide that both legislature and courts can amend rules.

[l] In CA, the Judicial Council is the body with power to adopt court rules.

[m] In NC, the judiciary has exclusive authority to adopt appellate rules; as for trial courts, the legislature can delegate its authority or change a rule.

[n] In NY, judicial branch court rulemaking authority is subject to the legislature's reserved powers under the state constitution.

NOTES

1. Roscoe Pound, "The Rule-Making Power of the Courts," *ABAJ* 12, no. 9 (1926): 599–603.

2. John Wigmore, "All Legislative Rules for Judiciary Procedure Are Void Constitutionally," *Ill. L. Rev.* 23 (1928): 276.

Bibliography

Advisory Commission on Intergovernmental Relations. *Mandates: Cases in State-Local Relations*. Washington, DC: The Commission, Report M-173, 1990.

"AG Fires Rebuttal at Justices," *Portsmouth [NH] Herald*, April 5, 2000.

Alfini, James, Shailey Gupta-Brietzke, and James McMartin. "Dealing with Judicial Misconduct in the States: Judicial Independence, Accountability and Reform." *S. Tex. L. Rev.* 48 (2007): 889–1135.

Amoskeag Mfg. v. Head, 56 NH 386 (1876).

American Bar Association. Center for Professional Responsibility. "Client Protection Funds: Lawyers Put Their Money Where Their Mouths Are." Available at http://www.americanbar.org/groups/professional_responsibility/resources/client_protection/tplart02.html.

Anderson, Leon. *To This Day: The 300 Years of the New Hampshire Legislature.* Canaan, NH: Phoenix Publishing, 1981.

Andrews, John. "So It's A Mandate! Whattya Goin' to Do About It?" *New Hampshire Town and City,* November/December 2005. Available at https://www.nhmunicipal.org/TownAndCity/Article8.

Appeal of Naswa Motor Inn, 144 NH 89, 738 A.2d 349 (1999).

Arkansas. General Assembly. *Journal of the House of Representatives of the Twentieth General Assembly of Arkansas, 1874.* Little Rock, AR: The Assembly, 1874.

———. James Pomeroy. *Trial of Hon. John McClure, Chief Justice of the Supreme Court of the State of Arkansas, Before the Senate of the State of Arkansas on Impeachment by the House of Representatives*. Little Rock, AR: Price & McClure, 1872.

Ashman, Charles. *The Finest Judges Money Can Buy*. Los Angeles: Nash Publishing, 1973.

Associated Press, "2 Justices Broke Law, New Hampshire Attorney General Says," *New York Times*, April 1, 2000. Available at http://www.nytimes.com/2000/04/01/us/2-justices-broke-law-new-hampshire-attorney-general-says.html.

Backofen, Walter. "Claremont's Achilles' Heel: The Unrecognized Mandatory School-Tax Law of 1789." *NH Bar J.* 43, no. 1 (2002): 26–29.

Baker v. Carr, 369 U.S. 186 (1962).

Ballotpedia. "Amending State Constitutions." Available at https://ballotpedia.org/Amending_state_constitutions.

Ballotpedia, "List of New Hampshire ballot measures." Available at https://ballotpedia.org/wiki/index.php?title=List_of_New_Hampshire_ballot_measures&oldid=5330344.

Batchelder, William. "The Independence of the Judiciary in New Hampshire Revisited." *NH Bar J.* 39, no. 2 (1998): 62–71.

———. "The Judicial Journey of David A. Brock." *NH Bar J.* 47, no. 4 (2007): 5–9.

Batt, John. "Special Essay: American Legal Populism: A Jurisprudential and Historical Narrative, Including Reflections on Critical Legal Studies." *N. Ky. L. Rev.* 22, no. 3 (1995): 651–752.

Bauman, Richard, and Tsvi Kahana. *The Least Examined Branch: The Role of the Legislature in the Constitutional State.* New York: Cambridge University Press, 2006.

Beaumont, Elizabeth. *The Civic Constitution: Civic Visions and Struggles in the Path Toward Constitutional Democracy.* New York: Oxford University Press, 2014.

Bell, Charles. *The Bench and Bar of New Hampshire.* Boston: Houghton Mifflin, 1894.

Berger, Raoul. *Impeachment: The Constitutional Problems.* Cambridge, MA: Harvard University Press, 1973.

Berkson, Larry, Rachel Caulfield and Malia Reddick. *Judicial Selection in the United States: A Special Report.* Chicago, IL: American Judicature Society, 2010.

Berkson, Larry, Steven Hays and Susan Carbon. *Managing the State Courts: Text and Readings.* St. Paul, MN: West Publishing, 1977.

Bishop, Thomas. "Evidence Rulemaking: Balancing the Separation of Powers." *Conn. L. Rev.* 43, no. 1 (2010): 265–302.

Black, Charles. *Impeachment: A Handbook.* New Haven, Ct.: Yale University Press, 1974, 1998.

Bliss's Petition, 63 NH 135 (1884).

Boston & Maine Railroad v. Concord, 69 NH 91, 44 A. 808 (1896).

Bowen, Abel, and Jerome Smith. *The Boston News-letter, and City Record, Volume 1.* Boston, MA: Abel Bowen, 1826.

Bowman, Ann, and Richard Kearney. *The Resurgence of the States.* Englewood Cliffs, NJ: Prentice-Hall, 1986.

Boyte, Harry. *Civic Agency and the Cult of the Expert.* Dayton, OH: Kettering Foundation, 2009.

———. "Civic Populism." *Perspectives on Politics* 1, no. 4 (2003): 737–42.

———. *Everyday Politics: Reconnecting Citizens and Public Life.* Philadelphia: University of Pennsylvania Press, 2004.

Bradley, Charles. *The Methods of Changing the Constitutions of the States, Especially That of Rhode Island.* Boston: Alfred Mudge & Son, 1885.

Brettschneider, Corey. "Popular Constitutionalism and the Argument for Judicial Review." *Pol. Theory* 34, no. 4 (2006): 516–21.

Brown, Mary. *The Impeachment Trial of the New Hampshire Supreme Court Chief Justice.* Pittsfield, NH: Lynxfield Publishing, 2001.

Bryant's Case, 24 NH 149 (1851).
Bussiere v. Roberge, 142 NH 905, 714 A.2d 894, 1998).
Canovan, Margaret. *Populism*. New York: Harcourt Brace Jovanovich, 1981.
———. "Trust the People! Populism and the Two Faces of Democracy." *Political Studies* 47, no. 1 (1999): 2–16.
Carrington, Paul. "Hail! Langdell!" *Law & Social Inquiry* 20, no. 3 (1995): 691–760.
———. "Judicial Independence and Democratic Accountability in Highest State Courts." *Law & Contemp. Probs.* 61, no. 3 (1998): 79–126.
Charter of Manchester, 47 NH 277 (1867)
Chiacu, Donna. "Ex-Judge's Problems Mystify Newport Neighbors, Associates." *Concord [NH] Monitor*, October 30, 1989.
Citizens Conference on State Legislatures. *The Sometimes Governments: A Critical Study of the 50 American State Legislatures*. Kansas City, MO: The Conference, third printing, 1973.
Claremont School District v. Governor, 138 NH 183, 635 A. 2d 1375 (1993).
Claremont School District v. Governor, 142 NH 462, 703 A. 2d 1353 (1997).
Claremont School District v. Governor, 143 NH 154, 725 A. 2d 648 (1998).
Claremont School District v. Governor, 144 NH 210, 744 A.2d 1107 (1999).
Clark, Mary. *Parliamentary Privilege in the American Colonies*. New Haven, CT: Yale University Press, 1943.
Coffey's Case, 157 NH 156, 949 A. 2d 102 (2008).
Cohen, Andrew. "In New Hampshire, a GOP-Led Assault on the State Judiciary." *The Altantic* (October 13, 2011).
Concord Railway v. Greeley, 17 NH 47 (1845).
Connecticut General Assembly. Office of Legal Research. "Constitutional and Statutory Impeachment Provisions in 50 States." OLR Research Report 2004-R-0146 (2004). Available at https://www.cga.ct.gov/2004/rpt/2004-R-0146.htm.
Connolly, Bernadette. "The Judges' Trump Card." *Manchester [NH] Union Leader*, January 9, 2001, A8.
Conrad, Clay. *Jury Nullification: The Evolution of a Doctrine*. Washington, DC: Cato Institute, 2013.
Cooper v. Aaron, 358 U.S. 1 (1958).
Copp v. Henniker, 55 NH 179 (1875).
Coppes-Gathy, Nicole. "A Summary of the Public Protection Fund." *NH Bar J.* 20, no. 3 (1999), 20–25.
Corning, Charles. "The Highest Courts of Law in New Hampshire—Colonial, Provincial, and State," in Horace Fuller (ed.), *Green Bag* 2 (1890): 469–89.
Council of State Governments. *The Book of the States, Volume 42*. Lexington, KY: Council of State Governments, 2010.
Creel, Frank. "Court in Peril: The Legislative-Judicial Struggle." *Chronicles of Oklahoma*, 52 (1974): 220–36.
Curry v. Spencer, 61 NH 624 (1882).
Dacey, Norman. *How to Avoid Probate—Updated!* New York: Crown, 1980.
Dartmouth College v. Woodward, 1 NH 111 (1817), rev'd on other grounds, 17 U.S. 518 (1819).

DeBlack, Thomas. *With Fire and Sword: Arkansas, 1861–1874*. Fayetteville, AR: University of Arkansas Press, 2003.

DeFelice, Jonathan, and Wilfred Sanders. *Task Force for the Renewal of Judicial Conduct Procedures, Report to Supreme Court of New Hampshire*. Concord, NH: Supreme Court, 2001.

DeGrandpre, Charles. "Lex Loci: A Survey of New Hampshire Supreme Court Decisions." *NH Bar J.* 35, no. 1 (1994): 69.

———. "Lex Loci: A Survey of New Hampshire Supreme Court Decisions." *NH Bar J.* 45, no. 1 (2004): 91.

Demary, Michelle. "Legislative-Judicial Relations on Contested Issues: Taxes and Same-Sex Marriage." *Judicature* 89, no. 4 (2006): 202–211.

Deming v. Foster, 42 NH 165 (1860).

DeMitchell, Todd. "School Finance Reform: The Carousel Reform." *School Business Affairs* 65, no. 1 (1999): 42–47.

DeMitchell, Todd, and Barbara Krysiak. "School Finance Reform in the 'Live Free or Die' State: Personal, Legal, and Policy Responses to Claremont School District v. Governor." *IJER* 8, no. 1 (1999): 89–98.

DeMitchell, Todd, Joseph Onosko, and Mark Paige. "Amending the NH Constitution (CACR12): Education Will No Longer Be Fundamental to the Citizens of New Hampshire." Durham, NH: UNH Dept. of Educ. Policy Brief #12–02, March 2012. Available at www.unh.edu/education

Dinan, John. *The American State Constitutional Tradition.* Lawrence, KS: University Press of Kansas, 2006.

———. "Court-Constraining Amendments and the State Constitutional Tradition." *Rutgers L. J.* 38 (2006): 983.

———. "Independence and Accountability in State Judicial Selection." *Tex. L. Rev.* 91, no. 3 (2013): 633–649.

———. *Keeping the People's Liberties: Legislators, Citizens, and Judges as Guardians of Rights*. Lawrence, KS: University Press of Kansas, 1998.

Dishman, Robert. *A New Constitution for New Hampshire?* Durham, NH: University of New Hampshire, 1956.

DiStaso, John. "Separation-of-powers: NH Supreme Court offers compromise on rule-making constitutional amendment plan." *NH Union Leader,* May 3, 2012, http://www.unionleader.com/article/20120503/NEWS06/120509947&template=mobileart.

Dodd, Walter. *The Revision and Amendment of State Constitutions*. Baltimore, MD: Johns Hopkins Press, 1910.

Douglas, Charles, and Jay Surdukowski. "The New Hampshire Supreme Court: A History of Change." *NH Bar J.* 51, no. 2 (2010): 10–18.

Duncan v. State, 166 NH 630, 102 A.3d 913 (2014).

Durkee v. Moses, 67 NH 115 (1891).

East Kingston v. Towle, 48 NH 57(1868).

Education Law Center. Available at http://www.edlawcenter.org/.

Elder, Sonja. "Enforcing Public Educational Rights via a Private Right of Action." *Duke FL & Soc. Change* 1, no. 1 (2009): 137–70.

Ellingwood, Albert. *Departmental Cooperation in State Government.* New York: Macmillan, 1918.

Ellis, Richard. *The Jeffersonian Crisis: Courts and Politics in the Young Republic.* New York: W. W. Norton, 1974.

Epp, Charles. *The Rights Revolution: Lawyers, Activists, and Supreme Courts in Comparative Perspective.* Chicago: University of Chicago Press, 1998.

Ewing, Cortez. "Arkansas Reconstruction Impeachments." *Ark. Historical Q.* 13, no. 2 (1954): 137–53.

Fautsko, Timothy, Steven Berson, and Steve Swensen. *Status of Court Security in State Courts: A National Perspective.* Williamsburg, VA: National Center for State Courts, 2013.

Feingold, Jeff. "A Legal Black Eye: Cases like the one involving Judge Fairbanks have taken a sizable chunk out of the public's regard for the legal profession." *The Spectator* (September 1999), 11.

Ferguson, Margaret, ed. *The Executive Branch of State Government: People, Process, and Politics.* Santa Barbara, CA: ABC-CLIO, 2006.

Ferry, Luc. *Rights: The New Quarrel Between the Ancients and the Moderns.* Chicago: University of Chicago Press, 1990.

Finn, John. *Peopling the Constitution.* Lawrence, KS: University Press of Kansas, 2014.

Flamm, Richard. *Judicial Disqualification: Recusal and Disqualification of Judges.* 2nd ed. Berkeley, CA: Banks & Jordan, 2007, with updates through 2015.

Flango, Victor. "Court Unification and Quality of State Courts." *Just. Sys. J.* 16, no. 3 (1994), 33–55.

Ford, Royal. "Scandalous Judge's Legacy Won't Die: Rural NH town reels from tale of disorder in the court." *Boston Globe,* September 18, 1997, B1. Available at http://www.scribd.com/doc/229520210/John-C-Fairbanks-Scandalous-Judge-s-Legacy-Won-t-Die-Rural-n-h#scribd.

Friedberg, Aaron. "The Merger of Law and Equity." *St. John's L. Rev.* 12, no. 2 (1938)

Friedman, Lawrence. *The New Hampshire State Constitution.* New York: Oxford University Press, 2015.

———. "On the Justifications for Constitutional Amendment Concurrent Resolution 5," *NH Bar J.* 43, no. 3 (2002): 46–49.

Friedman, Lawrence M. *A History of American Law.* New York: Simon & Schuster, 1973.

Garabedian v. William Company, 106 NH 156, 207 A. 2d 425 (1965).

Garrell-Michaud, Virginia. *An Evaluation of the Supreme Court of New Hampshire Committee on Judicial Conduct and Professional Conduct Committee.* Concord, NH: Governor's Commission on Crime and Delinquency, Grant No. 78-I-A2001 E07, 1979.

Garrison, Marsha. "How Do Judges Decide Divorce Cases—an Empirical Analysis of Discretionary Decision Making." *N.C. L. Rev.* 74, no. 2 (1996): 401–552.

Gerber, Scott. *A Distinct Judicial Power: The Origins of an Independent Judiciary 1606–1787.* New York: Oxford University Press, 2011.

Gerber v. King, 107 NH 495, 225 A.2d 620 (1967).

Gerhardt, Michael. *The Federal Impeachment Process: A Constitutional and Historical Analysis*. Chicago, IL: University of Chicago Press, 2000.

Geyh, Charles. *Courting Peril: The Political Transformation of the American Judiciary*. New York: Oxford U. Press, 2016.

———, James Alfini, Steven Lubet and Jeffrey Shaman. *Judicial Conduct and Ethics*. 5th ed. Newark, NJ: Matthew Bender and Company, 2013.

Gray, Cynthia. "Controversy and Reform in New Hampshire." *Judicial Conduct Reporter* 23, no. 1 (2001), 1, 5–7.

———. "Judicial Conduct Commissions: How Judicial Conduct Commissions Work." *Just. Sys. J.* 28, no. 3 (2007): 405–18.

Goldberg, Cary. "In the Live-Free-or-Die State, An Unpalatable Tax Decision." *New York Times,* July 29, 1998. Available at http://www.nytimes.com/1998/06/29/us/statehouse-journal-in-the-live-free-or-die-state-an-unpalatable-tax-decision.html.

Grimes, Warren. "Hundred-Ton Gun Control: Preserving Impeachment as the Exclusive Removal Mechanism for Federal Judges." *UCLA L. Rev.* 38, no. 5 (1991): 1209.

Grossi, Simona. "The Courts and the People in a Democratic System: Against Federal Court Exceptionalism." *Notre Dame L. Rev. Online* 92 (2017): 106–111. Available at http://ndlawreview.org/wp-content/uploads/2017/04/Grossi_Final.pdf.

Guare v. State,—NH --, 117 A. 3d 731 (2015).

Hall, Douglas. *Plumbing the Numbers #2: Using Per Capita Income in A School Aid Formula: Concerns and Suggestions*. Concord, NH: New Hampshire Center for Public Policy Studies, 2001.

Hall, Kermit. "The Judiciary on Trial: State Constitutional Reform and the Rise of an Elected Judiciary, 1876–1860." *Historian* 45, no. 3 (1983): 337–354.

Hall, Kermit, and Kevin McGuire, eds. *Institutions of American Democracy: The Judicial Branch.* New York: Oxford University Press, 2005.

Hamilton, Alexander, James Madison, and John Jay. *The Federalist Papers.* New York: New American Library, 1961.

Hannaford-Agor, Paula. "Judicial Nullification? Judicial Compliance and Non-compliance with Jury Improvement Efforts." *N. Ill U. L Rev.* 28 (2008): 407–24.

Hardy, Leroy, Alan Heslop and Stuart Anderson. *Reapportionment Politics: The History of Redistricting in the 50 States*. Beverly Hills, CA, and London: Sage, 1981.

Hastings v. U.S., 802 F. Supp. 490 (US D.D.C, 1992).

Hersey, Thomas. *The Claremont Education Lawsuit: Bridging the Educational Divide*. Concord, NH: Wiss Institute for Public Policy and Claremont Lawsuit Coalition, 1998.

Hesse, Richard. "The Legislature, the Court, and the Constitution." *NH Bar J.* 41, no. 1 (2000): 38–45.

Higginson, Stephen. "A Short History of the Right to Petition Government for the Redress of Grievances." *Yale L. J.* 96, no. 1 (1986): 142–66.

Hirsch, Alan. *A Citizen's Guide to Impeachment*. Washington, DC: Essential Books, 1998.

Hoffer, Peter, and N. E. H. Hull. *Impeachment in America, 1635–1805*. New Haven, CT: Yale University Press, 1984.

Home Gas v. Strafford Fuels, 130 NH 74, 534 A. 2d 390 (1987).

Horton v. McLaughlin, 149 NH 141, 821 A. 2d 947 (2003).

Hubsch, Allen. "Note: The Emerging Right to Education Under State Constitutional Law." *Temple L. Rev.* 65 (1992): 1325.

Hudzik, John. *The Effects of State Financing: Summary Findings from the Four-State Study*. Williamsburg, VA: National Center for State Courts, 1990.

Hurn, Marcus. "State Constitutional Limits on New Hampshire's Taxing Power: Historical Development and Modern State." *Pierce L. Rev.* 7, no. 3 (2009): 252–325.

Ignatieff, Michael. *The Rights Revolution*. Toronto: House of Anansi, 2000.

Institute for the Advancement of the American Legal System. "Judicial Performance Evaluation." Available at http://iaals.du.edu/quality-judges/projects/judicial-performance-evaluation.

Ionescu, Ghita, and Ernest Gellner, eds. *Populism: Its Meaning and National Characteristics*. London: Weidenfield and Nicholson, 1969.

Isenbergh, Joseph. "Impeachment and Presidential Immunity from Judicial Process." *Yale Law & Policy Rev.* 18, no. 1 (1999): 53–109.

Itse, Daniel. *The People's Liberty: A Commentary on Constitution of the State of New Hampshire*. 4th ed. Concord, NH: House Republican Alliance, 2007.

Jameson, John. *The Constitutional Convention: Its History, Powers, and Modes of Proceeding*. New York: Scribner, 1867.

Jesseman v. State, NH Superior Court, Merrimack County, Docket No. 82-E-038 (1982).

Kaplan, Benjamin, and Warren Greene. "The Legislature's Relation to Judicial Rule-Making: An Appraisal of Winberry v. Salisbury." *Harv. L. Rev.* 65, no. 2 (1951): 234–52.

Kazin, Michael. *The Populist Persuasion: An American History*. New York: Basic Books, 1995.

Kiernan, Laura. "Bills Hang on Definition of What Is 'Adequate.'" *Boston Globe,* January 16, 1994. Available at https://www.highbeam.com/doc/1P2–8262426.html.

Kirschner, Otto. *Political Justice: The Use of Legal Procedure for Political Ends.* Princeton, NJ: Princeton University Press, 1961.

Kitch, Michael. "Legal Lion Arthur Nighswander Dies at 100." *NH Bar News,* January 16, 2009. Available at https://www.nhbar.org/publications/display-news-issue.asp?id=4906.

Knightly, Dot. "New Hampshire's Corrupt Family Courts: Be amazed at the abuses NH Families suffer in NH Family Courts!" *Merrimack, NH Patch,* June 13, 2014. Available at https://patch.com/new-hampshire/merrimack/be-amazed-at-the-abuses-nh-families-suffer-in-nh-family-courts.

Kramer, Larry. *The People Themselves: Popular Constitutionalism and Judicial Review*. New York: Oxford University Press, 2004.

Krauss, Stanton. "An Inquiry into the Right of Criminal Juries to Determine the Law in Colonial America." *J. Crim. Law Criminol.* 89, no. 1 (1998): 111–214.

Kurland, Philip, and Ralph Lerner, eds. *The Founders' Constitution.* Chicago: University of Chicago, 1987.

Kyvig, David. *The Age of Impeachment: American Constitutional Culture since 1960.* Lawrence, KS: University Press of Kansas, 2008.

Laconia Board of Education v City of Laconia, 111 NH 389, 285 A.2d 793 (1971).

Lambert, Richard. "The 'Ten Pound Act' Cases and the Origins of Judicial Review in New Hampshire." *NH Bar J.* 43, no. 1 (2002): 37–54.

Lawrie, Timothy. "Interpretation and Authority: Separation of Powers and the Judiciary's Battle for Independence in New Hampshire, 1786–1818." *Am. J. Legal Hist.* 39, no. 3 (1995): 310–336.

Leidinger, Jeffrey. "The Move Toward State Financing: A New Hampshire Approach." *Just. Syst. J.* 7, no. 1 (1982): 103–123.

Lessner, Richard. "Bait and Switch—Judicial Magic: Now You See It, Now You Don't." *Manchester [NH] Union Leader*, August 7, 1998, C1.

Lever, Jeremy. "Why Procedure Is More Important than Substantive Law." *Int'l Comp. L. Q.* 48, no. 2 (1999): 285–301.

Libertarian Party. "2016 Platform" (May 2016). Available at https://www.lp.org/platform/.

Little, Thomas, and David Ogle. *The Legislative Branch of State Government: People, Process, and Politics*. Santa Barbara, CA: ABC-CLIO, 2006.

Londonderry School District v. State, 154 NH 153, 907 A.2d 988 (2006).

Londonderry School District v. State, 157 NH 734, 958 A. 2d 930 (2008).

Looney, J. W. *Distinguishing the Righteous from the Roguish: The Arkansas Supreme Court, 1836–1874*. Fayetteville, AR: University of Arkansas Press, 2016.

Love, Norma. "Judge Coffey Resigns." *Seacoast [NH] Online,* April 21, 2008. Available at http://www.seacoastonline.com/article/20080421/NEWS/80421015.

Lynch, Tim. "Jury Nullification Law Signed by New Hampshire Governor." *PoliceMisconduct.net,* June 27, 2012. Available at https://www.policemisconduct.net/jury-nullification-law-signed-new-hampshire-governor/?+Policemisconductnet+%28PoliceMisconduct.net%29.

Lynn, Robert. "Judicial Rule-Making and the Separation of Powers in New Hampshire: The Need for Constitutional Reform." *NH Bar J.* 42, no. 1 (2001): 44–69.

MacIntosh, John. "The New Hampshire General Court: A Legislative Primer." *NH Bar J.* 42, no. 2 (2001): 19–22.

Maddex, Robert. *State Constitutions of the United States*. 2nd ed. Washington, DC: CQ Press, 2006.

Marbury v. Madison, 5 U.S. 137 (1803).

Mark, Gregory. "The Vestigial Constitution: The History and Significance of the Right to Petition." *Fordham L. Rev.* 66, no. 6 (1998), 2153–2231.

Marshall, Susan. *The New Hampshire State Constitution*. New York: Oxford University Press, 2011.

Matton, Danielle. "An Examination of Federal Rules of Evidence 413, 414, and 415 and the Adoption of These Rules by the States." *NH Bar J.* 41, no. 3 (2000): 28–35.

McDuffy v. Secretary of Executive Office of Education, 415 Mass. 545, 615 N.E.2d 516 (1993).

McNamara, Richard. "The Separation of Powers Principle and the Role of the Courts in New Hampshire." *NH Bar J.* 42, no. 2 (2001): 66–87.

Merrill v. Sherburne, 1 NH 199 (1818).

Millimet, Joseph, Richard Upton and Stanley Brown. "A Modern Constitution for New Hampshire." *NH Bar. J.* 6, no. 3 (1964): 208–211.

Minnesota. House of Representatives. Research Department. "Separation of Powers: When Statutes and Court Rules Conflict" (2005). Available at http://www.house.leg.state.mn.us/hrd/pubs/ss/ssseppw.pdf.

Missouri. Secretary of State. "2014 Ballot Measures." Available at http://www.sos.mo.gov/elections/2014ballot/.

Moneyhon, Carl. *The Impact of the Civil War and Reconstruction on Arkansas: Persistence in the Midst of Ruin.* Fayetteville, AR: University of Arkansas Press, 2002.

Monopoli, Paula. *American Probate: Protecting the Public, Improving the Process.* University Press of New England, 2003.

Montgomery, Paul. "Small-town Scandal Still Casts a Long, Dark Shadow." *New Hampshire Magazine* (July 1999): 8–13. Available at http://www.gnbtaxpayers.com/FAIRBANKS,%20JOHN,%20JUDGE%20-%20SCANDAL%20&%20COVER-UP.pdf.

Mooney, Christopher. "Measuring U.S. State Legislative Professionalism: An Evaluation of Five Indices." *State & Local Govt. Rev.* 26, no. 2 (1994): 70–78.

Morison, Samuel. "Custom, Reason, and the Common Law—a Reply to Hasnas." *NYU J. L & Liberty* 2 (2007): 209–40.

Mosca, Edward. "New Hampshire's *Claremont* Case and the Separation of Powers." *Pierce L. Rev.* 4, no. 3 (2006): 409–34.

Murphy, Jane. "Eroding the Myth of Discretionary Justice in Family Law: The Child Support Experiment." *N.C. L. Rev.* 70, no. 1 (1991).

Mussman's Case, 111 NH 402, 286 A.2d 614 (1971).

Mussman, In re, 112 NH 99, 289 A. 2d 403 (1972).

Mussman, In re, 113 NH 54, 302 A. 2d 822 (1973).

Nassif Realty v. National Fire Insurance, 107 NH 267, 220 A.2d 748 (1966).

Natapoff, Alexander. "1993: The Year of Living Dangerously: State Courts Expand the Right to Education." *W. Educ. L. Rep.* 3, no. 4 (1994) 639–71.

Nebraska Legislature ex. rel. State v. Hergert, 271 Neb. 976, 720 N.W.2d 372 (2006).

Nelson, Caleb. "A Re-Evaluation of Scholarly Explanations for the Rise of the Elective Judiciary in Antebellum America." *Am. J. Legal Hist.* 37, no. 2 (1993): 190–224.

Neumann, Richard. "The Revival of Impeachment as a Partisan Political Weapon." *Hastings Const. L. Q.* 34, no. 2 (2007): 161–327.

New Hampshire Bar Association. "CACR 5: Reform Linchpin or Mischief-Maker? A Bar Journal Roundtable Discussion." *NH Bar J.* 43, no. 2 (2002): 38–47.

New Hampshire Court Rules Annotated, 2015–2016 Edition (eBook). Charlottesville, VA: LexisNexis/Matthew Bender, 2016.

New Hampshire. Commission to Study the State Constitution. *Report to the Fifteenth Constitutional Convention.* Concord, NH: Evans Printing, 1964.

———. *[Journal of the] Convention to Revise the Constitution, May 1964.* Concord, NH: Evans Printing 1964.

———. *Journal of the Convention to Revise the Constitution, May 1974.* Concord, NH: Evans Printing, 1975.

———. *Journal of the Convention to Revise the Constitution, May 1984.* Concord, NH: Evans Printing, 1984.

———. *Manual for the General Court*. Concord, NH: Secretary of State [annual publication, various dates].

———. Attorney General. Jeffrey Howard. Letter to Robert Lockwood, Chairman, House Judiciary & Family Law Committee, Re: HB1593, Investigation of John C. Fairbanks (April 25, 1996).

———. Philip McLaughlin. *Report of the attorney general: in re: W. Stephen Thayer, III and related matters*. Concord, NH: The Office, 2000.

———. General Court. Bill Status System. Available at http://www.gencourt.state.nh.us/bill_status.

———. *Impeachment of David A. Brock, Chief Justice of the New Hampshire Supreme Court: before the New Hampshire Senate sitting as a Court of Impeachment*. Concord, NH: The Senate, 2000.

———. *Investigation by the House Judiciary Committee pursuant to House Resolution 50: Depositions*. Concord, NH: The Committee, 2000.

———. *Journal of the House of Representatives of the State of New Hampshire, 1963*. Concord, NH: George Hough, 1963.

———. *Journal of the House of Representatives of the State of New Hampshire, 1983*. Concord, NH: George Hough, 1983.

———. *Journal of the House of Representatives of the State of New Hampshire, 1985*. Concord, NH: George Hough, 1985.

———. *Journal of the House of Representatives of the State of New Hampshire, 1986*. Concord, NH: George Hough, 1986.

———. *Journal of the House of Representatives of the State of New Hampshire, 1987*. Concord, NH: George Hough, 1987.

———. *Journal of the House of Representatives of the State of New Hampshire, 2000*. Concord, NH: The House, 2000.

——— House of Representatives, Commission to Study the State Constitution, *Research Report*, April 25, 1995 (partial reproduction of "Summary Report: A Modern Constitution for New Hampshire" as attachment).

———. House of Representatives. Paul Mirski. Letter to Henry Mock, Re: House Address #1 (March 16, 1999). Available at http://mainstream.net/nhpolitics/mirski.letter2.html.

———. Judiciary Committee. *Investigation pursuant to House Resolution 50: Final Report of special counsel Joseph D. Steinfield*. Concord, NH: The Committee, 2000.

———. *Investigation pursuant to House Resolution 50: Interim report of special counsel Joseph D. Steinfield*. Concord, NH: The Committee, 2000.

———. *Investigation pursuant to House Resolution 50: Supplemental memorandum of law by special counsel Joseph D. Steinfield*. Concord, NH: The Committee, 2000.

———. Governor. Jeanne Shaheen. "Advancing better classrooms: Governor proposes the ABC Plan to address Claremont decision" (1998). Available at http://www.library.unh.edu/digital/object/claremontpapers:0015.

———. Governor and Council. Minutes, June 2, 2004. Available at http://sos.NH.gov/2004–2005_Governor_and_Council_Minutes.aspx.

———. Justice Department. Christopher Domian. Memorandum of Interview, Eileen Fox. March 27, 2000.

———. Memorandum of Interview, Sherman Horton. March 10, 2000.

———. Memorandum of Interview, William Johnson. March 8, 2000.

———. Memorandum of Interview, Howard Zibel. March 3, 2000.

New Hampshire Revised Statutes Annual. Available online at http://www.gencourt.state.nh.us/rsa/html/indexes/default.html

Nixon v. United States, 506 U.S. 224 (1993).

North Carolina. *Trial of David M. Furches, Now Chief Justice and Formerly Associate Justice and Robert M. Douglas, Associate Justice of the Supreme Court of North Carolina, on Impeachment by the House of Representatives for High Crimes and Misdemeanors*. Raleigh, NC: Edwards & Broughton, and E.M. Uzzell, 1901.

Obituary. "Martin L. Gross (1938–2016)." *Concord Monitor,* January 31, 2016. Available at http://www.legacy.com/obituaries/concordmonitor/obituary.aspx?pid=177510052.

Odden, Allen R. and Lawrence Picus. *School Finance: A Policy Perspective*. 3rd ed. New York: McGraw-Hill, 2004.

———, eds. "Table of School Finance Legal Cases." Available at http://highered.mheducation.com/sites/0072823186/student_view0/table_of_school_finance_legal_html.

Oklahoma. *Journal of the Proceedings of the State Senate Sitting as a Court of Impeachment.* Oklahoma City, OK: State of Oklahoma, 1927.

———. *Transcript of Proceedings of the Senate of the Twelfth Legislature, State of Oklahoma, by Fletcher Riley*. Oklahoma City, OK: Leader Press, 1929.

Olabisi, Oyebola. *New Hampshire's Quest for a Constitutionally Adequate Education: NEPPC Discussion Paper 06–2*. Boston: New England Public Policy Center, Federal Reserve Bank of Boston, 2006.

Oleck, Howard. "Historical Nature of Equity Jurisprudence." *Fordham L. Rev.* 20, no. 1 (1951); 23–44.

Opinion of the Justices (1816), 62 NH 704 (first published, 1883).

Opinion of the Justices, 62 NH 706 (1877).

Opinion of the Justices, 143 NH 429, 725 A.2d 1082 (1999).

Opinion of the Justices, 145 NH 474, 765 A.2d 673 (2000).

Opinion of the Justices (Appointment of Chief Justice of the Supreme Court), 150 NH 355, 842 A.2d 816 (2003).

Opinion of the Justices (Domicile for Voting Purposes), 167 NH 539, 115 A.3d 257 (2015).

Opinion of the Justices (Prior Sexual Assault Evidence), 141 NH 562, 688 A.2d 1006 (1997).

Opinion of the Justices (Reformed Public-School Financing System), 145 NH 474, 765 A.2d 673 (2000).

Opinion of the Justices (Requiring Attorney General to Join Lawsuit), 162 NH 160, 27 A.3d 859 (2011).

Opinion of the Justices (School Financing), 142 NH 892, 712 A.2d. 1080 (1998).

Owens, Ryan, Alexander Tahk, Patrick Wohlfarth, and Amanda Bryan. "Nominating Commissions, Judicial Retention, and Forward-Looking Behavior on State

Supreme Courts: An Empirical Examination of Selection and Retention Methods." *St. Pol. & Pol'y Q.* 15, no. 2 (2015): 211–38.

Park, Roger. "Exporting the Hearsay Provisions of the Federal Rules of Evidence." *BU Int'l L.J.* 33, no. 2 (2015): 327–42.

Paynter, Sharon, and Richard Kearney. "Who Watches the Watchmen: Evaluating Judicial Performance in American States." *Admin. & Soc'y* 41, no. 8 (2010): 923–953.

Pennsylvania. William Hamilton. *Report of the Trial and Acquittal of Edward Shippen, Esq., Chief Justice, and Jasper Yeates and Thomas Smith, Esquires, Assistant Justices of the Supreme Court of Pennsylvania, on an Impeachment before the Senate of the Commonwealth, January 1805.* Lancaster, PA: Lancaster Journal, 1805.

People v. Molineux, 168 N.Y. 264, 61 N.E. 286 (1901).

Perry, Darryl. "NH House Removes the Grievance Committee." *Free Keene,* January 2, 2013. Available at http://freekeene.com/2013/01/02/nh-house-removes-the-grievance-committee/.

Petition of Burling, 139 NH 266, 651 A. 2d 940 (1994).

Petition of Governor and Executive Council, 151 NH 1, 846 A. 2d 1148 (2004).

Petition of Judicial Conduct Committee, 145 NH 108, 751 A. 2d 514 (2000).

Petition of Mone, 143 NH 128, 719 A.2d 626 (1998).

Petition of Southern N. H. Medical Center, 164 NH 319, 55 A.3d 988 (2012).

Pickering, Octavius, and William Gardiner. *Report of the Trial by Impeachment of James Prescott, Esquire, Judge of the Probate of Wills, &c. for the County of Middlesex, for Misconduct and Maladministration in Office: Before the Senate of Massachusetts in the Year 1821, with an Appendix, Containing an Account of Former Impeachments in the Same State.* Boston, MA: Daily Advertiser, 1821.

Pomeroy, John. *Pomeroy's Equity Jurisprudence and Equitable Remedies* (San Francisco, CA: Bancroft-Whitney, 1905), Vol. 1, §98.

Posner, Richard. *An Affair of State: The Investigation, Impeachment, and Trial of President Clinton.* Cambridge, MA: Harvard University Press, 1999.

Pound, Roscoe. "The Causes of Popular Dissatisfaction with the Administration of Justice." *Ann. Rep. ABA* 29 (1906): 395.

———. "The Rule-Making Power of the Courts." *ABAJ* 12, no. 9 (1926): 599–603.

Powell, William, ed. *Dictionary of North Carolina Biography.* Chapel Hill, NC: University of North Carolina Press, 2000.

———. *North Carolina through Four Centuries.* Chapel Hill, NC: University of North Carolina Press, 2010.

Powell v. McCormack, 395 U.S. 486 (1969).

Proposed Public Protection Fund Rule, 142 NH 588, 707 A. 2d 125 (1998).

Porteous v. Baron, U.S. D.D.C, Case No. 1:09-cv-2131 (2009).

Rao, Vivek. "So Ordered? Scrutinizing the Massachusetts Judiciary's Role in the State's Sweeping Education Reform Plan" (2011). Available at https://www.law.berkeley.edu/files/So_Ordered_Rao.pdf.

Redish Martin, and Dennis Murashko. "The Rules Enabling Act and the Procedural-Substantive Tension: A Lesson in Statutory Interpretation." *Minn. L. Rev.* 93, no.1 (2008): 26–95.

Reed, Douglas. *On Equal Terms: The Constitutional Politics of Educational Opportunity*. Princeton, NJ: Princeton University Press, 2001.

———. "Popular Constitutionalism: Toward a Theory of State Constitutional Meanings." *Rutgers L. J.* 30 (1999): 871–932.

Reid, John Phillip. "The Arena of the Giants: Rockingham County, New Hampshire." *ABAJ* 46, no. 2 (1960): 163–66, 214–16.

———. *Chief Justice: The Judicial World of Charles Doe*. Cambridge, MA: Harvard University Press, 1967.

———. *Controlling the Law: Legal Politics in Early National New Hampshire*. DeKalb, IL: Northern Illinois University Press, 2004.

———. "Doe of New Hampshire: Reflections on a Nineteenth Century Judge." *Harv. L. Rev.* 63, no. 3 (1950): 513–19.

———. "From Common Sense to Common Law to Charles Doe: The Evolution of Pleading in New Hampshire." *NH Bar J.* 1, no. 2 (1959): 27–44.

———. *Legislating the Courts: Judicial Dependence in Early National New Hampshire*. DeKalb, IL: Northern Illinois University Press, 2009.

———. *Legitimating the Law: The Struggle for Judicial Competency in Early National New Hampshire*. DeKalb, IL: Northern Illinois University Press, 2012.

"Report of Governor's Commission on Court System Improvement." *NH Bar J.* 11, no. 4 (1969): 217–61.

"Report of Governor's Commission on Court System Improvement." *NH Bar J.* 16, no. 1 (1974): 1–125.

Reporters Committee for Freedom of the Press. "Secret docket for disciplinary cases shocks public, legislators," September 12, 2000. Available at http://www.rcfp.org/browse-media-law- resources/news/secret-docket-disciplinary-cases-shocks-public-legislators.

Ricker's Petition, 66 NH 207, 29 A. 559 (1890).

Riddick, Floyd, and Robert Dove. *Procedure and Guidelines for Impeachment Trials in the United States Senate: Prepared Pursuant to Senate Resolution 439, 99th Congress, 2d Session*. Washington, DC: US Government Printing Office, 1986.

Rinden, Constance, and Janet Lyman. *New Hampshire Constitutional Amendment Proposals. 3rd Ed.* Concord, NH: State Law Library, 1984.

Rorick, Beverly. "Maurice Geiger Dedicates Life to Judicial Reform." *NH Bar News,* May 7, 2004. Available at https://www.nhbar.org/publications/archives/display-news-issue.asp?id=1640.

Rose v. Council for Better Education, 60 Ky. 1289, 790 S.W.2d 186 (1989).

Rosenthal, Alan. *The Decline of Representative Democracy: Process, Participation and Power in State Legislatures*. Washington, DC: Congressional Quarterly Press, 1981.

Sabato, Larry. *Goodbye to Good-time Charlie: The American Governorship Transformed.* 2nd Ed. Washington, DC: CQ Press, 1983.

Sampson, Kathleen. *Judicial Conduct Organizations, Governing Provisions*. 2 Vols. Chicago: American Judicature Society, 1982, 1984.

Schauer, Frederick. "On the Supposed Jury-Dependence of Evidence Law." *Univ. of Pa. L. Rev.* 155, no. 1 (2006): 165–202.

Scheflin, Alan, and Jon Van Dyke. "Merciful Juries: The Resilience of Jury Nullification." *Wash. & Lee L. Rev.* 48, no. 1 (1996): 165–83.

Schneider, Carl. "The Tension Between Rules and Discretion in Family Law: A Report and Reflection." *Fam. L. Q.* 27, no. 2 (1993): 229–45.

Schneider, Rhoda. "The State Constitutional Mandate for Education: The *McDuffy* and *Hancock* Decisions." Available at http://www.doe.mass.edu/lawsregs/litigation/mcduffy_hancock.html.

SchoolFunding.Info (formerly National Education Access Network). Available at http://schoolfunding.info/.

Senz, Kristen. "Measuring Judicial Performance." *NH Bar News,* February 19, 2014. Available at https://www.nhbar.org/publications/display-news-issue.asp?id=7197.

Serrano v. Priest, 5 Cal. 3d 584, 487 P.2d 1241 (1971), modified, 20 Cal.3d 25, 569 P.2d 1303 (1977).

Shklar, Judith. *Legalism.* Cambridge, MA: Harvard University Press, 1964.

Shugerman, Jed. "Economic Crisis and the Rise of Judicial Elections and Judicial Review." *Harv. L. Rev.* 123, no. 5 (2010): 1061–1150.

———. *The People's Court: Judicial Independence in America.* Cambridge, MA: Harvard University Press, 2012.

Simpson v. Hill, 128 Okl. 269, 263 P. 635 (1927).

Sirkin, J.R. "New Hampshire Districts Drop Finance Lawsuit." *Education Week* 5, no. 2 (1985): 9.

Sirrell v. State, 146 NH 364, 780 A.2d 494 (2001).

Smith, Steven. "Impeachment, Address, and the Removal of Judges in Arkansas: An Historical Perspective." *Ark. L. Rev.* 32 (1978): 253–68.

Soltani, et al., v. Hollingworth, NH Superior Court, Merrimack County, Docket No. 00-E-240 (2000).

Squire, Peverill. *The Evolution of American Legislatures: Colonies, Territories, and States, 1619–2009.* Ann Arbor, MI: University of Michigan Press, 2012.

Squire, Peverill, and Keith E. Hamm. *101 Chambers: Congress, State Legislatures, and the Future of Legislative Studies.* Columbus, OH: Ohio State University Press, 2005.

Stafford, Scott. "The Arkansas Supreme Court and the Aftermath of the Civil War." *U. Ark. Little Rock L. Rev.* 23, no. 2 (2001): 355–407.

———. "Judicial Coup D'état: Mandamus, Quo Warranto and the Original Jurisdiction of the Supreme Court of Arkansas." *U. Ark. Little Rock L. J.* 20, no. 4 (1998), 891–984.

State Justice Institute. "About SJI." Available at http://www.sji.gov/about-sji/.

State v. Campbell, 64 NH 402, 13 Atl. 585 (1887).

State v. Collins, 67 NH 540, 42 A. 51 (1893).

State v. Graf, 143 N. H. 294, 726 A. 2d 1270 (1999).

State v. Hayes, 61 NH 264 (1884).

State v. Jackson, 69 NH 511, 43 A. 749 (1898).

State v. LaFrance, 124 NH 171, A 2d 340 (1983).

State v. Lapage, 57 NH 245 (1876).

State v. Moore, 69 NH 102, 40 A. 702 (1896).

State v. Paul,—NH—, 104 A. 3d 1058 (2014).

State v. Ploof, 162 NH 609, 34 A.3d 563 (2011).

State v. Ray, 63 NH 406 (1885).

State v. Wilson, 48 NH 398 (1869).

Steelman, David, John Goerdt and James McMillan. *Caseflow Management: The Heart of Court Management in the New Millennium*. Williamsburg, VA: National Center for State Courts, 2004.

Steelman, David, and Ann Skove. "Creation of State Court Administrative Offices and Selection of State Court Administrators: Technical Assistance Report" (Denver, CO: National Center for State Courts, Court Consulting Services Division, 2007).

Story, Joseph. *Commentaries on the Constitution of the United States*. 3 Vols. Boston: Billiard, Gray, 1833.

Strickland, Shauna, Richard Schauffler, Robert LaFountain and Kathryn Holt, eds. *State Court Organization.* Last uploaded June 30, 2017. Williamsburg, VA: National Center for State Courts. Available at www.ncsc.org/sco.

Sunstein, Cass. *After the Rights Revolution: Reconceiving the Regulatory State*. Cambridge: Harvard University Press, 1990.

Talbot, Roger. "Fairbanks Case Prober Puzzles, then Startles, NH Lawmakers." *Manchester Union Leader,* November 14, 1996. Available at http://www.gnbtaxpayers.com/FAIRBANKS,%20JOHN,%20JUDGE%20-%20SCANDAL%20&%20COVER-UP.pdf.

———. "Fairbanks' Delinquency Tolerated; Officials Trusted Ex-Judge." Manchester *Union-Leader*, April 30, 1995.

Tarr, G. Alan. "Arthur T. Vanderbilt (1888–1957)," in *Great American Judges: An Encyclopedia,* ed. John Viles (Santa Barbara, CA: ABC-CLIO, 2003), Vol. 2, 775–82.

———. *Without Fear or Favor: Judicial Independence and Judicial Accountability in the States*. Stanford, CA: Stanford University Press, 2012.

Teaford, Jon. *The Rise of the States: Evolution of American State Government.* Baltimore, MD: Johns Hopkins Press, 2002.

Thro, William. "Judicial Analysis during the Third Wave of School Finance Litigation: The Massachusetts Decision as a Model." *BC L. Rev.* 35, no. 3 (1994): 592–617.

Tobin, Robert. *Creating the Judicial Branch: The Unfinished Reform.* Williamsburg, VA: National Center for State Courts, 1999.

———. *An Overview of Court Administration in the United States.* Williamsburg, VA: National Center for State Courts, 1997.

———. "Managing the Shift to State Court Financing." *Just. Sys. J.* 7, no. 1 (1982), 70–102.

Toobin, Jeffrey. "The Judge Hunter." *The New Yorker*, January 12, 2000, 49–54.

Topf, Mel. *A Doubtful and Perilous Experiment: Advisory Opinions, State Constitutions, and Judicial Supremacy*. New York: Oxford University Press, 2011.

Treanor, William. "Judicial Review Before Marbury." *Stanford L. Rev.* 58, no. 2 (2005): 455–562.

Tuccille, J.D. "Hit and Run Blog: Jury Nullification Law Gutted by New Hampshire Supreme Court." *Reason.com,* October 24, 2014, http://reason.com/blog/2014/10/24/jury-nullification-law-gutted-by-new-ham.

Tushnet, Mark. *Taking the Constitution Away from the Courts*. Princeton, NJ: Princeton University Press, 1999.

Umpstead, Regina. "Determining Adequacy: How Courts Are Redefining State Responsibility for Educational Finance, Goals, and Accountability." *BYU Educ. & L. J.* 2007, no. 2 (2007): 281–320.

Unification of NH Bar, 109 NH 260, 248 A.2d 709 (1968).

United States. Senate. "Impeachment." Available at http://www.senate.gov/artandhistory/history/common/briefing/Senate_Impeachment_Role.htm#2.

Upton, Richard. "The Independence of the Judiciary in New Hampshire." *NH Bar J.* 39, no. 2 (1998): 56–61.

Urofsky, Melvin. "State courts and protective legislation during the Progressive Era: A reevaluation." *J. Am. History* 72, no. 1 (1985): 63–91.

Van Dyke, Jon M. "Merciful Juries: The Resilience of Jury Nullification." 48 *Wash. & Lee L. Rev. 165* (1996).

Van Loan, Eugene. "Ten Pound Acts: An Introduction to Original Research on the Origins of Judicial Review." *NH Bar J.* 43, no. 1 (2002): 34–36.

Vanderbilt, Arthur. *The Challenge of Law Reform*. Princeton, NJ: Princeton University Press, 1955.

———. *The Doctrine of the Separation of Powers and Its Present-Day Significance*. Lincoln, NE: University of Nebraska Press, 1953.

———. *Judges and Jurors: Their Functions, Qualifications, and Selection*. Boston, MA: Boston University Press, 1956.

———, ed. *Minimum Standards of Judicial Administration*. New York: NYU Press, 1949.

Vernhoff, John. *New Hampshire State Court Organization Profile*. Williamsburg, VA: National Center for State Courts, 1978.

Volinsky, Andru. "New Hampshire's Education-Funding Litigation: Claremont School District v. Governor, 635 A.2d 1375 (NH 1993), modified, 703 A.2d 1353 (NH 1997)." *Neb. L. Rev.* 83, no. 3 (2004): 836–55.

Walker, Samuel. *The Rights Revolution: Rights and Community in Modern America.* New York: Oxford University Press, 1998.

White, Penny. "The Continuing Evolution of the Federal Rules of Evidence," in Gordon Griller and Keith Stott, eds., *The Improvement of the Administration of Justice* (Oak Park, IL: American Bar Association, 2002).

White, Thomas. "Amendment and Revision of State Constitutions." *U. Pa. L. Rev.* 100, no. 8 (1952): 1132–52.

Wigmore, John. "All Legislative Rules for Judiciary Procedure Are Void Constitutionally." *Ill. L. Rev.* 23 (1928): 276.

Winberry v. Salisbury, 5 N.J. 240, 74 A.2d 406 (1950).

Index

About the Authors

John Cerullo received his BA in History (Honors) and PhD in History from the University of Pennsylvania. He is Professor Emeritus (History) at the University of New Hampshire at Manchester, where his courses' subject matter included the "rights revolution" of recent times and the historical evolution of the idea of the "rights-bearing" citizen. A former visiting scholar at Boston College Law School, his publications include work on "wrongful life" litigation and a book on French military justice, entitled, *Minotaur: French Military Justice and the Aernoult-Rousset Affair* (2011).

David C. Steelman graduated Phi Beta Kappa from the University of New Hampshire with a BA and MA in History. After graduating from the Boston University School of Law, he joined the National Center for State Courts, working as a staff attorney, then a regional vice president, and finally a principal court management consultant, until his retirement at the end of 2013. In 2004, he was a visiting scholar at the University of Bologna's Research Institute on Judicial Systems. His recent books include *Caseflow Management: The Heart of Court Management in the New Millennium* (lead author) (2000, 2004) and *Model Time Standards for State Trial Courts* (co-author, with Richard Van Duizend and Lee Suskin) (2011).

www.ingramcontent.com/pod-product-compliance
Ingram Content Group UK Ltd.
Pitfield, Milton Keynes, MK11 3LW, UK
UKHW040155091026
15587UKWH00018B/270

9 781498 56589